# Biographies of the Tibetan Spiritual Leaders Panchen Erdenis

*By*
Ya Hanzhang

*Translated by*
Chen Guansheng and Li Peizhu

Foreign Languages Press Beijing

First Edition 1994

Hardcover: ISBN 7-119-01687-3
Paperback: ISBN 7-119-01688-1

© Foreign Languages Press, Beijing, 1994

Published by Foreign Languages Press
24 Baiwanzhuang Road, Beijing 100037, China

Printed by Beijing Foreign Languages Printing House
19 Chegongzhuang Xilu, Beijing 100044, China

Distributed by China International Book Trading Corporation
35 Chegongzhuang Xilu, Beijing 100044, China
P.O. Box 399, Beijing, China

*Printed in the People's Republic of China*

# Preface

*Biographies of the Tibetan Spiritual Leaders Panchen Erdenis* and *The Biographies of the Dalai Lamas* are companion volumes. They are works in a biographical style which describe the past six hundred years of Tibetan history. The history of this period begins at the juncture of the Yuan and Ming dynasties and continues to 1951, when Tibet was peacefully liberated and the Panchen Lama returned to Tashilhunpo Monastery.

Tibet is an inseparable part of China. Its history has been an integral part of the history of China for more than six hundred years. However, while its history has some common ground with that of other ethnic groups in other areas of China, at the same time it is different.

The history of Tibet in the last six hundred years or more may be roughly divided into two periods. From the closing years of the Yuan Dynasty (1271-1368) and the early years of the Ming Dynasty (1368-1644) to the middle of the Qing Dynasty (1644-1911), the eighteenth century, is the first period. This is a period in which all the nationalities of China developed peacefully in a unified motherland under the rule of the central governments of the Yuan, Ming and Qing dynasties. Tibet was not an exception. Although two foreign invasions (one by the Dzungar Mongols, and the other by Gurkhas) and two internal rebellions (one when Khangchennas was murdered and the other was the rebellion staged by Gyumey Namgyal), occurred, in general, it was a period of peaceful development.

The second period is from the middle of the Qing Dynasty to the peaceful liberation of Tibet in 1951. This period, viewed from the situation of the whole country, is the period in which imperialism invaded China and the Chinese people staged an anti-imperialist struggle, fighting for national liberation. Tibet was not

i

an exception at that time either, but the situation there certainly had its own features. In any case, the Tibetans faced the problem of anti-imperialism and patriotism just as the other nationalities in China did. They all suffered from the imperialist invasion and were weighed down upon by the three big mountains (imperialism, feudalism and bureaucrat-capitalism).

But the content of the anti-imperialist struggle in Tibet was not exactly the same as that of other nationalities in other areas. In Tibet it was mainly a problem of fighting against British imperialism. Another feature is the problem of subordinacy—a problem rather unique to Tibet. Among the Tibetans there has always been a small clique of people who, lacking common sense and having been propped up by British imperialism for a long time, take a quite wrong attitude towards the unity of Tibet with the motherland. They attempt to separate Tibet from China. This incorrect attitude works against the fundamental interest of all the nationalities of China, including the Tibetans, so it could not enjoy popular support even among the Tibetans. Many well-known Tibetan political and religious leaders have strongly opposed this separatist attitude—among them the Ninth Panchen Erdeni was a remarkable representative. When I wrote *The Biographies of the Dalai Lamas* and *Biographies of the Tibetan Spiritual Leaders Panchen Erdenis*, I took the problems of anti-imperialism, patriotism and subordinacy as the central theme.

To write the history of Tibet of those more than six hundred years, especially the modern history before the peaceful liberation, we have to write at full length the lineages of the Dalai Lamas and the Panchen Lamas. Although the Dalai Lamas and the Panchen Lamas are both Tsongkhapa's disciples, being adherents of the Gelug order of Tibetan Buddhism (also called Lamaism or the Yellow sect) founded by Tsongkhapa, it was nonetheless the successive Dalai Lamas and Panchen Lamas who developed the order into the biggest and the most influential Buddhist sect in Tibet and secured the local political power. They ruled over Tibet for the more than three centuries from the time of the Fifth Dalai Lama to the time of the peaceful liberation of Tibet (from the middle of the seventeenth century to the middle of the twentieth century). As to the Dalai Lamas, I have given a detailed introduction of them in *The Biographies of the Dalai Lamas*. *Biographies of the Tibetan Spiritual Leaders Panchen Erdenis* will give a systematic record of the Panchen Lamas.

My purpose in writing these two books is not simply to write the biographies of the Dalais and the Panchens, but to expound upon the Tibetan history of the last six hundred years in a biographical style—the style loved by the broad masses of the Tibetan people. Therefore, when I wrote the two books I did not confine myself to the two lineages. For instance, when I wrote *The Biographies of the Dalai Lamas*, I did not confine myself to the successive Dalai Lamas, and I gave a brief account of the Yuan Dynasty, and talked about how Tibet was officially incorporated into the territory of the Yuan Empire, how the Yuan court instituted the *Xuanzheng Yuan* system to take charge of Tibetan affairs and instituted a Pacification Commissioners General Office for the Three Regions of U (Anterior Tibet), Tsang (Ulterior Tibet) and Ngari, and instituted thirteen *wan hu fu* (ten-thousand-household districts) in the regions of U and Tsang. All this has surpassed the limitation of describing the lives of the Dalai Lamas. At the same time, when I was writing *The Biographies of the Dalai Lamas* I was under many restrictions, and there were many questions that should have been discussed but which I was unable to. In order to let my readers have a better understanding of the history of Tibet in the last six-hundred-odd years, all the questions that I had no time to examine in *The Biographies of the Dalai Lamas* have been put into *Biographies of the Tibetan Spiritual Leaders Panchen Erdenis*, and some facts which were not correctly presented in the previous book have been corrected·here.

There are two questions that need an explanation.

(1) Since the lineages of the Dalais and Panchens share an identical history of six-hundred-odd years, the material I could use in *Biographies of the Tibetan Spiritual Leaders Panchen Erdenis* would sometimes unavoidably repeat what has already been written in *The Biographies of the Dalai Lamas*. In such cases I here only give a brief and necessary supplement to what has been expounded in detail in *The Biographies of the Dalai Lamas*; for instance, the First Anti-British War in 1888, the Second Anti-British War in 1904, the first treaty about Tibet contracted in 1890 between China and

Britain, the second (1906) Sino-British treaty concerning Tibet and the Simla Conference in 1914 have all been expounded at full length in *The Biographies of the Dalai Lamas,* therefore I made in this book only a brief and necessary reference to them when they concern the Panchen Lamas.

(2) While writing *The Biographies of the Dalai Lamas* and *Biographies of the Tibetan Spiritual Leaders Panchen Erdenis,* I have cited historical data from books in Tibetan, Chinese and foreign languages. The dates given in Tibetan historical documents follow the Tibetan calendar, the dates given in Chinese documents follow the lunar calendar, while the dates given in foreign books follow the Gregorian calendar. Upon comparison, the dates are not always consistent. To put them right needs the time and help of many people, and it is beyond my capability. Here I raise the question and hope other Tibetologists would do some textual research into them.

I am glad the English edition of this book will soon be published and readers will have one more channel to learn Tibetan history. For this I am grateful to the staff members with the Foreign Languages Press.

Ya Hanzhang
Beijing
December 1988

Tashilhunpo Monastery, the Panchen Erdeni's residence.

The Jetsun Jampa Chapel in
Tashilhunpo Monastery.

The statue of Jampa in
Tashilhunpo Monastery.

Scripture Repository in
Tashilhunpo Monastery.

**An embroidered map of the Tashilhunpo, dating back to the time of the Seventh Panchen.**

The stupa of Tsongkhapa and statues of Tsongkhapa Gyeltsab Je and Khedrup Je (the First Panchen Lama).

Photo of Ninth Panchen
Lama Choskyi Nyima.

The stupa of Fourth Panchen
Lama Lozang Choskyi.

The stupas of the Fifth through the Ninth Panchen Lamas.

The mausoleum of the Sixth Panchen—the Pagoda
of Purification in Beijing's West Yellow Temple.

The gold seals of authority of the Fifth Panchen
Erdeni, granted by Qing Emperor Shengzu.

The jade seal of authority of the Sixth Panchen
Lama, granted by Qing Emperor Gaozong.

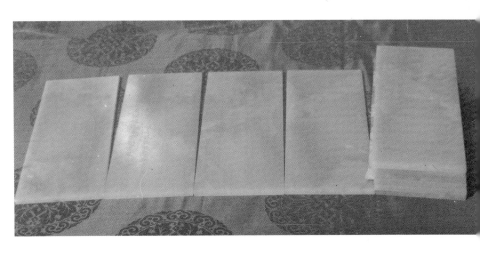

The jade album inscribed with the edict of Qing Emperor Gaozong conferring the recognition of the Sixth Panchen Lama.

The gold album inscribed with the edict of Qing Emperor Gaozong
conferring recognition of the Seventh Panchen Lama.

The portrayal of Qing Emperor Gaozong granted
by the Emperor to the Sixth Panchen Lama.

The gold seal bearing the inscription "Propagator of Honesty, Saviour of the World," granted to the Ninth Panchen by the Interim Governor of the post-imperial Northern Government.

The Tenth Panchen Lama presenting a banner to Chairman Mao Zedong to express respects to him.

The gold seal inscribed with the title "Great Master of Infinite Wisdom, Defender of the Nation and Propagator of the Doctrine," bestowed upon the Ninth Panchen Lama by the Nationalist Government.

Choskyi Gyaltsen, the Tenth Panchen Lama.

# CONTENTS

## Chapter One

# The First, the Second and the Third Panchen Lamas

## 1. Khedrup Je, the First Panchen Lama

The First Panchen,* given the religious name Khedrup Je Geleg Palzang, was born on the eighth day of the fourth month of the Wood-Ox Year of the sixth Tibetan calendrical cycle** (1385, or the eighteenth year of Ming Emperor Taizu's reign) in the village of Chewo in Latu Toshong in Tsang. His father and mother were Kunga Drashi and Phazhen Gyelmo. As a boy, Khedrup Je became a lamaist monk at Sakya Monastery after taking vows as a *getsul* before Sengge Gyaltsen of the Sakya order. At sixteen, he won a debate with Putong Chogle Namgyal at Ngamring Monastery, thereby earning some passing renown. Then he studied esoteric doctrines under the guidance of Jetsun Reponwas at Sakya Monastery, thus becoming versed in both exoteric and esoteric Buddhism.

In 1403, or the first year of Ming Emperor Chengzu's reign, Khedrup Je travelled to Phalafen of U to study the Tripitaka (the Buddhist canon, which has three divisions) and take initiation

---

* The title "Panchen Erdeni" was granted to Lozang Yeshe, the Fifth Panchen Lama, by Qing Emperor Shengzu in 1713, or the fifty-second year of the Kangxi reign period. Before this, the title "Panchen Pokto" had been given to Lozang Choskyi, the Fourth Panchen, by Gushri Khan, a Mongol chieftain. Khedrup Je was posthumously recognized as the First Panchen Lama. This author here adopts the traditional assertion.

** The Tibetan calendar is based on a sixty-year cycle, with each year designated by a combination of one of the names of twelve animals and that of the five elements, i.e., Wood-Ox year, Iron-Horse year, Water-Tiger year, etc.

rituals under the guidance of Tsongkhapa, who at that time enjoyed a very high reputation in Tibetan Buddhist circles. Then he
returned to Tsang and took his *gelong* vows before the eminent
monk Rendawa.* Khedrup Je lived at Jamla Monastery in Nyangto
and at Palkhor Chode Monastery in Gyantse, where he made
further study of exoteric and esoteric Buddhism.

On Rendawa's recommendation, Khedrup Je was accepted by
Tsongkhapa as a disciple in U in 1407, or the fifth year of Ming
Emperor Chengzu's reign. He was thereby a desciple of Tsongkha-
pa at the latter's founding of the Gelug sect.

Tsongkhapa was a native of Tsongkha (now Huangzhong County, Qinghai Province), Amdo. He was born on the tenth day of the
tenth month of the Fire-Cock year of the sixth Tibetan calendrical
cycle (1357, or the seventeenth year of Yuan Emperor Shundi's
Zhizheng reign period) and given the name Lozang Drakpa. His
father and mother were Nubumug and Shangsha Ache. His father
was an official in the post of *darkhache*.

Tsongkhapa became a monk at the age of seven and took his
*getsul* vows before Dondrup Rinchen at Sharjong Monastery. In
1372, or the fifth year of Ming Emperor Taizu's reign) he went to
Tibet to study Buddhist philosophy, learning mainly the Five
Doctrines of Exoteric Buddhism first at Drigung Monastery of the
Kagyu order and then at Diwajian Monastery in Nietang. At that
time the local Tibetan government established by the Sakya sect
had already been taken over by the Phagmo Drupa family of the
Kagyu sect, the third Desi of which, Drakpa Changchub, was
holding ruling power when Tsongkhapa came to Tibet. From the
religious aspect, however, the Sakya sect had a number of eminent
monks. The most famous of them was Rendawa, who went to
Gyantse when Tsongkhapa was studying Buddhist sutras there.
Tsongkhapa thereafter studied the *Abhidharma-kosa-sastra* under
the guidance of Rendawa, and the two men developed a close
master-disciple relationship. In 1385, Tsongkhapa was ordained
into full monkhood by Tsultrim Rinchen at Namgyal Lhakhang in
Yalung and since then became qualified to give sermons and

---

* Rendawa, given the religious name Shunu Lodru, was born in 1349, or the
ninth year of the Zhizheng reign period of Yuan Emperor Shundi, and died in 1412,
or the tenth year of Ming Emperor Chengzu's reign.

recruit disciples.

By 1391, or the twenty-fourth year of Ming Emperor Taizu's reign, Tsongkhapa had recruited thirteen disciples. It was the first step he took to found the Gelug sect. Together with Tsongkhapa, they travelled widely, preaching the Gelug doctrines. Wherever they went, they enjoyed the financial support of the local *dzongpon* (the local official of the Phagmo Drupa regime, equal to a county magistrate in inner China). This shows that the Tibetan ruling class was giving active patronage to their movement to form a new religious sect. In 1396, or the twenty-ninth year of Ming Emperor Taizu's reign, Tsongkhapa had more than thirty disciples; none of them was very eminent, however, as the later records tell us. His most brilliant disciple was Gyeltsab Je (1364-1432), who took Tsongkhapa as his tutor in 1397, or the thirtieth year of Ming Emperor Taizu's reign, and became Tsongkhapa's chief assistant in the founding of the Gelug sect. Gyeltsab Je was originally one of the seven chief disciples of Rendawa—Tsongkhapa was the most famous and Gyeltsab Je was most eloquent. It was said that Gyeltsab Je admitted defeat in a debate with Tsongkhapa in 1397, and then took the latter as his tutor and helped Tsongkhapa to found the Gelug sect. On Rendawa's recommendation, Khedrup Je was also accepted by Tsongkhapa as his disciple at Sera Choding Monastery in Lhasa in 1407, or the fifth year of Ming Emperor Chengzu's reign, and became another of Tsongkhapa's chief assistants. In 1415, or the thirteenth year of Ming Emperor Chengzu's reign, Gedun Truppa, the First Dalai Lama,* took Tsongkhapa as his tutor at Ganden Monastery. By then Tsongkhapa had recruited several hundred converts, bringing a new lamaist sect into being.

The new religious sect founded by Tsongkhapa was called the Gelug sect (*gelug* means "Virtuous Order"), or popularly the Yellow Hat sect (later simply Yellow sect for short), since its monks all wore yellow hats, or New Katampa, because the Gelug sect was based on the Katam sect's doctrines. Subsequently it incorporated

---

* The title "Dalai Lama" was granted to the Fifth Dalai Lama, Lozang Gyatso, by Qing Emperor Shizu in the tenth year of the Shunzhi reign period. Before that, the title of Dalai Lama had been conferred on Sonam Gyatso, the Third Dalai Lama, by the Mongol leader Altan Khan. Gedun Truppa (1391-1474) was posthumously recognized as the First Dalai Lama. This author here adopts the traditional assertion.

the Katam sect, and as a result the latter sect no longer existed as an independent body. Tsongkhapa's reforms for the revival of Buddhism met the needs of the Phagmo Drupa regime of the Kagyu order, the then ruling power in Tibet. So Tsongkhapa enjoyed the regime's patronage. With the financial support of the local *dzongpons* and *depas*, Tsongkhapa was able to engage in religious activities (giving sermons and recruiting converts). He also made direct contacts with the Desi—the highest ruler of the Phagmo Drupa regime. In 1385, or the eighteenth year of Ming Emperor Taizu's reign, he went to pay respects to Drakpa Changchub, the abbot of Dansa Thel Monastery in Lhoka, who had been the third Desi of the Phagmo Drupa regime. Drakpa Changchub also regarded Tsongkhapa highly. (Their meeting has been described in the *Records of Tibetan Kings and Ministers* written by the Fifth Dalai Lama.) It was the first contact between a resigned Desi and Tsongkhapa after Tsongkhapa had come to Tibet. Thanks to Drakpa Changchub's support, Tsongkhapa was able to meet his successor, the current Desi.

In 1398, or the thirty-first year of Ming Emperor Taizu's reign, Tsongkhapa wrote a letter to the fifth Desi of the Phagmo Drupa regime, Drakpa Gyaltsen, Propagation Prince of Persuasion (the latter title having been granted by Ming Emperor Chengzu). The letter, which has been included in the second volume of *The Complete Works of Tsongkhapa*, is obviously a reply to a letter from Drakpa Gyaltsen. This shows that Tsongkhapa then had close relations with Drakpa Gyaltsen. At the invitation of Drakpa Gyaltsen, Tsongkhapa went to Dechenteng Monastery of Wen in 1403, or the first year of Ming Emperor Chengzu's reign, to preach his *Complete Course of the Graded Path of Bodhi*. Drakpa Gyaltsen was his sponsor. In 1407 (the fifth year of Ming Emperor Chengzu's reign) Tsongkhapa and Drakpa Gyaltsen decided that in 1409 they would institute the Monlam Festival, also known as "the Great Prayer Festival," at Lhasa and then began to make preparations for it. In 1408 (the sixth year of Ming Emperor Chengzu's reign), Drakpa Gyaltsen invited Tsongkhapa to Jomonang Monastery to preach *Complete Course of the Graded Path of Bodhi* to more than a thousand monks who came from various areas with the financial help of Drakpa Gyaltsen.

The Monlam Festival, held in the first lunar month of 1409, was attended by more than ten thousand monks and tens of thousands of laymen. It was held at Jokhang Temple in Lhasa from the first day through the fifteenth of the first month of the seventh year of Ming Emperor Chengzu's reign. The most important sponsor of the festival was Drakpa Gyaltsen. Namkha Zangpo, the *dzongpon* of Newu. Dzong, and his nephew Paljor Gyalpo were responsible for the arrangement and organization of the festival. Because of the large attendance and the length of time involved, the festival's daily expenses were large. According to *The Biography of Tsongkhapa* written by Lozang Trinley Namgyal, the first day's expenses were provided by Tsongkhapa and his disciples; the second day's by Drakpa Gyaltsen; the third, fourth, fifth and thirteenth days' by the local officials (mostly *dzongpons*) under Drakpa Gyaltsen; the eighth day's by Namkha Zangpo; the fifteenth day's by the middle- and lower-level monk and lay officials from other districts; the sixth, seventh and fourteenth days' by officials of the Phagmo Drupa regime and those who had close relations with Drakpa Gyaltsen; and the twelfth day's by the monks of Jomonang, Tsel-gungtang and six other monasteries that had close relations with Tsongkhapa. According to *The Biography of Tsongkhapa* written by Khedrup Je, the total donations were 931 *shiao* of gold (a unit of weight equivalent to 5 grams), silver ingots equal to 550 pieces of gold, 37,060 *jin* (a unit of weight equivalent to half a kilogramme) of butter, 18,211 *khal* (a unit of measure equal to about 32 pounds) of *qingke* barley and *tsamba* (parched *qingke* barley or pea flour), 416 bricks of green tea, 163 bricks of black tea, the cured meat of 2,172 yaks and sheep, cattle and sheep worth 2,073 *shiao* of gold, and a large amount of other materials. The festival relied on the economic power of the whole of Tibet, especially the huge donations given by Drakpa Gyaltsen, who ruled Tibet at that time.

During the Monlam Festival, Tsongkhapa and Drakpa Gyaltsen decided to build a monastery for the monks of the Gelug sect. Tsongkhapa selected Mt. Drokri, 30 kilometres to the east of Lhasa, as the site for the monastery. After the festival Tsongkhapa himself went to have a survey of the mountain and worked out a plan for the monastery. Ganden Monastery—as it was called—was completed in 1410 (the eighth year of Ming Emperor Chengzu's reign) to accommodate his several hundred monks. The expenses for the construction were all provided by Drakpa Gyaltsen. However, in order to provide for the several hundred monks who were to live in the monastery over a long period of time, the monastery needed a stable income and could not rely only on indefinite donations. According to *Records of Tibetan Kings and Ministers*, Desi of the Phagmo Drupa regime Drakpa Gyaltsen, along with Shika Drakawa Nangso Rinchen and his brother Nangso Gyawu and a few others, donated a number of manorial estates (known as *shika* in Tibetan) to the monastery. These manors provided labour service and land rent in kind for the daily expenses of the monks. Obviously, Ganden Monastery, accepting these manorial estates as its establishment, functioned as a manorial lord.

Later, the Drepung, Sera and Tashilhunpo monasteries of the Gelug sect all took Ganden Monastery as their example. In 1416 (the fourteenth year of Ming Emperor Chengzu's reign), Jamyang Chosje, a disciple of Tsongkhapa, founded Drepung Monastery in Lhasa with donations from Namkha Zangpo, the *dzongpon* of Newu. In 1418 (the sixteenth year of Ming Emperor Chengzu's reign), with donations from inner China, Shakya Yeshe, another disciple of Tsongkhapa, founded the Sera in Lhasa.

Here we shall add a few words about the relations between the Ming emperors and Tsongkhapa. In 1408 (the sixth year of Chengzu's reign), the Ming Emperor sent envoys to Tibet to invite him to preach Buddhism in inner China. The envoys went first to meet Drakpa Gyaltsen, the Propagation Prince of Persuasion, then on his recommendation the envoys paid a visit to Tsongkhapa at Sera Choding. At that time, however, the sect's founder was too busy with the preparations for the Monlam Festival (held in the first lunar month of 1409) to go in person. So he wrote a letter (which is in the second volume of *The Complete Works of Tsongkhapa*) to the Emperor to express his thanks and explain why he could not travel to inner China. The date of the letter is the nineteenth day of the sixth month of the Earth Rat year of the Tibetan calendrical cycle (1408).

In 1415 (the thirteenth year of Chengzu's reign), the Ming Emperor again sent envoys to invite Tsongkhapa. Being in poor health after a serious illness, he could not go; but he also could not very well refuse the Emperor's invitation, so he sent his disciple, Shakya Yeshe, to Nanjing. That year, the Ming Emperor granted Shakya Yeshe the title "Grand State Tutor of Western Buddhism." Shakya Yeshe returned to Tibet the following year. In 1434 (the ninth year of the Xuande reign period of Ming Emperor Xuanzong) he went again to preach Buddhism in inner China, and Emperor Xuanzong bestowed on him the title "Great Mercy Prince of the Dharma."

When Ganden, Sera and Drepung monasteries had been built, Tsongkhapa's task of founding the Gelug sect was accomplished. The converts to the sect, only thirteen in 1394 (the twenty-seventh year of the Hongwu reign period of the Ming Dynasty), were four or five thousand when Sera Monastery was built in 1418. In 1409, when the Ganden was built, it had several hundred monks. In 1419 when Tsongkhapa visited the Drepung it had more than two thousand monks. The Sera had 2,850 monks in 1697, and it was estimated at that time that it had had more than one thousand monks when it was built. So totally there were about four or five thousand monks in the Three Major Monasteries (Ganden, Sera and Drepung in Lhasa.) It took only twenty-four years for Tsongkhapa to set up a new religious sect that overpowered all the old sects.

In the winter of the seventeenth year of the Yongle reign period of the Ming Dynasty (1419), Tsongkhapa fell ill. On the twenty-third day of the tenth month he passed the mantle of succession to Gyeltsab Je, his foremost disciple, who succeeded him as Ganden Tripa ("Throne Holder of Ganden," i.e., abbot). Two days later, on the twenty-fifth of that month, Tsongkhapa died at the age of sixty-three. At his death Gyeltsab Je succeeded him, becoming the second Ganden Tripa.

### Khedrup Je

Khedrup Je, as the second leading disciple of Tsongkhapa, did a lot of work in preaching the doctrines of the Gelug sect which Tsongkhapa founded. Carrying his mantle and alms-bowl, he went, always on foot, to all the monasteries in U and Tsang, preaching Tsongkhapa's *Complete Course of the Graded Path of Bodhi* and *Complete Course of the Graded Path of Tantric Buddhism* to persuade

the monks of other sects to convert to the Gelug sect. His missionary effort brought the Yellow Hat sect even more converts.
On the other hand, the old sects, opposing the Gelug sect, tried
to disparage it. In particular, a ruling lama of the Red Hat sect (Red
sect for short) named Renchenpa played the Gelug sect down
among the Tibetan people. Khedrup Je therefore travelled to find
Renchenpa and had a lengthy debate with him. Renchenpa admitted defeat and Khedrup Je gained high prestige among the converts of the Yellow Hat sect. *The Complete Works of the Panchen
Masters* compiled by Liu Jiaju also reflects this respect for Khedrup
Je, saying that he "worked hard to defeat heresies and finally
achieved his great goal."

Khedrup Je had close relations with Gedun Truppa, the First
Dalai Lama, who was six years younger and became Tsongkhapa's
disciple eight years later than Khedrup Je. After the death of
Tsongkhapa, Gedun Truppa continued his study of many essential
theories under Khedrup Je.

In 1432 (the seventh year of the Xuande reign period of Ming
Emperor Xuanzong) Gyeltsab Je, the second Ganden Tripa, died.
Khedrup Je was unanimously chosen as the third Ganden Tripa by
the Ganden monks. During his eight years as Ganden Tripa he did
much towards consolidating the Gelug order, of which two things
were most praiseworthy. First, Khedrup Je exerted great effort to
collect huge donations, including gold, iron and copper, that were
enough for him to have a Han-style roof with gold tiles built on a
Tibetan-style hall. In the hall stood the huge silver stupa keeping
Tsongkhapa's remains. It was the first temple built with gold tiles
in the history of the Ganden.

Second, Khedrup Je wrote the *Biography of Tsongkhapa*. As his
second chief disciple, Khedrup Je had followed Tsongkhapa for
twelve years since being recruited by Tsongkhapa as a disciple in
1407. He took part in developing the doctrines of the Gelug sect,
stipulating its rules and disciplines and sutra-study programme and
establishing the administrative system of monasteries of the Yellow
Hat sect. So he had a good understanding of Tsongkhapa's achieve-
ments. Although many eminent monks of later generations of the
Yellow Hat sect also wrote a number of other biographies of
Tsongkhapa, none of their works excelled Khedrup Je's *Biography*

*of Tsongkhapa.*
On the twenty-first day of the second month of the Earth-Horse year of the seventh Tibetan calendrical cycle (1438, or the third year of the Zhengtong reign period of Ming Emperor Yingzong), Khedrup Je died at the age of fifty-three. Both Gyeltsab Je and Khedrup Je made great contributions to the founding of the Gelug sect, so Tsongkhapa and these two disciples of his were honoured by the Tibetans as "the revered trinity—father and sons."
Khedrup Je was posthumously recognized as the First Panchen Lama by Tibetan historians.

## 2. Sonam Choglang, the Second Panchen Lama

The Second Panchen, given the religious name Sonam Choglang, was a native of Bensa in Tsang. Bensa is today's Jiangdang District in Shigatse County, to the south of the Yarlungzangbo River. He was born on the tenth day (or the fifteenth day, according to *The Political and Religious History of the Tibetan Nationality*) of the first month of the Earth-Sheep year of the seventh Tibetan calendrical cycle (1439, or the fourth year of the Zhengtong reign period of Ming Emperor Yingzong). The names of his father and mother are unknown. Since his childhood he was a monk at Ganden under the guidance of Baso Choskyi Gyaltsen, the then Ganden Tripa. According to Tibetan records, when Sonam Choglang paid respects to the abbot, he was asked by the latter what his name was. He answered: "My name is Bewu" (meaning "calf"). The abbot said: "A calf will grow into an ox," and thus gave him the religious name Sonam Chosje Langbu (usually given as Sonam Choglang for short).
After learning Buddhist scriptures at the Ganden for many years, Sonam Choglang had a good command of exoteric and esoteric doctrines and was especially good at open debate. Of the three thousand lamas at the Ganden, those who had debated with him all admitted defeat. Thus Sonam was known for his eloquence and was considered to be the reincarnation of Khedrup Je at Ganden Monastery.
At middle age Sonam Choglang left the Ganden for his home-

town Bensa, where there was originally a temple built by the lamas of the Sakya sect. It was called Bensa Gompa (meaning Bensa Monastery) or Bengom for short. (The Chinese records call it Bengom Monastery, so this author also uses this name here.)

After returning home, Sonam Choglang lived in Bengom Monastery, recruiting converts and preaching doctrines of the Yellow Hat sect, and eventually converting the Sakya temple to the Gelug sect. He then sent his sixteen chief disciples to preach the Gelug doctrines throughout the Tsang region, making considerable contributions to the development of the Gelug sect there. Sonam Choglang had Choskyi Phodrang Hall built in the monastery for his residence, took the abbotship of Bengom Monastery and engaged in writing books on the doctrines of the Gelug sect as laid down by Tsongkhapa. The printing blocks of his many works are still kept in the monastery. In the years when he was the abbot of the Bengom, the monastery had close relations with Tashilhunpo and Tashilganbe monasteries (Tashilganbe was in Shetongmoin Shika to the west of Shigatse). By Sonam Choglang's order, the monks of the Bengom were to go to study scriptures in turns and attend discussions in the two monasteries. Thus, Sonam Choglang enjoyed a high reputation in Tsang. He was respectfully called Bengom Living Buddha.

Gedun Gyatso, the Second Dalai Lama, was born in 1475 (the eleventh year of the Chenghua reign period of the Ming Dynasty), thirty-six years later than Sonam Choglang, though they were contemporaries. Gedun Gyatso served variously as the fifth abbot of the Tashilhunpo, the tenth abbot of the Drepung and the ninth abbot of the Sera. At that time Gedun Gyatso seemed to have won a high status—second only to the Ganden Tripa—in the Gelug sect. But we have not found any records to show that he and Sonam Choglang had any contact.

Sonam Choglang died at the age of sixty-five in the Choskyi Phodrang Hall of Bengom Monastery on the twenty-fifth day of the third month of the Wood-Rat year of the eighth Tibetan calendrical cycle (1504, or the seventeenth year of the Hongzhi reign period of Ming Emperor Xiaozong). Gedun Gyatso died at the Drepung at the age of sixty-seven in the Water-Tiger year of the ninth Tibetan calendrical cycle (1542, or the twenty-first year of the Jiaqing reign period of the Ming Dynasty), thirty-eight years later.

Sonam Choglang was posthumously recognized as the Second Panchen Lama by Tibetan historians.

## 3. Lozang Dondrup, the Third Panchen Lama

The Third Panchen Lama, given the religious name Lozang Dondrup, was born on the fourth day of the first month of the Wood-Ox year of the eighth Tibetan calendrical cycle (1505, or the eighteenth year of the Hongzhi reign period of Ming Emperor Xiaozong) at Bensa in Tsang. His father and mother's names were Sonam Dorje and Peldzonji, respectively. According to *The Complete Works of the Panchen Masters* by Liu Jiaju, the second and third Panchen Lamas were born in the same place and of the same clan. Lozang Dondrup, the Third Panchen Lama, was also called Bensa-pa.*

In 1516, or the eleventh year of the Zhengde reign period of Ming Emperor Wuzong, when he was eleven years old, Lozang Dondrup took his vows as a *getsul*, and was given the religious name by Gebel Kanchin** at Lharintse Monastery.

In his youth, Lozang Dondrup studied mainly exoteric Buddhism. However, he also studied the tantras under the guidance of Choskyi Lodro Gyaltsen, abbot of the Tashilganbe in Tsang. He also then studied *A Complete Course of the Graded Path of Bodhi* and *The Wheel of Time* and other scriptures under the guidance of Lozang Shine, Jotsewa, Thubten Namgyal, Gyalpodup Palzangpo and other eminent monks of Tashilhunpo Monastery. He thereby got a solid knowledge of esoteric and exoteric Buddhism.

At the age of sixteen (in 1521, or the sixteenth year of the Zhengde reign period of Ming Emperor Wuzong), Lozang Dondrup was infected with smallpox, which at that time was widespread in Tsang. Fortunately, a lama named Chuchin Chosje Dorje

---

* There are different versions about his birthplace. Judged by the title "Bensapa" (meaning "a native of Bensa"), he was a native of Bensa in Tsang.
** Drakpa Dondrup, according to *The Complete Works of the Panchen Masters* by Liu Jiaju.

cured him of the illness. He spread the secret prescription to the masses, and   many people were therefore able to survive the epidemic. Owing to this good deed, he earned a high reputation among the people in Tsang.

.   Lozang Dondrup spent his middle age travelling in many areas of Tsang and preaching the doctrines of the Gelug sect. He recruited many disciples and played an active role in the development of the Gelugpa sect in Tsang. In his old age, Lozang Dondrup came back to his hometown, Bensa. He secluded himself at Bengom Monastery and wrote a book about the doctrines of the Gelug sect.

Lozang Dondrup died at the age of sixty-one at Bengom Monastery on the twenty-third day of the second month of the Fire-Tiger year of the ninth Tibetan calendrical cycle (1566, or the forty-fifth year of the Jiaqing reign period of Ming Emperor Shizong). In the concluding years of his life, Lozang Dondrup came to be regarded as the reincarnation of Sonam Choglang, the former Bengom Living Buddha, by the monks of Bengom Monastery. He was posthumously recognized as the Third Panchen Lama by Tibetan historians.

Third Panchen Lama Lozang Dondrup was a contemporary of Third Dalai Lama Sonam Gyatso (but it seems there was no contact between these two, either). Sonam Gyatso, the Third Dalai Lama, was born in 1543 (the twenty-second year of the Jiaqing reign period of Ming Emperor Shizong), thirty-eight years later than Lozang Dondrup, the Third Panchen Lama. At the age of eleven, Sonam Gyatso was chosen as the Drepung's twelfth abbot. At the age of twenty-two, he became concurrently the Sera's thirteenth abbot.

In 1577 (the fifth year of the Wanli reign period of Ming Emperor Shenzong), at Mongol chief Altan Khan's invitation, Sonam Gyatso went to meet him at Yanghua Monastery in Qinghai. In 1583 (the eleventh year of Wanli) Altan Khan died and his son asked Sonam Gyatso to come to Inner Mongolia to pray for Altan Khan's soul. Sonam Gyatso accepted the invitation. He left Qinghai in 1584 (the twelfth year of Wanli) and arrived in Inner Mongolia the following year.

In 1587 (the fifteenth year of Wanli) Shelik, the Mongol Prince of Shunyi, in a letter to the Ming government, asked it to grant the title *Dorje Chang* to Sonam Gyatso. *Dorje Chang* in Tibetan means "Holder of the Vajra," a title usually granted to eminent monks in Tibet and Mongolia. His request was granted by Emperor Shenzong in the tenth month of that year. Emperor Shenzong decreed that "the Tibetan monk Dalai may be given the title of *Dorje Chang* and the official certificate for it" (see *Imperial Records of the Ming Dynasty*). Emperor Shenzong, as requested by Shelik, sent officials to Inner Mongolia with an invitation to Sonam Gyatso to meet the Emperor in Beijing and give sermons there. The Dalai Lama accepted the invitation and left for the Ming capital. But death intervened. On March 26, 1588, he died at Kha'otomi in Inner Mongolia at the age of forty-six, twenty-two years after Lozang Dondrup.

From the historical records cited above, it is evident that Third Dalai Lama Sonam Gyatso was much higher in status, both political and religious, than Third Panchen Lama Lozang Dondrup.

# Chapter Two
# Lozang Choskyi, the Fourth Panchen Lama

## 1. He Becomes the Bengom Living Buddha at Fourteen

The Fourth Panchen Lama, given the religious name Lozang Choskyi, was born at Drugya Bewa Village in Lanrin Rabu Shika (to the west of Shigatse; a *shika* is equivalent in size to a *dzong*) on the fifteenth day of the fourth month of the Iron-Horse year of the tenth Tibetan calendrical cycle (1570, or the fourth year of the Longqing reign period of Ming Emperor Muzong).* His father was Dzongcho Kunga Ushe, alias Tsering Paljor, and his mother Tsokye. Lozang Choskyi, named Choskyi Palden Zangpo by his father and mother, was, according to his *Autobiography*,** thin, small and homely as a boy. At that time monks of Bengom Monastery were searching for the "soul boy" of Lozang Dondrup, the deceased abbot of the monastery and the Third Panchen Lama. At the age of five (in 1575, or the third year of the Wanli reign period of Ming

---

* Most works about the Panchen Lamas say that the Fourth Panchen Lama was born in the Fire-Rabbit year of the tenth Tibetan calendrical cycle (1567, or the first year of the Longqing reign period of the Ming Dynasty). According to Lozang Choskyi's *Autobiography*, his mother did give birth to a boy in 1567, but the boy soon died. Lozang Choskyi himself was born in the Iron-Horse year of the tenth Tibetan calendrical cycle (1570, or the fourth year of the Longqing reign period of Ming Emperor Muzong). The dead boy was his elder brother. So we cite here the birth date given by Lozang Choskyi himself.

** The sections of the Tibetan-language *Biography of the Fourth Panchen Lama, Lozang Choskyi* before the Water-Tiger year of the tenth Tibetan calendrical cycle (1662) were written by Lozang Choskyi himself (so this author calls it *Autobiography*), and those after the Water-Tiger year by Lozang Yeshe, the Fifth Panchen Lama.

Emperor Shenzong), Choskyi Palden Zangpo met monk officials of Bengom Monastery, who had come to Drugya Bewa Village on some errands. One of the monk officials was Khedrup Sangye Yeshe, a chief disciple of Third Panchen Lama Lozang Dondrup. He stayed in the village for more than a month to observe Choskyi Palden Zangpo and inquire of his parents about him, while the other monks continued on, begging for alms. His father told Khedrup Sangye Yeshe that his son might become a monk, as the boy showed an affinity for monks.

At the age of thirteen, Choskyi Palden Zangpo was brought by his father to the monastery and became a monk after being ordained and taking his vows as a *getsul* before khedrup Sangye Yeshe at Bengom Monastery on the tenth day of the first month of the tenth year of the Wanli reign period (1582). He was given the religious name of Lozang Choskyi Gyaltsen (Lozang Choskyi for short). Lozang Choskyi studied scriptures and attended debates. One day when Trichen, an eminent monk from the Shrine Drat-sang of Palkhor Chode Monastery in Gyantse (Gyangze), came to give sermons and have a debate with the monks at Bengom Monastery, he was surprised to find Lozang Choskyi had a good understanding of Buddhist scriptures and had defeated other monks in debates. The eminent monk invited Lozang Choskyi to his residence, offering him a cup of tea and a suit of the yellow mantle worn by monks of the Gelug sect, and asked Lozang Choskyi to give a sermon to him. The thing caused a stir among the monks, who assumed that this meant Lozang Choskyi was the soul boy of Lozang Dondrup, the Bengom Living Buddha. But Lozang Choskyi said that he was only an ordinary monk with a superficial knowledge of Buddhism and he hoped to do nothing but to devote himself to monastic study of esoteric and exoteric Buddhism. After repeated discussions, the monks of Bengom Monastery enthroned Lozang Choskyi as the Bengom Tripa (abbot) in Choskyi Phodrang Hall on the third day of the second month of the eleventh year of the Wanli reign period (1583), when Lozang Choskyi was fourteen years old.

Lozang Choskyi, though the abbot of the Bengom, put management of the monastery into the hands of Khedrup Sangye Yeshe and devoted himself to studying scriptures and writing books. He wrote five books in all. His second work is *The Biography of God Gonpo Shiwa.*

On the third day of the eleventh month of the fourteenth year of the Wanli reign period, Lozang Choskyi left for the Tashilhunpo to further study Buddhist scriptures and attend debates. At that time the Tashilhunpo had only three *dratsangs*—Tsosamling, Shartse and Kyilkhang—all of which were dedicated to exoteric Buddhism. He therefore studied in Tsosamling Dratsang, with only Geshe Paljor to keep him company. On meeting Samdrup Palzang (the thirteenth abbot of the Tashilhunpo), Lozang Choskyi exchanged *katags* (ceremonious scarves) with him, but they did not kowtow to each other. However, the other monk officials and *dratsang khenpos* of the Tashilhunpo kowtowed to him, in recognition of his status as the Bengom Living Buddha. Lozang Choskyi attended scripture chantings and debates at the Tashilhunpo. In these activities, he refused at first to sit on the higher chair specially prepared for Living Buddhas, for he preferred to sit among ordinary monks. Then, when the abbot insisted that he do so, he reluctantly agreed to take the seat for Living Buddhas. In 1586 Lozang Choskyi received the academic degree of *Rachin* (an abbreviation of *Rabjamchenpo*, an honorific title granted to learned lamas in the early period of the Gelug order).

On the third day of the seventh month of the nineteenth year of the Wanli reign period (1591), Lozang Choskyi took his *gelong* vows—before Tangcho Yonphel, the then fourteenth abbot of the Tashilhunpo. Usually, a grand ceremony should be held when a monk takes the *gelong* vows—that is, when he is initiated into full monkhood. This is an important matter for the monks. At the ceremony there should be a *khenpo* (tutor), a *Sangton* (ordination tutor), an *atcharya* (a teacher of morals), a *leje lopon* (the one who reads the code of discipline at the ceremony), a *tsepabo* (the one who holds a wooden box with *tsamba* in it), a *lelo* (the one who puts questions before the novice) and a *dukhorwa* (the one who gives a sermon on the *Wheel of Time* sutra). The discipline code that a *gelong* should abide by has 253 rules. There are strict and detailed regulations about monks' clothing, food, language, living, chanting of scriptures, worshipping of Buddha, etc. Monks were subject to rigid discipline. In this aspect lay the difference between the Gelug

and other lamaist sects, and discipline was what Tsongkhapa laid
special emphasis on when founding the sect.

After taking his *gelong* vows, Lozang Choskyi left for Lhasa, first
worshipping the image of Sakyamuni brought by Tang Dynasty's
Princess Wen Cheng to Tibet and holding a grand prayer and
sacrifice offering ceremony at Jokhang, and then settling in to
study scriptures at the Ganden, the monastery founded by Tsongkhapa himself. Tangcho Palpa, the abbot of the Ganden, asked
Lozang Choskyi to attend scripture chantings at the Great Chanting
Hall and the debates at the *dratsangs* so that he could enlarge his
knowledge. But Lozang Choskyi hesitated to do so, thinking he had
learnt too little to be qualified to take part in the debates with
learned monks who came to the Ganden from various places. At
the abbot's insistence, however, he chose "The Middle Way" and
"Cause and Logic" as the two courses for his study. In debate, he
answered all questions raised by the learned monks and pointed
out some *geshes'* misunderstanding of Buddhist scriptures. As a
result, he won high regard from all the monks at the Ganden.

## 2. The Sixteenth Tripa of the Tashilhunpo

In 1598, or the twenty-sixth year of the Wanli reign of the Ming
Dynasty, Lozang Choskyi left the Ganden for the Bengom to take
over the administration of that monastery, give sermons and
recruit disciples. At that time Ganjan Chosphel Monastery, which
was one day's journey to the west of the Tashilhunpo, had no
abbot and all the monks of the monastery and the local official
*depa* decided to ask Lozang Choskyi to fill the post. Lozang
Choskyi accepted the request. On the twenty-fifth day of the tenth
month (the anniversary of Tsongkhapa's death) of the twenty-
sixth year of the Wanli reign period, he became concurrently the
*tripa* of Ganjan Chosphel Monastery. He then moved between the
Bengom and the Ganjan Chosphel, being in charge of the two
monasteries' routine duties.

When the fifteenth Tashilhunpo abbot, Lhawang Lodro, was
relieved from his office, Lozang Choskyi was requested to be
concurrently the sixteenth Tashilhunpo abbot. He declined, saying

that he was too busy with the management of Bengom and Ganjan Chosphel monasteries. But the high-ranking monk officials, on behalf of all the monks of the Tashilhunpo, came to request insistently, saying that they would not go back until he had acceded to their request. With the above situation in view, Lozang Choskyi promised to be their *tripa*, but he set a time limit of two years.

On the third day of the second month of the twenty-ninth year of the Wanli reign period (1601), Lozang Choskyi became the sixteenth Tashilhunpo abbot. First of all, he gave the 250-odd newly-recruited monks their *getsul* vows. Then he began to solve the problem of the food supply for the monks of the Tashilhunpo who were living a hard life there. He had a big cooking pot made, which could cook sixty-three *khal* (787.5 kilos) of rice for two thousand monks for a meal. Then three big tea-boilers and eighteen teakettles were made to provide tea for the monks chanting scriptures in the Great Chanting Hall. At that time the Tashilhunpo had only a few *choshi* (manorial estates of monasteries) and the monastery's annual income was insufficient to provide for the monks. The monks could drink tea only once or twice a day. Lozang Choskyi gave sermons to the manorial lords and asked them to give donations to the Tashilhunpo, so the lords gave a number of *choshi* to the monastery. With the increased income of the monastery, its monks could drink tea five or six times a day. As the problem of food and tea was thereafter basically solved, all the monks at the Tashilhunpo highly praised Lozang Choskyi for his good management.

Besides, Lozang Choskyi established the Monlam Festival of the Tashilhunpo in 1603, or the thirty-first year of the Wanli reign period of the Ming Dynasty. The festival was thereafter held during the third through the sixteenth day of the first month of each year, as was stipulated by him. It had the same activities as the festival at the Jokhang in Lhasa. Thus, the monks could obviate the hardship necessary for the long and difficult journey to attend the Monlam Festival at Lhasa.

Usually the "Sunning the Buddha Festival" was held on the fourteenth, fifteenth and sixteenth days of the fifth month each year. At that time a large piece of cloth about three hundred feet long with the image of the Buddha on it would be hung on a hill to be exhibited to the public. Lozang Choskyi found that the cloth painting was too old, so he ordered that a new painting be made with the donations he collected from manorial lords. He also built a new chanting hall called Lima Lhakang. As a result, the Tashilhunpo took on an entirely new look.

In 1607 (the thirty-fifth year of the Wanli reign period), Lozang Choskyi proposed that the Ngapa Dratsang be established at the Tashilhunpo for the study of esoteric Buddhism. His proposal was accepted by all the monks at the Tashilhunpo. For this purpose he himself went to Don in U and Samdrup Ganden and other places in Tsang to collect donations. The *dratsang* was built in front of Lharang Hall in the centre of the Tashilhunpo in the same year. Since then the monks of the Tashilhunpo, after accomplishing the study of exoteric Buddhism, could also study esoteric Buddhism at the Tashilhunpo, instead of going to Gyu-to (Upper Tantric College) or Gyu-me (Lower Tantric College) in Lhasa to study esoteric Buddhism. Thus the Tashilhunpo had a complete system for studying Buddhism of both the exoteric and esoteric orders.

In the winter of 1613, or the forty-first year of the Wanli reign period, Lozang Choskyi, having held the abbotship at the Tashilhunpo for thirteen years, submitted his resignation, hoping that a learned high monk would be chosen to be the *tripa* of the Tashilhunpo and he could go back to the Bengom to seclude himself for a further study of Buddhism. But his request for resignation was not accepted. All the monks at the Tashilhunpo asked him to stay on the post. So Lozang Choskyi was obliged to promise to be the *tripa* for another period of time.

# 3. The Gelug Sect Is Persecuted by the Kagyu Sect and Two Other Forces

Lozang Choskyi lived in an age when the Gelug, headed by the Dalai and Panchen lamas, was persecuted by the ruling lama of the Karma Kagyu Sect, who was holding ruling power over Tibet, and Tsangpa Khan, who was then the head of Tibetan serf owners.

Because of the unique conditions in Tibet, the persecution, though it was actually political and military, was carried out in the name of religion. The struggle of persecution and anti-persecution, which lasted for dozens of years, occurred when Lozang Choskyi was the de facto leader of the persecuted Gelug sect. At that time the feudalist serf system in Tibet was in its ascendancy. Meanwhile, the reform of Lamaism sponsored by Tsongkhapa was playing a progressive role in the ideological sphere, wiping out what blocked the forces of production and developing what promoted production. So it was supported by the masses of the Tibetan people, including the Desi of the Phagmo Drupa regime.

All progressive social movements surely have to come into a conflict of interest with and be persecuted by conservative forces and have to struggle against persecution—only in this way can the new progressive forces survive and accomplish their historical tasks. This was why the struggle between the Gelug sect and the conservative forces was unavoidable.

Except the Phagmo Drupa Kagyu sect, nearly all the other old religious sects were hostile to the Gelug. The most hostile and powerful force consisted of the Karma Kagyu and Drigung Kagyu sects, and Tsangpa Khan, who together took the cruelest measures to persecute the Gelug sect. After the Phagmo Drupa Kagyu's third ruling lama, Drakpa Changchub, became Tsongkhapa's disciple, the regime's successive Desis all supported the Gelug. But after its fifth ruling lama, Drakpa Gyaltsen, the Phagmo Drupa Kagyu regime declined, and the Rinpungpa and Shingshapa (Tsangpa Khan's grandfather) successively held independent feudal authority in Tsang. The Black Hat and Red Hat subsects of the Karma Kagyu there then enjoyed greater development. When the Phagmo Drupa regime was taken over by the conservative religious and secular forces, the Desi of Phagmo Drupa became powerless, and the position continued to exist in name only.

The Karma Kagyu, one of the four subbranches of the Dakpo Kagyu, was founded by Dusum Khyenpa, a native of Shol in Kham. As a boy, he became a monk and studied esoteric Buddhism. In 1147, or the seventeenth year of the Shaoxing reign period of Southern Song Emperor Gaozong, he established Karma Dansa Monastery at Karma near Riwoche. The Karma Kagyu sect derived its name from the monastery. In 1187, or the fourteenth year of the Chunxi reign period of Southern Song Emperor Xiaozong, he established Tsurpu Monastery at Tsurpu in U, which became the leading monastery of the Karma Kagyu order. He was therefore called Tsurpu Karmapa by later generations.

In the Karma Kagyu branch there were two different sub-branches—the Black Hat line and the Red Hat line. This sect initiated the system of the reincarnation of Living Buddhas. The Black Hat line's first ruling lama was Dusum Khyenpa, while the second ruling lama was Karma Pakshi (1204-1283, or from the fourth year of Southern Song Emperor Ningzong's Jiatai reign period to the twentieth year of Yuan Emperor Shizu's reign). The subbranch derived its name from a gold-brimmed black hat bestowed on Karma Pakshi by Mongka Khan, Yuan Emperor Xianzong. In 1283 (the twentieth year of Yuan Emperor Shizu's reign) Karma Pakshi died at Tsurpu Monastery. The third ruling lama of the Black Hat line, Rangjung Dorje (1284-1339, or from the twenty-first year of Yuan Emperor Shizu's reign to the fifth year of the Zhiyuan reign period of Yuan Emperor Shundi), came to Beijing in 1322 (the second year of the Zhizhi reign period of the Yuan Dynasty) and again in 1338, at the invitation of Yuan Emperor Yingzong and Emperor Shundi, respectively. He died at Beijing in 1339.

Rolpai Dorje, the Black Hat's fourth ruling lama (1340-1383, or from the sixth year of the Zhiyuan reign period of Yuan Emperor Shundi's reign to the sixteenth year of Ming Emperor Taizu's reign), came to Beijing in 1356 (the sixteenth year of the Zhizheng reign period of Yuan Emperor Shundi) at the invitation of the Emperor.

Deshin Shekpa, its fifth ruling lama (1384-1415, or from the seventeenth year of the Hongwu reign period to the thirteenth year of the Yongle reign period, both of the Ming Dynasty), came to Nanjing in 1407 at the invitation of Ming Emperor Chengzu and was granted the title "Great Treasure Prince of the Dharma." He went back in 1408 and died at Tsurpu Monastery in 1415.

Tongwa Donden, its sixth ruling lama (1416-1453, or from the fourteenth year of the Yongle reign period to the fourth year of the Jingtai reign period, both of the Ming Dynasty), was invited to

Beijing by the Ming Emperor. However, he sent envoys to offer tribute to the Emperor instead of going himself.

Chosdrak Gyatso, its seventh ruling lama (1454-1506, or from the fifth year of the Jingtai reign period to the first year of the Zhengde reign period, both of the Ming Dynasty), began the struggle with Tsongkhapa's Gelug order.

Mikyo Dorje, its eighth ruling lama (1507-1554, or from the second year of the Zhengde reign period to the thirty-third year of the Jiaqing reign period, both of the Ming Dynasty), refused to meet Liu Yun, an eunuch envoy sent by Ming Emperor Wuzong to invite him to Beijing. Liu threatened to take the lama away by force. Some Tibetans then robbed Liu of his treasure and weapons. Liu fled to Chengdu and warned his subordinates against disclosing what had happened. By the time he sent a false report to the imperial court, Ming Emperor Wuzong had died. Emperor Shizong ordered Liu to come back to the capital, Beijing, and had him imprisoned (see *History of the Ming Dynasty*).

Wangchuk Dorje, its ninth ruling lama (1556-1603, or from the thirty-fifth year of the Jiaqing reign period to the thirty-first year of the Wanli reign period, both of the Ming Dynasty), did nothing particular in his life.

Choyin Dorje, its tenth ruling lama (1604-1674, or from the thirty-second year of the Wanli reign period of the Ming Dynasty to the thirteenth year of the Kangxi reign period of the Qing Dynasty), collaborated with Tsangpa Khan to fight against both the Gelug order and the Phagmo Drupa regime.

The following are the ruling lamas of the Red Hat line.

Drakpa Sengge, its first ruling lama (1283-1349, or from the twentieth year of Yuan Emperor Shizu's reign to the ninth year of the Zhizheng reign period of Yuan Emperor Shundi's reign), was said to have had a gold-brimmed red hat bestowed upon him by the Emperor, and thus claimed himself to be the "Red Hat Prince of Dharma." He was a contempory of Rangjung Dorje, the third ruling lama of the Black Hat line. With his disciples growing in number, he established the Red Hat line.

Khachog Wangpo, its second ruling lama (1350-1405, or from the tenth year of the Zhizheng reign period of Yuan Emperor Shundi to the third year of Ming Emperor Chengzu's reign), expanded his influence to the Bomi area, giving sermons and recruiting disciples wherever he could. He was a contempory and tutor of Deshin Shekpa, the fifth ruling lama of the Black Hat line. Chosphel Yeshe, its third ruling lama (1406-1452, or from the fourth year of Chengzu's reign to the third year of Daizong's reign, both of the Ming Dynasty), was bestowed an image of Vajrapani, a Buddhist bell and club, etc., by the Ming Emperor.

Chosdrak Yeshe, its fourth ruling lama (1453-1524, or from the fourth year of Daizong's reign to the third year of Shizong's reign, both of the Ming Dynasty), was once the acting regent of the Phagmo Drupa regime and collaborated with Rinpungpa Tsokye Dorje to persecute the Gelug sect.

Konchok Yenlha, its fifth ruling lama (1525-1583, or the fourth year of Shizong's reign to the eleventh year of Shenzong's reign, both of the Ming Dynasty), and Migyur Wangchuk, its sixth ruling lama (1584-1635, or from the twelfth year of Shenzong's reign to the eighth year of Sizong's reign, both of the Ming Danasty), collaborated with Tsangpa Khan to expand their influence from Tsang to U, and together they intensified their persecution of the Gelug order.

Supported by Tsangpa Khan, head of the serf owners in Tsang, the Black Hat and Red Hat lines of the Karma Kagyu became religiously and politically very influential in Tibetan areas in the late period of the Phagmo Drupa regime. Shingshapa Tseten Dorje, grandfather of Tsangpa Khan, was originally a subordinate of Ngawang Jigme Drakpa, the last chief of the Rinpungpa family. Taking advantage of the Rinpungpas' trust in him, he seized the family's power. In 1565 (the forty-fourth year of Ming Emperor Shizong's reign) Shingshapa Tseten Dorje usurped the Rinpungpas' leadership and claimed himself to be the "Tsangtod Gyalpo" (King of Upper Tsang). He established his capital at Samdrutse (modern Shigatse). Shingshapa had nine sons. His eldest son, Padma Gyalpo, helped him to overthrow the Rinpungpas' leadership. His second son, Tensung Wangpo (also called Tensungpa), captured Phunyu in U in 1605 (the thirty-third year of Ming Emperor Shenzong's reign). His third son, Phuntsok Namgyal, captured Yargyab in U in 1610 (the thirty-eighth year of Shenzong's reign). The father and sons of the Shingshapa family were of the Karma Kagyu sect, which was hostile to Tsongkhapa's Gelug sect. So Phuntsok Namgyal and Choyin Dorje, the tenth ruling lama of the Karma Kagyu Black Hat line, allied themselves against the Yellow Hat sect and the Phagmo Drupa regime.

One of the feudal groupings which persecuted the Gelug was the Drigung Kagyu, a subbranch of the Phagmo Drupa Kagyu, founded by Drigungpa Rinchenpal (1143-1217, or from the thirteenth year of Southern Song Emperor Gaozong's Shaoxing reign to the tenth year of Southern Song Emperor Ningzong's Jiading reign), a native of Danma in Kham (modern Dengke County in Sichuan). Drigungpa, who became a monk at the age of nine, went to Dansa Thel Monastery to study esoteric doctrines under the guidance of Phagmo Drupa at the age of sixteen. In 1179 (the sixth year of Southern Song Emperor Xiaozong's reign) he expanded a small temple into the Drigung Thel Monastery of Drigung (modern Medrogungkar County in Tibet), and he, as the first abbot of the monastery, was called Drigungpa. With the number of his followers growing increasingly, he established the Drigung Kagyu sect.

The Drigung Kagyu had become influential due to the support of the Kyura family, a local chief serf-owning family. Abbots of Drigung Monastery were all from that family. One of those appointed by Kublai Khan to be heads of the thirteen *wan hu* (ten thousand households) in Tibet in 1268 (the fifth year of Yuan Emperor Shizu's reign) was Dorjedrag, the abbot of Drigung Monastery, who was later concurrently one of the Pacification Commissioners for the Three Regions of U, Tsang and Ngari.

In 1290 (the twenty-seventh year of Yuan Emperor Shizu), the head of the Drigung *wan hu*, Dorjedrag, who worked hand-inglove with Hulagu, a Mongolian prince, rebelled against the authority of the Sakya sect. The Sakya *ponchen* (administrator), with the approval of Yuan Emperor Kublai, united with the other twelve *wan hu* heads, dispatching an allied force to suppress the rebellion of the Drigung sect. The Sakya *ponchen*'s army defeated the Drigung troops and burned Drigung Monastery. The incident caused considerable damage to the influence of the Drigung sect.

But soon the Drigung recovered its influence and the monastery was reconstructed. In 1413 (the eleventh year of the Yongle reign period of Ming Emperor Chengzu) the Ming court conferred upon

Wang Rimpoche Rinchen Paljor, the thirteenth abbot of Drigung Monastery, the title "Propagation Prince of the Doctrine," making him one of the five princes in Tibet.

The three main forces—the Karma Kagyu and Drigung Kagyu sects and Tsangpa Khan—which persecuted the Gelug sect, had not only their own manorial estates and serfs but also their own troops, and had the local regime under their control. On the other hand, the Gelug order, relying on strict monastic organization, monastic influence and the support of a number of small serf owners, had its own local regime and troops, though it was not so strong as its opponents.

The Kagyu sect began its persecution of the Gelug from the sixteenth century, when Chosdrak Yeshe, the fourth ruling lama of the Red Hat line of the Karma Kagyu, and Rinpungpa Tsokye Dorje became "acting regents" and ran administrative affairs on behalf of the tenth Desi of the Phagmo Drupa regime, Ngawang Drashi Drakpa, who was then too young to wield power. During a period of nineteen years (1498-1517, or from the eleventh year of Ming Emperor Xiaozong's reign to the twelfth year of Ming Emperor Wuzong's reign), they had military control of Lhasa and forbade the monks of Drepung and Sera monasteries to attend the Monlam, the annual prayer festival instituted by Tsongkhapa that took place in the first month of every year. At that time the Second Dalai Lama, Gedun Gyatso, was the Living Buddha of the Drepung, and the Second Panchen Lama, Sonam Choglang, was a junior Living Buddha of the Bengom. They could do nothing to prevent the persecution. It was not until 1518 (the thirteenth year of Ming Emperor Wuzong), when the tenth Desi took over administrative power and drove the Rinpungpas' troops out of Lhasa, that the ban was lifted. But, instead of ceasing, the persecution was intensified. In 1526 (the fifth year of the Jiaqing reign period of Ming Emperor Shizong), the Drigung *Ponchen*, Kunga Rinchen, led troops of Gongpo and Sholka to capture the manorial estates belonging to Ganden Monastery in Drigung and Medro. In 1537 (the sixteenth year of the Jiaqing reign period of Ming Emperor Shizong), Kunga Rinchen led troops to attack Ganden Monastery, but was defeated by the supporters of the Gelug sect—the *dzongpon* of Newu Dzong, Depa Kyishopa and Donyo of Wolka. The Drigung troops

had to retreat to Druda. Their hope to destroy Ganden Monastery
did not come true. Nevertheless, the Drigung sect captured eighteen Gelug monasteries and forced the monks there to "change
their hats," that is, to convert their faith to the Kagyu sect. (The
monks of the Gelug sect wore yellow hats, and they were popularly called the Yellow Hat sect.)

In 1605 (the thirty-third year of the Wanli reign period of Ming
Emperor Shenzong), Tsangpa Khan and Kunga Rinchen led their
troops to attack the Gelug. They defeated Depa Kyishopa and
killed five thousand monks and laymen on the hills behind the
Drepung and the Sera. The surviving monks planned to flee to
Qinghai. When they arrived at Taklung, the abbot of Taklung
Monastery (a monastery of another Kagyu sect, Taklung Kagyu),
Shadrung Ngawang Namgyal, admonished them not to go to
Qinghai but to stay in the monastery for four months—where food
and housing would be supplied. At the same time he asked
Tsangpa Khan to allow the monks to go back. Tsangpa Khan
approved his request. (Later, in order to show thanks for the
abbot's help, Ganden, Drepung and Sera monasteries decided to
give Taklung Monastery all tea left over from the Monlam Festival
of the first month of every year, while each monk of the Taklung
would have a share of the donations for that festival.) In order to
punish Drepung and Sera monasteries, Tsangpa Khan imposed a
severe fine on the two monasteries and forbade the Fourth Dalai
Lama, Yonten Gyatso, to "reincarnate."

# 4. The Panchen and the Dalai Establish a Tutor-Disciple Relationship

Yonten Gyatso, the great-grandson of Altan Khan of Mongolia
and son of Sumirtechin Hongteji, was born in 1589 (the seventeenth year of Ming Emperor Shenzong's reign or the Earth-Ox
year of the tenth Tibetan calendrical cycle). When he was a boy,
he was identified by the native Mongols as the reincarnation of
Sonam Gyatso, the Third Dalai Lama, and was invited to reside in
a local monastery. In 1602 (the thirtieth year of Ming Emperor

Shenzong's reign), the Three Major Monasteries in Tibet (Drepung, Ganden and Sera) sent their representatives to Inner Mongolia to give their official recognition of Yonten Gyatso. Escorted by Mongolian cavalrymen, he was brought to Tibet the following year to be enthroned in Radreng Monastery. Then he was invited to reside in Ganden Phodrang Hall, where Second Dalai Lama Gedun Gyatso and Third Dalai Lama Sonam Gyatso had resided. According to a decision of all the monks of the Three Major Monasteries, Lozang Choskyi, the Tashilhunpo's abbot, was invited to hold the *getsul* ritual for Fourth Dalai Lama Yonten Gyatso. When Lozang Choskyi arrived in Lhasa he stayed at Drepung Monastery and had a meeting with Yonten Gyatso. Then Yonten Gyatso took the vows of a *getsul* from Lozang Choskyi and Gedun Gyaltsen, the Ganden Tripa, and was given the religious name Yonten Gyatso. After that, the relationship of tutor and disciple was instituted between the Dalai and Panchen lamas, the elder being the tutor and the younger the disciple. The exceptions emerged only in cases when both of them were too young. During the ritual, Lozang Choskyi gave out alms and sweet buttered-tea to the monks of the Drepung. Thereafter, Yonten Gyatso studied under Lozang Choskyi and became the abbot's good friend. In 1604 (the thirty-second year of the Wanli reign period of Ming Emperor Shenzong), Lozang Choskyi attended the Monlam Festival held at Jokhang Temple in the first month of the Water-Dragon year of the Tibetan calendar, giving out alms and sweet buttered-tea to the monks and delivering a sermon to them. After that, he left for Radreng Monastery, where his preaching was warmly welcomed. Coming back to Lhasa from the Radreng, he was about to return to the Tashilhunpo, when Yonten Gyatso invited him to go to Chokhorgyal Monastery, which had been established by Second Dalai Lama Gedun Gyatso at Lhamo Latso in Lhoka, together with him. Yonten Gyatso and Lozang Choskyi first went to Dechen, where they retreated into seclusion for twenty-one days and Yonten Gyatso studied the works of Tsongkhapa under Lozang Choskyi. When they were at Dechen, Mowang Yugyawa, Yangsi Sharchun and Gongyuyang Bonpa (members of the local upper stratum and followers of the Gelug sect) visited them and asked them to give sermons. After that, they spent half a month at Wolka. They then left for Chokhorgyal Monastery at Lhamo Latso. Lozang Choskyi and Yonten Gyatso went on foot from Lhasa to Lhamo Latso.

After visiting Lhamo Latso and Chokhorgyal Monastery, Lozang Choskyi bade farewell to Yonten Gyatso and went to Wolka and then from Wolka to Sangri, where a local prince named Lhagari (a descendant of an ancient Tibetan king) came to pay his respects to him and asked him to give sermons to him. Then Lozang Choskyi left Sangri for Samye Monastery (an ancient monastery built in the Tang Dynasty). On the third day of the seventh month of that year he returned to the Tashilhunpo.

In 1605 (the thirty-third year of the Wanli reign period of Ming Emperor Shenzong), Lozang Choskyi went from the Tashilhunpo to Lhasa to give sermons to Yonten Gyatso at the latter's invitation. At Lhasa he lived with Yonten Gyatso in Ganden Phodrang Hall of Drepung Monastery. It was said that Lozang Choskyi at that time initiated Yonten Gyatso into the secrets of Kalachakra (Vajrapani of the Wheel of Time).

In 1607 (the thirty-fifth year of the Wanli reign period of Ming Emperor Shenzong), Yonten Gyatso came to visit Lozang Choskyi at the Tashilhunpo. At this time the Gelug sect was being persecuted by Tsangpa Khan and the Karma Kagyu and Drigung Kagyu and thus needed a leader to mobilize all its strength to resist the persecution. So Lozang Choskyi decided to give Yonten Gyatso an unprecedented grand reception to raise his prestige. On the day of Yonten's arrival, Lozang Choskyi himself led more than a hundred monk officials of the Tashilhunpo, all wearing new clothes and riding on horseback, to welcome Yonten Gyatso at the bank of the Nyangchu River. Meanwhile, several hundred monks were blowing *suona* horns on the roofs of all the *dratsangs* of the Tashilhunpo, and three thousand monks stood in two rows in front of the monastery, holding burning joss sticks in their hands. This was Lamaism's most grand reception of honoured guests.

While staying at the Tashilhunpo, Yonten Gyatso lived with Lozang Choskyi in Lharang Hall and his entourage were put up in the best living quarters for monks, with the Tashilhunpo's supply of food and tea at their disposal. Yonten Gyatso spent a month and a half in the Tashilhunpo, studying Buddhist doctrines with Lozang Choskyi every day. When Yonten Gyatso took his leave, Lozang

Choskyi gave him several spirited horses and accompanied him to Ganjan Chosphel Monastery to see him off. Yonten Gyatso then left for other places of Tsang to give sermons.

In 1608 (the thirty-sixth year of the Wanli reign period of Ming Emperor Shenzong), Lozang Choskyi left the Tashilhunpo for Lhasa to give sermons to monks of the Drepung at the invitation of the Fourth Dalai Lama. When he arrived at Lhasa, Yonten Gyatso gave him as grand a reception at the Drepung as had been given in the Tashilhunpo. A group of people were dispatched to welcome the Panchen at the big bridge on the Kyichu River (ten kilometres from the Drepung), while the Fourth Dalai Lama, Yonten Gyatso, and Zimkhang Gongma Rimpoche Sonam Geleg Palzang waited with all the monks of the Drepung at the front gate. When Yonten Gyatso met with Lozang Choskyi, they exchanged *katags* and saluted each other.

While at Lhasa, Lozang Choskyi gave sermons of the Vajra-yana (Diamond Vehicle) to Yonten Gyatso and monks of the Drepung and collected more than a hundred kilos of metal and five hundred taels of gold leaf as donations from the feudal lords of Lhasa. After going back to the Tashilhunpo, he built a Chinese-style gilded roof on Jetsun Jampa Chapel, the first gilded-roof chapel in the Tashilhunpo.

In 1613 (the forty-first year of the Wanli reign period), Fourth Dalai Lama Yonten Gyatso sent people to invite Lozang Choskyi to officiate at the Monlam Festival at Lhasa (according to the tradition of the Yellow Hat sect, the Monlam Festival was to be presided over by the Dalai Lama; but as Yonten Gyatso was too young to do this, he asked his tutor, Lozang Choskyi, to act on his behalf). At first Lozang Choskyi declined, but, as the envoy insisted, he then accepted the invitation reluctantly. Lozang Choskyi held the Monlam of 1613 at Lhasa and ordained into full monkhood the Zimkhang Gongma Rimpoche of the Drepung and more than forty monks of the Sera and the Drepung. Then he went to Don to give sermons to Tenzin Wangyal, the local *depa* (chief administrator), and his parents.

In 1614 (the forty-second year of the Wanli reign period), Lozang Choskyi came to Lhasa to ordain Yonten Gyatso into full monkhood at the latter's invitation. A thousand monks of the

Drepung also took *getsul* or *gelong* vows before him. Shortly afterwards, at the invitation of Radreng Monastery, he went there to preside over a ceremony in which more than a hundred monks of that monastery took *getsul* or *gelong* vows from him.

While en route to Lhasa, Panchen Lama Lozang Choskyi collected donations of seventy loads of metals and four hundred taels of gold leaf, with which he built the second gilded-roof chapel at the Tashilhunpo.

In the winter of 1614 Tsangpa Khan Phuntsok Namgyal and his son invited the tenth ruling lama of the Black Hat line of the Karma Kagyu sect, Choyin Dorje, to Samdrutse (modern Shigatse) and ordered the ruling lamas of all religious sects and all *dzongpons* in the Tsang region to meet at Samdrutse. They wanted the monastic and secular leaders to support Choyin Dorje to be the Desi. Being afraid of their power, the monastic and secular leaders had to obey them. On December 11, 1614, Choyin Dorje was enthroned as the Desi, with the real power being in the hands of Phuntsok Namgyal and his son, Tanchong Wangpo.

On December 15, 1616 (the forty-fourth year of Ming Emperor Shenzong's reign), Yonten Gyatso died suddenly in Drepung Monastery at the age of twenty-eight. Public opinion held that he was murdered by Tsangpa Khan, but there was no evidence to support the claim. Lozang Choskyi hurried to Lhasa to hold the ceremony to release the deceased from worldly cares and engaged in the preparations for his reincarnation. He felt very sad at Yonten Gyatso's death, but he did not say anything against Tsangpa Khan, for at that time the Gelug sect was under the pressure of persecution.

After Yonten Gyatso's death, the abbotship of Drepung and Sera monasteries became vacant (according to tradition, the abbotship of the Drepung and Sera should be taken by the Dalai Lama), so monks of the two monasteries requested Lozang Choskyi to be their abbot. The request, however, was turned down, for Lozang Choskyi said that he had little talent and less learning and, in addition, was too busy with his abbot's work in the Tashilhunpo to assume the abbotship of the two monasteries.

In 1617, Lozang Choskyi went to give sermons in Ngari at the invitation of Ngari's monks and laymen, for he wanted to make a pilgrimage to the Gang Rimpoche (Mt. Kailas) and the lake of Tso Mapham (Manasarovar) in Ngari, which are Buddhist sacred places and attract thousands of pilgrims from India and Nepal every year. Lozang Choskyi travelled to Ngari on foot, giving sermons and recruiting disciples all the way. After a month's journey, on April 23, 1617, he arrived at Tso Mapham and took a bath in the lake. The following day, he went on a pilgrimage to Mt. Kailas, where he held a ritual offering. Then he traveled to Bedin in Shangshung, where he was warmly greeted by local monks and laymen; he therefore preached Tsongkhapa's doctrines to them. On May 13, Shadrung, king of Ngari, invited Lozang Choskyi to Toling Monastery, offering him a *mandral*; Lozang Choskyi then preached sermons to him. On October 13, Lozang Choskyi returned to the Tashilhunpo.

# 5. The Fourth Panchen Leads the Gelug Sect in an Alliance with Gushri Khan to Defeat Tsangpa Khan

After Yonten Gyatso's death, his *changzod* (chief administrator), Sonam Rabten, together with Depa Kyishopa Tsokye Dorje, mobilized the troops of all the *dzongs* and *shikas* in U who supported the Gelug and the two thousand Mongolian cavalrymen who had escorted Yonten Gyatso to Tibet to attack Tsangpa Khan's troops. The latter retreated to Jangtanggang and Chakpori. The fight came to a stalemate. Lozang Choskyi, Ganden Tripa Konchok Chosphel and Taklung Shadrung Ngawang Namgyal acted as mediators between the two parties. They made mediation proposals as follows:

(1) The Lharang of Ganden Phodrang would enjoy the ownership of all the monasteries and manorial estates in Lhasa and in the lower reaches of the Lhasa River;

(2) Yonten Gyatso's Chief administrator, Sonam Rabten, would reside in Ganden Phodrang Hall of the Drepung to take charge of administrative and religious affairs of the Gelug sect;

(3) Tsangpa Khan would return to the three monasteries of

Ganden, Sera and Drepung their manorial estates he had seized;

(4) Tsangpa Khan would allow the monks in Dechen, Samyang and Kari, whom he had converted from their faith by force, to return to their belief in the rites of the Gelug order;

(5) Depa Kyishopa could take over Phanpo Kartse Dzong captured by Tsangpa Khan; and

(6) Tsangpa Khan would lift the ban on the search for the reincarnation of Fourth Dalai Lama Yonten Gyatso.

Tsangpa Khan accepted all the proposals except the last one. Under such circumstances, the search for the reincarnation of the Fourth Dalai Lama had to be done secretly.

In 1618 (the forty-sixth year of the Wanli reign period of Ming Emperor Shenzong), Tsangpa Khan's troops captured U, surrounded Nedong Palace and overthrew the Phagmo Drupa's eleventh ruling lama, Drowai Gonpo, who had fled. The *Records of Tibetan Kings and Ministers*, written by the Fifth Dalai Lama, does not tell in what month and year Drowai Gonpo died, though the author points out clearly that Drowai Gonpo died. After overthrowing the last ruling lama of the Phagmo Drupa regime, Tsangpa Khan made Choyin Dorje (the tenth ruling lama of the Black Hat line of the Karma Kagyu) Desi. The latter is referred in Tibetan historical materials as Karma Desi. His capital was Samdrutse (modern Shigatse). The real power of the Karma regime was in the hands of Tsangpa Khan Tanchong Wangpo, who claimed himself to be the King of Tsang, while he is referred in Chinese historical materials as Tsangpa Khan. The Karma regime, a new regime as it was, also belonged to the Kagyu sect, so the ruling power remained in the hands of the Kagyu sect. But it was still different from the Phagmo Drupa regime. For one, the Karma regime existed only for a short time. The main difference, however, was that the Phagmo Drupa regime supported the Gelug sect, while Tsangpa Khan persecuted it.

When Tsangpa Khan overthrew Drowai Gonpo, the eleventh ruling lama of the Phagmo Drupa regime, his troops captured the Lhasa area and plundered Drepung and Sera monasteries. At this very unhappy news, Lozang Choskyi immediately gave a large amount of relief to the two monasteries and five times gave out alms and sweet buttered-tea to the monks there.

Tsangpa Khan's troops soon attacked the Drepung again, destroying Third Dalai Lama Sonam Gyatso's stupa and taking away the gold, silver, pearls and jewels inlaid on the stupa. So Lozang Choskyi, to express his sympathy and solicitude for the monks, collected donations, with which he reconstructed the Third Dalai's stupa, gave out sweet buttered-tea and alms to the monks of the Ganden, Sera and Drepung, and gave each monk a small image of Buddha and a *katag*.

By now Tsangpa Khan was seriously ill. He had undergone various treatments without success. Some people recommended that, as Lozang Choskyi was skilled at medicine, he could doubtless be able to cure Tsangpa Khan. However, Tsangpa Khan was not willing to ask Lozang Choskyi, his mortal enemy, for help. But in order to save his own life, he could not but ask Lozang Choskyi to give him medical treatment. Lozang Choskyi accepted his invitation with pleasure. After giving medical treatment to him, Lozang Choskyi cured Tsangpa Khan of his serious illness. To express his gratitude to Lozang Choskyi, Tsangpa Khan prepared to donate a manorial estate to the Ngapa Dratsang of Tashilhunpo Monastery. Lozang Choskyi declined the donation. But he requested Tsangpa Khan to permit the search for the soul boy of Yonten Gyatso. It was after the repeated pleas of Lozang Choskyi that Tsangpa Khan lifted the ban and the search began. Not long afterwards, the monks of Drepung Monastery found the soul boy, who later became the Fifth Dalai Lama.

The Fifth Dalai Lama, Ngawang Lozang Gyatso (Lozang Gyatso, for short), was born in 1617 (the forty-fifth year of Ming Emperor Shenzong's reign, or the Fire-Snake year of the tenth Tibetan calendrical cycle) in the Chonggye region (modern Lhoka) in U. As the soul boy of the Fourth Dalai, he was moved to Drepung Monastery by the monks of the Three Major Monasteries. He took his *getsul* vows from and was given his religious name by Lozang Choskyi at Lhasa in 1625 (the fifth year of the Tianqi reign period of Ming Emperor Xizong). So the Fifth Dalai Lama was the disciple of the Fourth Panchen Lama. On the fifth day of the fourth month of the eleventh year of the Chongzhen reign period of Ming Emperor Sizong (1638), the Fifth Dalai Lama was initiated into full monkhood by Fourth Panchen Lama Lozang Choskyi. That year smallpox was widespread in Lhasa, so Lozang Choskyi moved the Fifth Dalai to Ganden Khangsar (behind Radreng Monastery in Northern Tsang) and took the opportunity to teach him all the works of Tsongkhapa. At that time Tsangpa Khan was again trying every means to stamp out the Gelug sect, so it was necessary for the Fourth Panchen and the Fifth Dalai to unite to stem the tide of persecution Tsangpa Khan was bringing upon them.

In 1631 (the fourth year of the Chongzhen reign period of Ming Emperor Sizong), Tanchong Wangpo (1606-1642) succeeded his father Phuntsok Namgyal (1586-1621) as Tsangpa Khan. He persecuted the Gelug even more cruelly. But the Gelug sect had become a very popular religious faith in Qinghai, Kham, U, Tsang and even Mongolia; in its more than two centuries of development since Tsongkhapa, the sect had won the popular support of the Tibetan people. Tsangpa Khan knew it would not be easy to stamp it out. For this purpose he had to seek help from outside. So Tsangpa Khan Tanchong Wangpo secretly sent for Lindan Khan* of the Chahar (Qahar) tribe of Inner Mongolia, asking him to lead his troops into Tibet. Lindan Khan, originally a follower of the Gelug sect, had later converted to the Karma Kagyu sect after being won over by Tsangpa Khan. At that time it was hard for him to remain active in Mongolia, so he accepted Tsangpa Khan's request. His troops captured Qinghai in 1633 (the sixth year of Chongzhen). But in 1634 (the seventh year of Chongzhen), when his army reached a place called Shartala, he died suddenly of illness. Tsangpa Khan therefore failed in stamping out the Gelug sect by way of alliance with Lindan Khan.

That same year (1634) Chogthu Khan, the head of seven Kharkha tribes from the north of the Gobi desert, led his troops to invade Qinghai after he had been defeated in a war by other Mongolian chieftains. It was said that his cavalrymen, thirty thousand in number, and their families totalled more than a hundred thousand. Chogthu Khan soon subdued the Tibetan and Mongolian tribes in

---

* Lindan Khan (1592-1634), a descendant of the thirty-seventh generation of the Mongolian royal family since the overthrow of the Yuan Dynasty, united with the Ming court to fight against the Manchu regime. He died of illness in Qinghai in 1634 (the seventh year of the Chongzhen reign period of Ming Emperor Sizong), after he had been defeated in a war and had retreated to the west.

Qinghai and became the real king of Qinghai.

Tsangpa Khan secretly sent for Chogthu Khan in Qinghai, asking him for help. Chogthu Khan, as a follower of the Karma Kagyu, promised to send at the proper time an army of ten thousand cavalrymen under his son's command to put an end to the Gelug sect. At that time (1634, or the seventh year of Chongzhen), the Fifth Dalai Lama was a young man of seventeen and inexperienced in politics, while the Fourth Panchen Lama, at sixty-three, was politically mature and religiously enjoyed high authority. They therefore necessarily consulted with each other to decide how to deal with Tsangpa Khan's secret plots. The natural result was that the Gelug sect sought support from Mongolian chieftains just as Tsangpa Khan had done.

The Fifth Dalai and the Fourth Panchen, after consulting with Sonam Chosphel (also known as Sonam Rabten, the Fifth Dalai's *changzod*, who was in charge of the daily administrative and religious affairs of the Gelug) and Depa Kyishopa Tsokye Dorje (a feudal lord in U and a supporter of the Gelug, who held a part of military and ruling power), secretly sent for Gushri Khan, chief of the Qoshot Mongols in Xinjiang, asking him to lead his army into Tibet to defend the Gelug. The situation at the time was very tense. It was said that the Fifth Dalai and the Fourth Panchen had sent some monks of Drepung Monastery to take a confidential letter to Ngachen Garu and Sheni Garchin, instructing them to disguise themselves as members of other sects and go to Xinjiang to make contacts with Gushri Khan.

Gushri Khan (1582-1655, or from the tenth year of the Wanli reign period of Ming Emperor Shenzong to the twelfth year of the Shunzhi reign period of Qing Emperor Shizu), also called Tulubaihu, was a leader of the Qoshot tribe of the Oylut Mongols (the Oylut were also called Oirat in the Ming Dynasty). The Oylut comprised four big tribes—the Durbat, Turgut, Dzungar and Qoshot—and were very strong. They captured the western part of both Outer and Inner Mongolia in 1435 (the tenth year of the Xuande reign period of Ming Emperor Xuanzong). Fifty years later, Dayan Khan (a twenty-ninth-generation descendant of Genghis Khan) and the Tatar Mongols defeated the Oylut Mongols and drove them to the south and north of the Tianshan Mountains in

Xinjiang. In 1543 (the twenty-second year of the Jiaqing reign period of Ming Emperor Sizong), when Dayan Khan died, the Tatar Mongols were divided into five large tribes: the Chahar (whose chieftain was Lindan Khan), Karashin, Ordos, Tumet (whose chieftain Altan Khan had invited the Third Dalai Lama Sonam Gyatso to Qinghai) and Kharkha. The former four tribes lived to the south of the Gobi desert, while the last one lived to the north of it. Of the four tribes to the south of the Gobi, the strongest was the Tumet tribe, whose chieftain Altan Khan had once led his army into Qinghai. Altan Khan was granted the title "Prince of Compliance and Righteousness" by the Ming court in 1571 (the fifth year of the Longqing reign period of Ming Emperor Muzong). Grand Secretary Zhang Juzheng asked Third Dalai Sonam Gyatso to persuade Altan Khan to go back to Inner Mongolia. Altan Khan accepted the Dalai's suggestion. He led most of his tribesmen back to Inner Mongolia in 1578 (the sixth year of the Wanli reign period of Ming Emperor Shenzong), leaving a small part in Qinghai.

The Oylut Mongols in Xinjiang lived a pastoral life to the south and north of the Tianshan Mountains. The Qoshot and Durbat Mongols resided in the areas of the Emba and Kharakum rivers bordering on Tsarist Russia.

From 1632 to 1634 (from the fifth to the seventh year of the Chongzhen reign period of Ming Emperor Sizong), Gushri Khan moved the Qoshot tribe to the Tobel valley of the Irtysh River. In 1634 (the seventh year of the Chongzhen reign period of Ming Emperor Sizong) the Qoshot tribe, under Gushri Khan's command, joined in the war Durbats and Dzungars were making on Kazaks. The Mongols won the war and captured Yanggil, son of Eshim Khan, the chieftain of the Kazaks.

In the same year Gushri Khan captured several Russians from Tara and Chiumin, which were under Russian's occupation, while the Russian side captured Katse, an envoy sent by Gushri Khan. After negotiation, the Russians released Katse, and Gushri Khan set a Russian free. Gushri Khan proposed that the other captured Russians should be exchanged with the two grandsons of Kuchen Khan captured by the Russians. (As to the results of the negotiation, no record can be found in historical documents.) It was at the time when Gushri Khan was negotiating with the Russians on the exchange of captives that the Fifth Dalai Lama and the Fourth Panchen Lama secretly sent emissaries to Gushri Khan. Gushri Khan, as a devoted follower of the Gelug sect, accepted their request and prepared to help the Gelug sect in Tibet. Gushri Khan, clever and resourceful, never took a rash act. He knew it would not be easy to win the war against Chogthu Khan, who had thirty thousand cavalrymen, while he had only ten thousand. Besides, Tsangpa Khan was wielding power over Tibet, and Gushri Khan did not know how big Tsangpa Khan's forces were. In order to find out Tsangpa Khan's real power and the Gelug converts' number and power, Gushri Khan, in the disguise of a pilgrim, went to Tibet in 1635 (the eighth year of the Chongzhen reign period of Ming Emperor Sizong). Making a field investigation on his journey from Xinjiang through Qinghai to Tibet, Gushri Khan met Arsalang, Chogthu Khan's son, at the upper reaches of the Tongtian River in Qinghai as the latter was leading an army of ten thousand Mongolian cavalrymen to Tibet to help Tsangpa Khan to fight the Gelug sect. It is said that Gushri Khan pressed Arsalang not to persecute the Gelug. Arsalang was convinced. Instead of helping Tsangpa Khan, his cavalrymen attacked and defeated Tsangpa Khan's troops at Yamdrok. Choyin Dorje, the ruling lama of the Black Hat line of the Karma Kagyu, wrote to Chogthu Khan about his son's rebellion. Chogthu Khan was so angry that he sent a secret order to his son's chief assistant, Daichen, instructing him to put his son to death. Arsalang was thus assassinated.* Tsangpa Khan failed again in engineering the plot of using Chogthu's armed forces to get rid of the Gelug sect.

According to Lozang Choskyi's *Autobiography*, when Gushri Khan arrived safely at Lhasa in the disguise of a Buddhist pilgrim, he had a secret meeting with the Fifth Dalai Lama and the Fourth Panchen. Gushri Khan paid respects to them. He gave the Fifth Dalai Lama a treasure in gold, silver, pearls and jewelry and was

---

* According to the *Political and Religious History of Amdo*, after defeating Tsangpa Khan, Arsalang defeated Beri Tusi and seized large amounts of war spoils on his way back to Qinghai. In the scramble for the spoils, his subordinates assassinated him and his trusted followers, thirteen in all.

granted the title Guardian Prince of the Doctrine.* He also gave two
thousand taels of silver as a gift to the Panchen, and the Panchen
chanted scriptures for him at his request. After consulting with the
Fifth Dalai Lama and the Fourth Panchen, Gushri Khan decided to
lead his army from Xinjiang to Qinghai to get rid of Chogthu Khan
first, and then to Kham to wipe out Donyo Dorje, the local lord
(*tusi*) of Beri, and, finally, to Tibet to overthrow Tsangpa Khan. The
measures were necessary in order that the Gelug sect preserve itself
in the urgent situation at that time.

The areas under Tsangpa Khan's jurisdiction were U, Tsang and
Ngari. Kham was ruled by the local lord of Beri, Donyo Dorje, a
follower of the Bon (Black) religion. He opposed the Gelug sect as
well as the Kagyu and the Sakya. He was especially hostile to the
Gelug sect and persecuted it more cruelly than Tsangpa Khan did,
killing and imprisoning many monks of the Gelug. So the Dalai
and Panchen asked Gushri Khan to get rid of him before dealing
with Tsangpa Khan.

After going back to Xinjiang, Gushri Khan made military arrangements for waging a life-and-death battle with Chogthu Khan.
Considering Chogthu Khan's superior forces, Gushri Khan asked
the chieftain of the Dzungar tribe, Batur Hongteji, for help, but
even the combined force of Qoshot and Dzungar cavalrymen
totaled only a little more than ten thousand, and was still numer-
ically inferior to Chogthu Khan's force.

In 1637 (the tenth year of the Chongzhen reign period of Ming
Emperor Sizong), Gushri Khan and Batur Hongteji led their cavalrymen to attack Chogthu Khan in Qinghai. They fought a great
battle after several skirmishes in a valley. Gushri Khan won the
battle. (Since that time the two mountains on either side of the
valley have been known as the Greater and Lesser Ulan Qoshot.)
The battle is referred to in the history of Qinghai as the Battle of
Blood Mountain. Gushri Khan's son Dalai Teji closely pursued the
enemy and killed Chogthu Khan. This put an end to Chogthu      ·
Khan's rule over Qinghai. Gushri Khan thereby overthrew Chog-

---

* According to the *Political and Religious History of Amdo*, it was in 1637 (the
tenth year of the Chongzhen reign period of the Ming Dynasty) that Gushri Khan
was granted the title "Tenzin Choskyi Gyalpo" (Guardian Prince of the Doctrine)
by the Fifth Dalai Lama.

thu Khan and became the ruler of Qinghai. To express gratitude for Batur Hongteji's help, Gushri Khan married his daughter to him and gave him a large amount of the treasure captured from Chogthu Khan. Afterwards Batur Hongteji went back to the Dzungar tribe's pastureland in Xinjiang.

Chogthu Khan's death caused Donyo Dorje, the local lord of Beri, great alarm and anxiety, and he became all the more hostile to the Gelug. In 1639 (the twelfth year of the Chongzhen reign period of Ming Emperor Sizong), he wrote a letter to Tsangpa Khan, asking the Khan to send troops to support him in an attack on Gushri Khan in the next year. But the letter was intercepted by Gelug monks and was sent to Gushri Khan. So Gushri Khan decided to get rid of Donyo Dorje as soon as possible.

In May 1639 (the twelfth year of the Chongzhen reign period of Ming Emperor Sizong), Gushri Khan led his troops to attack the lord of Beri in Kham. The war lasted for a year and ended with Gushri Khan's victory. In 1640 (the thirteenth year of the Chongzhen reign period of Ming Emperor Sizong), Gushri Khan killed Donyo Dorje and occupied the territory that had been ruled by him. Gushri Khan set free all the monks of the Gelug, Sakya, Kagyu and Nyingma sects that had been imprisoned by the lord of Beri. Thus, except the Bon, all Tibetan religious sects were pleased and supported Gushri Khan with admiration and gratitude.

Before 1641 (the fourteenth year of the Chongzhen reign period of Ming Emperor Sizong), when Gushri Khan led his army into Tibet, Tsangpa Khan Tanchong Wangpo had already seemingly changed his attitude towards the Gelug, for he knew that he was in a disadvantageous position. In order to curry favour with Fourth Panchen Lozang Choskyi, Tsangpa Khan donated the prosperous Shetongmoin Shika and Lanrenrabu Shika (equal to two *dzongs*) to the Tashilhunpo. The donations made Lozang Choskyi well off and he began to build Lharang Hall at the Tashilhunpo. It took seven months to build the hall. After Gushri Khan's troops had captured a large part of U, Tsangpa Khan retreated to Tsang and meanwhile asked the Fourth Panchen to mediate. The Panchen agreed to act as a mediator. He visited Gushri Khan when the Khan stationed his troops at a place called Pad'onakha, five kilometres from the Tashilhunpo in Samdrutse (modern Shigatse), the capital

of the Karma Desi's regime. Gushri Khan said that he would take
over the whole of Tibet from Tsangpa Khan, but he would permit
Tsangpa Khan to spend his old age in a *shika*, if the latter
surrendered his military and administrative power. Tsangpa Khan
refused the proposal. So the war dragged on between the two
parties in Tsang.

Meanwhile, two *dzongpons* of Dechen Dzong (appointed by the
Karma Kagyu Desi) wrote to Lozang Choskyi, asking him to
mediate between them and the local inhabitants, who had determined to kill them. Lozang Choskyi went to Dechen Dzong at their
invitation. With his mediation, the two *dzongpons* were set free
from the original punishment of death when they accepted the
conditions of handing the ruling power over to Kyishod Depa, a
Gelug supporter, and offering five hundred loads of *tsamba*. After
settling the problem, Lozang Choskyi, on the pretense of giving
sermons, went to Drepung Monastery at Lhasa to consult with the
Fifth Dalai Lama Lozang Gyatso on how to deal with the situation
after Tsangpa Khan's overthrow.

In 1642 (the fifteenth year of the Chongzhen reign period of
Ming Emperor Sizong), Tsangpa Khan, after having been once
again defeated and with a greater part of the Tsang region being
occupied by Gushri Khan, again invited Lozang Choskyi to act as
a mediator. So Lozang Choskyi left for Tsang. But on his way he
received at Linggar Dzong a letter from Gushri Khan, who asked
him to invite Choyin Dorje, the tenth ruling lama of the Black Hat
line and the Desi of the Karma Kagyu regime, to meet him. Choyin
Dorje dared not accept the invitation, though Lozang Choskyi
stayed at Linggar Dzong for almost two months trying again and
again to persuade Choyin Dorje to go to meet Gushri Khan. So
Gushri Khan ordered that Choyin Dorje be deprived of the title of
Desi, forbidding anyone, however, from taking away his property.
As for Tsangpa Khan, Gushri Khan still insisted that he should
hand over his troops. Knowing that he had no other way out and
being persuaded by Lozang Choskyi, Tsangpa Khan surrendered.
He offered a thousand loads of tea, butter, grain, gold, silver and
other treasures and pleaded guilty before Gushri Khan.

After capturing Tsangpa Khan, Gushri Khan, not intending to
kill him, imprisoned him at Newu Shika. But then a secret docu-

ment was discovered on a cook of Choyin Dorje. The document, sealed by the ruling lamas of the Karma Black Hat and Red Hat lines and Tsangpa Khan, showed that the three parties intended to destroy Ganden, Sera and Drepung monasteries, take away their *shikas* and imprison the Fifth Dalai Lama and the Fourth Panchen at Gongpo. So Gushri Khan put Tsangpa Khan to death by tying him in a wet ox-hide bag and drowning him in the river near Newu Shika. Thus the Karma regime of the Kagyu sect that had ruled over Tibet for twenty-four years (1619-1642) came to an end.

The *Records of Tibetan Kings and Ministers*, written by Fifth Dalai Lama Lozang Gyatso, does not give a detailed account of the incident. It only says:

> Then the chief of Samdrutse, a subordinate of Rinpungpa, united many officials in the north and south, such as Nathangpa, Lhochongpa and Gyatsowa, to stage a rebellion. The rebellion grew in scale, but under the command of the King of Man who was stationed in Tsang [Gushri Khan], all those in authority were subdued by the rule of one man, who is the *Tchakra Vartti Radja* [a ruler, the wheels of whose chariot roll everywhere without hindrance] of this *kalpo*—Tenzin Choskyi Gyalpo.

The book does not mention Tsangpa Khan, from whom the Fifth Dalai Lama took over the administration of Tibet with the help of Gushri Khan's military power.

The Fifth Dalai Lama devoted a whole chapter of his *Records of Tibetan Kings and Ministers* to Gushri Khan. He said:

> The Great King of the Dharma Tenzin Choskyi Gyalpo fiGushri Khanfl led a great army of a million soldiers to occupy the southern border-land. On the twenty-fifth day of the second month of the year *ren-wu* [that is, the fifteenth year of the Chongzhen reign period of Ming Emperor Sizong, or 1642] all Tibetan families and all officials gave allegiance to him. Therefore he completed the unification of Tibet and became the king of the three regions of the whole of Tibet on the fifteenth day of the third month of the first year of the "Wheel of Time." His command was as great as the sacred white canopy that covers the sky.

Gushri Khan invited Fifth Dalai Lama Lozang Gyatso to Samdrutse to celebrate his victory over Tsangpa Khan. He offered the Dalai Lama all the treasures found in Tsangpa Khan's palace at Samdrutse. The palace was dismantled at his order. He further

ordered that all the timber from the dismantled palace be sent to
Lhasa for the extension of Jokhang Temple and the Potala. All the
monks of the monasteries of the Black Hat line were forced to
convert to the Gelug sect.

The tenth ruling lama of the Black Hat line, Choyin Dorje, fled
to Lhodak and united with the local Karma Kagyu in rebellion
against Gushri Khan. The rebellion was quelled by Gushri Khan's
son Tenzin Dalai Khan, who forced the local monks of the Karma
Kagyu sect to convert to the Gelug sect. Choyin Dorje then fled to
Lijiang in Yunnan to seek refuge with Mu Tusi (a descendant of
Mu Ying, the Prince of Ning in Guizhou in the early Ming Dynasty).
He thereafter lived there in exile. His property and monasteries in
Tibet were under the charge of his representative, Gyaltsab Chen-
po Drakpa Choyang. In 1653 (the tenth year of the Shunzhi reign
period of Qing Emperor Shizu), Shadrung Rimpoche of Taklung
Monastery, acting as a mediator, went to Lhasa, together with
Choyin Dorje's representative, to ask the Fifth Dalai Lama to permit
Choyin Dorje to come back to Tibet and asked the Dalai to return
Choyin Dorje's property confiscated in the war. The Dalai Lama
agreed, on the condition that the Kagyu sect recognize the Dalai's
rule over them. After the mediation, in 1661 (the eighteenth year
of the Shunzhi reign period of Qing Emperor Shizu), Choyin Dorje
came back. He settled in Tsurpu Monastery after paying his respects to the Fifth Dalai Lama. In 1671 (the tenth year of the
Kangxi reign period of the Qing Dynasty), he died at Tsurpu
Monastery.

Gushri Khan ordered that the annual income of tax revenue in
Tibet be given to the Dalai for his financial support and appointed
the Dalai's *changzod*, Sonam Chosphel (alias Sonam Rabten), to be
Depa to take charge of the political and religious administration
under the leadership of Gushri Khan and the Fifth Dalai Lama. The
capital of Tibet was moved from Samdrutse to Lhasa, and the Fifth
Dalai Lama's residence was also moved from Ganden Phodrang
Hall of the Drepung to the Potala.

The rivalry between the Gelug and Kagyu sects ended with the
Gelug's victory. Fourth Panchen Lozang Choskyi was the backstage
manipulator, though on surface he acted as a humble "mediator."
He was generally acknowledged as the real leader in the rivalry.

Following the example of Altan Khan, who had given Sonam Gyatso the title "Dalai Lama," Gushri Khan granted Lozang Choskyi the title "Panchen Pokto" in 1645 (the second year of the Shunzhi reign period of Qing Emperor Shizu). *Pan* is an abbreviation of the Sanskrit word *pandita*, meaning "wisdom"; *chen* is an abbreviation of the Tibetan word *chenpo*, meaning "great"; and *pokto* means "a wise and brave man" in Mongolian. Besides, Gushri Khan donated dozens of *shikas* in Tsang to the Tashilhunpo.

Though the Fifth Dalai Lama, the Fourth Panchen and Gushri Khan had gothen rid of Tsangpa Khan and taken over the Tibetan regime, the Kagyu sect still enjoyed authority in various regions and staged a number of armed rebellions. The rebellions were suppressed one after another by Gushri Khan's cavalrymen.

After suppressing the Kagyu rebellions, Gushri Khan returned to Samdrutse in 1645 (the second year of the Shunzhi reign period of Qing Emperor Shizu). He forbade local chieftains to communicate with each other and gave the order that those who acted against his order be punished. Lozang Choskyi persuaded Gushri Khan not to do so. When Gushri Khan lifted the ban upon the Panchen's persuasion, the social order became gradually stable.

Not long after its establishment, the Gelug regime took severe measures to punish those who had been against the Gelug sect, imposing heavy fines on them. Many people complained of their sufferings. So Lozang Choskyi wrote to the Depa, asking that the fines be reduced. At his proposal, the Depa gave the order to reduce the fines by one-third.

Apart from staging rebellions, the overthrown Kagyu sect prepared public opinion for attacking the Gelug sect and the Dalai and Panchen. A lama of the Kagyu sect named Drakpa Sherab Rinchen wrote books to attack the Gelug doctrines. Block-printed, his books became widespread among the people. His arguments could not be refuted, even by many learned lamas of the Gelug sect.

On hearing of this, Lozang Choskyi, in his old age, wrote a book *The Roar of a Lion* to refute the Kagyu lama's arguments. In the debate Drakpa Sherab Rinchen admitted defeat and his influence was soon wiped out.

After the Karma Kagyu regime was overthrown by Gushri Khan, the Fourth Panchen and the Fifth Dalai, the whole of Tibet was put under the jurisdiction of the local Tibetan regime (*Depashung* in Tibetan) established by the Gelug sect.

The Bhutanese, called *Drukpa* in Tibetan, are similar in language, writing, habits and customs to Tibetans. Religiously, the Bhutanese were followers of the Kagyu sect (the White sect). Bhutan's local Kagyu sect, one of the eight subsects of the Phagmo Drupa Kagyu, was called Drukpa Kagyu. It had its own ruling lama, who was under the rule of the Phagmo Drupa Desi. When Tsangpa Khan overthrew the Phagmo Drupa regime, Bhutan was still ruled by the ruling lama of the Drukpa Kagyu sect. After getting rid of Tsangpa Khan, Gushri Khan, busy suppressing rebellions, had no time to deal with Bhutan.

In 1656 (the thirteenth year of the Shunzhi reign period of Qing Emperor Shizu), Fifth Dalai Lama Lozang Gyatso began to pay attention to Bhutan. He sent a letter to the religious king of the Bhutan Drukpa Kagyu, asking him to submit to the Gelug regime. The religious king would not even consider this, because he was not a Gelug follower. When the Fifth Dalai dispatched a militia from Gongpo, Dakpo and Lhoka to attack Bhutan, the religious king of the Bhutan Drukpa Kagyu sent Bhutanese militiamen to put up resistance. At that time Gushri Khan had just died and his eldest son, Dayan Khan, was still in Qinghai, so only a part of the Mongolian cavalrymen stationed in Tibet were sent to assist the Dalai's troops. The war lasted for a year, but neither side won a clear victory. Fifth Dalai Lozang Gyatso asked Depa Kyishopa to persuade the religious king of Bhutan to submit himself to the Gelug regime, but Depa Kyishopa was also refused by the religious king. So the Fifth Dalai could not but ask Fourth Panchen Lozang Choskyi to act as a mediator. The Panchen did not refuse the Dalai's request, though he was at the advanced age of eighty-five and was too old to go to Bhutan himself. He sent Chosje Sonam Phuntsok, Kachin Tsoksopa, and Trulgyi Legpa of the Tashilhunpo to take his letters to Tuncho Rimpoche, the religious king of Bhutan, and to Depa Changzodpa, the commander-in-chief of the force that the Fifth Dalai had sent to the front. They gave a hundred *katags*, a thousand taels of silver, a hundred bolts of silk fabric, fifty bolts of satin and three taels of gold to each side and extended their greetings. Through the Fourth Panchen's mediation, the two sides ceased the war and withdrew their troops. But the Fourth Panchen could not settle the problem of subordinating Bhutan to the Tibetan Gelug regime either.

# 6. The Relations Between the Fourth Panchen and the Central Government of the Qing Dynasty

A short overview of the relations between the Fifth Dalai, the Fourth Panchen and Gushri Khan on the one side and the central government of the Qing Dynasty on the other is now necessary. In 1642 when Gushri Khan seized Tibetan political power after overthrowing Tsangpa Khan's regime, although the central government of the Ming Dynasty had not yet collapsed, the Qing Emperor Taizong Huangtaiji had extended his domain to the whole Northeast China outside the Shanhaiguan Pass, as well as Inner Mongolia to the south of the Gobi Desert, and at the same time Li Zicheng and Zhang Xianzhong's peasant re- bellious troops had spread all over the country. In 1637 (the tenth year of the Chongzhen reign period of Ming Emperor Sizong, or the second year of the Chongde reign period of Qing Emperor Taizong), after occupying Qinghai, Gushri Khan went from Qinghai to Lhasa publicly for a meeting with the Fifth Dalai Lama and the Fourth Panchen, not secretly in the disguise of a lamaist pilgrim as he had two years before. They all sensed that the Ming rule was tottering and the Manchu rulers would not take long to occupy Central China. Therefore, the two lamas decided to jointly send a goodwill mission to Shengjing (modern Shenyang) to give allegiance to the Manchus. The mission would consist of Sanchen Choje as the envoy of the Dalai and Panchen, and Dechen Dorje as the representative of Gushri Khan.

When the Fifth Dalai, the Fourth Panchen and Gushri Khan told the real ruler of Tibet at that time, Tsangpa Khan, about this, the latter agreed, but he did not send his representative to join the mission. Instead, he wrote a letter to Qing Emperor Taizong.

When the mission had set off, Gushri Khan went back to Qinghai to make preparations for wiping out the *tusi* of Beri.

After a five-year journey by way of Xinjiang and Outer and Inner Mongolia to the north and south of the Gobi, the mission, which had set off in 1637, arrived at Shengjing in October 1642, and was given a hearty reception by Qing Emperor Taizong. The reception was vividly recorded in *Imperial Records of the Qing Dynasty*:

> In the tenth month of the seventh year of the Chongde reign period [1642] Sanchen Choje Hutuktu and Dechen Dorje sent by the Dalai Lama of Tibet arrived at Shengjing. The Emperor, his princes and court officials greeted them outside the Huaiyuan Gate. After the Emperor and his retinue performed the prostration rituals to heaven at the reception house, Sanchen Choje Hutuktu kowtowed and delivered to the Emperor a letter from the Dalai Lama. The Emperor showed him special respect by taking the letter in a standing position and granted the two envoys the honour to take seats on his right side.... By the Emperor's order, Gushian read the letters from the Dalai Lama and Tibetan Tsangpa Khan. The guests were entertained with tea. The monks chanted scriptures before drinking it. Then a welcome banquet was held in the envoys' honour. Sanchen Choje and his company offered gifts such as camels, horses, Buddhist rosaries, black fox-fur, blankets, carpets, wolfskin and tea. The Emperor accepted a part of them.

In 1643 (the eighth year of the Chongde reign period of Qing Emperor Taizong, or the sixteenth year of the Chongzhen reign period of Ming Emperor Sizong), the envoys asked to go back to Tibet. On their departure Qing Emperor Taizong held a grand farewell ceremony in their honour.

The letter delivered to the Dalai Lama by Qing Emperor Taizong was quoted in my *Biographies of the Dalai Lamas*. As to the letter to the Panchen, the *Imperial Records of the Qing Dynasty* says: "It was the same as that to the Dalai Lama in language and style and was accompanied by the same gifts." This showed that the Qing Emperor had accorded the Dalai and Panchen the same treatment. The Emperor's letter to Tsangpa Khan reads:

> I, the wise, tolerant and benevolent Emperor of the Great Qing Empire, am writing to you, Tsangpa Khan. With great pleasure I received your letter through your envoy and am pleased to know of your intention of salvaging the worldly people through spreading the teachings of the Buddha among them. I have heard that you were defeated by Gushri

Khan and I would like to know the details. I hope there will be friendly relations between yourselves from now on. I shall send you what you need. Accompanying this letter are my gifts for you, which include a hundred taels of silver and three bolts of brocade.

The Emperor's letter to Gushri Khan reads:

I, the wise, tolerant and benevolent Emperor of the Great Qing Empire, am writing to you, Gushri Khan. I have heard that you have punished those who have broken the laws. I think the teachings of the Buddha have not come to an end since sacred emperors managed state affairs in ancient times. Now I take the opportunity to tell you that I have sent envoys to go with Sanchen Choje to Tibet to invite high monks, regardless of their costume's colour, whether red or yellow. They will be invited to spread Buddhism and to safeguard our country's happiness. Accompanying this letter is a suit of armour, my gift to you.

Sanchen Choje and his party did not return to Tibet until the first year of the Shunzhi reign period of Qing Emperor Shizu (1644). By that time the Fifth Dalai Lama and Gushri Khan had become the genuine rulers of Tibet after Tsangpa Khan had been put to death.

In the second year of the Shunzhi reign period (1645), Gushri Khan, after suppressing rebellions in Tibet, sent his eldest son to lead the main forces of his army back to Qinghai, leaving only a detachment of Mongolian cavalrymen in Tibet for urgent needs. Gushri Khan made Shigatse his headquarters.

When the Ming Dynasty was overthrown by Manchu troops and the Qing Dynasty was founded, the Tibetan local regime was put all the more obviously in a subordinate position to the central government of the Qing Dynasty. In 1645, the Fifth Dalai Lama dispatched Sanchen Choje again to Beijing with a letter to Qing Emperor Shizu. In the letter the Fifth Dalai expressed his thanks brimming with warm feeling. It started with a poem in Tibetan in which the Qing Emperor was compared to *Tchakra Vartti Radia* (a god "the wheels of whose chariot roll everywhere without hindrance"). The letter reads:

In a turbulent period *Tchakra Vartti Radja* raises an all-conquering banner atop the three regions. He safeguards people with a white umbrella of law. Under him, people live a happy life.

Accompanying this letter were gifts, which included the *sarira* of Sakyamuni, a bronze image of the Buddha made in India, a collection of the essential teachings of Buddhism, Tsongkhapa's *Complete Course of the Graded Path of Bodhi*, Atisha's pagoda with an iron-cap and a lotus-base, a Vajra-knot amulet, coral and amber rosaries, etc. The letter was delivered by Ngorpa Shika. It was written on the third day of the third month in the Wood-Cock year of the Tibetan calendrical cycle (the second year of the Shunzhi reign period of the Qing Dynasty) at Jokhang Temple in Lhasa (see *The Biography of the Fifth Dalai Lama*).

The *Imperial Records of the Qing Dynasty* says:

> Chahan Lama, who was sent to visit the Dalai Lama, came back in the third year of the Shunzhi reign period [1646]. The Dalai Lama and Gushri Khan of the Oylut tribe sent Pandita Lama and Darhan Lama together with him to Beijing with gifts and a memorial paying respects to the Emperor. The gifts included gold images of the Buddha, rosaries, woolen fabric, suits of armour, horses, etc. The Emperor bestowed suits of armour, bows and arrows, quivers for arrows, knives, saddles, silver articles, bolts of brocade, animal hides, etc., in return.

In the same year the Fifth Dalai Lama wrote to the Qing Emperor again. The letter also started with a poem, praising Qing Emperor Shizu for "having achieved a great sea of merit, having everything accomplished by the Heaven, knowing everything about Sakyamuni and bestowing happiness to the earth he ruled." A part of the letter reads:

> I have achieved the eight great powers of self-manifolding. I sit in the full lotus posture of Fearless Vajrapani, facing towards the throne of Great Emperor Manjushri and hearing the good news that the wide world has been ruled very smoothly by His Majesty.

The letter was accompanied with gifts. It was written on the sixteenth day of the second month in the Fire-Dog year of the Tibetan calendrical cycle (the third year of the Shunzhi reign period) at a monastery in U (see *The Complete Works of the Fifth Dalai Lama*).

The *Imperial Records of the Qing Dynasty* also has an account of this as follows:

> In the early fourth year of the Shunzhi reign period fi1647fl, the Dalai

Lama, Panchen Hutuktu, Baha Hutuktu, Rukba Hutuktu, Ildzarsabu Hutuktu, Sashsha Hutuktu, Erchidong Hutuktu, Ishda Gelong Hutuktu and Nomihan sent their men to Beijing with Tibetan local products as gifts and letters paying homage to the Emperor. Therefore, lamas, *gelongs* and officials were sent to Tibet with greetings and gifts from the Emperor, including gold and jade articles, silk and satin, saddles and suits of armour.

In the same year the Fifth Dalai wrote again to Qing Emperor Shizu. The letter also started with a poem, in which the Qing Emperor was called *Pradjapati* (Great Lord of Life) and asked to "give his gold-like orders to all the people, high or low in status, far or near in distance." The letter says:

For a time the world was thrown at into darkness and chaos as the last emperor, Chongzhen, of the Ming Dynasty was overthrown by the rebel Li Zicheng. In the Fire-Hog year of the Tibetan calendrical cycle fithe fourth year of the Shunzhi reign periodfl, four years after the Holy Emperor, son of the Later Jin Emperor Huangtaiji, came to the imperial throne of Manjushri, he gave out light of happiness and virtue, and Chahan Lama and many other envoys were sent to me by His Majesty with much silk and satin as well as an imperial edict. Enclosed is my memorial to the throne as a reply.

The letter was dated from Lhasa the tenth day of the ninth month in the Fire-Hog year of the Tibetan calendrical cycle and delivered by Chahan Lama to Beijing (see *The Complete Works of the Fifth Dalai Lama*).

According to Fourth Panchen Lozang Choskyi's *Autobiography*, in the third year of the Shunzhi reign period (1646), Qing Emperor Shizu sent envoys to Tibet with greetings and valuable gifts to the Fifth Dalai and the Fourth Panchen, and alms (tea and one tael of silver for each monk) for the major monasteries in Tibet, including the Three Major Monasteries in Lhasa and the Tashilhunpo. Letters from the Dalai and Panchen expressing thanks to Qing Emperor Shizu were brought by the envoys back to Beijing.

In the fifth year of the Shunzhi reign period (1648), Qing Emperor Shizu sent Sherab Lama Khangsar Kagyupa to Tibet with · a letter paying greetings to the Dalai and Panchen and alms and buttered-tea for the Three Major Monasteries in Lhasa, the Tashilhunpo and some other monasteries in Tibet.

In 1648, the Fifth Dalai was invited for an audience with Qing Emperor Shizu in Beijing. The *Imperial Records of the Qing Dynasty* says:

In the fifth year of the Shunzhi reign period [1648], Sherab Lama Gelong and others were sent to Tibet with the Emperor's invitation to the Fifth Dalai Lama for an audience with him in Beijing, and greetings and a letter to Panchen Hutuktu, asking him to persuade the Dalai to come to Beijing. Gifts such as gold belts inlaid with jade and silver tea-boxes were given to them.

In the sixth year of the Shunzhi reign period [1649] the Dalai Lama sent an envoy to Beijing with his answer to the invitation, saying he would come to Beijing for paying homage and offering Tibetan local products as gifts to the Emperor in the summer of the year of *ren-chen* [1652].

According to Fourth Panchen Lozang Choskyi's *Autobiography*, when the Fifth Dalai Lama received Qing Emperor Shizu's letter of invitation, due to some people's opposition, he could not decide whether he should accept it or not. So he wrote to Lozang Choskyi for advice whether such a visit was necessary. Lozang Choskyi suggested that he should go to Beijing, but he might delay his departure for a few years. Thus the Dalai decided to go to Beijing, but postponed his departure to the ninth year of the Shunzhi reign period (1652). The Dalai wrote to the Qing Emperor about his decision, which the Emperor approved. The Emperor ordered that the Yellow Temple (Huangsi) be built in Beijing for his accommodations.

Before going to Beijing in the ninth year of Shunzhi at the invitation of Qing Emperor Shizu, the Fifth Dalai Lama invited Fourth Panchen Lozang Choskyi for a consultation at Yangpachen in U. Lozang Choskyi, despite his eighty-two years of age, still left the Tashilhunpo for Yangpachen on the tenth day of the third month of that year at the Dalai's invitation. They were in consultation about the visit for seven days. Gushri Khan and his son, Prince Lhagyalrin of Lhoka, the Kyishod Depa and his son, and other prominent political and religious figures also came to Yangpachen to see the Dalai off. After exchanging farewells with them, the Fifth Dalai Lama left for Beijing with a large entourage of three thousand Tibetan officials, attendants and guards via Qinghai and

Inner Mongolia. As for his arrival and stay at Beijing, my *Biographies of the Dalai Lamas* (published by The Foreign Languages Press in 1991) has a detailed description of it, and we shall not repeat it here.

In the eleventh month of that year, the Qing Emperor sent Kha Lama, Dagen Chosje and Segan Kagyupa to bring his autographed letter and a suit of fur clothes as gifts to the Panchen, who wrote in return to express his thanks to the Emperor.

In the tenth year of the Shunzhi reign period (1653), Fifth Dalai Lama Lozang Gyatso, having received a title-conferring gold album and a gold seal of authority from the central government of the Qing Dynasty, returned to Tibet from Beijing. The title was "Dalai Lama, Overseer of the Buddhist Faith on the Earth Under the Great Benevolent Self-subsisting Buddha of the Western Paradise." And the Emperor sent his attendant lama Nangnuk and court official Shushidai as special envoys to accompany the Fifth Dalai to Tibet. There, a gold album and seal of authority were bestowed on Gushri Khan at a ceremony conducted by Nangnuk and Shushidai.

In the fifth month of the eleventh year of the Shunzhi reign period (1654), the Dalai Lama arrived back in Tibet. It being difficult for him to go to Lhasa at the advanced age of eighty-four, the Fourth Panchen sent monk officials of the Tashilhunpo to extend a warm welcome to the Fifth Dalai on his return from Beijing. On his arrival at Lhasa, the Dalai sent Depa Kyishopa to the Tashilhunpo to convey his greetings and respects to the Panchen. In the seventh month of that year Fifth Dalai Lama Lozang Gyatso went to visit Fourth Panchen Lozang Choskyi at the Tashilhunpo, staying there for five days and giving sweet buttered-tea and alms to the monks. Then the Dalai went to stay with Gushri Khan in the fort of Shigatse Dzong for a month. It was said that during that time the Dalai often went to learn scriptures from Lozang Choskyi. In the eighth month of that year, at the Fifth Dalai's proposal, Gushri Khan went to the Tashilhunpo, giving alms and sweet buttered-tea to the monks. And then he asked the Fourth Panchen to sit on the chair of the *tripa* in the Great Chanting Hall and offered him a *mandral* to show his highest respects to him. After that, the Fifth Dalai bid farewell to the Fourth Panchen and Gushri Khan and went back to Lhasa.

In the fifth month of the twelfth year of the Shunzhi reign period (1655), Qing Emperor Shizu sent Sherab Lama and Albu'ongba to the Tashilhunpo to convey his greetings and to present a complete *Kangyur* (the Tripitalaa) of an Indian Sanskrit edition to the Fourth Panchen, who wrote a letter in return to express his thanks to the Emperor.

In the winter of that year Gushri Khan bid farewell to Lozang Choskyi and left Shigatse for Lhasa to take medical treatment. But his disease resisted all treatment and not long afterwards, at the age of seventy-four, he died. Emperor Shizu sent officials to hold a memorial ceremony for Gushri Khan at Lhasa and instructed the Board for National Minority Affairs:

> I heard that Gushri Khan of the Oylut tribe had died. For his allegiance and loyalty to our country, a memorial ceremony shall be held for him. Your Board and the Ministry of Rites shall arrange the matter and report it to me.

In the third year after Gushri Khan's death, or the fifteenth year of the Shunzhi reign period (1658), Gushri Khan's eldest son, Dayan Khan, came to Tibet from Qinghai and succeeded the throne left by Gushri Khan.

In the eighth month of the thirteenth year of the Shunzhi reign period (1656), Emperor Shizu sent Changling Anjie and others to Tibet with his autographed letters to and gifts for the Dalai and Panchen. After arriving in Tibet, Changling Anjie first paid a visit to the Fifth Dalai Lama at the Potala, and then went to visit Lozang Choskyi at the Tashilhunpo. He acknowledged Lozang Choskyi as his tutor and took his vows as a *getsul* before Lozang Choskyi.

In the fifteenth year of the Shunzhi reign period (1658), envoys were sent again by the Qing Emperor with his autographed letter to and gifts for Lozang Choskyi, who wrote a letter in return and presented Tibetan local products as gifts to the Emperor.

# 7. The Death of the Fourth Panchen Lama

According to Lozang Choskyi's *Autobiography*, in 1658, when Lozang Choskyi was in the last years of his life, Shadrung (a descendant of Phagspa), the ruling lama of Sakya Monastery, while on his way to Lhasa for paying respects to the Dalai Lama, came to the Tashilhunpo. He asked to visit Lozang Choskyi, who was recuperating at Samdrup Temple after a long illness. Considering that the ruling lamas of the Sakya sect had once been kings of Tsang, Lozang Choskyi received the lama on his sickbed. The ruling lama of the Sakya sect read prayers for Lozang Choskyi's health. Soon afterwards Dagen Noryan Khan from Outer Mongolia made his pilgrimage to Tibet. He visited Lozang Choskyi at the Tashilhunpo and was received at the latter's sickbed. The Khan was there initiated into full monkhood by Lozang Choskyi. The Khan's concubine also took her vows as a *getsul* before Lozang Choskyi.

Lozang Choskyi was by now in very poor health. All monks of the Tashilhunpo were worried about his health and prayed for him. On learning of this, the Fifth Dalai sent high monk officials from the Potala to convey his cordial regards and presented a suit of monk clothes and a written prayer for longevity to Lozang Choskyi.

Lozang Choskyi's health was getting worse in the Water-Tiger year in the eleventh Tibetan calendrical cycle, or the first year of the Kangxi reign period in Qing Emperor Shengzu's reign (1662). He died on the thirteenth day of the second month at the age of ninety-two. His body was placed in the great Maitreya Chapel of the Panchen Lama's Lharang Hall in the Tashilhunpo. Forty high priests chanted sutras for fourteen days for his early reincarnation. Fifth Dalai Lozang Gyatso was in deep grief at the news of Lozang Choskyi's death and sent the chief *khenpo* of the Potala as his representative to the Tashilhunpo to offer a *tingcha katag*, one hundred gold coins and four bolts of satin, and to pray for the Panchen Lama's early reincarnation. By order of the Dalai Lama, all the monks of the Three Major Monasteries in Lhasa and of the Gelug monasteries in U, Tsang, Ngari, Kham and Qinghai chanted sutras and prayed for the Panchen's early reincarnation.

The chief *khenpo* of the Tashilhunpo was sent to Lhasa to offer many of the things left by the deceased Fourth Panchen to the Fifth Dalai as souvenirs, and gave alms and sweet buttered-tea for the Three Major Monasteries of Lhasa, as well as the Gelug monasteries in U, Tsang, Ngari, Kham and Qinghai.

As to the treatment of the Panchen Lama's body, a decision was made jointly by the Lharang Changzod and *khenpos* of the *dratsangs* of the Tashilhunpo. By the decision, a gold stupa was to be made for interment of his body and Lharang Changzod Lozang Geleg was made responsible for the preservation of the body and the building of the stupa. When the stupa was built, the Fifth Dalai Lama and Depa sent their representatives to honour the memory of the deceased and offer prayers for the Panchen Lama. A hall, named Chokhang, crowned with a golden roof, was specially built for keeping the stupa. Four monks resided in it and were responsible for chanting sutras, lighting lamps and keeping watch on the hall and the stupa. The Fifth Dalai Lama sent the Depa to place a satin canopy over the stupa and various satin decorations on the pillars in the hall.

The Fifth Dalai and monk officials of the Tashilhunpo reported the death of the Fourth Panchen to the Qing court, and Qing Emperor Shengzu sent Migen Choskyi and Ake Kagyu as special envoys to Tibet to hold a memorial ceremony for the Fourth Panchen at the Tashilhunpo. The *Imperial Records of the Qing Dynasty* says: "In the eighth month of the second year of the Kangxi reign period [1663], Panchen Hutuktu died in Tibet and officials were sent there to hold a memorial ceremony for him".

# 8. An Appraisal of the Fourth Panchen Lama

Fourth Panchen Lozang Choskyi was not only a distinguished religious leader, but also an outstanding political leader. His life can be summed up in the following five aspects:

(1) He safeguarded national unification and promoted the friendship and unity between different nationalities of China. Before defeating Tsangpa Khan, the Dalai, Panchen and Gushri Khan jointly sent a goodwill mission to Shengjing to establish a good relationship with the Qing regime of Emperor Taizong. When

the Qing Dynasty was established in Beijing, they sent envoys to Beijing to express congratulations. When the Fifth Dalai paid a visit to Beijing to show his support for the Qing Dynasty, he was conferred a honorific title by the Qing court, and thus established Tibet's official subordination to the central government. The Dalai and Panchen made great contributions to the cause of safeguarding national unification and promoting the unity among the Hans, Manchus, Mongols and Tibetans.

(2) To the Gelug sect, the struggle against Tsangpa Khan's persecution was a serious problem of life and death. As the Fifth Dalai Lama was too young, the Fourth Panchen naturally had to shoulder the leadership in the struggle with the hostile powers headed by Tsangpa Khan. The Fourth Panchen was so experienced and capable in exercising his leadership in the rivalry with Tsangpa Khan that the rivalry ended with the Gelug's complete triumph. Tsangpa Khan's rule of Tibet was replaced by the Gelug regime. The Fourth Panchen's role was a deciding factor in the achievement of the final victory by the Gelug sect.

(3) The close relationship of tutor and disciple was established between the Fourth Panchen and the Fifth Dalai. Prior to them, First Dalai Lama Gedun Truppa and First Panchen Lama Khedrup Je were the disciples of the same tutor, while the Second Dalai and the Second Panchen, as well as the Third Dalai and the Third Panchen, did not know each other. The Fourth Dalai Yonten Gyatso took his vows as a *getsul* and then as a *gelong* under the guidance of the Fourth Panchen, and so did the Fifth Dalai. At that time the tutor-disciple relationship between the Panchen and Dalai was officially set up. The relationship is especially evident when considering the endeavour by the Fourth Panchen to have Tsangpa Khan lift the ban on seeking the Fourth Dalai's reincarnation after the latter's death. The matter was significant in the history of the Gelug sect.

(4) Thanks to the Fourth Panchen's painstaking efforts, the Tashilhunpo became the largest monastery of the Gelug sect in Tsang. During the reign of Fourth Panchen Lozang Choskyi, the Tashilhunpo had five thousand monks, three thousand rooms, fifty-one subordinate monasteries with four thousand monks, sixteen *shikas* (manorial estates) and more than ten pastures. So it was

also the largest feudal-lord monastery in Tsang. What was important was that under the Fourth Panchen's leadership the Tashilhunpo achieved the same status as that of the Three Major Monasteries in Lhasa by setting up its own monastic study system. After the Fourth Panchen Lama, all the successive Panchen Lamas were recognized as the *tripa* (abbot) of the Tashilhunpo by its monks. That the life tenure of the abbot of the Tashilhunpo replaced the rotation system was also established by Lozang Choskyi.

(5) Fourth Panchen Lozang Choskyi was modest and lived a simple life. Although he enjoyed high status in religious circles, he always went on foot and carried his luggage on his shoulder when he went out to give sermons. He kept the genuine qualities of a monk and thus got near to the masses of the people. According to his *Autobiography*, he recruited a hundred fifty thousand disciples, of whom about five hundred were initiated into full monkhood, a hundred thousand took *getsul* vows and fifty thousand took vows to be lay Buddhists. This shows that Lozang Choskyi played a significant role in spreading Tsongkhapa's doctrines and recruiting followers for the Gelug sect.

# Chapter Three
# Lozang Yeshe, the Fifth Panchen Lama

## 1. The Search for the Soul Boy, His Enthronement and the Vows-Taking Ceremony

The Fifth Panchen Lama (1663-1737), given the religious name of Lozang Yeshe, was born on the fifteenth day of the seventh month in the Water-Rabbit year of the eleventh Tibetan calendrical cycle (1663, or the second year of the Kangxi reign period of Qing Emperor Shengzu). His father was Sonam Wangdrak and his mother, Tseten Butri. He was a native of Chutsang Village of Thobgyal Shika in Tsang, where his father was a minor aristocrat. When Lozang Yeshe was born, the Fourth Panchen Lama's *Solpon Khenpo*, on behalf of the Tashilhunpo, paid a visit to his family and offered his parents a *katag*, a silver *mandral* and a bale of tea as gifts for congratulations. Meanwhile, the Tashilhunpo sent messengers to Lhasa to make a report to the Fifth Dalai Lama and to ask the Dalai Lama whether the child was the soul child reincarnating the Fourth Panchen. The Dalai's answer was that the child should be protected, but he did not confirm that the child was the reincarnation.

By the Fifth Dalai's order, the child was invited by the monks of the Tashilhunpo to Namdo Phodrang Monastery near Thobgyal Shika on the eighth day of the sixth month in the Wood-Dragon year (1664, or the third year of the Kangxi reign period). In the following year the boy was invited to the Panchen Lharang Hall of Tashilhunpo Monastery. Owing to the fact that opinions differed on whether or not the child's soul boy status could be established, he was sent back to Namdo Phodrang Monastery in Thobgyal Shika on the second day of the tenth month of that year, after having resided in the Tashilhunpo for four months. The Tashilhunpo again asked the Fifth Dalai Lama for instructions. The Dalai answered in his letter that an investigation should be made of the boy. So the Tashilhunpo sent three groups of high monks with various articles, of which some belonged to the Fourth Panchen and the others did not, for the boy to distinguish the true from the false. The three groups were: (1) Lopon Konchok Gyaltsen and Dronyer Gedun Tsultrim from Ngapa Dratsang with medicine, dice, tweezers, a bell and other things left by the Fourth Panchen; (2) Changzod Phuntsok Rabten with the Fourth Panchen's rosary, small and big drums, etc.; (3) Pontsang Gelong Lozang Wangyal and Odser Choyin Gyatso with the Fourth Panchen's picture, Tsongkhapa's picture and two other picture, and the Fourth Panchen's *Solpon* and *Zimpon*. When each group exhibited the things to the boy, he picked out the things left by the Fourth Panchen. At last the three groups agreed that the boy was indeed the Panchen Lama incarnate.

Tashilhunpo Monastery sent Solpon Lozang Tenzin and Jedrung Lama to report the results of the investigation to the Fifth Dalai Lama. On hearing the news, the Dalai Lama acknowledged that the boy was the reincarnation of the Fourth Panchen Lama and ordered that the boy should be invited to the Panchen Lharang Hall of the Tashilhunpo and a grand enthronement ceremony be held for him.

On the seventh day of the tenth month in the sixth year of the Kangxi reign period (1667), Changzod Phuntsok Rabten of Tashilhunpo Monastery, along with two hundred monk officials, went to the Namdo Phodrang Hall in Thobgyal Shika to pay their homage to the five-year-old reincarnation. On the eleventh day of the tenth month the soul boy's hair was tonsured and he was dressed into a suit of monk robes. The *Solpon* then carried him on his back to his family in the village of Chutsang. Meanwhile, the Fifth Dalai Lama's representatives—Zimpon Choskyi Apa, Khenchung Jampa Rinchen and Dronyer Gyalpa Dorje Wangchuk—the *Depa's* representative, Dapon Ngogne, and two representatives of Dayan Khan (son of Gushri Khan) came to give congratulations and *katags* to the soul boy of the Fourth Panchen Lama. On the seventeenth day of the tenth month the boy was invited to Tashilhunpo Monastery. He was warmly greeted by monks of the Tashilhunpo and its subordinate monasteries and tens of thousands of local inhabitants lined both sides of the road, holding burning joss sticks in their hands and chanting sutras. He resided in the Gyaltsen Tongbo Lharang Hall of the Tashilhunpo. By the Fifth Dalai Lama's order, he was enthroned on the third day of the first month of the Earth-Monkey year of the Tibetan calendrical cycle (1668, or the seventh year of the Kangxi reign period in Qing Emperor Shengzu), for that day was chosen as the day of good omen. He was given the religious name Lozang Yeshe Palzangpo (Lozang Yeshe for short).

Thus the six-year-old Lozang Yeshe took the chair of the Fourth Panchen Lama and became the Fifth Panchen Lama on the third day of the first month in the seventh year of Kangxi. In the tenth month of that year Qing Emperor Shengzu sent an envoy, Jamling Anchen Sangye Gyaltsen, to the Tashilhunpo to visit the Fifth Panchen and to deliver an imperial decree and gifts to express his congratulations. After being enthroned, the Fifth Panchen Lama began to study Tibetan and Buddhist sutras under the guidance of Lopon Lozang Tenzin, who was invited from Ganden Rabje Monastery in Thobgyal Shika by Tashilhunpo Monastery.

In the eighth year of Kangxi (1669), Tashilhunpo Monastery sent Dronyer Karchen Gedun Tsultrim to Lhasa to express thanks to the Fifth Dalai Lama for the Fifth Panchen's enthronement and wish him peace and longevity. He also gave alms and sweet buttered-tea for the Three Major Monasteries at Lhasa, as well as those of U, Tsang, Ngari, Qinghai and Kham. The gifts amounted to 72,999 *khal* of *qingke* (highland barley), 92 horses, more than 40 cows and 6,250 *katags*.

In the ninth year of Kangxi (1670), Lozang Yeshe was eight years old. According to the rules of the Yellow Hat sect he should take the vows of a *getsul*, and it was decided that he should take the vows before the Fifth Dalai Lama. Lozang Yeshe left the Tashilhunpo on the first day of the sixth month of that year and arrived at Lhasa via Yangpachen on the fourteenth day of the sixth month of that year. He was greeted by monk and lay officials of the Tibetan local government, as well as all monk officials of the Drepung and Sera, in the outskirts of Lhasa. He was lodged in Yangsigang Hall in the Potala. On the next day the Fifth Panchen paid respects to the Fifth Dalai at the Great Chanting Hall in the Potala, offering a *mandral*, an image of the Buddha, twenty-five bolts of silk and satin, thirty horses, gold and silver, gold and silver saddles, pearls, etc., as gifts to the Dalai. He kowtowed to the Fifth Dalai and acknowledged him as his tutor. The ceremony was followed by a grand *gadro* celebration in the Great Chanting Hall. Beginning on the twenty-first day of the sixth month, the Fifth Panchen studied many scriptures under the guidance of the Fifth Dalai. On the third day of the seventh month, envoys from the Qing Emperor arrived at Lhasa with an imperial decree and gifts to the Fifth Dalai and the Fifth Panchen to express congratulations for the vows-taking ceremony for the Fifth Panchen. The Fifth Panchen officially took his vows as a *getsul* before the Fifth Dalai at Khensong Namgyal Hall in the Potala Palace on the fifteenth day of the seventh month. On the thirteenth day of the eighth month, the Fifth Panchen bid farewell to the Fifth Dalai, intending to leave for the Tashilhunpo. On his departure, the Fifth Dalai gave him many rare gifts and advised him to continue his sutra studies, especially emphasizing Tsongkhapa's works. On the fifteenth day of the eighth month, monk and lay officials of the Tibetan local government saw the Fifth Panchen off on the outskirts of Lhasa.

In the eleventh year of Kangxi (1672), Qing Emperor Shengzu sent envoys with an imperial decree, greetings and gifts to call on the Fifth Panchen at the Tashilhunpo. The envoys were accompanied by Lozang Thuthop, the Depa of that time, who offered gold, silver, silk and satin to the Fifth Panchen.

In the thirteenth year of Kangxi (1674), the Fifth Panchen was twelve years of age. According to the tradition of the Yellow Hat sect, he attended the collective debates on the Buddhist doctrines in the Tashilhunpo. This marked the beginning of his official monastic studies.

In the fifteenth year of Qing Emperor Shunzhi's reign (1658), three years after the death of Gushri Khan, Dayan Khan (Gushri Khan's eldest son) came from Qinghai to Lhasa to succeed to the throne as Khan and appointed Trile Gyatso as the Depa. Two years later Dayan Khan and Trile Gyatso died one after another. The Fifth Dalai Lama appointed his *Chopon Khenpo*, Lozang Thuthop, as the Depa. In the tenth year of Kangxi (1671), Dalai Khan, Dayan Khan's son, came from Qinghai to Lhasa to succeed his father as the Khan. Four years later Depa Lozang Thuthop was relieved of his post. Dalai Khan appointed the Fifth Dalai's *Dratsang Yerpa*, Lozang Jimpa, as the Depa. In the eighteenth year of Kangxi (1679), Lozang Jimpa was relieved from his post and Sangye Gyatso was appointed as the Depa by Dalai Khan.

In the twentieth year of Kangxi (1681), the king of Lhadak, Deleg Namgyal, led his army to invade Ngari, but was defeated by Dalai Khan and Sangye Gyatso's Mongolian and Tibetan troops led by Dalai Khan's brother Ganden Tsewang Palzang, who followed up the victory and captured the city of Leh, capital of Lhadak. In the twenty-second year of Kangxi (1683), the king of Lhadak surrendered, returning to Tibet Guge and Rutog of Ngari, which it had occupied since 1630. Since then Lhadak acknowledged its vassal status to the Qing Empire by offering tribute to Lhasa every year. Also at this time the Tibetan government agreed not to impose restrictions on brick-tea export to Lhadak.

In 1682, Fifth Dalai Lama Lozang Gyatso died in the Potala at the age of sixty-six. Depa Sangye Gyatso kept the death of the Fifth Dalai a secret, saying that the Dalai was too deep in meditation to be disturbed, and forged the Dalai's instructions for the decisions he made. This abnormal state lasted for fifteen years.

In the twenty-second year of Kangxi (1683), it was time that Fifth Panchen Lozang Yeshe, twenty-one years old, be ordained into full monkhood. So Tashilhunpo Monastery sent its *Changzod* to Lhasa to ask the Fifth Dalai Lama to hold the ceremony. But Depa Sangye Gyatso refused his request, saying the Fifth Dalai Lama was too deep in meditation to be disturbed and that another high lama might be invited to hold the ceremony for the Fifth Panchen.

On returning to the Tashilhunpo, the *Changzod* consulted with other monk officials and they decided to invite Konchok Gyaltsen, the *khenpo* of Ngapa Dratsang of the Tashilhunpo, to preside over the *gelong* ceremony of the Fifth Panchen. On the eighth day of the twelfth month of the twenty-third year of Kangxi (1684), Fifth

Panchen Lama Lozang Yeshe, at the age of twenty-two, became a fully ordained monk after taking his *gelong* vows before Konchok Gyaltsen at the Tashilhunpo. In the fifth month of the following year (1685), Qing Emperor Shengzu sent an envoy, Ajithu Choskyi, to the Tashilhunpo to deliver an imperial decree and gifts to the Fifth Panchen Lama, expressing congratulations for his taking the *gelong* vows. The Fifth Panchen wrote a letter in return to show thanks to the Qing Emperor. In the same year Dalai Khan and Depa Sangye Gyatso also sent gifts and congratulations to the Fifth Panchen. To pray for the Fifth Dalai Lama's "well-being and longevity," the Fifth Panchen sent representatives with alms and buttered-tea to the monks of the three main monasteries, their expense equivalent to 135 loads of butter and 37,385 *khal* of *qingke* barley.

## 2. Relations Between the Fifth Panchen Lama and the Central Government of the Qing Dynasty

The historical period in which the Fifth Panchen Lama lived witnessed the establishment of the Great Qing Empire, a period full of serious conflicts between separatism and unification. As a part of the Qing Empire, Tibet could not be an exception. It was influenced especially by three big events: (1) Wu Sangui rebelled in Yunnan; (2) the Dzungar chieftain Galdan twice invaded Outer and Inner Mongolia; (3) the Dzungar chieftain Tsewang Rabten dispatched his general Tsering Dondup to invade Tibet. In these conflicts the Dalai and Panchen lamas could choose to stand either on the side of Wu Sangui, Galdan and Tsewang Rabten, who attempted to split the national unification, or to support the central government of the Qing Dynasty in safeguarding the cause of China's unification. A third way did not exist. Both the Fifth Dalai Lama and the Fifth Panchen Lama played an important role in these conflicts.

Wu Sangui rebelled against the Qing Dynasty in Yunnan in the thirteenth year of the Kangxi reign period (1674). In a letter to the Qing Emperor the Fifth Dalai Lama said:

I am dismayed to know that Wu Sangui has rebelled. . . .If Wu Sangui surrenders, please spare his life, and if he persists in what he is doing now, it might be advisable to cede territories to him and make peace with him.

The Emperor refused. In his decree to the Dalai Lama, the Emperor said:

Wu Sangui was originally a low-ranking officer of the Ming Dynasty. His father was killed by rebelling peasants. He came to ask for our help. Emperor Shizu bestowed upon him the title of prince and married a royal princess to his son. I favoured him with another title of prince, and I bestowed upon him more privileges and honour than any ministers in the court, which has rarely been seen in history. Wu Sangui was unworthy of our trust and he caused much harm and damage to the people. Heaven and the people are filled with anger. I am the lord of all the people under Heaven. How can I cede territories to him and make peace with him? But if he repents, I will spare his life.

However, taking the opportunity of Wu Sangui's rebellion, the Fifth Dalai Lama sent a Tibetan army to capture two cities of Yunnan—Yangdamu and Jiedamu. In a report to the Qing court, he said:

Yangdamu and Jiedamu were originally under the jurisdiction of two Karmapas [the ruling lamas of the Black Hat and Red Hat lines of the Karma Kagyu], but later they were occupied by Wu Sangui. So I have sent troops to take them back.

Taking into consideration the overall situation, the Qing Emperor did not make known his stand on this, but ordered that "military and civil officers of all levels who were sent to suppress the rebellion investigate the letters between Wu Sangui and the Fifth Dalai Lama and hand them in as soon as they are intercepted."

In the nineteenth year of Kangxi (1680), internal conflicts occurred between the seven banners in Outer Mongolia. The Board for National Minority Affairs reported to the Qing court:

In former days, Kharkha Mongols used to send a delegation headed by Chechen Kyirong to offer tribute. Now Drashakatu Khan has replaced Chechen Kyirong and put Erdeni Kyirong at the head of the delegation. However, the name of Erdeni Kyirong was never mentioned in the reports sent by the Fifth Dalai Lama. We asked the envoys from the Dalai Lama to give us a report about it. As to whether the tribute is to be accepted or not, we are to report it to Your Majesty after getting a report from the Dalai Lama.

The Emperor criticized the Board for National Minority Affairs, saying:

> Whether the tribute from various Mongolian chieftains is to be accepted or not should be discussed by yourselves, not according to the Dalai Lama's report. Otherwise, the Mongolian chieftains in our territories would do as told by the Dalai Lama. From now on whenever the Mongolian chieftains come to offer tribute, the Board for National Minority Affairs should discuss the matter and report it for me to decide whether the tribute should be accepted. The matter should be decided not on the basis of the Dalai Lama's report.

On the other hand, the Qing court attached much importance to the respective influence of the Dalai and Panchen among the Mongolian people. Emperor Gaozong wrote in *On the Lamas*:

> Buddhism originated in India. Then it spread east to Tibet. The Tibetan high monks are called lamas. . . . The titles of the Dalai Lama and Panchen Lama have been inheritable since the Yuan and Ming dynasties. The two lamas, being the leaders of the Yellow Hat sect, have the absolute allegiance of all Mongol tribes. Patronizing the sect means keeping the Mongols in peace, which is something of great significance. That is why the two lamas deserve our protection.

This is a concrete reflection of the Qing Dynasty's policies towards national minorities and religion.

In the twenty-first year of Kangxi (1682), Fifth Dalai Lozang Gyatso died. As mentioned above, Depa Sangye Gyatso kept the death of the Fifth Dalai a secret in an attempt to monopolize political and religious power. Beginning then, a split developed between the Tibetan local government and the central government of the Qing Dynasty, because Sangye Gyatso was "obedient" to the Qing court on the surface, but secretly supported those who acted against the Qing's cause of unification.

Nevertheless, in order to consolidate his rule over Tibet, Sangye Gyatso had to ask the Qing Dynasty for support. In the thirty-second year of Kangxi (1693), he presented the Qing Emperor with a forged letter in the name of the Dalai Lama, which said: "Because of my advanced age I have left all my administrative responsibilities to the Depa, so the Depa needs an honorific title."

Then he instructed Gelong Yeshe to report to the Emperor orally: "Our state affairs are all run by the Depa, who needs a seal of authority granted by Your Majesty. The Depa will hand in the jade seal if a gold one is bestowed on him."

The following year the Qing Emperor granted Sangye Gyatso a title-bearing seal with the inscription "Seal of Butada Ahbadhi, Mentor of the Faith of the Vajra-Holding Dalai Lama, King of the Propagation of the Doctrine of the Buddha" (see the *Imperial Records of the Qing Dynasty*). Butada Ahbadhi in Sanskrit means Sangye Gyatso. The title granted was "King of the Propagation of the Doctrine of the Buddha."

Before that, Depa Sangye Gyatso colluded with Galdan, the chieftain of the Dzungar Mongols, to act against the Qing Dynasty. The Dzungars, one of the four Oylut Mongol tribes, were a nomadic tribe in the Ili valley of Xinjiang. When Gushri Khan led the Qoshot tribe into Qinghai, he got rid of Chogthu Khan with the support of Batur Hongteji, chieftain of the Dzungars. In the tenth year of the Shunzhi reign period of Qing Emperor Shizu (1653), Batur Hongteji died. He was succeeded by his eldest son, Sengge. Galdan, Sengge's younger brother, became a monk and went to the Three Major Monasteries in Lhasa for monastic studies. He acknowledged the Fifth Dalai Lama as his tutor and had close relations with Sangye Gyatso. In the tenth year of the Kangxi reign period of Emperor Shengzu (1671), Sengge was murdered by his stepbrothers Chechen and Chotbar Batur. On hearing of his brother's death, Galdan returned to his tribe with the Fifth Dalai Lama's approval. He avenged his brother's death upon the murderers. Chechen was killed and Chotbar Batur fled to the Qoshot tribe in Qinghai for refuge.

Sengge was succeeded by his son Sonam Rabten. In the fifteenth year of Qing Emperor Shengzu's reign (1676), Galdan usurped the Dzungar khanship after murdering his nephew, Sonam Rabten. He won the Fifth Dalai Lama's support, who granted him the honorific title of *Boshoktu Khan*. He sent missions to Beijing, offering tribute to the Qing Emperor, and was thus recognized by the Qing court.

In the sixteenth year of Qing Emperor Shengzu's reign (1677), Galdan's troops annexed the Durbat and Turgut tribes of the Oylut Mongols and subdued the Uygurs in Xinjiang. After occupying the wide territories to the south and north of the Tianshan Mountains, Galdan established the Dzungar Khanate. Then he led an army of thirty thousand soldiers to attack the seven banners of the Kharkha Mongols on the pretext of avenging his brother Dorje Drak's death on two murderers—Tushetu Khan and Jetsun Dampa Hutuktu —who had killed Drashakatu Khan and Dorje Drak. Being defeated by Galdan, the seven banners asked the Qing court for help. Qing Emperor Shengzu took into consideration the survival of the Kharkha Mongols as well as the preservation of the Outer Mongolian territory. Aware that Galdan was the Fifth Dalai Lama's disciple and was in close relation with the Dalai, the Emperor sent an envoy to Tibet to ask the Dalai Lama to mediate peace between Galdan and the Kharkha Mongols.

In the twenty-ninth year of Qing Emperor Shengzu's reign (1690), Depa Sangye Gyatso, in the name of the Fifth Dalai Lama, sent Shanpaling Khenpo to offer tribute and pay respects to the Qing Emperor. Shanpaling Khenpo reported secretly to the Emperor:

> When I went to bid farewell to the Dalai Lama, he did not come out to meet me. Instead, the Depa came out to say that the Dalai Lama ordered me to report to Your Majesty that if Your Majesty would capture Tushetu Khan and Jetsun Dampa and hand them over to Galdan, this will be good to the people and the Dalai Lama will guarantee their lives.

The Qing Emperor did not agree and sent the Dalai Lama a decree which says:

> You as a lama should do good things for worldly beings. I don't believe what Shanpaling Khenpo has reported is your intention. Why did you not write a report to me? I have doubts about this. So I send you this decree and order you to report to me about this matter in detail (see the *Imperial Records of the Qing Dynasty*).

Seeing that his plot did not work, Depa Sangye Gyatso, in the name of the Fifth Dalai Lama, sent Kyirong Hutuktu to the Dzungars. By the Depa's order, Kyirong, while pretending to try to win Galdan's submission to the Qing, plotted an invasion of Inner Mongolia by the Dzungar chieftain. The Qing army, led by Hoshoyu Prince Fu Quan, the Frontier Pacification General, defeated the Dzungars at Ulanpudong, and Galdan fled with the remnants of his troops. Several years later, Galdan's troops again invaded Outer Mongolia. In the thirty-fifth year of Qing Emperor Shengzu's reign (1696), a punitive expedition led by the Emperor himself routed the Dzungars on the Kalulun River in Outer Mongolia, and Galdan fled back to his home base in Xinjiang.

When the Emperor learned from the Tibetans taken captive by the Qing army that the Dalai Lama had died many years ago, he wrote a letter to Sangye Gyatso denouncing him in stern language. The letter, which threatened with the might of the Qing Dynasty, sent Depa Sangye Gyatso into great panic. The next year (1697) he wrote a confidential letter to Emperor Shengzu and sent Nyima-thang Hutuktu to deliver the letter to the Emperor at the Emperor's military headquarters of the military expedition (in present-day Yinchuan city of Ningxia Hui Autonomous Region).

The *Imperial Records of the Qing Dynasty* says:

On the *geng-wu* day of the third month of the thirty-sixth year of Emperor Shengzu's reign [April 10, 1697], Nyimathang Hutuktu came to deliver the Depa's confidential letter and offer an image of the Fifth Dalai Lama to the Emperor at his military headquarters. After reading the letter, the Emperor had the letter and the image sealed up before the Hutuktu, and said, "Several years ago I knew that the Fifth Dalai had died. If he were alive, Sengpa Chenpo Hutuktu, Galdan Sheletu, Chichike Dalai Khenpo and Kyirong Hutuktu would not have acted so wildly and the Kharkha and Oylut would not have suffered so much damage. So I denounced the Depa in stern language. Now, since he has confessed the truth in his confidential letter to me, I will also keep it a secret.

After this, the Fifth Dalai Lama's death was made known publicly in Tibet. In September of the same year Depa Sangye Gyatso brought Tsangyang Gyatso to the Potala, where he was enthroned as the Sixth Dalai Lama.

# 3. The Fifth Panchen Lama Tonsures the Sixth Dalai Lama and Gives Him *Getsul* Vows

Tsangyang Gyatso, the Sixth Dalai Lama, was born in the Water-Hog year of the eleventh Tibetan calendrical cycle (1683, or the twenty-second year of Emperor Shengzu's reign) in the Monyul region in southern Tibet. According to the Tibetan-language biography of Fifth Panchen Lama Lozang Yeshe, the Fifth Panchen did not know of the Fifth Dalai's death until the fourth of the seventh month of the Fire-Ox year (1697) when Depa Sangye Gyatso wrote a letter to inform him:

> The Fifth Dalai passed away several years ago. Under his orders, his death was not announced. Now I have reported through Nyimathang Hutuktu to the Emperor what has happened in Tibet since the Fifth Dalai Lama's death. The reincarnation of the Fifth Dalai will be invited to the Potala Palace via Nankartse Dzong....

On the sixteenth of the eighth month of that year Depa Sangye Gyatso wrote again to the Fifth Panchen:

> The reincarnation of the Fifth Dalai Lama was born in Tsona [at that time the Monyul was under the jurisdiction of Tsona Dzong] several years ago and will be secretly invited to Nankartse Dzong on the fourteenth of the ninth month and will take the vows there on the seventeenth of the ninth month. You are invited to tonsure him and initiate him into monkhood and give him a religious name.

The letter was delivered to the Fifth Panchen by Bindu Darhan Wangpo, who was responsible for accompanying the Fifth Panchen to Nankartse.

On the eighth of the ninth month, the Fifth Panchen left the Tashilhunpo by way of Rinpung Dzong and arrived at Nankartse Dzong on the tenth of the ninth month. A grand welcoming ceremony was held for him by the Tibetan local government. En route to Lhasa, the soul boy met with Lozang Yeshe, the Fifth Panchen, at Nankartse Dzong on the seventeenth of the ninth month. After giving the soul boy large quantities of gold, silver, silk and satin as gifts, the Fifth Panchen tonsured him and gave him the religious name Lozang Rinchen Tsangyang Gyatso. Then the Fifth Panchen gave Tsangyang Gyatso instructions on *Genyen, Gezho, Padmarabjung* and other Buddhist rules. The Sixth Dalai Lama thereby became a disciple of the Fifth Panchen. To express his gratitude to the Fifth Panchen, the Sixth Dalai offered him gold and silver, silk and satin, and tea as gifts. At the ceremony for the Dalai to take his *getsul* vows, the Panchen and the Dalai exchanged gifts. The Panchen's gifts consisted of a long *katag* with Tibetan words on it, an image of Sakyamuni Buddha, Buddhist scriptures, a small gold pagoda, white jade teacups, a gold vase, a Buddhist robe, satin cushions, a gold *mandral* and other rare objects. The lay and monk officials of the Tibetan local government asked the Fifth Panchen to take the seat of honour and let the Sixth Dalai Lama kowtow to the Panchen to show thanks to him. Meanwhile, the Panchen also came down from his seat and kowtowed in return to the Dalai.

Sixth Dalai Tsangyang Gyatso left Nankartse Dzong for Lhasa on the twenty-first of the ninth month. En route to Lhasa, he arrived at Netang, where he was warmly welcomed by Dalai Khan and Depa Sangye Gyatso, together with lay and monk Mongolian and Tibetan officials as well as representatives of the Three Major Monasteries in Lhasa—about a thousand in all. The following day Fifth Panchen Lozang Yeshe also arrived there from Nankartse to hold consultations and make decisions on the ceremony of the Dalai's enthronement.

A grand ceremony for the Sixth Dalai's enthronement was held at the Potala on the twenty-fifth in the tenth month. At first the Fifth Panchen intended to attend the ceremony in person, but the Sixth Dalai Lama, out of politeness, said that it was not necessary for his tutor, the Panchen, to attend, and that it would be all right for him to send a representative to the ceremony. So the Fifth Panchen sent the *Changzod* of the Tashilhunpo as his representative to attend the Sixth Dalai Lama's enthronement ceremony and offer a *katag* to the Dalai. After staying in the Potala for two days, the Fifth Panchen moved to Tengyeling Monastery at Lhasa.

On the thirtieth of the tenth month, the Fifth Panchen went from Tengyeling Monastery to the Potala and had a long talk with the Sixth Dalai Lama in Nyiod Khang Hall. He told the Sixth Dalai the great contributions the Fifth Dalai had made to the development of Tibetan Buddhism and to the happiness of worldly beings, and urged the Sixth Dalai Lama to devote himself to the study of Tsongkhapa's works to make great contributions to the Tibetan people's peace and happiness.

By then the construction of the Fifth Dalai's stupa was completed. At Depa Sangye Gyatso's invitation, the Fifth Panchen held the initiation ceremony for it. In the ceremony, which was quite simple, the Panchen grasped a handful of Tibetan barley grains, had them consecrated, and then threw them onto the stupa. After the initiation ceremony, Depa Sangye Gyatso offered the Fifth Panchen many gifts to express his thanks to him.

Fifth Panchen Lozang Yeshe went to give sermons in Ganden Monastery on the thirteenth of the twelfth month at the invitation of Tsultrim Dargye, the Ganden Tripa. He gave a sermon expounding the scripture entitled "Sude" to more than three thousand monks of the monastery in the Great Chanting Hall of the Ganden. He also ordained many monks into full monkhood. He left the Ganden on the seventeenth of the twelfth month on a pilgrimage to Yerpa. He arrived back in Lhasa on the twenty-second of the twelfth month and moved to the Potala at the invitation of the Sixth Dalai. On the next day, at the Dalai Khan's invitation, he went to Samdrup Phodrang, the Khan's residence, to spend a day there to give sermons to the Khan. He bid farewell to the Sixth Dalai Lama, Dalai Khan and Depa Sangye Gyatso and a grand farewell ceremony was held for him on the twenty-fourth of the twelfth month. En route to the Tashilhunpo he stayed for more than a month at Palkhor Chode Chapel in Gyantse. He arrived back at the Tashilhunpo on the seventh of the second month in the thirty-seventh year of Qing Emperor Shengzu's reign (1698).

According to *The Biography of Lozang Yeshe*, Sixth Dalai Lama Tsangyang Gyatso showed little interest in either religious observances or monastic study. On hearing this, the Fifth Panchen wrote letters to the Dalai and Depa Sangye Gyatso, urging the Dalai to study Buddhist scriptures and attend debates with other monks to carry on the cause of the Fifth Dalai Lama. In reply, Depa Sangye Gyatso asked the Panchen to come to persuade the Sixth Dalai to devote himself to monastic study, for the Dalai would not listen to him. The Depa also invited the Panchen to ordain the Dalai into full monkhood, as he would soon reach the age of twenty. Tsangyang Gyatso sent a confidential letter to the Fifth Panchen, saying that he did not like by nature to attend debates with monks and was not willing to take the *gelong* vows, though he hoped to meet the Panchen. Being displeased at the letter, the Panchen resolved not to go to Lhasa to meet Tsangyang Gyatso.

In another letter to the Fifth Panchen, Tsangyang Gyatso said he would go himself to the Tashilhunpo, if the Panchen did not come to meet him at the Potala. As soon as he received the letter, the Fifth Panchen sent men to stop the Sixth Dalai, saying that he would soon go to Lhasa. The Fifth Panchen left the Tashilhunpo by the north route for Lhasa on the sixth of the sixth month in the forty-first year of Qing Emperor Shengzu's reign (1702). At Thobgyal, en route to Lhasa, he met envoys from the Potala, who told him that the Sixth Dalai had left Lhasa by the south route for the Tashilhunpo. So the Panchen immediately went from Thobgyal to Yamdrok Lake and met Tsangyang Gyatso at Taklung. As Tsangyang Gyatso had decided to go to the Tashilhunpo, and the Fifth Panchen could not very well stop him, he went back to the Tashilhunpo via Rinpung Dzong earlier than the Dalai in order to make preparations for a warm welcome.

Sixth Dalai Tsangyang Gyatso arrived at the Tashilhunpo on the twentieth of the sixth month of that year. As it was the first time he visited the Tashilhunpo, a grand ceremony was held by the monastery to welcome him. Several thousand monks holding various Buddhist ritual objects in their hands lined up along the road to welcome the procession. From the roofs of all the buildings at the Tashilhunpo, which were decorated with various flags, monks beat drums and blew horns. The inhabitants of Shigatse also danced and sang songs. The monks and local inhabitants extended a royal welcome to the Sixth Dalai, just as they had done to the Fifth Dalai. After arriving at the Tashilhunpo, the Sixth Dalai Lama resided in Gyaltsen Tongbo Lharang, the Fifth Panchen Lama's usual residence. The Fifth Panchen took the opportunity to ask the Sixth Dalai to give a sermon to the monks and to take his *gelong* vows. But the Sixth Dalai Lama refused both requests. After spending several days there, he performed three kowtows to the Fifth Panchen and then, begging his pardon, left the Tashilhunpo for the fort of Shigatse. There he stayed for thirteen days and then left for Lhasa. It was the last meeting between the Fifth Panchen and the Sixth Dalai Lama.

## 4. The Fifth Panchen Lama Is Prevented from Meeting Qing Emperor Shengzu

In the forty-second year of Qing Emperor Shengzu's reign (1703), Dalai Khan died and his son Lhazang Khan was enthroned as the Khan. The relationship between the new Khan and Depa Sangye Gyatso began to sour. In order to moderate contradictions between himself and the Khan, Depa Sangye Gyatso made his son Drosha the acting Depa, but in reality he still controlled all political and religious affairs.

While instigating the Dzungars to attack the Kharkha Mongols, Depa Sangye Gyatso made a conspiracy to prevent the Fifth Panchen from going to Beijing to meet the Qing Emperor.

The reason why the Qing court patronized the Dalai and Panchen was that they had great influence over the Mongols, as we have explained above. Jetsun Dampa Hutuktu of the Kharkha Mongols was a follower of the Gelug sect. Mongolian chieftains all listened to the Dalai and Panchen. So Qing Emperor Shengzu, following Emperor Shizu's policy towards Tibet, invited the Panchen to Beijing to meet him. On the surface, the invitation gives the impression that the Qing court wanted to mete out the same treatment to the Dalai and the Panchen. But the real purpose of the Qing court was to calm down things in Mongolia and cause the Mongolian chieftains to give their allegiance to the Qing Dynasty. In the eighth month of the thirty-second year of Qing Emperor Shengzu's reign (1693), the Qing Emperor sent Yeshe Gelong, Bo Sholka and sixty other men to deliver two letters to the Fifth Panchen, one of which announced that the Qing government had conferred on Depa Sangye Gyatso the title "King of the Propagation of the Doctrine of the Buddha," and the other gave greetings from the Emperor. Yeshe Gelong said to the Panchen that the Emperor invited him to Beijing for an audience. The Panchen replied that he could not go to Beijing at that time for fear of a smallpox epidemic and he would go to pay respects to the Emperor after the epidemic had passed.

In the thirty-fourth year of Qing Emperor Shengzu's reign (1695), the Qing Emperor sent an imperial envoy to the Tashilhunpo to give two hundred taels of gold and a letter to the Fifth Panchen. The letter said:

> My father invited the Fifth Dalai Lama to Beijing for an audience. The invitation played an important role in developing Buddhism and promoting friendship between the Hans and Tibetans. Now the Fifth Dalai was too old to come to Beijing. So if you come to Beijing it will be a good thing for the development of Buddhism and the promotion of the well-being of the people.

At that time Fifth Panchen Lozang Yeshe, at thirty-three, was young and strong. He hoped to go to Beijing as the Fifth Dalai had done, for an audience with Qing Emperor Shengzu would raise his social status and widen the influence of Tashilhunpo Monastery. But as Depa Sangye Gyatso controlled the ruling power over Tibet, the Panchen had to ask the Depa for approval. So, after receiving the letter of invitation from the Qing Emperor, he sent men to deliver confidential letters to Lhazang Khan and Depa Sangye Gyatso, asking for their instructions. In response, the Depa sent his trusted official, Dronyer Trilung, to tell the Panchen to refuse the invitation under the pretext of fearing a smallpox outbreak. The Panchen replied to the Qing envoy as the Depa instructed.

In the eighth month of the thirty-fifth year of Qing Emperor Shengzu's reign (1696), when the Emperor had defeated Galdan on a punitive expedition, he sent Jimpa Dramusu Rimpoche and others to Tibet to deliver letters to the Dalai, Panchen, Dalai Khan and Sangye Gyatso. The Emperor said in his letter to the Panchen:

> All the states are under my command and I treat them equally. I respect Buddhism and hope that the Buddhist doctrines will prevail everywhere. The Dalai Lama is old now. You, Hutuktu, devote yourself to Buddhism, chanting sutras and doing good things. So I have invited you to Beijing. I will help you to preach Buddhist doctrines. But the Depa was jealous of you and colluded with Galdan. He prevented you from coming to Beijing by frightening you that you would be killed by Galdan's soldiers on the way to Beijing. . . . I have criticized the Depa for what he has done in helping Galdan and preventing you from coming to Beijing (see the *Imperial Records of the Qing Dynasty*).

Apparently the Emperor knew quite well that the Panchen's failing to come to Beijing was due to the Depa's intervention.

In the eleventh month of that year the Qing Emperor again sent Onchang and Dinggye Gelong to invite the Panchen, and meanwhile Depa Sangye Gyatso sent Dronyer Trilung to escort the envoys to the Tashilhunpo. The envoys said to the Panchen that the Emperor was angry at his declination with the excuse of fearing the smallpox outbreak, and that the Emperor was again inviting him to Beijing. In the first month of the next year (1697, or the thirty-sixth year of Qing Emperor Shengzu's reign), when the envoys went back to Beijing, they brought to the Emperor a letter from the Panchen. In the letter the Panchen asked the Emperor's pardon, for he could not go to Beijing, the only reason being the smallpox epidemic. Meanwhile, the Panchen asked Dronyer Trilung to report to Depa Sangye Gyatso on what he had written to the Emperor. Obviously, the Panchen wrote the letter according to the Depa's instructions. About this incident, the *Imperial Records of the Qing Dynasty* has an account as follows:

> In the thirty-fifth year of Emperor Shengzu's reign [1696] the Emperor sent envoy Zhong Shenbao and others to summon Panchen Hutuktu to Beijing. The imperial envoy went to Xining in the company of envoys from the Dalai Lama. It was reported to the Emperor in the name of the Dalai Lama and Dalai Khan that the Emperor's invitation had been given to the Panchen, but that he could not go to Beijing for fear of the smallpox outbreak. Panchen Hutuktu also reported to the Emperor: "I should have gone to Beijing at Your Majesty's summons, but our tradition takes smallpox outbreaks as a taboo, so I could not go as Your Majesty asked me to do." The Depa reported: "On hearing that Your Majesty had sent a summons to the Panchen Lama, Galdan sent men to prevent the Panchen from going to Beijing. This was why the Panchen did not go." So the Emperor ordered the Dalai Lama to send men to Beijing.

The account shows that it was Depa Sangye Gyatso who conspired to attribute the Panchen's declination of the Emperor's invitation to Galdan's threats and the smallpox outbreak, and thus shifted his culpability onto others.

In the tenth month of the thirty-seventh year of Qing Emperor Shengzu's reign (1698), the Emperor sent Boja Guchi and Chakcha Guchi to the Tashilhunpo. The envoys told the Panchen:

In the year before last you were prevented by the Depa from going to Beijing at the summons of His Majesty, though you intended to go. Now we are sent by His Majesty to invite you again to Beijing. If the Depa does not prevent you, all the people of the thirteen provinces and forty Mongolian tribes under the command of His Majesty will be overjoyed, for it will play an important role in promoting friendship between the Hans and Tibetans as well as in developing Buddhism. Otherwise, His Majesty will punish the Tibetan authorities. We hope you will think this over.

So, the Panchen sent Dronyer Karchu Dondrup to Lhasa to ask Depa Sangye Gyatso for instructions. The Depa sent his men to the Tashilhunpo to instruct the Panchen to write a reply to the Emperor in which the Panchen should promise to go to Beijing to pay his respects to the Emperor in the Iron-Dragon Tibetan calendrical year (1700, or the thirty-ninth year of Qing Emperor Shengzu's reign). The Depa told the Panchen to send Lozang Drashi to Beijing in the meantime to report to the Emperor in person that the Panchen requested an exemption from going to Beijing for fear of the smallpox outbreak, or that he be allowed to go to the Kumbum Monastery in Qinghai for an audience with the Emperor, if the Emperor would be kind enough to go there.

The *Imperial Records of the Qing Dynasty* says: "The Emperor approved the Panchen's request for an exemption from coming to Beijing on the grounds of his fear of the smallpox outbreak."

After his sinister plot was realized, Depa Sangye Gyatso was swollen with arrogance. He thereafter tried every conspiracy to drive the power of Lhazang Khan out of Tibet. In the forty-fourth year of Emperor Shengzu's reign (1705), one of Lhazang Khan's attendants, hired by Sangye Gyatso, attempted to kill Lhazang Khan with poisoned food. When the attempt became known to the Khan, the *Depa* hastily assembled his militiamen in U-Tsang and secretly sent his men to Xinjiang to ask Dzungar Khan Tsewang Arabten to attack Qinghai, the rear of Lhazang Khan, in a bid to drive Lhazang Khan out of Tibet.

# 5. Rivalry Between Sangye Gyatso and Lhazang Khan

Tsewang Arabten was the son of the deceased Dzungar Khan Sengge. He challenged the authority of Galdan after the latter proclaimed himself Khan and his military presence posed a threat to Galdan. In the thirty-fifth year of Emperor Shengzu's reign (1696), Galdan, after being defeated by the Qing army on the Kalulun River, had to flee back to Xinjiang. There he came under military attack from Tsewang Arabten, and, in complete despair, Galdan committed suicide in 1697. Tsewang Arabten collected the remnants of Galdan's troops and proclaimed himself Dzungar Khan. He sent envoys to acknowledge allegiance to the Qing court in the thirty-seventh year of Emperor Shengzu's reign (1698). In the same year the Emperor sent Assistant Secretary of the Grand Secretariat Yi Dao and others to deliver his letter to Tsewang Arabten, which said:

> What you reported to me about how Depa Sangye Gyatso had kept the Dalai's death in secret and despised the Panchen and prevented him from coming to Beijing was true. Your report on the Depa's conspiracy was correct.... So I sent envoys—Assistant Secretary of the Grand Secretariat Yi Dao, Imperial Guard La Shi, Imperial Guard of the second rank Ke Shitu, Assistant Secretary of the Grand Secretariat Tu Changming and Imperial Guard of the third rank Jing Ba—with my letter and ten bolts of imperial satin to you (see the *Imperial Records of the Qing Dynasty*).

From this letter it was obvious that Dzungar Khan had pledged allegiance to the Qing Empire, so the Qing government recognized Tsewang Arabten as the Chief of the Dzungar Khanate.

Even as Depa Sangye Gyatso was colluding with Tsewang Arabten, Lhazang Khan also sent men with many gifts to Tsewang Arabten and made an offer of marriage to Tsewang Arabten's daughter for his son. Tsewang Arabten promised the marriage. Lhazang Khan was overjoyed at this and sent his son to invite the bride, according to Mongolian custom. Thinking that, since Tsewang Arabten was his relative by marriage, he would not act against him, Lhazang Khan relaxed his vigilance against Tsewang

Arabten and thought it was a good time to settle with Depa Sangye Gyatso.

In the forty-third year of Emperor Shengzu's reign (1704), when the attempt of Sangye Gyatso to use Lhazang Khan's attendant to kill the Khan with poisoned food became known to the Khan, the relations between the Khan and the Depa became extremely tense. The Tibetan people were worried about it. The abbots of the Three Major Monasteries in Lhasa invited the Fifth Panchen to mediate. The Panchen sent Dronyer Karchen Dorje to mediate together with representatives of the Three Major Monasteries between Lhazang Khan and Depa Sangye Gyatso. In the sixth month of the next year Dronyer Karchen Dorje came back to report to the Panchen on the result of the mediation, saying that Lhazang Khan had promised to leave Tibet for Qinghai soon. A month later Lhazang Khan left Lhasa for Nagchu in the north of Tibet. Thinking that his attempt of driving Lhazang Khan's power out of Tibet was realized, Depa Sangye Gyatso relaxed vigilance against the Khan.

But in reality the Khan's withdrawal was to carry out his tactics for attacking and getting rid of Depa Sangye Gyatso's power. He stayed at Nagchu and secretly mustered ten thousand crack Mongolian cavalrymen from Qinghai for his plan to march southward. On learning of this, the Sixth Dalai Lama immediately sent a letter to Lhazang Khan, asking him not to resort to force, and meanwhile sent letters to the Three Major Monasteries and the Fifth Panchen to ask them to mediate. Dronyer Karchen Dorje, on behalf of the Fifth Panchen, and the representatives of the Three Major Monasteries went to Nagchu to persuade Lhazang Khan not to use force. But Lhazang Khan refused their request. At the same time Depa Sangye Gyatso called in militiamen from U, Tsang, Ngari and Kham to Lhasa for resistance against Lhazang Khan's attack.

On learning that Lhazang Khan's army had already reached Pondo Dzong, north of Lhasa, the Fifth Panchen left for Lhasa on the ninth of the seventh month, hoping to mediate in person. On the way he stayed at a place called Wuyou and sent a letter to the Sixth Dalai, inquiring about the state of affairs. The Sixth Dalai told him in his reply that the representatives of the Three Major Monasteries had gone to see Lhazang Khan, but the result was still not known. He asked the Panchen not to come to Lhasa for the time being. So the Panchen stayed at Wuyou for more than ten days. On the nineteenth of the seventh month the Panchen received a letter from the Dalai to the effect that Lhazang Khan had occupied Lhasa after defeating the Depa's army. Sangye Gyatso and the remnants of his routed army had fled to Gongkar in Lhoka. At first the Panchen decided to go to Lhoka, but after careful consideration he sent a representative there to ask the two fighting parties to agree to a cease-fire and to say that he would go there himself if the two parties agreed to his intervening. When his representative arrived at Gongkar, Sangye Gyatso had been captured by the Mongolian troops and sent to Doilung and executed there.

As to the appraisal of Sangye Gyatso, he has been cast in a completely negative light by the Chinese historical documents. His major wrongdoings were that he sent Kyirong Hutuktu to instigate Galdan in Xinjiang to attack Outer Mongolia and then invade Inner Mongolia, acting against the Qing court's cause of unification of China; and that he prevented the Fifth Panchen from going to Beijing, that is, preventing him from playing the important role of pacifying the people of the upper and lower strata of Outer and Inner Mongolia and helping to bring about their allegiance to the Qing central government. In a word, Depa Sangye Gyatso stood opposed to the Qing regime when the latter was engaged in its struggle against the country splitting up. As to his keeping the Fifth Dalai Lama's death secret, it has not been considered as a serious problem.

But in recent years, the Chinese Tibetologists have had differing opinions about him. Some scholars hold that, for all his wrongdoings, Sangye Gyatso did a number of good things. For instance, he put an end to the long-standing feudal separatism in Tibet, making Lhasa the political, economic and cultural centre of Tibet; for decades he extended the Potala with all the manpower, materials and financial resources of Tibet, making the Potala one of the rare, magnificent buildings in the world; and he presided over the editing of works on Tibet's medicine, calendar, literature, history and biographies—endeavours that furthered the development of Tibetan culture. He wrote three major books: *Yellow Glaze*, on the religious history of the Yellow Hat sect; *Blue Glaze*, on Tibetan medicine; and *White Glaze*, on Tibetan calendrical calculation. The other more than twenty books written by him were all great contributions to Tibetan culture. Sixth Dalai Lama Tsangyang Gyatso, whom he enthroned, was so yearned for by the Tibetan people, lay and monk alike, that the Qing government finally could not but give tacit recognition of his status as Dalai Lama after dethroning him. Tsangyang Gyatso's lyric poems have enjoyed great popularity in Tibet, which shows that he was an outstanding figure. How to correctly appraise Sangye Gyatso remains a problem to be discussed.

After killing Depa Sangye Gyatso, Lhazang Khan sent men to Beijing to report to Emperor Shengzu on the Depa's conspiracy and ask the Emperor to dethrone Tsangyang Gyatso on the ground that he was a "sham" Dalai Lama. In response, Emperor Shengzu sent envoys, Protector-Military Commander Xi Zhu and Chancellor of the Hanlin Academy Shu Lan, to Tibet to extend his support to Lhazang Khan in the forty-fifth year of the Kangxi reign period (1706). The *Imperial Records of the Qing Dynasty* has an account of this as follows:

> The forty-sixth year of the Kangxi reign period [1707]. In the past, the Depa kept the Fifth Dalai Lama's death secret and instigated the Oylut and Kharkha to fight against each other. He enthroned a sham Dalai Lama to confuse the people's minds and attempted in vain to poison Lhazang Khan and drive the Khan out of Tibet. Lhazang Khan hated the Depa so much he captured and killed the Depa. The Khan reported to the Emperor on the sham Dalai Lama. So the Emperor sent Pertector-Military Commander Xi Zhu and Chancellor Shu Lan to grant the Khan the title "Supporter of the Doctrine, the Obedient Khan" and ordered that the sham Dalai Lama be brought to Beijing.

The dethronement of the Sixth Dalai Lama caused a big stir in Tibetan religious circles, especially in the Three Major Monasteries. In fear that something untoward might happen, Lhazang Khan sent men to ask the Fifth Panchen for advice. The Panchen said that he could not give his opinion, but suggested that a ceremony for divine revelation be held by Lhazang Khan and the abbots of the Three Major Monasteries. The result of the divine revelation is not mentioned in Tibetan historical documents.

In the eleventh month of the forty-fifth year of the Kangxi reign period (1706), Lhazang Khan sent Tsangyang Gyatso and Sangye Gyatso's wife and children to Beijing under escort. It was said that Tsangyang Gyatso died en route at Kokonor at the age of twenty-four. The *Imperial Records of the Qing Dynasty* has an account of this as follows:

> The Board for National Minority Affairs reported to the Emperor that "according to Shangnan Dorje, a lama in charge of Xining, the sham Dalai Lama deported to Beijing by Lhazang Khan died of illness in Xining. The sham Dalai had acted against Buddhist discipline, so a written order should be given to Shangnan Dorje to throw away his body." The Emperor approved the report.

After dethroning Sixth Dalai Lama Tsangyang Gyatso, Lhazang Khan had to seek another Dalai to replace the dethroned one. He knew this was an important event in the religious society of Tibet. The reincarnation of the Sixth Dalai had to get the endorsement of the Panchen before he could be accepted by others. So Lhazang Khan himself went to visit the Panchen at the Tashilhunpo and said that he would give all the pastoral land and farmland in Tanarinchen, Lipu and Yerepa as donations to Tashilhunpo Monastery, just as he had given many manorial estates to the Three Major Monasteries to support the Yellow Hat sect. The Fifth Panchen accepted the donation and expressed thanks to the Khan. After several days Lhazang Khan said to the Panchen that the genuine reincarnation of the Dalai Lama had been found and he invited the Panchen to go to Lhasa to ordain the boy into monkhood. The Fifth Panchen accepted the invitation.

# 6. Qing Emperor Shengzu Grants a Title to the Fifth Panchen

On the eleventh day of the second month of the forty-sixth year of the Kangxi reign period (1707), the Fifth Panchen left for Lhasa at the invitation of Lhazang Khan. He was greeted by Lhazang Khan's wife on behalf of the Khan at Doilung, west of Lhasa. The following day, when he arrived at the suburbs of Lhasa, a grand welcoming ceremony was held for him by more than a thousand people led by Lhazang Khan, Depa Ngawang Rinchen (appointed by Lhazang Khan to replace Depa Sangye Gyatso), Changling Khenpo and representatives of the Three Major Monasteries. The Panchen resided in the Sesong Namgyal Lharang Hall of the Potala. On the twenty-fifth day of the second month the soul boy met with the Fifth Panchen in the Seshi Phuntsok Hall of the Potala. The soul boy kowtowed to the Panchen and they exchanged *katags*. Lhazang Khan presented a gold wheel of life, a conch and other Buddhist objects to the soul boy. The Panchen also gave him many rare objects as gifts.

On the eighth day of the third month the Fifth Panchen and the soul boy went together to Jokhang Temple. The boy took the vows of a *getsul* under the guidance of the Fifth Panchen. The ceremony was held in front of the statue of Sakyamuni Buddha. The master of the ceremony was Ganden Tripa Dondrup Gyatso. The Panchen gave the boy the religious name of Yeshe Gyatso Palzangpo (Yeshe Gyatso for short).

On the seventeenth day of the fourth month the Panchen and Yeshe Gyatso went to Drepung and Sera monasteries where the Panchen held *getsul* and *gelong* vows-taking ceremonies for hundreds of monks. From the twenty-seventh of the fourth month through the twelfth day of the seventh month, Yeshe Gyatso studied sutras of exoteric and esoteric Buddhism under the guidance of the Panchen at the Potala. During that time the Panchen gave alms and sweet buttered-tea to the monks of the Three Major Monasteries in Lhasa at an expense of 54,226 *khal* of Tibetan barley.

On the thirteenth day of the seventh month the Panchen left Lhasa for the Tashilhunpo. Again, a grand farewell ceremony was held for him. To show his gratitude to the Panchen's support, Lhazang Khan gave many manorial estates in Tsang to Tashilhunpo Monastery.

The enthronement of Yeshe Gyatso as the Sixth Dalai Lama by Lhazang Khan caused strong opposition not only among the Tibetan monks and laymen, but also among the Mongols in Qinghai. They lodged complaints against it with the Qing government. Emperor Shengzu sent Academician of the Grand Secretariat Laduhun, together with the representatives of all the *tejis* (adminis-

trators) of Qinghai, to look into the matter. Lhazang Khan said to
the imperial envoy that Panchen Hutuktu told him that Yeshe
Gyatso was the authentic Dalai Lama, so he enthroned Yeshe
Gyatso. When this was reported to the Emperor, the Emperor
ordered the cabinet ministers to have a discussion of it. The
ministers reported to the Emperor:

> There should be no problem about the authenticity of the Dalai Lama,
> since Lhazang Khan enthroned him after asking the Panchen Hutuktu
> for advice. . . . The *tejis* in Qinghai are not in good relations with
> Lhazang Khan. Therefore, it will not be convenient for Lhazang Khan
> to rule over Tibet alone. An official should be sent to Tibet to run
> Tibetan affairs together with Lhazang Khan.

The imperial edict was: "Your suggestion is approved. Vice-
Minister Heshou is to go and take charge of Tibetan affairs" (see
the *Imperial Records of the Qing Dynasty*).

In response to the suggestion of Lhazang Khan and Heshou,
Qing Emperor Shengzu granted Yeshe Gyatso the title "The Sixth
Dalai Lama" and an album of appointment and a seal of authority
in the forty-ninth year of the Kangxi reign period (1710).

Emperor Shengzu knew that the political situation in Tibet was
not stable and that Yeshe Gyatso, enthroned by Lhazang Khan, did
not enjoy the support of the Tibetan people. In order to calm
things down in Tibet, the Emperor conferred on the Fifth Panchen
Lozang Yeshe the title of "Panchen Erdeni" in the fifty-second year
of the Kangxi reign period (1713). The *Imperial Records of the Qing
Dynasty* says:

> The Emperor gave orders to the Board for National Minority Affairs as
> follows: Panchen Hutuktu, being calm by nature, devotes himself to the
> study of Buddhist doctrines. He deserves praise. I order to grant him
> the title of Panchen Erdeni and an album of appointment and a seal of
> authority in the same honour as that given to the Dalai Lama.

The Tibetan-language *Biography of Lozang Yeshe* says:

> In the fourth month of the Fire-Serpent year [the fifty-second year of
> the Kangxi reign period, or 1713] the Emperor sent Norbu and Jiare
> Koje, grand lamas from Tserenkya, and other officials to take an
> imperial edict to the Tashilhunpo to grant the Fifth Panchen the title
> "Panchen Erdeni" and bestowed upon him a gold album and a gold seal
> of authority.

The gold seal remains intact, but the album was lost. According to the biography, the imperial edict was to the following effect: "All the Panchens spread Buddhism to benefit the masses of the people. I also support Buddhism to bring about a happy life to them. We have the same purpose. To show my respect to you, I order to grant you the title of Panchen Erdeni and bestow on you a gold seal and a gold album with inscriptions in Manchu, Han and Tibetan writings on them."

The Emperor granted the Panchen the title in order that the Panchen, his social status being raised, could better assist Lhazang Khan to stabilize the state of affairs in Tibet. To stabilize the state of affairs in Tibet was also the reason why the Panchen gave support to Lhazang Khan and acknowledged Yeshe Gyatso as the Sixth Dalai.

In spite of all this, Mongolian monks, lay people, and the *teji* of the Qoshot tribe in Qinghai, as well as members of upper religious status of the Three Major Monasteries in Lhasa, still refused to recognize the enthronement of Yeshe Gyatso. They found another reincarnation of the Dalai Lama at Litang in Xikang (Kham) in the fifty-fourth year of the Kangxi reign period (1715) and asked the Qing court for recognition of him. According to the *Imperial Records of the Qing Dynasty*.

> On the *xin-wei* day of the fourth month in the fifty-fourth year of the Kangxi reign period, the Board for National Minority Affairs reported to the Emperor that Right Wing Prince of Qinghai Daichen, Shochi and Charhan Tenzin asked the Emperor to recognize the authentic reincarnation of the Dalai Lama, who was newly found at Litang, and to dethrone the sham one, the one enthroned by Panchen Hutuktu and Lhazang Khan.

So, Emperor Shengzu sent officials in charge of Buddhism to inquire with the Panchen about the authenticity of the reincarnation at Litang. The officials came back and reported that the Panchen said the reincarnation at Litang was a sham one. As a result, Emperor Shengzu ordered that the soul boy found at Litang be moved to Hongshan Monastery in Qinghai (later he was moved to Kumbum Monastery).

After overthrowing Depa Sangye Gyatso, Lhazang Khan entrusted all political and religious affairs to the care of Ngawang Rinchen, the Depa he appointed, and took to drinking, not taking precautions against Tsewang Arabten—a relative by marriage.

After Lhazang Khan's son Galdan Tenzin had lived in Xinjiang for three years after marrying Tsewang Arabten's daughter and had three children by her, Arabten sent a crack army of six thousand under the command of Tsering Dondup on the pretext of escorting Galdan Tenzin and his family back to Tibet. The army arrived in Ngari in the west of Tibet in the fifty-sixth year of the Kangxi reign period (1717). Heshou, who had come back to Beijing from Tibet and was appointed the Minister of the Board for National Minority Affairs, reported to the Emperor on the army movement, saying that "Arabten is cunning and can not be trusted." The Emperor ordered him to write in his name to Lhazang Khan, warning the Khan to pay attention to the situation.

It was not until the seventh month of the fifty-sixth year of the Kangxi reign period (1717), when the army led by Tsering Dondup arrived at Nam Tso, a place not far from Lhasa, via grasslands in the north of Tibet, that Lhazang Khan came to realize the army's intention. He hurriedly assembled the Dam Mongols and militiamen from U and Tsang regions in an attempt to make resistance, and meanwhile he asked the Panchen and representatives of the Three Major Monasteries to mediate. After receiving Lhazang Khan's letter for help, the Panchen immediately left the Tashilhunpo, starting out on the nineteenth of the seventh month via Mt. Gola for Dam, where the Panchen and the representatives of the Three Major Monasteries had a meeting with Lhazang Khan.

After the meeting they were sent by the Khan to ask Tsering Dondup, commander of the Dzungar army, not to wage a war on Tibet. They arrived at Lower Dam on the thirtieth of the seventh month and paid a visit to the commander, who told them he would use force if Lhazang Khan would not come to meet him in person. The Panchen passed the message to Lhazang Khan. The Khan dared not go in person. The Panchen and the representatives then continued to mediate between the two parties, but failed to make peace.

Tsering Dondup sent word to the Panchen, asking him to go back to the Tashilhunpo. The Panchen first sent letters to Tsering Dondup and Lhazang Khan, respectively, bidding them farewell and asking them to settle their matters without bloodshed for the sake of Buddhism. Then, on the thirty-first of the eighth month, the Panchen left Dam for the Tashilhunpo.

After leaving Dam, the Panchen did not go back to the Tashilhunpo directly, but broke off his journey at several places over a month in order to observe the changes of the state of affairs in Tibet. He reached Lhasa on the eighth of the tenth month and resided in the Potala, where he met with Yeshe Gyatso. Soon Lhazang Khan was defeated and fled back to Lhasa. The Khan resided in Khensong Namgyal Hall in the Potala and consulted with the Panchen and Yeshe Gyatso on the defence of Lhasa. He sent men to Beijing to ask the Qing court for military help.

The *Imperial Records of the Qing Dynasty* says:

Lhazang Khan reported to the Emperor: "My family has been under Your Majesty's benevolence for several generations. Unexpectedly the evil Tsewang Arabten sent six thousand soldiers to make war upon Tibet. After two months of fighting, the war has not yet been won by either side. Now the enemy is coming to attack Lhasa, which I am now defending. But what makes me worry is that the Tibetan forces are too weak. If Kham, U and Tsang fall into the enemy's hands, Lamaism will be wiped out. So I beg Your Majesty to send his troops and those in Qinghai to rescue Lhasa as soon as possible."

On the seventeenth of the tenth month, Tsering Dondup's army of Dzungar soldiers marched to Lhasa and stationed itself at Chunmai, Langyul and Changtanggang. Again the Panchen sent men to mediate, but without any success. On the twenty-ninth of the tenth month the Dzungar army captured Lhasa and the Tibetan militiamen were dispersed. The next day the Panchen went to meet Tsering Dondup at Jokhang Temple, offering him tea, silk and satin and other gifts and asking him to spare Lhazang Khan's life and put the Khan in the custody of the Panchen. The commander replied that his requests could be accepted if Lhazang Khan came to meet him. Lhazang Khan dared not go to meet him. Instead, he tried to flee with his wife and children on the night of the first of the eleventh month. He was captured and killed by Dzungar soldiers in the suburbs of Lhasa. His family was also captured. The Panchen again went to ask the commander to put the captives in his custody, but his request was refused. Nevertheless, the commander promised to spare the lives of the Khan's family. Tsering Dondup advised the Panchen to go back to the Tashilhunpo as soon as possible and asked him to give a sermon to the four thousand Dzungar soldiers before his leaving Lhasa. At his invitation the Panchen gave a sermon to the Dzungar soldiers at Seshi Phuntsok Hall in the Potala. The Panchen left Lhasa for the Tashilhunpo on the third of the eleventh month under the escort of the Dzungar soldiers sent by Tsering Dondup.

## 7. Qing Emperor Shengzu Defeats the Dzungars' Invasion of Tibet

According to Tibetan historical documents and the *Imperial Records of the Qing Dynasty*, one of the reasons why Tsering Dondup so quickly occupied Tibet and killed Lhazang Khan was that some local officials betrayed Lhazang Khan's regime.

Gelong Sakdur Gyalpo of the Tibetan local government defected to the Dzungars on the thirtieth day of the tenth month in the fifty-sixth year of the Kangxi reign period (1717) when Tsering Dondup's troops marched to Lhasa after defeating Lhazang Khan. Owing to the *gelong*'s defection, Tsering Dondup soon captured Lhasa. Teji Namgyal opened the north gate to the Potala for the Dzungars, so they soon occupied the Potala. Not long afterwards, Tsering Dondup confined Yeshe Gyatso at Chakpori and appointed Taktsewa Lhagyal Rabten as the Depa to take charge of Tibetan political and religious affairs in accordance with his intentions. By then the seventy-five-year-long regime of the Gushri Khan family in Tibet (1642-1717) was ended forever.

Lhazang Khan's son Sultsa was also captured by the Dzungars, but Sultsa's wife fled to Qinghai and begged the Qing court to suppress the rebellion in Tibet. After reading the report about the matter, Emperor Shengzu immediately sent Hua Se, Assistant Secretary of the Hanlin Academy, to Qinghai to give one thousand taels of silver to Sultsa's wife for her living expenses.

At the same time the Emperor ordered Governor-General Erentai of Xi'an and General Seleng of the Imperial Guards to lead an army of several thousand men into Tibet. To lure the Qing army in deep, Tsering Dondup's troops feigned retreat. So Erentai and Seleng's troops advanced smoothly, without meeting much resistance. When they arrived at Karawusu (now Nagchukha) in the ninth month of the fifty-seventh year of the Kangxi reign period (1718), the enemy suddenly blocked their advance and attacked them from the rear, cutting off their food supply lines. Though the Qing army held out for a month, they were annihilated when they ran out of food. Governor-General Erentai and General Seleng were killed in action.

The tragic defeat of the Qing army in Tibet gave rise to debates in Beijing. All agreed that no more military action should be attempted in Tibet. But Emperor Shengzu thought otherwise. He said that, as Tibet was the shield of Qinghai, Yunnan and Sichuan, its seizure by the Dzungar barbarians would mean no peace on the frontier. Thus, a second military expedition was planned for the fifty-eighth year of the Kangxi reign period (1719). The Emperor's fourteenth son, Yunti, was appointed as the General of Frontier Pacification. With his headquarters at Xining, he was commander-in-chief of several contingents. A Manchu-Han army from Shaanxi and Gansu struck out from Xining under the command of generals Yan Xin, Ma Jibo and Li Lin on its expedition along the middle route. Meanwhile, generals Galbi and Yue Zhongqi led another Manchu-Han army, formed by troops from Yunnan, Sichuan, Hubei and Zhejiang, out of Tachienlu (modern Kangding also spelled as Dajianlu) on a march along the southern route. General Fu Ning'an's army was to pin down the Dzungars out of Hami on a march to Urumchi along the northern route, keeping the Dzungars from sending more troops to Tibet.

In the same year, Emperor Shengzu conferred the title of Sixth Dalai Lama (renamed as the Seventh Dalai Lama in the forty-fifth year of the Qianlong reign period, or 1780) on the soul boy found at Litang (residing by then at Kumbum Monastery in Qinghai), and ordered him to be taken to the Potala for enthronement by an escort led by General Yan Xin.

Also, by order of the Emperor, units of the armed forces of Mongol khans, princes and *tejis* in Qinghai, each numbering from several hundred to several thousand men, joined the Qing escort in accompanying the Dalai Lama to Tibet. Judging by the size of the escort, at least twelve thousand men must have been involved, not including the five thousand officers and men marching on Urumchi.

At that time Khangchennas, the Galpon (an official title) of Ngari, assembled all the militiamen in Ngari. He occupied Ngari and then sent his men on a march to Tsang and occupied the whole area to the west of Ngamring Dzong. Thus he blocked the invading Dzungars' contacts with their home base in Xinjiang. Under such circumstances, Tsering Dondup begged the Fifth Panchen to mediate. The Panchen sent Kyirong Legpa Kachin Lozang Dargye to Ngari to meet Khangchennas. In order to show due respect to the Panchen, Khangchennas withdrew his army a little from Latu towards Shol. According to the *Imperial Records of the Qing Dynasty*, when the Dzungars occupied Tibet, Khangchennas was very hostile to the Dzungars, blocking their retreat and capturing their men. To reward his meritorious service, the Qing court granted him the title of Beizi (prince).

During the occupation of Tibet by the Dzungars, the Fifth Panchen always acted as a mediator, so the Dzungars showed their respect for him. The invaders pillaged the Three Major Monasteries at Lhasa and sent the loot back to Xinjiang, but did not touch the Tashilhunpo's property. Dzungar officers Dorkha Chesang, Chosphel Chesang and Sangye Chesang paid respects to the Panchen at the Tashilhunpo and asked him to give them a sermon in the fifty-seventh year of the Kangxi reign period (1718). The Dzungar commander-in-chief, Tsering Dondup, with two hundred officers also came to ask the Panchen to give a sermon on the twenty-third day of the seventh month in the same year.

In the fifty-eighth year of the Kangxi reign period (1719), Dzungar Khan Tsewang Arabten sent Wubashi and three others from Xinjiang to Tibet. In his letter to the Panchen Lama, Tsewang Arabten said that he sent Tsering Dondup with an army to occupy Tibet the year before because Lhazang Khan was hostile to the Depa Sangye Gyatso and the Tibetan people suffered much and Buddhism was harmed under Lhazang's rule. He asked the Panchen to send two *khenpos* and one representative from each *dratsang* of the Three Major Monasteries to Xinjiang to consult with him on

Tibetan affairs. The Panchen sent Zimpon Chunrapa Khedrup Chosphel and Chopon Tsoso Lozang Sangpo, together with the representatives of the Three Major Monasteries, to Xinjiang. In his letter to Tsewang Arabten, the Panchen explained that Lhazang Khan and Depa Sangye Gyatso had not caused damage to the Yellow sect and its monks, and asked for sparing the lives of Lhazang Khan's family and his subordinates. He also asked for the release of the deposed and jailed Kalons of the Tibetan local government and that they not be sent to Xinjiang.

Meanwhile, Tsering Dondup donated to Panchen all the manorial estates of Rinchentse Dzongpon of Tsang and Tsangtse Dzongpon of Gyantse. At first the Panchen refused the donation, but when Tsering Dondup threatened that the Dzungar Khan would be angry at his refusal, he reluctantly accepted it.

In the winter of the same year, Prince Yunti, General of Frontier Pacification, dispatched Sherab Thangkha and four other officials, accompanied by Changzod Kagyu Ngawang Bagon and Dronyer Konchok, as well as representatives of Qoshot Mongols in Qinghai, to Tibet with a letter from the prince to Tsering Dondup, in which the prince said that he would like to hold peace negotiations with the Dzungars.

In July the following year this group of representatives went to visit the Fifth Panchen at the Tashilhunpo and was warmly received by him. The Panchen wrote a letter to the prince, asking him to solve the problems of Tibet through peace negotiations instead of force and to convey his suggestions to the Emperor. But the Dzungars did not show the least desire to withdraw from Tibet, so Emperor Shengzu decided to drive them out of Tibet by force.

To solve the problems of Tibet by force, the Qing court first of all had to solve the problems of food supply and communication for the troops that marched to Tibet. So, a number of army service stations were set up along the routes. There were fifteen stations with twenty horses each from Ashihan to Solomu, and five stations with fifteen horses each from Solomu to Chaidam. Each station had ten men of the Green Banner from Guyuan and ten men from Qinghai on guard.

In order to strengthen military discipline, Prince Yunti reported to the Emperor that Vice-Minister of Personnel Seltu and General

Hu Xitu should be punished severely, because the former delayed the military supply and the latter caused losses of men and horses in the army. Thus the two officials were arrested. Seltu was sentenced to death, and Hu Xitu was deposed and put in jail.

In the fifty-ninth year of the Kangxi reign period (1720), by the Emperor's order Prince Yunti moved his headquarters from Xining to Muluswusu (modern Tongtianhe). He was responsible for military affairs and food supply for the Qing expeditionary troops. The troops marched to Tibet along the middle, southern and northern routes.

The southern contingent led by General Galbi did not meet resistance from the local Tibetan chieftains, as Galbi took the strategy of pacification towards them. He had marched smoothly to the suburbs of Lhasa by the eighth month of that year. Taktsewa, the Depa appointed by the Dzungars, surrendered. On the twenty-third day of the eighth month, the southern contingent marched into Lhasa. Soon after he took Lhasa, Galbi arrested all the one hundred and one Dzungar monks who were hiding in the Three Major Monasteries. He had five of them, leaders of the arrested monks, executed summarily and the rest thrown into jail. He then declared the Emperor's intention to save Tibetan people to all officials, chieftains and monks, and had the Dalai Lama's storehouses closed up.

Meanwhile, Yan Xin's army, which was advancing along the middle route, broke the resistance of the Dzungars at the Bogchu River on the fifteenth day of the eighth month, at Chonengar on the twentieth day, and at Tshomorab on the twenty-second day of that month. Unable to return to Lhasa, Tsering Dondup fled back to Xinjiang by way of the grasslands of northern Tibet with what was left of his men. The Dzungars altogether occupied Tibet for a period of three years, from 1717 to 1720.

Early in the ninth month Yan Xin arrived at Lhasa with the seventh Dalai Lama. On the fifteenth day of that month Kelzang Gyatso was enthroned in the Potala. On the sixth day of the tenth month Yan Xin and the representatives of the Dalai Lama went to the Tashilhunpo to invite Fifth Panchen Lozang Yeshe to hold a *getsul*-vows-taking ceremony for the Dalai Lama at Lhasa. The Panchen accepted the invitation and left for Lhasa on the next day.

On the route he met Galpon Khangchennas from Ngari, who was also going to Lhasa. So they went together. At Doilung the Panchen was warmly greeted by Tenzin, Mongol Khan in Qinghai, Prince Galdan Erdeni Boshoktu, Lozang Tenzin, etc. On the following day, the Panchen and his party came to the suburbs of Lhasa and were greeted by Outer Mongolian Khan Kharkha Dondrup, Dalai's father Sonam Dargye, representatives of Drepung and Sera monasteries and lamas of the Namgyal Dratsang of the Potala. He was also welcomed by General Yan Xin and the Manchu and Han officers and officials and the monk and lay officials of the Tibetan local government in front of Drepung Monastery. The welcoming party was more than two thousand in number.

# 8. The Fifth Panchen Ordains the Seventh Dalai Lama

After arriving at the Potala, the Fifth Panchen went to meet the Seventh Dalai in Nyiod Khang Hall. They saluted each other and exchanged *katags*. The Panchen resided at the Deyangshar Mansion of the Potala.

On the nineteenth day of the tenth month, envoys from Qing Emperor Shengzu, Grand Lama Lozang Tsultrim and Thukwan Hutuktu arrived at Lhasa. Accompanied by General Yan Xin, they came to bestow an imperial edict in Han, Manchu and Tibetan scripts to the Panchen. The Panchen received the edict with both hands in a standing posture after kowtowing to it. The general idea of the edict was as follows: I protect Tibetan Buddhism as the sun shines on the earth. I hope the Panchen will be in peace and will preach Buddhism as before; each Tibetan religious sect will do as it thinks right according to traditional customs to promote Tsongkhapa's Buddhist doctrines in Tibet and to give peace and safety to the Tibetan people; and no internal revolt will occur again.

The Emperor bestowed twelve bolts of satin and two thousand taels of silver on the Panchen. The Panchen chanted sutras of peace and safety for the Emperor at General Yan Xin's request.

After receiving the imperial edict, the Panchen asked monks of the Tashilhunpo to chant sutras of longevity for Emperor Shengzu, who was advanced in age then. Besides, he wrote a letter in reply to express his many thanks to the Emperor. The letter was accompanied with an image of the Longevity Buddha, a set of satin cushions and a *katag* of longevity as gifts to the Emperor. He sent Kachin Tseten Gyaltsen with the letter and gifts to Beijing.

On the fifth day of the eleventh month, the Panchen gave the *getsul* vows to the Dalai. The vows-taking ceremony was held at the Sunlight Hall of the Potala. The Panchen gave the Seventh Dalai Lama the religious name of Lozang Kelzang Gyatso.

After the enthronement of the Seventh Dalai, the Qing Emperor had Yeshe Gyatso, the Dalai Lama installed by Lhazang Khan, taken out of Chakpori, where he had been jailed by the Dzungars, and ordered that he be brought to Beijing for a decision to be made on him. On departure, Yeshe Gyatso went to bid farewell to the Panchen and begged for his care. The Panchen gave Yeshe Gyatso many things for use on the route.

General Yan Xin arrested Depa Taktsewa, Gelong Tashi Drakpa, Achok and the *Jetsun* of the Tashilhunpo as well as other persons who had rendered their service to the Dzungars. The Panchen asked the general to spare their lives. But General Yan Xin refused his request. He had the Depa Taktsewa and Gelong Tashi Drakpa executed, while the *Jetsun* and other persons were taken to Beijing under escort. In order to show due respect for the Panchen's feelings, he set free a number of accessories. He abolished the post of "*depa*," delegating Tibetan administrative power to Khangchennas, who was appointed as the chief Kalon. He also installed Ngabopa, Lumpanas, Jaranas, and Pholhanas as kalons (Ministers of Council) to assist Khangchennas in handling day-to-day affairs. A stone slab bearing an inscription of the account of the Qing expedition, entitled "The Restoration of Peace in Tibet," was erected in front of the Potala. The next year (1721, or the sixtieth year of the Kangxi reign period) the expeditionary troops were pulled back to inner China.

Meanwhile, the Panchen sent men to give alms and sweet buttered-tea to the monks of the Three Major Monasteries at Lhasa and those in U and Tsang at an expense of more than 99,000 *khal* of Tibetan barley. He left for the Tashilhunpo on the twenty-eighth day of the first month of the sixtieth year of the Kangxi reign period. Before the Panchen's departure, Kelzang Gyatso went to bid him farewell, wishing him a good journey. The Panchen also wished the Dalai Lama safety and peace, and asked him to study Buddhist scriptures for the development of Buddhism. The Tibetan local government held a grand farewell ceremony for the Panchen. He arrived at Bengom Monastery on the sixth day of the second month. After staying there for several days, he went back to the Tashilhunpo on the tenth day of the second month.

In 1723 Qing Emperor Shengzu died, and Emperor Shizong came to the throne. The title of his reign period was Yongzheng. Emperor Shizong sent envoys to give alms and sweet buttered-tea to the monks of all monasteries in Tibet. In response, the Dalai and Panchen asked all monks in Tibet to pray in memory of Emperor Shengzu's death, and each sent a grand *khenpo* lama to Beijing to convey their congratulations on Emperor Shizong's enthronement. In the second year of Emperor Shizong's reign (1724), the Emperor sent a party of seventy persons headed by Dzasa Lama Lozang Paljor, Jiaguchi and Bichiche to bestow a gold seal upon the Dalai and to visit the Panchen.

In the fourth year of Emperor Shizong's reign (1726), the Seventh Dalai Lama made known his intention to go to Tashilhunpo Monastery to take *gelong* vows before the Panchen. But the Panchen wrote to the Dalai that he himself would go to Lhasa to ordain the Dalai. On the twenty-seventh day of the second month the Dalai sent Shodepa Kunga Jintan to the Tashilhunpo to invite the Panchen. The Panchen started óff on the twenty-third day of the second month, Kalon Jaranas and the *dzongpons* of Shigatse, Gyantse, Bainang and Namling going to see him off. When the Panchen and his party arrived at Chushui, Chief Kalon Khangchennas and his wife, together with a hundred-odd officials, came to welcome him at the bank of the Yarlungzangbo River. When he arrived at Yadang, he was welcomed by the Seventh Dalai's father, Sonam Dargye, and his hundred-member retinue.

On the fifth day of the fourth month, the Panchen arrived at Lhasa and was warmly welcomed by the *khenpos* of the Three Major Monasteries, all eminent hutuktu and representatives of all the *khangtsens* of the Three Major Monasteries, numbering over two hundred. Welcoming tents were set up at Tsannyid Lingkha in front of the Drepung. Kalons and two hundred monk and lay officials of the Tibetan local government also came to welcome him, setting their tents up at Sultsaitang. After taking a rest in these tents the Panchen came to the Potala and met with Seventh Dalai Lama Kelzang Gyatso at Nyiod Khang Hall. They exchanged *katags*. The Panchen resided at Deyangshar Mansion as he had done before.

On the ninth day of the fourth month the Panchen ordained the Seventh Dalai Lama as a *gelong*. The vows-taking ceremony was held before the image of Sakyamuni in Jokhang Temple. The three masters of ceremony were the abbot of the Ganden, the *khenpo* of the Lower Esoteric College and Kachin Molang Gyatso. After spending eight days at the Jokhang, the Dalai and Panchen went back to the Potala on the sixteenth day of the fourth month. The Panchen lived for a month in the Potala. During the month he gave sermons to the Dalai Lama every day. On the nineteenth day of the fifth month the Panchen left Lhasa for the Tashilhunpo.

# 9. Internal Conflicts in the Tibetan Local Government

Hostilities broke out between the Kalons, who were rival representatives of serf-owners in U and Tsang. Chief Kalon Khangchennas and Kalon Pholhanas were representatives of serf-owners in Tsang, while Kalons Ngabopa, Lumpanas and Jaranas, representatives of serf-owners in U. Lumpanas married his daughter to the Dalai's father, Sonam Dargye, and thus was in closer relation with the Dalai's family. The two local forces became more hostile to each other.

In the third year of the Yongzheng reign period (1725), the Emperor sent General Eqi, Chancellor of the Hanlin Academy Bandi, Dzasa Lama Geleg Dorje, etc., to make an investigation of the situation in Tibet. In the fifth year of the Yongzheng reign period (1727), after coming back from Tibet to Beijing, Eqi reported to the Emperor:

I went to Tibet and had made investigations of the political situation there. The leading administrators in Tibet are not on good terms with each other. The Dalai Lama is clever but still too young to be totally fair where his father is concerned. Khangchennas is a fairly decent man, but, being too conscious of his meritorious services, acts arrogantly towards the Kalons and is hated by them. Ngabopa is treacherous and quite different from Khangchennas. He has formed a clique with Sonam Dargye and Lumpanas, whose two daughters are married to Sonam Dargye. Their schemes to turn the Dalai Lama and Khangchennas against each other will inevitably cause troubles. Besides, there are too many Kalons to be of any help. As Lumpanas is impulsive and Jaranas incompetent, they should be removed from office as Kalons, so that Ngabopa will be left without any assistance and no one will be able to create trouble.

So Emperor Shizong sent Sengge, an Academician of the Grand Secretariat, and General Mala to Tibet to deal with the civil strife there. But before they arrived in Tibet, armed clashes had broken out. Ngabopa, Lumpanas and Jaranas, allying with each other in the clash, killed Khangchennas in the Jokhang, while Teji Pholhanas fled to Tsang.

After fleeing to Shigatse, Pholhanas collected militiamen of Tsang and Ngari, intending to go to Lhasa to quell the rebellion. Ngabopa and others, with militiamen of U, went to Bainang Dzong, threatening to arrest Pholhanas. A war broke outbetween the two parties at Bainang Dzong. At first Pholhanas' troops were defeated and retreated to Saga Dzong. The Dalai's uncle on his mother's side, Gushiang, led the militiamen from Lhasa and occupied Shigatse. He paid a visit to the Panchen at Tashilhunpo Monastery, but the Panchen did not receive him in person because of suffering from smallpox. The Panchen sent his *Changzod* to offer butter, barley, tea and dried meat to the troops of both parties to express sympathy and solicitude and convey his proposal that both parties should stop fighting for the sake of Tibetan people. Both sides ostensibly accepted his proposal, while actually preparing to fight a life-and-death battle.

Pholhanas retreated to Ngari. Gushiang chased him to Ngamring Dzong, but did not catch up to him. Pholhanas, with nine thousand men he collected in Ngari, came back into Tsang and staged a counterattack. He defeated the troops of U and seized Shigatse.

Pholhanas also paid a visit to the Panchen. Because of his smallpox, the Panchen did not come out to receive him in person, but sent advice to him not to seek revenge.

In the first month of the sixth year of the Yongzheng reign period (1728), troops of U and Tsang fought with each other at Gyantse, though neither side could win the battle. They stood deadlocked. The Panchen sent Dronyer Sagupa to Gyantse with the suggestion that they stop fighting and wait for imperial envoys from Beijing. Meanwhile, the Dalai also sent letters to both sides, asking them to accept the Panchen's proposal. In response, the two sides signed a truce agreement, according to which both sides withdrew troops from Gyantse and released the prisoners of war they held.

In the fifth month of the same year Pholhanas led his nine thousand men from Tsang and Ngari on a detour via the northern grasslands to attack Lhasa on the pretext that the truce agreement was broken by the officials of U who killed some of his men. He occupied Lhasa on the twenty-sixth day of the fifth month and, with the help of the monks of the Three Major Monasteries, captured Ngabopa, Lumpanas and Jaranas. Pholhanas put them into jail, waiting for the Emperor's decision. Thus the rebellion of Ngabopa and others ended up in failure.

Before Pholhanas occupied Lhasa, the imperial envoys, Sengge and Mala, had come into Tibet. Being without troops, they could not deal with the matter. So they reported to the Emperor immediately about the situation, asking him to send an army to quell the turmoil in Tibet. Emperor Shizong, upon the report, sent an army of 11,400 men, composed of 400 Manchu soldiers from Xi'an, 8,000 men of the Green Banner from Shaanxi and 3,000 men of the Green Banner from Yunnan, under the command of Jalangga, a Censor-in-chief, and General Mailu, to Tibet.

Before the Qing army reached Tibet, Pholhanas, in the seventh month of the sixth year of the Yongzheng reign period (1728), had already occupied Lhasa and captured Ngabopa, Lumpanas and Jaranas. When Jalangga and Mailu arrived in Lhasa, they formed a court of justice together with Sengge and Mala. The *Imperial Records of the Qing Dynasty* has an account of this as follows:

Ngabopa confessed that they had murdered Khangchennas. Now since

Ngabopa and other murderers, though officials under the benevolence of the state, had dared act against the laws, they needed to be punished separately, each according to his own crime. Ngabopa and Lumpanas were to be put to death by slicing. Ngabopa's three sons—Galdan Phuntsok, Yanchuk Lhajab and Odalhan Gyaltsen Chudar—and Lumpanas' son Shimpon Trudra should also be executed. Jaranas' wife and two sons, as well as the wives and daughters of Ngabopa and Lumpanas, should be exiled. Those who have assisted Ngabopa and his group in the rebellion were also punished accordingly.

The Emperor made Pholhanas the chief administrator of Tibet, and appointed, at Pholhanas' recommendation, Sedrut Sebten and Tsering Wangdrak as Kalons to assist Pholhanas in handling day-to-day affairs. In recognition of the contributions made by Pholhanas' troops to the termination of the turmoil, the Emperor ordered Jalangga to give thirty thousand taels of silver from the Qing army's supplies to Pholhanas' men. The Emperor, in addition to that, ordered General Mala and Academician of the Grand Secretariat Sengge to keep a close watch on Pholhanas on behalf of the Qing court.

Not long after Jalangga reached Tibet, on the twenty-fifth of the seventh month that year, the Fifth Panchen sent Dronyer Sagupa to present ten thousand *khal* of barley to the Qing army at Lhasa as an expression of gratitude and to ask the imperial envoys to lighten the punishment and spare the lives of the criminals. Jalangga accepted three thousand *khal* of barley and sent two officials to invite the Panchen for an audience at Lhasa.

The Panchen left for Lhasa on the thirteenth of the ninth month. When he reached Doilung, Chief Kalon Pholhanas and the Dalai's father, Sonam Dargye, with three hundred cavalrymen, came to welcome him. On the following day he arrived at Sucaitang in the suburbs of Lhasa and was warmly greeted by Mala and Sengge, representatives of the Three Major Monasteries and monk and lay officials of the Tibetan local government. After a short interview with them in the tents set up for welcoming him, the Panchen went to the Potala and had a meeting with the Seventh Dalai Lama at the Sunlight Hall. He put up in Deyangshar Mansion.

On the twenty-sixth of the ninth month, Jalangga, with more than twenty Manchu and Han officials, came to the Potala to read an imperial edict to the Panchen. The general idea of the edict was that the Emperor bestowed the areas from the west of the Tashilhunpo (or of Mt. Ganbala in some other records) to Ngari to the Panchen. The Panchen declined to accept the donation, saying the Tashilhunpo was well accommodated by the manorial estates it had and no more were needed. He asked that the order be countermanded by the Emperor. But Jalangga asked him not to refuse, for the Emperor made the donations not to increase the Panchen's personal wealth, but for the sake of Buddhism and worldly beings.

In reality, this was a part of the Qing court's policy towards Tibet of trimming off the power of the Tibetan hierarchies and keeping them divided. The Qing government gave orders that Tachienlu, Litang and Batang to the east of the Jinsha River come under the jurisdiction of Sichuan Province, that Gyalthang (modern Zhongdian) region be administered by Yunnan Province and that forty tribes of the seventy-nine tribes in Jyekundo (modern Yushu) be administered by the Xining Governor (the Grand Minister Superintendant of Qinghai), while the other thirty-nine tribes were later put under the jurisdiction of the Amban in Tibet. Tsang and Ngari were offered to the Panchen. As a result, what was to be left to the Tibetan local government would be only U and what is now the Chamdo region. The power of the Tibetan ruling groups would thus naturally be much weakened, which would be conducive to the rule of the Qing court.

But the Panchen thought that he, as a monk, should not be involved too deeply in worldly affairs, so he sent his *Changzod* the next day to ask Jalangga for the order to be countermanded. Later, he turned down a second offer, this one for six districts, including Lhatse, Ngamring, Phuntsoling, Kyirong, Tsongkha and Ngari, made by Jalangga. It was only when Jalangga said that the Emperor would be angry at his refusal that he finally, and with much reluctance, accepted three of them: Lhatse, Ngamring and Phuntsoling. Since that time there were two regimes in Tibet: one was the Tibetan local government headed by the Dalai Lama, and the other was the Panchen Lharang headed by the Panchen, both being under the supervision of the Resident Commissioner, namely imperial representative—Amban as he is known in Tibetan—appointed by the Qing government.

Pholhanas ruled over Tibet for nineteen years.

Before that, Lozang Tenzin's rebellion in Qinghai caused trouble to Tibet's political stabilization. Lozang Tenzin, son of Drashi Batur, the youngest son of Gushri Khan, had been granted the title of prince by the Qing court. After Lhazang Khan's death, he claimed himself to be the Khan, hoping to rule the Qoshot tribes in Qinghai. Refusing to be ruled by him, the tribes fought a bitter battle with Lozang Tenzin in the first year of the Yongzheng reign period (1723). The Emperor sent an army of nineteen thousand men under the command of Nian Gengyao, Governor-General of Sichuan and Shaanxi, and Yue Zhongqi, Provincial Military Commander of Sichuan, on an expedition to Qinghai along four routes —via Xining, Songpan, Ganzhou and Bulongjir—in the second year of the Yongzheng reign period (1724). Being defeated by the Qing troops, Lozang Tenzin fled from Qinghai to Xinjiang, where he entered into an alliance with the Dzungar Khan Tsewang Arabten. The two then proclaimed a renewal of the military attack on Tibet.

In order to ensure the Dalai's safety, in the sixth year of the Yongzheng reign period (1728) the Qing Emperor ordered that the Seventh Dalai Lama be moved to Litang Monastery in Kham under the protection of generals Mala and Naige. More than a year later, in the seventh year of the Yongzheng reign period, the Dalai Lama was moved from Litang Monastery to the Huiyuan Monastery in Taining. The Qing government then stationed 1,500 men in Tibet under the command of the Amban, and ordered that the Amban maintain a defense line on the Tengri Nor against military invasion by the Dzungars and conduct an inspection tour there every year.

During his rule over Tibet, Pholhanas solved the problem of Bhutan's submission. Bhutan (or Drukpa in the Chinese historical official records) was a protectorate of China. The ruling lama of the Drukpa Kagyu (White sect)—who was the ruler of Bhutan —would not submit himself to the Gelug (Yellow sect). As early as the thirteenth year of the Qing Shunzhi reign period (1656) a war broke out between Bhutan and Tibet when the Fifth Dalai tried to force the ruling lama of Bhutan to pledge allegiance to him. Owing to the Fourth Panchen's mediation, both sides agreed finally to a cease-fire. But the problem was not solved. In the eighth year of the Kangxi reign period of Emperor Shengzu (1669), when the Fourth Panchen had died and the Fifth Panchen was very young, a clash of arms broke out again. Mediation did not work, so the war lasted intermittently for sixty-two years.

In the ninth year of the Yongzheng reign period (1731), an internal struggle occurred in Bhutan. Pholhanas mediated between the two opposing sides, who both told him that they intended to pledge allegiance to the Qing Empire. Pholhanas and the Fifth Panchen took the opportunity to send representatives to make peace between them, and, as a result, the contradictions between Tibet and Drukpa were also completely solved. According to *Records of Tibet*:

> Drukpa is a month's journey to the southwest of Tibet. The tribe of Noryanlinchin is a follower of the Red Hat line. The climate there is rather warm and the products there are similar to China's. A month's journey to its south is India. It pledged allegiance to the Tang Dynasty and was bestowed an album and a seal with an inscription of six Chinese characters on it, meaning "State Treasure Bestowed by the Tang Dynasty."

Gabi, a sub-tribe of the Noryanlinchin, became stronger gradually. The Noryanlinchin Hutuktu, Chuknai Namchar, was detained by the Gabis when he passed the area inhabited by the Gabis. The inhabitants of Dina and Wana, two places under Noryanlinchin jurisdiction, secretly went to Gabi to pay homage to the Hutuktu. Being hostile to each other, Noryanlinchin and Gabi fought with each other.

Gabi asked Pholhanas for help in the tenth year of the Yongzheng reign period [1732], and defeated the Noryanlinchin with Pholhanas' help. The Noryanlinchin sent men to the Amban to pledge allegiance and asked to go to Beijing to offer tribute. At that time the two tribes sent men to Tibet, each making a report to the Qing court on pledging allegiance to the court and accusing the other of vengeful murder. The next year envoys were sent to mediate between them, but the mediation failed. In the tenth month of the same year Commander of the Shaanxi Independent Battalion He Shang, Kalon Tromtse under Pholhanas, and other envoys were sent to mediate between the two tribes at the city of Wangtse in Shizhong. The two tribes sent men to Beijing to offer tribute in the first month of the *jia-ying* year [1734]. Emperor Shizong bestowed seals to the two tribes and sent men to escort them back. They arrived in Tibet in the fifth month of the thirteenth year of the Yongzheng reign period [1735]. When Donglubu Lama of the Gabi tribe died, the Gabi land and people were put under Noryanlinchin rule. About a hundred households who would not submit themselves to the Noryanlinchin were settled by the Qing court at Wantse of Shangyue. Noryanlinchin Chilapuji came in person to pay respects to the Dalai Lama in Tibet in the spring of the first year of the Qianlong reign period [1736] and went back on the fifth day of the eighth month of that year.

The following is a memorial of the ruling lama of Drukpa to the Qing Emperor recorded in *A General History of U-Tsang*:

> We, Noryanlinchin Chilapuji and Dzasa Liburukguji, lamas of Drukpa, prostrate ourselves with joined palms before the imperial court and beg to speak to Your Majesty, the Great Lord of Manchu supported by all worldly beings under heaven.
>
> We, foolish people of the Western borderland and ignorant of what is good or bad, were once engaged in vengeful killing. We were overjoyed at receiving the letter from the Tibetan Beile that conveyed to us Your Majesty's benevolence. So we sent men to His Excellency Beile to ask that we be allowed to submit ourselves to your imperial court. Your Majesty bestowed on us so many favours that we could not repay them even after ten thousand generations.
>
> But the Drukpa people, foolish as wild animals and ignorant of laws, often engaged in wars with the Gabi. Upon reports from the Amban, Your Majesty sent officials to mediate between us. The Tibetan Beile came in person to Wangtse to pass on the order of Your Majesty to us. We felt very grateful for Your Majesty's kindness and readily restored peace between ourselves. To repay Your Majesty's kindness, we will remain forever friendly to each other.
>
> We beg Your Majesty to grant us a seal of authority so that we might put the Drukpa people under control, because many of them are ignorant of laws.... We sent Gelong Barchong to present our deepest respects and some of our local products to Your Majesty. They are five *kachi* belts in various colours, a bolt of *kachi* satin, a string of 108 coral beads, four bolts of patterned cloth, twenty bolts of Drukpa cloth, a small *kachi* knife and a silver bowl. Written on the auspicious day of the month.

According to the *Imperial Records of the Qing Dynasty*, in the ninth year of Yongzheng reign period (1731) the Emperor wrote to Beile Pholhanas, saying:

I, as the Lord of the World, treat all people equally and impartially. I have been much worried about the internal strife of the Drukpa people. You knew what I was worried about and sent your men with those from Panchen Erdeni to mediate. You also sent men to pass on my favour to the people. I am glad to know that the Drukpa people now have ceased the strife and are enjoying good relations between themselves and beg me to give them more instructions. If they safeguard peace on the borderlines, live in amity and adhere to Buddhism, I will give them more favours. The Noryanlinchin of Drukpa and others will be rewarded. Donglubu Lama of the Gabi pledged allegiance to us earlier than others, so he deserves praise and shall be richly rewarded. You should pass my decree on to the Drukpa people.

In the same year, the Emperor ordered the Board for National Minority Affairs to grant the title of Beile to Beizi Pholhanas because he had sent men to mediate between the rival tribes in Drukpa and had made known the Emperor's authority and benevolence; and to grant the title of Duke of State Succour to his son Gyumey Tseten with the first rank of Teji for his military merits in safeguarding borderlands.

Since then, Drukpa restored its submission to the Qing Empire and frequently sent envoys with tribute to Beijing via Tibet. The Qing Emperor bestowed gifts in return whenever they came to offer tribute.

During the period when Pholhanas ruled over Tibet, Balebu (a name for Nepal in Chinese historical records) also set up good relations with the Qing Empire via Tibet. The *Records of Tibet* has an account of it as follows:

> In a period of more than ten years since the fifty-ninth year of the Kangxi reign period, thanks to the Qing officers and men who went to and fro, high mountains and narrow paths in Tibet became wide and flat roads, and poor and remote places were benefited. Balebu is two months' journey to the southwest of Tibet. It has warm weather and many peacocks. Its people consist of three parts: Buyanhan, Yelenghan and Kukumhan. In the tenth year of the Yongzheng reign period [1732] Balebu sent envoys to Tibet to pledge allegiance to the Qing. Upon the Amban's report on them, the Emperor permitted them to give their submission, and in the eighth month of the next year [1733], sent envoys to Tibet to bestow on them three official documents as well as satin, glass, porcelain, etc.

In the first month of the twelfth year of the Yongzheng reign period [1734], the three districts again sent men to Tibet, asking for permission for them to go to Beijing to offer memorials and tribute. Upon the Amban's report, the Emperor gave them permission to come to Beijing and ordered that they be well accommodated on the road. They started off from Tibet on the twentieth of the fourth month, bringing with them three memorials and their tribute. The following is the memorial of the Chief of Buyanhan:

"I, Buyanhan Zazagemar, prostrate myself with joined palms before the court and beg to speak to Your Majesty. I was much honoured at receiving an official document, as well as satin, glass, porcelain, etc., from Your Majesty. I have long intended to pay my respects to Your Majesty, ever since the benevolence of Your Majesty has been made known to me. But Lhazang Khan would not transmit my memorial to Your Majesty. Now, on the Beile's report, Your Majesty bestows favours on me and permits me to offer tribute to Your Majesty. I beg Your Majesty to give us instructions from time to time, so that we may have the Heavenly benevolence of Your Majesty. The report is accompanied by a *katag*, a coral tree, a string of 55 coral beads, a string of 108 small coral beads, a string of 41 amber beads, 3 big and five small *kachi* belts woven with gold silk, 3 bolts of *kachi* satin in various colours, 4 bolts of white *kachi* cloth, a rhinoceros horn, a fan made of peacock feathers, a bunch of peacock feathers, a pack of black perfume and a pack of various medicinal herbs. Written on the twenty-eighth day of the twelfth month of the *kui-chou* year [the eleventh year of the Yongzheng reign period, or 1733]."

The content of the memorials and tribute of Kukumhan and Yelenghan and the time of their offering were similar to those of Buyanhan.

In a decree to Buyanhan, Kukumhan and Yelenghan, the Emperor said:

I am very glad to know that you, who have not communicated with China since ancient times, now pledge loyalty to me from thousands of *li* [1 *li* = 1/2 km] away. I received the local products you offered to me. Considering that it is very difficult to make a long journey, I ordered that your envoys be escorted back from Tibet. I hope that you will cooperate with Beile Pholhanas in Tibet to develop Lamaism, as I wish you to do for the good of all worldly beings.

In the tenth year of the Yongzheng reign period (1732), Ladakhi Khan Dezhong Namgyal also pledged allegiance to the Qing government through Pholhanas. In a decree to the Ladakhi Khan, Emperor Shizong said:

> I was very glad to read the memorial you, Dezhong Namgyal, made through your envoy to the Amban, in which you said that you would do your best to run state affairs and to support Buddhism, try to uncover information about the Yelchim Dzungars and report to Beile Pholhanas, and asked me for instructions.
>
> I bestowed special favours on your father, Nyima Namgyal, for he and Beizi Khangchennas helped each other to serve the imperial court. Now you take your father as your example in assisting Beile Pholhanas to show loyalty to the court. I will also extend special favours to you as I have done before.

Pholhanas improved the relations between Tibet and Bhutan, Nepal and Ladakh, and, in particular, put an end to the war that had lasted for seventy-five years between Tibet and Bhutan, thus giving the Tibetans and Bhutanese a chance to recuperate and build up strength. Therefore, Tibet enjoyed a period of peace and economic growth and witnessed an improvement in the people's life. This was one of Pholhanas' major contributions to Tibet.

# 10. Contributions Made by the Fifth Panchen Lama

In the twelfth year of the Yongzheng reign period (1734), when Dzungar Khan Tsewang Arabten died, his son Galdan Tsering succeeded the throne of the Khan and sent envoys to Beijing to appeal for peace and suggested that "the boundaries be defined and hostilities be ceased." The Qing government approved his appeal and granted him the title of Teji. Thus the threat of Xinjiang to Tibet was removed.

On the instructions of the Emperor, the Seventh Dalai Lama was sent back from Taining to Tibet under the escort of Changkya Hutuktu, Prince Guo (named Yunli) and General Naige. Overjoyed at the news, the Fifth Panchen wrote a letter and sent Lozang Yonphel to Xikang to welcome the Dalai Lama. After starting the journey, the Dalai Lama also sent Sengge Gedun Gyaltsen to the Tashilhunpo with a letter paying respect to the Panchen. In his letter, the Dalai said that he would pay a visit to the Panchen after he came back to Lhasa.

The Seventh Dalai Lama Kelzang Gyatso arrived at Lhasa on the ninth day of the eighth month in the thirteenth year of the Yongzheng reign period (1735), after living for seven years at Taining in Xikang. Having learned that the Dalai had come back to Lhasa, the Panchen sent Dzasa Lama Lozang Gedun with gifts to tender his congratulations to the Dalai at the Potala. On the ninth day of the tenth month, Changkya Hutuktu, with the party of three hundred men that had escorted the Dalai back to Lhasa, came to the Tashilhunpo to pay a visit to the Panchen. The monastery held a grand welcoming ceremony. The Fifth Panchen received Changkya Hutuktu at the Sunlight Hall and ordained him as a *getsul* and gave him the religious name Yeshe Tenpa Drokmi.

Qing Emperor Shizong died in the same year, and Emperor Gaozong came to the throne. On the twenty-third day of the tenth month, on the instructions of the Panchen, a memorial ceremony for the Emperor's death was held at the Tashilhunpo. Changkya Hutuktu went back to Lhasa as soon as he learned of the Emperor's death.

In the second month of the first year of Qing Emperor Gaozong's reign (1736), the Emperor sent grand lamas Chosphel Dargye and Lozang Paljor to pay a visit to the Fifth Panchen at the Tashilhunpo in the company of Amban Nasutai. A grand welcoming ceremony was held at the Tashilhunpo, with Buddhist flags decorating the roofs, big horns being blown and incense being burnt. The envoys from the Emperor read an imperial decree to the Panchen and then celebrations were held. When the envoys were to leave for Beijing, the Panchen wrote a memorial to the Emperor expressing his thanks, and selected Lozang Drashi to send along with them to Beijing to offer his congratulations on Emperor Gaozong's enthronement.

On the sixteenth day of the seventh month, the Seventh Dalai Lama sent Malpon Rabten Dondrup from Lhasa to Tashilhunpo Monastery to inform the Panchen that he would soon come to pay him a visit. Early in the ninth month the Seventh Dalai went to the Tashilhunpo by way of Gyantse, where he was greeted by a party of thirty people, headed by Dronyer Kachin Peljam Jedrung and

Drongkhor, sent by the Panchen. At Bainang Dzong the Dalai was also greeted by another party of thirty people headed by Dzasa Lama Lhundrup Lingpa. When the Dalai arrived at the Tashilhunpo on the thirteenth day of the ninth month, a party of four hundred, including all the *lopons* of its *dratsangs* and lay and monk officials, went to the suburbs to welcome him, all monks waiting at the gate of the monastery, holding burning incense and various Buddhist objects, and with monks of the Ngapa Dratsang beating drums and cymbals and blowing horns on the house roofs.

The Dalai Lama took a rest in the Tsosamling Dratsang at the Tashilhunpo and then went to visit the Fifth Panchen. Being old and sick, the Panchen received the Dalai at his residence. The Dalai, as a disciple, kowtowed to the Panchen and the Panchen drew his sleeves three times to express his respects in a Buddhist way. Then they exchanged *katags* and saluted each other. Soon afterwards they went to take seats at the Sunlight Hall. Pholhanas and other officials that followed the Dalai to the Tashilhunpo came to offer *katags* to the Panchen, who in response touched each of them on the head with his hand and gave them *jiakas*. A grand welcoming banquet was held for the Dalai in the monastery. The Dalai and Panchen exchanged gifts at the banquet. The Dalai then took up temporary residence in the Tsosamling Dratsang.

The Dalai spent almost a month at the Tashilhunpo. During that time the Panchen taught him many exoteric and esoteric sutras. On the eighteenth day of the ninth month, at the monks' request, the Seventh Dalai took the seat of the First Dalai Lama at the Great Chanting Hall of the Tashilhunpo and gave them a sermon on *Complete Course of the Graded Path of Bodhi* written by Tsongkhapa. On the twenty-eighth day of the ninth month the monastery held a grand farewell banquet for the Dalai. The Panchen also held a grand farewell banquet for the Dalai's sutra teacher, Ganden Tripa Nomihan, Beile Pholhanas and his son Ngarigong, and gave them many gifts.

On the second day of the tenth month, the Seventh Dalai, accompanied by a few khenpos, went to bid farewell to the Panchen at his residence, the Panchen Lharang. The Panchen gave the Dalai an image of Sakyamuni Buddha and said that he wished the Dalai longevity and hoped the Dalai would study Buddhist scriptures diligently for the development of Buddhism and peace of the worldly beings, and that he himself was quite old then and would not live long. The Dalai also wished the Panchen longevity and good health. It was the last time the Seventh Dalai met with the Fifth Panchen.

On the third day of the tenth month the Dalai left for Lhasa.

In the seventh month of the second year of the Qianlong reign period (1737), the Panchen's health condition became critical and failed to respond to any medical treatment. On the fifth day of that month he was put on a high seat in a sitting position facing the east. He soon died, at the age of seventy-four. When he died, all the *khenpos* of the Tashilhunpo, Dronyer Sagupa, Dronyer Peljampa, Solpon Rabten and his lama physicians kowtowed to his body, wishing that he would be reincarnated as early as possible. Meanwhile men were sent by them to report to the Dalai Lama and the Amhan on how the Panchen died and ask the Dalai to pray for the Panchen's reincarnation. On their instructions, all monks of the Tashilhunpo chanted sutras for the Panchen, and men were sent to give alms and sweet buttered-tea to the monks of the Three Major Monasteries of Lhasa and those in U, Tsang, Ngari, Xikang and Qinghai, who also chanted sutras for the Panchen.

After repeated consultation, all monk officials of the Panchen Lharang decided to build a stupa to keep his body.

In the ninth month of the same year, upon the Amban's report, Emperor Gaozong sent Chobten Karpo Lama Shashapal, Narenkha, Jiaguchi and Bichiche Chosje from Beijing to the Tashilhunpo to offer gifts, which consisted of ten bundles of incense of the best quality, a gold *mandral* weighing fifty taels, a white jade vase, a white jade plate, a silver plate weighing fifty-two taels, a silver tea-pot, five loads of dried fruits, two boxes of dyestuff, nine bolts of silk and satin, etc.

Mongolian Jetsun Dampa offered a silver *mandral* weighing fifty taels, five bolts of cloth for making *katags*, ten bolts of satin and silk and one thousand taels of silver as gifts. Pholhanas offered ten silver ingots, twenty bales of tea and thirty bolts of satin. The Dalai Lama's father, the Amban, the Sakya ruling lama, the *Kalons* and many others also offered sacrifices. The silver collected for the sacrifice was 60,480 taels, enough for building the Panchen's stupa.

The stupa was built in the fifth year of the Qianlong reign period (1740), and the Panchen's body, after embalmment, was put into it. The Seventh Dalai Lama sent men to offer a box of barley, over which sutras had been chanted, to be sprinkled over the stupa at the initiation ceremony. Let us have a review of the Fifth Panchen's life. He lived in a period of time full of conflicts between separatists and those who supported unification of his country. He firmly stood on the side of the central government of the Qing Dynasty, doing his best to make contributions to the cause of safeguarding the unification of his country and promoting the friendship between Manchus, Hans, Mongols and Tibetans. While he should have been able to play a more important role in calling on the Outer and Inner Mongols to rally around the Qing Dynasty and in the struggle against Galdan of Dzungar, owing to Depa Sangye Gyatso's interference, he could not do what he had hoped to, and was even prevented from having an audience with Qing Emperor Shengzu. Not long after Depa Sangye Gyatso was overthrown, Tsering Dondup of the Dzungar Mongols came from Xinjiang and occupied Tibet. The Fifth Panchen had to deal with the enemy. Taking advantage of his political and religious prestige among the Dzungars, he did what was in his power to protect the Tibetan people and Tashilhunpo Monastery from the enemy. So Qing Emperor Shengzu trusted him and gave high praises on his contributions to the cause. The title of Panchen Erdeni was given to the Fifth Panchen by Emperor Shengzu. Since then the title has been inherited by all the succeeding Panchen Lamas, and the two main reincarnation systems of the Dalai and Panchen were thereby formed in Tibetan history.

Emperor Shizong trusted the Fifth Panchen so much that he decided to put the regions of Tsang and Ngari under his jurisdiction, taking this as an important measure to stabilize the political situation in Tibet. But, considering the importance of the internal unification of Tibet, the Fifth Panchen gently declined. He did not take Tsang and Ngari over from the Dalai, because he hoped to moderate the conflicts between the local forces of U and Tsang and strengthen his good relations with the Dalai. (Since Gushri Khan occupied Tibet, all the *dzongpons* of Tsang and *gyapons* of Ngari had been appointed by the Dalai and under the administration of the Depa.) For fear of being accused of resisting an imperial edict, he reluctantly accepted three *dzongs*. But, as a result, the Dalai lost the three *dzongs*. This was perhaps one of the reasons why the relations between the Dalai and Panchen systems became sour afterwards. Viewing the situation objectively, we may find that the Fifth Panchen took great pains to guard the authority of the central government of the Qing Dynasty, the internal unity of Tibet and his good relations with the Dalai. This is worthy of praise.

## Chapter Four
# Palden Yeshe, the Sixth
# Panchen Lama


## 1. The Enthronement of the Sixth Panchen

The Sixth Panchen Lama (1738-1780), given the religious name of Palden Yeshe, was a native of Trashitse Shika of Namling Dzong in Tsang. He was born to Tangla and Tangla's wife, Nyingda Wangmu, on the eleventh day of the eleventh month of the Earth-Horse year in the twelfth Tibetan calendrical cycle (the third year of the Qianlong reign period of the Qing Dynasty, or 1738). (The date here is taken from the Tibetan historical records. The birth date is given as the third day of the eleventh month in *The Complete Works of the Panchen Masters* compiled by Liu Jiaju, and as the third day of the seventh month in *The Biographies of the Panchen Erdenis* written by Zhang Bozhen; nevertheless, the *Political and Religious History of the Tibetan Nationality* compiled by Fa Zun and the Tibetan-language version of *The Biography of Palden Yeshe* put it on the eleventh day of the eleventh month.)

At that time the reincarnation of the Fifth Panchen Lama, who had been dead for more than a year, was being searched for by Tashilhunpo Monastery. When the chief monks heard that a boy was born to Tangla's family at Trashitse Shika in Namling Dzong, they sent Dronyer Sagupa Lozang Drondro to report the news to Pholhanas, the chief administrator of Tibet at that time, for instructions. Pholhanas told the *dronyer* that reliable monk officials should be sent to examine the boy by way of having him pick up articles used by the deceased Panchen. The *dronyer* was sent out again by the monastery to accomplish the task.

On the pretext of taking a bath in a hot spring there, he went

to Namling Dzong on the thirtieth day of the seventh month of
the fifth year of the Qianlong reign period (1740) to check every
detail of Tangla's family history, his social relationships, behaviour,
etc., and to ask about the unusual circumstances surrounding the
birth of the young child. As he found out nothing bad about the
family and the child, he paid a visit to the family, meeting the boy
on the twelfth day of the eighth month. He placed before the boy,
so goes the Tibetan biography of Palden Yeshe, many articles,
among which were a small statue of the Buddha, a bell, a monk's
staff, a rosary and a tea-box the deceased Fifth Panchen had used.
He was surprised to see that the boy picked out only the objects
of the Panchen. He soon went back and reported this to the Dzasa
Lama of the Tashilhunpo. The Dzasa Lama sent Paljor Gyaltsen as
the representative of the Tashilhunpo to Lhasa to report investigation results to Seventh Dalai Lama Kelzang Gyatso and Pholhanas.

On the second day of the eighth month Dronyer Ngawang
Lozang and Paljor Gyaltsen and others on behalf of the Seventh
Dalai Lama, Pholhanas and Tashilhunpo Monastery, respectively,
went to Ganden Khangsar Monastery in Lhasa to ask Chosgyong,
a professional oracle, to invoke a revelation as to whether or not
the boy was the reincarnation of the deceased Panchen. The oracle
confirmed the boy was the former Panchen's reincarnation. So the
Seventh Dalai Lama informed the Tashilhunpo in a letter that the
boy should be taken good care of. Meanwhile, the Dalai Lama
reported in detail the discovery of the reincarnation to Amban Ji
Shan and, through the Amban, asked Emperor Gaozong for approval. Not long afterwards the Emperor gave a decree of approval
to the Dalai. Thus the identity of the candidate as the Panchen's
reincarnation was confirmed by all the formalities necessary for his
selection.

On the ninth day of the ninth month the Tashilhunpo was
officially informed that the Seventh Dalai had given the Sixth
Panchen the religious name of Lozang Palden Yeshe (Palden Yeshe
for short). Drongkhor and others on behalf of the monastery were
sent to tell the Tangla family that their son was the reincarnation
of the Fifth Panchen, i.e., the Sixth Panchen Erdeni. The envoys
held a *gadro* (a Tibetan-style celebration) over the event in the
*shika*. Monks from the Tashilhunpo played Buddhist musical in-

struments at the simple but grand ceremony. A physician was sent from Lhasa by Pholhanas to make a physical examination of the boy. He brought a letter of congratulation from Pholhanas to the Sixth Panchen, in addition to many gifts from Pholhanas, including a suit of monk's robes, a small statue of Buddha, a wheel of Dharma, a horn, a bell, a monk's staff, etc. After the celebrations the Sixth Panchen was carried in a sedan chair by the monks of the Tashilhunpo to the Dondrup Minkhang Phodrang Hall at Ludong Shika, which bordered on Trashitse Shika. There he remained, being in the good care of monks from Tashilhunpo Monastery.

On the ninth day of the fifth month of Iron-Cock year (the sixth year of the Qianlong reign period, or 1741), Lharamgangpa Jetsun Lozang Tsewang was appointed as the Dzasa Lama of Tashilhunpo Monastery, and therefore he would be responsible for the enthronement of Sixth Panchen Palden Yeshe. On the first day of the sixth month the Dzasa Lama, Solpon Khenpo, Zimpon Khenpo, Dronyer Dechong, envoys from Pholhanas and Draya Pandita went to Ludong Shika. The Dzasa Lama tonsured the Sixth Panchen and put on him a monk's robe. On the second day of the sixth month the Sixth Panchen was invited to Tashilhunpo Monastery. He took residence in Kadam Phodrang Hall, where the Fifth Panchen had once lived.

By that time the Grand Lama Totsange, *jiaguchis* and *bichiches* —envoys sent by Emperor Gaozong to preside over the ceremony of enthronement—had arrived at Tashilhunpo Monastery in the company of Pholhanas. The Seventh Dalai Lama also sent Dedru Khenpo Lozang Norbu as his representative to attend the ceremony.

On the fourth day of the sixth month the grand ceremony of enthronement of the Sixth Panchen was held at the Sunlight Hall of the Tashilhunpo in the presence of all the lay and clerical officials of the monastery, its subordinate monasteries and its *dratsangs*, as well as officials and chiefs of all the *dzongs* and *shikas*.

The ceremony of enthronement began with the Sixth Panchen being placed on the official seat of the deceased Panchen. First of all, the imperial envoys on behalf of the Emperor gave the Sixth Panchen a *Nangzho katag*, various silver articles, silk and satin, and three thousand taels of silver. Then the Seventh Dalai Lama's representatives offered him a *katag*, a silver *mandral*, a statue of the Buddha, a suit of monk's robes, a set of religious objects and twenty-one *ping* of Tibetan silver. Pholhanas offered the Panchen a *katag*, a silver *mandral*, a Statue of the Buddha, a suit of monk's robes, a wheel of the Dharma, a horn, religious objects and thirty-one *ping* of Tibetan silver. The representatives of the Amban, the Ganden Tripa and abbots of the Three Major Monasteries also offered *katags* to the Panchen. Then all the lay and clerical officials of the Tashilhunpo, its subordinate monasteries and its *dratsangs* and all guests offered *katags* to the Panchen. The king of Bhutan, the lord of Ngari and the Sakya ruling lama also sent representatives to tender their congratulations.

On the seventh day of the sixth month, envoys from Beijing on behalf of the Emperor gave sweet buttered-tea, rice, alms of five *qian* (twenty-five grams) of silver to each of the monks of the Tashilhunpo, and they sent people to give sweet buttered-tea and alms of five *fen* (two and a half grams) of silver to each of the monks of the 379 lamaseries in the region of Tsang. The Tashilhunpo wrote a memorial in the name of the Sixth Panchen to Emperor Gaozong and sent tribute of Tibetan local products to express gratitude for the Emperor's benevolence. Before the imperial envoys left for Beijing, rare and precious gifts and a farewell banquet was given for them by Tashilhunpo Monastery.

According to the Tibetan biography of the Sixth Panchen, in the same year (1741) the Qing central government granted Pholhanas the title "prince" (*junwang*). The Sixth Panchen and Tashilhunpo monastery sent representatives to Lhasa to offer *katags* and many gifts to Pholhanas to express their congratulations. The *Imperial Records of the Qing Dynasty* gives an earlier date, saying that Pholhanas was granted the title in the fifth year of the Qianlong reign period (1740):

> The Emperor ordered that the Tibetan Beile Pholhanas be granted the title of prince, for he had acted in accordance with the Emperor's orders, adhered to the Yellow sect, developed Buddhist doctrines and drilled troops to safeguard the borders.                    .

Apparently, the Qing central government decided to bestow the title of prince to Pholhanas in 1740, but the ceremony was held in

Tibet in the next year.

Pholhanas, as the *Imperial Records of the Qing Dynasty* goes, settled two important things concerning the friendly relations between the states bordering with Tibet. First, in the third year of the Qianlong reign period (1738), Hang Yilu, an imperial representative stationed in Tibet, reported to the Emperor:

> Beile Pholhanas asked me to pass on the memorial and tribute of the Ladakhi Khan of the Enatkok tribe, Dedrung Namgyal, to Your Majesty. Dedrung Namgyal and his father, Nyima Namgyal, with grateful feelings for our country's benevolence, have always given information about the Dzungars to Pholhanas. Emperor Shengzu and Emperor Shizong gave them favours. If Your Majesty grants them an edict and other favours when they offer tribute, they will be more loyal to the imperial court.

So the Emperor gave Dedrung Namgyal an edict and such gifts as satin and porcelain.

In the fourth year of the Qianlong reign period (1739) Hang Yilu again reported to the Emperor:

> Kukumu, Buyan and Yeleng, the three khans of the Balebu tribes, three thousand *li* away to the southwest of Tibet, sent envoys to pay respects to His Majesty in the twelfth year of the Yongzheng reign period. In recent years the three khans became hostile to each other and have constantly battled with each other. I sent Pholhanas to inform them that Your Majesty is benevolent and treats the people inside and outside the borders equally, and to persuade them to cease battles and restore good relations. The three khans gladly obeyed. They reported the number of households of their tribes and offered tribute to the imperial court.

The Emperor ordered that gifts be bestowed on them.

The two events concerned deeply the stability of Tibet. At that time the Dzungars in Xinjiang had not submitted themselves to the Qing Dynasty and were intending to attack Tibet. So it was necessary for Pholhanas to get information about the Dzungars' intention through the Ladakhi Khan. Balebu (modern Nepal) and Tibet had trade relations, which helped to supply each country's wants and were an important aspect of the economic development of Tibet. Any internal strife in Balebu would exert negative influence on the local trade relations between Balebu and Tibet. The

Emperor appreciated very much Pholhanas' prompt settlement of the two problems, so it was only natural that he should be granted the title of prince.

On the third day of the tenth month of the seventh year of the Qianlong reign period (1742), Gonye, Ramjiangpa and Kunsang, the envoys sent to Beijing by Tashilhunpo Monastery to report on the enthronement of the Sixth Panchen to the imperial court, came back from Beijing with an edict from the Emperor to the Sixth Panchen in which the Emperor instructed the Panchen to study scriptures diligently for the development of the Yellow Hat sect. The edict was accompanied with twenty-four bolts of satin for the Panchen.

On the tenth day of the tenth month of the same year the Sixth Panchen took *getnian* vows before Phurchok Ngawang Champa of the Tashilhunpo and acknowledged the Phurchok as his tutor.

In the eighth year of the Qianlong reign period the Sixth Panchen invited Ngachen Lozang Supa to be his sutra teacher, and the latter thereafter taught him lessons every day. On the third day of the ninth month in the ninth year of the Qianlong reign period (1744), the Sixth Panchen, at the age of seven, took *getsul* vows before his sutra teacher.

In the twelfth year of the Qianlong reign period (1747) Prince Pholhanas died. He had two sons—the younger one was Gyumey Namgyal, and the elder one Gyumey Tseten. The latter, as the lord of Ngari, was put in charge of the regional administration and defence of Ngari and was granted the title of *Zhenguo Gong* (Duke of State Defence) by the imperial court in the eleventh year of the Qianlong reign period. He was the lord of Ngari who sent men to congratulate the Sixth Panchen on the ceremony of his enthronement.

The Tibetan biography of Pholhanas holds a good opinion of Pholhanas, because in the nineteenth years when he was the chief administrator of Tibet he consistently safeguarded the state and national unification, adhered to the central authority of the Qing government and recognized Tibet as a part of the Qing empire. So the central government of the Qing Dynasty trusted him. During his regime Tibet was a scene of peace and economic growth, so the Tibetan people keep a good memory of him. According to the

*Imperial Records of the Qing Dynasty*, on the third month of the twelfth year of the Qianlong reign period, the Emperor wrote in a communication:

> I was sad to know that Prince Pholhanas had died of illness, when General Fu Qing reported to me. He worked hard at handling Tibetan affairs and was loyal to the imperial court. I ordered that one thousand taels of silver be given to pay for his funeral expenses. Minister Solbai should be sent to Tibet to hold a sacrificial ceremony for him. . . . Now that Pholhanas has gone, I have decided to allow his son, Gyumey Namgyal, to inherit his title of prince [*junwang*] and be put in his position as the chief administrator of Tibet. As Gyumey Namgyal is still quite young, all Kalons should help him in handling affairs just as in the time when Pholhanas was alive. Fu Qing should be told to make the decree known to the public.

When Pholhanas died the Sixth Panchen and the Tashilhunpo sent men to offer sacrifices to him at Lhasa. In response, Pholhanas' family sent men with gifts to the Panchen and gave sweet buttered-tea and alms to all monks of the Tashilhunpo and asked the Sixth Panchen and the monks to chant sutras to release the deceased from the life of misery. When Gyumey Namgyal was enthroned as a successor to his father, the Sixth Panchen sent men to Lhasa to give the new prince a *katag* and gifts for congratulation.

In the thirteenth year of the Qianlong reign period (1748), Prince Gyumey Namgyal (or Dechen Badu in the Tibetan *Biography of the Sixth Panchen*), accompanied by a party of over a hundred persons, including his three concubines, the son of the lord of Ngari, three Kalons and the *dapons* of the U and Tsang regions, came from Lhasa to pay a visit to the Sixth Panchen at the Tashilhunpo. On the fifteenth day of the fifth month, Gyumey Namgyal offered a *katag* to the Panchen at the Sunlight Hall. The Panchen touched the prince on the head with his hand. The prince gave the Panchen a rosary string which was said to have been given to Pholhanas by the Qing Emperor and was worth a hundred thousand taels of silver. After staying over a month at the Tashilhunpo, Gyumey Namgyal left for Lhasa.

In the fourteenth year of the Qianlong reign period (1749) Gyumey Namgyal sent a letter to the Sixth Panchen, inviting him to come to Lhasa for an audience with the Seventh Dalai Lama

Kelzang Gyatso. The Seventh Dalai Lama also wrote a letter of the same content to the Panchen Lama. The Sixth Panchen wrote back to the Seventh Dalai and the newly-appointed prince, saying that he accepted gladly their invitation.

On the twenty-ninth day of the ninth month of that year the Sixth Panchen, accompanied by his attendant *khenpos*, left for Lhasa. On the ninth day of the tenth month the party arrived at Doilung near Lhasa and was greeted by Dronyer Kelzang Dondrup on behalf of the Seventh Dalai, Da Xing on behalf of Amban Ji Shan and representatives of the Three Major Monasteries. On the tenth day of the tenth month the Panchen arrived at Xingdamkhar, thirty *li* from Lhasa, where he was welcomed by Prince Gyumey Namgyal himself. At Sucaitang were tents that had been set up by the Tibetan local government and a welcoming party of about 130 people, including all Kalons, *Tse Dronyers Drungkhors* and clerical officials of the Potala. Besides, over two hundred Kashmirian Moslems and Kharkhas also were waiting there to welcome the Panchen. Over four hundred Tibetan cavalrymen were on guard. People, lay and monk, crowded on both sides of the road leading to Lhasa. On the roofs of the Potala flags were hung and monks were playing Buddhist musical instruments.

When the Sixth Panchen arrived at the Potala, he was warmly received by the *Solpon, Zimpon* and *Chopon*—the three grand Khenpos of the Seventh Dalai Lama—at the gate of the Potala. The Panchen went to the Great Chanting Hall, where the Seventh Dalai's sutra instructor, Ganden Tripa Nomihan Ngawang Chorten, offered the Panchen a *katag* and invited him to take a rest at Deyangshar Mansion. Then the Panchen met with the Seventh Dalai Lama at the old chanting hall. Being younger, the Sixth Panchen kowtowed to the Dalai, and then they exchanged *katags*. They took seats of the same order of honour. The Dalai inquired of the Panchen concerning his health on the journey and said that he himself would teach the Panchen the scriptures he had learned under the instruction of the deceased Fifth Panchen. So the Seventh Dalai became the Sixth Panchen's tutor. The Sixth Panchen resided at the Potala and the Seventh Dalai Lama taught him lessons every day. The Panchen spent half a year there.

In the fourth month of the fifteenth year of the Qianlong reign period (1750), the Sixth Panchen asked to return to the Tashilhun-po. His request was approved by the Seventh Dalai Lama. On the fifteenth day of the fourth month the Seventh Dalai and the Sixth Panchen went to Jokhang Temple to worship the statue of Sakya-muni Buddha and gave donations of one thousand butter-lamps and one thousand joss sticks. They resided in the temple. On the nineteenth day of the fourth month the Seventh Dalai bid farewell to the Sixth Panchen and went back to the Potala, while the Sixth Panchen went to reside in the Prince's residence hall at Ganden Khangsar at the invitation of Gyumey Namgyal. On the twenty-ninth day of the fourth month the Sixth Panchen left Lhasa for the Tashilhunpo by way of Yangpachen in the north. En route, the Panchen spent three days in his hometown, the Trashitse Shika of Namling Dzong. On the fifteenth day of the fifth month he arrived at the Tashilhunpo. At that time the Panchen was only twelve years old. He studied Buddhist scriptures assiduously under the guidance of his sutra teacher.

## 2. The Activities of the Sixth Panchen Lama During the Time When the Reactionary Tibetan Nobles Acted Against the Central Government of the Qing Dynasty

The Sixth Panchen lived at a time when China was in conflict between separatism and unification. Though the Qing Dynasty was in its zenith during the reign of Emperor Gaozong, the struggle for unification and against separation still continued in China. The same was true in Tibet, but with some special characteristics. This struggle in Tibet was reflected in the fact that some Tibetan nobles, acting against the central government, plotted secretly to drive away the Amban and the Qing troops stationed in Tibet. The central regime of the Qing Dynasty therefore had to wage a struggle against the reactionary movement.

The conflicts took place after Pholhanas' death. His son Gyumey Namgyal began to act in collusion with the Dzungars in Xinjiang and came to resent the Qing resident officials in Tibet. His actions aimed at overthrowing the Qing's rule over Tibet and splitting the country.

Unlike his father, Gyumey Namgyal was very despotic. He had no respect either for the Amban or for the Seventh Dalai Lama. When Pholhanas died in 1747, the Seventh Dalai Lama asked to offer sacrifices and chant sutras for Pholhanas, but his request was refused by Gyumey Namgyal. The *Imperial Records of the Qing Dynasty* has the following record:

> Amban Solbai reported to the Emperor in his memorial: When the Dalai Lama learned about the death of Pholhanas, he planned to offer his condolences to him on the sad event and to chant sutras for him, but his son Gyumey Namgyal refused the offer. General Fu Qing criticized Gyumey Namgyal for his behaviour, and the latter repented of his wrongdoing and accepted the offer of the Dalai Lama. Now they are in good relations. After learning about this, the Emperor said that he was released from anxiety about the situation in Tibet.

In the fourteenth year of the Qianlong reign period (1749) Gyumey Namgyal falsely accused his elder brother, Gyumey Tseten, of intending to invade Tibet by stationing troops on strategic roads. While sending troops to guard Gobinai, Gyumey Namgyal reported this to the Emperor. Being cautious, the Emperor sent Changkhyim to Ngari to see whether Gyumey Tseten was really acting in defiance of the central authorities.

Emperor Gaozong said:

> Gyumey Tseten has never caused trouble, but Gyumey Namgyal is violent-tempered, unlike his father, calm and kind. Probably it is because he has always been on bad terms with his brother, so he tried to frame his brother and tried to instigate Ji Shan and the Dalai Lama. Ji Shan should think this over.

In a communication to the Amban, Ji Shan, the Emperor said: "How could Gyumey Tseten try to mount an invasion, since he and his father had enjoyed so much benevolence from the court?" The Emperor said on another occasion: "Being isolated and surrounded by men of Gyumey Namgyal, Ji Shan has never been able to provide me with true information."

The fact was that Ji Shan had accepted a precious ancient statue of the Buddha, a horse, over ten lynx pelts and one thousand taels of silver as gifts from Gyumey Namgyal. They became so intimate with each other that they gave oaths of alliance and even had their names signed side-by-side on Ji Shan's memorial to the Emperor. For having accepted bribes and dereliction of duty, Ji Shan was removed from the post of Amban by the Emperor in the fourteenth year of the Qianlong reign period (1749), and Vice-Minister of Works Labdon was ordered to replace him.

In February of the fifteenth year of the Qianlong reign period (1750), when Labdon, Celeng and Yue Zhongqi reported to the Emperor that Gyumey Tseten had died on the eighteenth day of the twelfth month in the previous year (1749), Emperor Gaozong said:

> Gyumey Tseten was said to be healthy and to have intentions to invade Tibet. Why did he die so suddenly? His death is a mystery.... In a word, Gyumey Namgyal is treacherous and Ji Shan's wrong actions have given way to Gyumey Namgyal's conspiracy.

In the same year the Emperor wrote in a communication:

> Gyumey Tseten did not rebel against the government. He did not die of illness as it was claimed, but was framed and then murdered by his brother Gyumey Namgyal. As the case is clear now, I order that Gyumey Tseten's son inherit his father's title and position in charge of Ngari (see *Imperial Records of the Qing Dynasty*).

The true reasons that caused hostility between Gyumey Namgyal and the Amban were the following events:

(1) Gyumey Namgyal plotted to drive the Qing troops out of Tibet. In the fifteenth year of the Qianlong reign period (1750), Celeng, Governor-General of Sichuan Province, and Provincial Military Commander Yue Zhongqi reported to the Emperor: "Gyumey Namgyal told his subordinates that four hundred Han soldiers had been withdrawn as a result of his plot and he would kill all the rest if they would not withdraw in time."

(2) Gyumey Namgyal cut off the transmission of letters and documents between the central government and the Amban. Emperor Gaozong wrote in a communication to the Grand Ministers of State:

> Gyumey Namgyal is treacherous...and will be a danger to the Dalai Lama. Recently he cut off transmission of letters and documents. His wild ambition to be an overlord is quite obvious.

As inspection discovered, Zanda, Medrogungkar, Wusu, Jangtud and Lumaling—the five post-stations near Lhasa—were under the administration of Lozang Drashi. Whenever letters and documents from inner China reached there, he forbade the delivery of them, threatening to kill the messengers and making them flee back —and the communications were cut off. As a result the central government lost contact with the resident officials in Tibet.

(3) Gyumey Namgyal asked the Dzungars to invade Tibet and to help him to stage a rebellion. In the sixteenth year of the Qianlong reign period (1751), in a report to the Emperor, resident officials in Tibet Celeng and Bandi said:

> Gyumey Namgyal is acting in defiance of the central authorities. He sent Gyaltsen Drashi and his other trusted aides on a secret mission to the Dzungars to establish illicit relations with them. He illegally granted Tsewang Dorje Namgyal the title of Khan and asked the Dzungar chief to dispatch troops to Ladakh to express support for him. Fortunately, he did that at a time when the Dzungar barbarians were being torn by internal strife, and his envoys to the Dzungars were captured together with illicit letters and gifts on their return to Tibet. He is guilty of crimes for which even death is an insufficient punishment.

(4) Gyumey Namgyal pushed aside those who had formerly served under Pholhanas in order to materialize his plot of rebelling against the central government. In a report to the Emperor, the resident officials in Tibet, Fu Qing and Labdon, said:

> Gyumey Namgyal seized the property of Kalon Depa Phulungtsan and others of Tsang on false charges against him and distributed it among his trusted associates. He drove away Gyumey Tseten's son Gyumey Wangdrala. As to those who had formerly served under Pholhanas, they were killed, thrown into prison or removed from their official posts, and their property was confiscated.

(All the above-mentioned facts are recorded in the *Imperial Records of the Qing Dynasty*.)

As the proof of Gyumey Namgyal's crime was conclusive, Fu Qing and Labdon, in a report to Emperor Gaozong, said that "Gyumey Namgyal is now deploying his forces with evil intentions. So we intend to put him under arrest and wipe him out when he comes back from Daksa."

But the Emperor did not agree to their suggestion, saying that

Fu Qing and Labdon's suggestion is hazardous. I know Gyumey Namgyal is a danger to us. But the time is not yet ripe. We have to wait and
see. If he can be captured easily and his conspiracy is thwarted, it will
be a good thing to our country. Now Fu Qing and Labdon are far away
in Tibet without our active help. It is advisable to win some of Gyumey
Namgyal's men over to our side. Otherwise, if the resident officials
handle the affair rashly, disastrous results will be made. But Fu Qing
and Labdon have asked me for a carte blanche in dealing with Gyumey
Namgyal so that the danger might be removed once and for all. I have
ordered them to be cautious, because Tibet is too far for us to decide
things in time.

Unfortunately, the imperial decree did not reach Lhasa in time,
for post connections were cut off. Fu Qing and Labdon handled
the affair with a preemptive action before the decree came to
Lhasa.

On the thirteenth day of the tenth month of the fifteenth year
in the Qianlong reign period (1750), when Gyumey Namgyal
returned to Lhasa, the resident officials in Tibet, Fu Qing and
Labdon, sent for Gyumey Namgyal to discuss instructions from the
Emperor at the office of the Amban. Namgyal did not suspect
anything when he was sent for. He went to the Amban's office,
which was located at Tromzekhang in Lhasa, with only a few
attendants. When he arrived, he walked up to the upper room
where Fu Qing and Labdon were waiting. As soon as he showed
himself in the room, Fu Qing cut at him with a sword. Then Fu
Qing's attendants rushed over and hit him on the head with
bludgeons, killing him instantly. His attendants, four or five, were
also killed. Only Lozang Drashi fled through a window and informed his gang of the incident. Immediately men of Namgyal's
gang were gathered by Lozang Drashi and swarmed to the Amban's office, attacking it with guns from all sides. Fu Qing sent men
to ask Kalon Doring Pandita for military assistance. Being too weak
in forces, Doring Pandita reported it to the Dalai Lama. The Dalai
sent men to prevent them from attacking the office. However, the
gang did not listen to the Dalai Lama. They lit stacks of firewood
below the upper room. Thus the resident officials, Fu Qing and
Labdon, died at their post. Besides, forty-nine officers and soldiers
and seventy-seven Han inhabitants and traders were also killed,

and 85,000 taels of silver were robbed from the state treasury.
Soon after the tragic event happened, the Seventh Dalai Lama
reported it to the central government of the Qing Dynasty and
meanwhile had the chief culprits arrested and the robbed silver
taken back. He ordered the Tibetans not to hurt the Han inhabitants and gave the order to restore the communications between
inner China and Tibet.

Emperor Gaozong, after receiving the Dalai's report, ordered
Celeng, Governor-General of Sichuan Province, and Yue Zhongqi,
Provincial Military Commander, to lead troops without delay to
Tibet and to search for the remaining rebels. On the Emperor's
order, Regional Commander Dong Fang led an army to assist them,
Yin Jishan went to Sichuan to take over the responsibility of
military supplies, Vice-Minister Namgyal went to Tibet to assist
Bandi, and Vice-Minister Zhao Hui went to Tibet to assist Celeng
to cope with aftermath of the incident.

Before Celeng and Bandi reached Tibet, the Seventh Dalai
appointed Doring Pandita acting chief administrator of Tibet.
Celeng reported to the Emperor:

> When General Fu Qing and others died on their post, the surviving Han
> people, eighty officers and men and over a hundred inhabitants, were
> brought to the Potala and put under the protection of and given
> financial supplies by the Dalai. Doring Pandita reported on the twenty-
> third day of the tenth month that he had Lozang Drashi, the chief
> criminal, and more than half of the culprits captured, and most of the
> robbed silver taken back. At Tromzekhang and other places things
> were calmed down. Chang Ming [the local Subprefectural Magistrate],
> together with his militiamen, went back to his office on the twenty-
> fourth day.

So the Emperor ordered Yue Zhongqi to cease his march into Tibet,
and to stay at Tachienlu in order to answer any urgent need.

Celeng and Bandi reached Lhasa on the first day of the twelfth
month of the fifteenth year of the Qianlong reign period (1750).
The first thing they did was to punish the criminals. Lozang Drashi
and other six chief criminals who were responsible for the death
of the resident officials were put to death by dismemberment.
Lhadrab and other two principal criminals were beheaded; Drashi
Rabten and other accessories were hanged. The bodies of Pelong

Shakpa and those who committed suicide were beheaded and displayed in public. The criminals' property was sold and the income put into the state treasury. Gyumey Namgyal's property was confiscated. His wife was also executed. His son Taktra Tsering was brought to Beijing. The Thirty-Nine Tribes of Northern Tibet and the Eight Banners of the Dam Mongols formerly in Gyumey Namgyal's charge were put under the authority of the Amban.

Fu Qing and Labdon were posthumously granted the title of *Bo* (Count) of the first rank and were worshipped in the Two Martyrs' Temples. Their descendants were granted the hereditary title of Viscount of the first rank. By the order of the Emperor, two Two Martyrs' Temples were built: one inside the Chongwenmen Gate in Beijing and the other at Lhasa in the sixteenth year of the Qianlong reign period (1751).

Emperor Gaozong attributed the tragic incident in Tibet to Ji Shan, who as the former Amban was feeble-minded, obeyed Gyumey Namgyal and gave way to the latter's evil intentions. The Emperor ordered that Ji Shan be punished: "He should be executed, but owing to his ancestor's military merit, I will treat him leniently and let him commit suicide."

After Gyumey Namgyal was killed by Fu Qing and Labdon, Lhasa was thrown into chaos for a time. In order to deal with the critical situation, the Seventh Dalai Lama appointed Doring Pandita acting chief administrator of Tibet without getting the approval of the Qing Emperor beforehand. When Celeng and Bandi came to Tibet, Doring Pandita made clear his intention to replace Gyumey Namgyal and take the post of the Depa (chief administrator of Tibet). Without the approval of Celeng and Bandi, he moved his residence into the mansion of Gyumey Namgyal and sent men to Ngari to take over the administrative power. He granted the title of *teji* upon those whom he chose, considering himself as the Depa.

Emperor Gaozong said that Doring Pandita could not be trusted: "Though Pholhanas was very obedient, his descendants could not be trusted. How can I know Doring Pandita is not as treacherous and troublesome as Gyumey Namgyal?" So the Emperor instructed the Grand Ministers of State:

> Now a good opportunity has offered itself to settle the Tibet issue.
> If the situation is handled properly, a lasting peace may be expected;

otherwise, there will be more trouble in a few dozen years. I told Bandi that Tibet should have many more chiefs so that the power will not be concentrated in the hands of one man. This should be done now when our troops are stationed there....

Accordingly, Celeng and Bandi, after consulting with the Seventh Dalai Lama, produced "A Programme for the New Administration of Tibet," consisting of thirteen items. The aim of the programme was obvious: to rescind the post of the Depa and to establish a Kashag in order to take over the administration of Tibetan affairs. The Kashag, which functioned immediately under the Dalai Lama and the Amban, consisted of four Kalons, one of whom was a monk and the rest laymen. With the recommendation of Celeng and Bandi, Doring Pandita, Celeng Wangdrala, Seyul Tseten (these three were aristocrats) and Nyima Jamchen (a monk) were appointed Kalons. The programme was approved by Emperor Gaozong. He instructed: "Communicate the programme as I have been informed of it to the Ministry."

Nevertheless, the Emperor found out that the important issue of communication was neglected in the programme. He instructed the Grand Ministers of State on several occasions:

> I have approved the programme for the administration of Tibet produced by Celeng and Bandi. Communication centres are of great importance in Tibetan affairs. When Gyumey Namgyal forbade the messengers to pass through the centres, the communication line was broken. Afterwards Pandita gave the order to allow them to pass, and the communication was resumed. Everything in this respect was decided by the Depa. The Amban had no say in the matter. Such a situation was really shocking. You have to pay attention to this.... Under such circumstances, of what use it will be to station ten thousand soldiers there?... Communication, a matter of great importance, could only be effective under the control of the Ambans.... In the past Gyumey Namgyal forbade the use of post stations in Tibet and said that if the stations were not dismantled, all the people there would be killed. Thus the document transportation was stopped. After Gyumey Namgyal and other rebels were eliminated, by Pandita's order the post stations were reopened. This is something we should pay attention to. I have pointed out repeatedly that the maintenance of communication is of great importance. Why did Celeng and Zhao Hui start on their journey in a hurry without making investigation in advance and without reporting

to me? You should give orders to Celeng and Zhao Hui that they should find out when Gyumey Namgyal began to shut down the post stations and what documents had been delayed, and report to me in every detail.

Accordingly, Celeng arranged the affairs of stationing troops and reestablishing post stations from Tachienlu in Sichuan to Lhasa in Tibet, and reported to the Emperor:

> By Your Majesty's order, we shall station five hundred soldiers in Tibet, and we have selected them from among those we brought into Tibet, and we shall send officers and men to guard the post stations all along the road. Those who are in charge of the post stations are a lieutenant colonel (*youji*), a captain (*shoubei*), ten lieutenants (*qianzong*) and sergeants (*bazong*) and one thousand soldiers. If there is any vacancy at one station, it will be filled with officers and men from the previous station, and so on. Then if there is any vacancy at the station at Tachienlu, it will be filled with those selected from inner China by the commander of the *Fuhe* Battalion.

In the sixteenth year of the Qianlong reign period (1751) Celeng admitted in a memorial to Emperor Gaozong that it was his negligence that he had not specially discussed the affair of communication centres. The Emperor remarked on this: "Of course it was."

When the incident of Gyumey Namgyal happened, the Sixth Panchen Palden Yeshe was twelve years old. The Tibetan-language *Biography of the Sixth Panchen* only says the incident was due to the fact that the subordinates of Depa Dechen Badu (Gyumey Namgyal) gathered to take revenge and killed the resident officials. It notes that when the Sixth Panchen learned about it he at once sent men to Lhasa to make inquiries and present rice, flour, Tibetan incense and silver to express his sympathy to the surviving two *bichiches*, two grain commissioners and 247 officials and men of the office of the Amban.

In the sixteenth year of the Qianlong reign period (1751), when the Emperor appointed Bandi and Namgyal the resident officials in Tibet, the Sixth Panchen sent Lozang Gyaltsen and Yeshe Chosphel with congratulations and gifts to the new resident officials. Soon the officials sent a *bichiche* and others to the Tashilhunpo with greetings and a letter from the Emperor to the Panchen.

On the twenty-third day of the first month of the seventeenth year of the Qianlong reign period (1752), the Sixth Panchen's sutra instructor, Lozang Supa, died. The *khenpos* of the Tashilhunpo decided to invite Lozang Chosphel to be the Panchen's sutra instructor. They made a written report of their decision to the resident officials, asking the Emperor for the approval of the appointment.

On the twenty-first day of the fifth month of that year, Dronyer Yonten Ledrup and Shodepa Lhalung Tsepa, on behalf of the Kashag, representatives of the Three Major Monasteries, and others, were sent to invite the Sixth Panchen to Lhasa. The Panchen accepted their invitation. On the twenty-fifth day of the fifth month he arrived at Lhasa by way of Yangpachen. He was welcomed by the officials of the Kashag, and resident officials Bandi, Namgyal and Dorje at Sucaitang. He exchanged *katags* with them. Then the four Kalons and all the Han and Tibetan officials of the Amban's office offered *katags* to him.

The Sixth Panchen went to the Potala and met with the Seventh Dalai at the Sunlight Hall. The Panchen kowtowed to the Dalai, and they exchanged *katags* and saluted each other. Then the Panchen, accompanied by the Dalai, went to the Great Chanting Hall, where celebrations were held to welcome the Panchen. After that, the Panchen took his residence in Deyangshar Mansion.

On the twenty-sixth, the officials sent by the Panchen went to the Amban's office and offered a box of Tibetan incense from Tsang to each of the three imperial envoys. The Panchen also sent officials to the town of Tashi to offer one tael of silver to each of the five hundred officers and men stationed there.

The Sixth Panchen spent half a year at Lhasa. During that time, as the Tibetan biography of the Sixth Panchen goes, the Panchen, Dalai, three imperial envoys, four Kalons and representatives of the Three Major Monasteries held detailed discussions about the reform of the Yellow Hat sect. But the biography does not mention concretely what they discussed. The Panchen at that time was only fourteen years old and was engaged in monastic studies. In fact, the reason why the Panchen was removed from the Tashilhunpo to Lhasa was connected with the Qing's war against the Dzungars in Xinjiang.

In the seventeenth year of the Qianlong reign period (1752), for fear that the safety of the Dalai and the Panchen might be threatened if the Dzungars fled into Tibet after being defeated in the war, the Emperor instructed the Grand Ministers of State:

> In the past the Dalai was removed to Taining. Now preparations should be made to remove him to Taining once more, in case the Dzungars flee to Tibet and the Tibetans are not able to resist them. Besides, you must know how far the Tashilhunpo, where the Panchen resides, is from Lhasa and whether the Dzungars will threaten its safety.

The *Imperial Records of the Qing Dynasty* says:

> Afterwards Bandi reported in his memorial: "The Tibetans, cowards as they are, have had over ten thousand cavalrymen and fifteen thousand soldiers since the time of Pholhanas. If the Dzungars invade by way of Ahayak and Tengri Nor, I shall order Tsering Wangdrala to resist with his Tibetan and Mongolian soldiers, and will send soldiers from Gongpo and Dakpo to assist him. If the Dzungars come by way of Naksang and Ngari, I shall order Seyul Tseten to resist with his soldiers and send soldiers from Ngari and other places to assist him. Pandita and Nyima Jamchen will stay at Lhasa to protect the Dalai Lama. The Tashilhunpo Monastery of the Sixth Panchen is seven hundred *li* from Lhasa and is on the way from Ngari to Lhasa. If war breaks out, the Panchen will be moved to live with the Dalai at Lhasa. If the Dzungars come into Tibet and the Tibetans are not able to resist them, the Dalai and Panchen will be escorted to Taining and meanwhile troops stationed in Tibet and the Tibetan soldiers will guard the passes and wait for the relief troops from Sichuan."

This was why the Amban moved the Sixth Panchen to Lhasa.

It was not until the eleventh month of the seventeenth year of the Qianlong reign period (1752), after the Qing troops had won several decisive battles against the Dzungars, that the Sixth Panchen was allowed to go back to the Tashilhunpo. On his departure the Kashag presented the Panchen a silver *Mandral*, a suit of monk's robes, 85 silver ingots (each weighing 50 taels), 108 bolts of silk and satin and 1,000 bricks of tea. On the seventeenth day of the eleventh month when the Sixth Panchen bid farewell to the Dalai at the Potala, the Dalai gave him a statue of Sakyamuni Buddha and wished him a good journey. The Dalai sent Dronyer Yonten Ledrup to escort the Sixth Panchen to the Tashilhunpo.

In the twentieth year of the Qianlong reign period (1755), the central government of the Qing Dynasty defeated the Dzungars in Xinjiang. The Emperor sent an envoy to inform the Dalai and the Panchen of the victory of the Qing troops over the Dzungars in Xinjiang. The Sixth Panchen wrote a letter of congratulation to Emperor Gaozong and offered a *katag* and three statues of the Buddha. The *Imperial Records of the Qing Dynasty* has an account of this as follows:

> In the seventh month of the twentieth year of the Qianlong reign period, the Emperor decreed: "The Dzungar chieftain Dawachi was captured and the Dzungar rebellion was quelled. Salashan should be sent to inform the Dalai of the victory to make them happy."

## 3. Qing Emperor Gaozong Grants an Honorific Title to the Sixth Panchen

In the eighth month of the twentieth year of the Qianlong reign period (1755), the Seventh Dalai sent a letter to the Sixth Panchen saying that he had been ill and had undergone all treatments without any improvement. No sooner had he received the letter than the Sixth Panchen sent a well-known physician of the Tashilhunpo to Lhasa to give treatment to the Dalai. But this was also without success.

On the third day of the second month of the twenty-second year of the Qianlong reign period (1757), Seventh Dalai Kelzang Gyatso died at the age of fifty. The Kalons of the Kashag and the *Chikyap Khenpo* of the Potala sent men to inform the Sixth Panchen of the death of the Seventh Dalai Lama and ask him to pray for the Dalai's early reincarnation. The Panchen was also asked to make an announcement of the Dalai's death to all the Tibetan clerical and lay people.

The Sixth Panchen was sad at the death of the Seventh Dalai. He ordered all the monks of the Tashilhunpo to go into mourning for three days, chanting sutras in the Great Chanting Hall. At the mourning ceremony all monks took off their yellow hats to mourn the death of the Seventh Dalai. The Sixth Panchen Lama gave every one of them a tael of silver as alms for their chanting service. Then he gathered all monks of the Tashilhunpo to chant sutras at the Jikang Hall of the monastery for forty-two days. Tea and food were supplied to them seven times a day during that time. Meanwhile the Panchen sent men to Lhasa to offer one thousand lamps, one thousand joss sticks, sixty silver ingots, forty horses and one hundred bolts of satin to the body of the deceased Dalai. The Panchen also sent men to give alms and sweet buttered-tea to the monks of the Three Major Monasteries at Lhasa, and the monasteries in U and Tsang, and asked them to pray for the Dalai's early reincarnation.

As the Seventh Dalai's death left the top spiritual and temporal position vacant, the Kalons of the Kashag, through resident officials Wu Mitai and Salashan, asked the Emperor to appoint Demo Hutuktu to act in the Dalai's place.

Emperor Gaozong said:

> The idea of the report is not clear. The Kalons have long intended to act in the Dalai's place and will likely take the ruling power some day if no measures are taken to prevent them. So I give orders to grant Demo Hutuktu the title of *Nomihan* and to appoint him to act in the Dalai Lama's place. In addition, I order Wu Mitai and Salashan to consult with Demo Hutuktu in handling all Tibetan affairs as was in the days when the Dalai Lama was alive. They should be careful and not allow the Kalons to take over power.

From then on, until the new Dalai Lama assumed temporal power, Demo Hutuktu acted in the Dalai's place. Traditionally he has been called the "Regent" (*Gyatsab* in Tibetan).

In that year the Sixth Panchen Palden Yeshe was nineteen years old. According to Lamaism, he should be ordained into full monkhood. The *khenpos* and other chief monk officials of the Tashilhunpo decided to invite the Panchen's sutra tutor, Lozang Chosphel, to ordain him. The Sixth Panchen took his *gelong* vows before Lozang Chosphel at the Great Chanting Hall of Tashilhunpo Monastery on the fourth day of the sixth month. The representatives of the Kashag, of the Amban, and of the Three Major Monasteries came to congratulate him on his ordination.

In the twenty-fourth year of the Qianlong reign period (1759), the Emperor sent Changkya Hutuktu to Lhasa to arrange the search for the reincarnation of the Seventh Dalai Lama. On the fifth day of the second month, Dronyer Kelzang Dondrup and Jepon Phurchok, on behalf of the Kashag, and Phodrang Dcpa, on behalf of Drepung Monastery, were sent to invite the Sixth Panchen to Lhasa for an audience with Changkya Hutuktu.

The Panchen left the Tashilhunpo on the ninth day of the second month and arrived at Lhasa on the twenty-second day of the second month. In the welcoming tents set up at Kidtsel Luding he met with Changkya Hutuktu and the resident officials, Wu Mitai and Guanbao. They exchanged *katags*. Then the Panchen went to the Potala. During his stay at Lhasa the Sixth Panchen and Changkya Hutuktu, strictly according to the Yellow sect traditions, first invoked an oracle and then asked the Nechung Chosgyong for divine revelations, seeking information on the direction in which the reincarnate Dalai Lama could be found. With the directions given by the oracle and divine revelations, a large party of officials was sent to search for the reborn person.

Soon afterwards Changkya Hutuktu returned to Beijing to report to the Emperor, and the Sixth Panchen went back to the Tashilhunpo. He left Lhasa on the eleventh day of the fifth month. On his homeward journey he visited Ganden, Radreng (Rating) and other monasteries, giving sermons to the monks there. He went back to the Tashilhunpo by the northern route, arriving there on the third day of the seventh month.

En route he was informed at his birthplace, Trashitse Shika of Namling Dzong, that a boy was born to an aristocratic family at Lharigang at Thobgyal in Tsang in the Earth-Tiger year of the Tibetan calendrical cycle (the twenty-third year of the Qianlong reign period, or 1758). Rumours had it that the boy was the reincarnate Dalai Lama. The Sixth Panchen asked the parents to bring their son to Kadam Rabgyal Monastery and entertained them there with cooked rice and peanuts. The Panchen made observations of the boy, but did not say anything.

In the twenty-fifth year of the Qianlong reign period (1760), the Sixth Panchen sent a *balyar khenpo* to Beijing to extend congratulations to the Emperor on his fiftieth birthday. In the fourth month of the twenty-fifth year of the Qianlong period, the Emperor gave an order to the ministers of the Grand Secretariat:

Guanbao reported that the Panchen Erdeni and Demo Hutuktu have sent men to congratulate me on my birthday. If the men come to Chengdu with some goods, their goods will be treated favourably as tribute and not taxed.

In the twelfth month, a comprehensive religious examination from all sides confirmed the boy examined by the Panchen was the soul boy, the reincarnation of the Seventh Dalai Lama. With Emperor Gaozong's approval it was decided that the boy should succeed as the Eighth Dalai Lama. By order of the Amban and Demo Hutuktu, a large party of clerical and lay officials was sent by the Kashag and the Three Major Monasteries to Lharigang in Thobgyal to escort the soul boy from his parents' house to the Tashilhunpo. There the boy kowtowed to the Sixth Panchen when he was received by the latter.

In the first month of the twenty-sixth year of the Qianlong reign period (1761), the Seventh Dalai's *Chopon Khenpo*, Dedru, was sent to the Tashilhunpo on behalf of the Kashag to express congratulations to the Eighth Dalai Lama and convey a letter to the Sixth Panchen, in which the Panchen was asked by the Regent Demo Hutuktu and four Kalons to preside at the tonsuring and name-giving ceremony for the Eighth Dalai Lama.

On the eleventh day of the first month, the Eighth Dalai was tonsured and given the religious name of Jetsun Lozang Tenpai Wangchuk Jampel Gyatso Palzangpo (Jampel Gyatso for short). Celebrations were held and financially supported by the Kashag at the Tashilhunpo.

On the fifth day of the third month a party of over two hundred people, headed by Regent Demo Hutuktu, Amban Jifu, Kalon Doring Pandita and Kalon Dzasa Ta Lama, went to the Tashilhunpo to invite the Eighth Dalai Lama to Lhasa. On the following day, at a grand assembly in the Tashilhunpo's Great Chanting Hall, the Regent, Amban and Kalons offered *katags* and precious gifts to the Sixth Panchen and the Eighth Dalai Lama. On the eighteenth day of the third month, as the Eighth Dalai was leaving the Tashilhunpo for Lhasa, the monastery's clerical and lay officials and monks all lined up in front of the monastery to bow farewell to the Dalai, the Amban, the Regent and others. The Sixth Panchen sent two *dronyers* to accompany the Eighth Dalai Lama to Lhasa.

In the fifth month of the twenty-seventh year of the Qianlong reign period (1762), Dronyer Kelzang Dondrup, Jepon Shadrag and Kyiso Yelpa of Sera Monastery and other persons were sent by Demo Hutuktu and resident officials Jifu, Funai and Fujing to inform the Sixth Panchen that Eighth Dalai Lama Jampel Gyatso would be enthroned in the seventh month and that the ceremony would be witnessed by Kharkha King Tseten Drakpa sent by Qing Emperor Gaozong. They invited the Panchen to preside over the ceremony at Lhasa and give the Dalai lectures on commandments against sins. On the seventh day of the sixth month the Sixth Panchen left for Lhasa in response to the invitation. En route the Panchen went to Riwo Dechen Monastery at Netang and consulted with Amban Jifu about how to hold the ceremony. On the sixth day of the seventh month the Dalai, the Panchen and the Regent went to Lhasa.

On the ninth day of the seventh month Lhasa's inhabitants and government officials lined the road to offer an unprecedented grand welcome to them. The Eighth Dalai ascended the throne of the Dalai Lama at the Potala's Sunlight Hall, where celebrations were held by the Kashag.

On the seventeenth day of the seventh month the Eighth Dalai learnt the commandments against sins from the Sixth Panchen at the Potala's Sunlight Hall.

In order to celebrate the Dalai's enthronement the Panchen sent men to give alms and sweet buttered-tea to the monks of the Three Major Monasteries and other ones at an expense of 15,179 taels of silver.

On the twenty-fourth day of the eighth month the Kashag presented gifts to the Sixth Panchen. On the fifth day of the ninth month the Panchen bid farewell to the Dalai, the Regent and the Amban. He arrived at the Tashilhunpo on the twenty-first day of the ninth month.

In the thirtieth year of the Qianlong reign period (1765) the Eighth Dalai Lama, at seven, was of the age when he should take the *getsul* vows. The Panchen was invited to give the vows to him. In the third month the Panchen received a letter of invitation from the Kashag. On the eleventh day of the fifth month the Kashag sent Dronyer Kelzang Dondrup, Jepon Palsa and other envoys again to invite the Panchen to Lhasa.

On the sixteenth day of the fifth month the Sixth Panchen left the Tashilhunpo for Lhasa. He arrived on the first day of the sixth month. He met with the Dalai at Kadam Yantse Hall in the Jokhang, where the Kashag held a welcoming ceremony. The Panchen took up temporary residence in the Jokhang's Songjiang Hall.

On the fourth day of the sixth month the Dalai took his *getsul* vows from the Panchen before the image of Sakyamuni Buddha at the Jokhang in the presence of Amban Funai and other officials who came to express congratulations on behalf of the Emperor, as well as Ganden Tripa Ngawang Chosdrak and Demo Hutuktu, who were masters of the ceremony. After the ceremony the Dalai and the Panchen went to the Potala. The Panchen spent over two months in the Potala, teaching the Dalai scriptures almost every day. The Panchen took his leave on the twenty-third day of the eighth month and returned to the Tashilhunpo on the fourteenth day of the ninth month.

In the seventh month of the thirty-first year of the Qianlong reign period (1766), the Sixth Panchen was informed by the Kashag that the envoys from the Emperor would soon come by way of Tachienlu to the Tashilhunpo to grant him an honorific title. The Panchen at once sent Bapon Yeshe to Tachienlu to welcome the imperial envoys and sent Dronyer Lozang Geleg and Lodrawa Lozang Kajue to Lhasa to wait for them.

On the seventeenth day of the ninth month the imperial envoys —Asahangan, Dzasa Lama Ngawang Bajue Hutuktu, Keya and Jarbi —and their party, dozens in all, arrived at the Tashilhunpo. The Panchen sent a party of over one hundred people, including all the Tashilhunpo's monk officials and heads of *dzongs* and *shikas*, to welcome them in the suburbs, dozens of *li* away from the Tashil- hunpo. Buddhist flags were hung on the roofs of the monastery. Several thousand monks were waiting outside the monastery's gate. Welcoming tents were set up on the east bank of the Nyangchu River.

The imperial envoys met with the Sixth Panchen at the Tashil- hunpo's Sunlight Hall. After receiving the Panchen's respects to the Emperor, the envoys read an imperial edict to the Panchen. It reads as follows:

> I, the Emperor who rules the world by the order of Heaven, declare: I, the Lord of all worldly beings, as everybody knows, give my protection and benevolence to all who obey me. The Panchen has profound knowledge of Buddhism and has taught the Dalai Lama the Buddhist disciplines very well. I am very glad to know that the present Panchen is a man of great learning, just as the former one was. So I also grant you the same title of *Panchen Erdeni* as I have granted to the former Panchen, and put you in charge of the Tashilhunpo's administrative and religious affairs for the development of the Yellow sect. I hope you will chant more sutras for our country's security. This decree is issued on the fourth day of the first month of the thirtieth year of the Qianlong reign period.

The Panchen was given an album of gold sheets and a gold seal. The gold album consisted of thirteen sheets made with 230 taels of gold. The inscription on the sheets was written in Manchu, Han Chinese and Tibetan scripts. The gold seal of authority, 208 taels in weight, bore the inscription of "The Seal of the Panchen Erdeni Granted by the Emperor" also in Manchu, Han and Tibetan scripts. Besides, the envoys brought many gifts from the Emperor to the Panchen, including silk and satin, tea and many jade articles. The Panchen kowtowed to the east, expressing thanks to the Emperor, and then held a grand welcoming banquet for the envoys.

The *Imperial Records of the Qing Dynasty* has a brief account of this:

> In the ninth month of the thirtieth year of the Qianlong reign period, the Emperor said Panchen Erdeni should be granted an honorific title for his advanced knowledge of Buddhism gained by diligent study and his teaching work for the Dalai Lama.

Nevertheless, the *Records* does not say a word about the inscriptions of the gold album and the seal. What I introduce here is according to the Tibetan-language *Biography of the Sixth Panchen*, without reference to the original inscriptions.

On the twenty-seventh day of the ninth month, the envoys from the Emperor left for Lhasa. Besides giving a grand farewell ceremony, the Panchen sent a *dronyer* and a *bapon* to escort the envoys to Lhasa. Then he sent Dronyer Lozang Geleg with a memorial to Beijing to express thanks to the Emperor. The *dronyer* left for

Beijing on the first day of the eleventh month.

## 4. The Sixth Panchen's Mediation Between Bhutan and India. Bogle Enters Tibet. The Sixth Panchen's Insistence on Tibet's Subordination to the Central Government of the Qing Dynasty

By this time the British invaders had occupied India and the East India Company had been established. The British government appointed a governor in India. In 1774 (the thirty-ninth year of the Qianlong reign period), military conflicts took place between Bhutan and Indian Bengal. Being a friend of the Fifth Panchen, the ruling lama of Bhutan sent men to the Tashilhunpo to ask the Sixth Panchen for mediation.

The Sixth Panchen accepted the Bhutanese ruling lama's request, because the Fourth and Fifth Panchen Lamas in the past had mediated between Bhutan and Tibet at the request of the ruling lama of Bhutan and the Dalai Lama when they were in conflict. So he wrote a letter to the British Indian authorities—in fact, to Warren Hastings, the British Governor of India.

*India and Tibet*, written by Francis Younghusband, has an account of the interviews between George Bogle and the Sixth Panchen. We can make reference to it in our study of the British intrusion of Tibet, though the author, taking the imperialist stance, groundlessly claims that Tibet was a "state."

According to the book, after receiving the letter from the Sixth Panchen, Warren Hastings stopped the invasion of Bhutan and took advantage of the chance to send George Bogle to meet the Panchen. Bogle left Calcutta in the middle of May 1774 (the thirty-ninth year of the Qianlong reign period) and arrived at Tashilhunpo Monastery in November of the same year.

The Sixth Panchen at first did not permit Bogle to come into Tibet. In a letter to Hastings, the Panchen asked him to call back Bogle because the Emperor of China did not allow any foreigners to come into Tibet, a part of China, and the Tashilhunpo was too far from Beijing to get the Emperor's approval of Bogle's coming (see *History of the British Invasion of Tibet in the Qing Dynasty* by She Su).

Nevertheless, Hastings disregarded the Panchen's refusal and Bogle continued on to the Tashilhunpo. Prior to Bogle's departure, Hastings had instructed him to make contact through the Panchen with the Regent Demo Hutuktu and the Kashag at Lhasa for the purpose of concluding a trade agreement between India and Tibet and having a British trade agency set up in Lhasa, and meanwhile to learn about roads and inhabitants along the routes from Bengal to Lhasa and from Lhasa to its adjacent areas and to investigate administration, finance and folklore of the areas. Bogle, an Englishman of twenty-eight years of age, held a post in the Revenue Department of the British East India Company.

The day after arriving at Shigatse, Bogle had an interview with the Sixth Panchen and delivered to him a letter and a pearl rosary as gifts from Hastings. Younghusband's book says:

> The Tashi Lama received Bogle with a very courteous and smiling countenance, seated him near him on a high stool covered with a carpet, and spoke to him in Hindustani, of which he had a moderate knowledge....
>
> Bogle says of him [the Sixth Panchen] that he was about forty years of age, that his disposition was open, candid and generous, and that the expression of his countenance was smiling and good-humoured. He was extremely merry and entertaining in conversation, and told a pleasant story with a great deal of humour and action.

In their conversation the Sixth Panchen stressed the following points:

(1) He pointed out that Bhutan was a vassal state of China, so Tibet could not but care for the fate of Bhutan. In his letter to Hastings the Panchen pointed out clearly:

> But I now take upon me to be his mediator, and to represent to you that, as the said Deb Raja [the ruling lama in Bhutan] is dependent upon the Dalai Lama . . . should you persist in offering further molestation to the Deb Raja's country, it will irritate both the Lama and all his subjects against you.

He again stressed the point in his conversation with Bogle: "The [British Indian] Governor had reason for going to war, but, as I am averse to bloodshed, and the Bhutanese are my vassals, I am glad it is brought to a conclusion."

(2) He pointed out that Tibet, as a part of China, was subject to the Emperor of China. According to Younghusband:

> Bogle then hinted at the advisability of the Tibetans coming into some form of alliance with the English.... The Tashi Lama said that the Regent's apprehensions of the English arose not only from himself, but also from his fear of giving offence to the Chinese, to whom Tibet was subject. The Regent wished, therefore, to receive an answer from the Court at Peking.

The representatives of Demo Hutuktu also said to Bogle: "Gesub Rimpoche [the Regent at Lhasa] will do everything in his power, but that he and all the country are subject to the Emperor of China."

(3) To the proposal of trade, the Sixth Panchen and the representative of the Regent agreed, but said:

> The Tibetans are afraid of the heat, and will proceed, therefore, only as far as Phari, where the Bhutanese bring the commodities of Bengal and exchange them for those of Tibet. This is the ancient custom, and should certainly be observed.

(4) As to the Regent of Lhasa not allowing Bogle to go to Lhasa and set up a trade office there, the Panchen said that "he himself would have been quite willing, but that the Lhasa Regent was very averse, and he dissuaded Bogle from going, saying that the Regent's heart was small and suspicious, and he could not promise that he would be able to procure the Regent's consent."

Having spent four months at Shigatse, Bogle, who gained nothing there, left in March 1775. At his farewell interview Bogle said that Warren Hastings would send letters to the Lama by his own servants, upon which the Lama said:

> I wish the Governor will not at present send an Englishman. You know what difficulties I had about your coming into the country, and how I had to struggle with the jealousy of Gesub Rimpoche [the Regent].... I wish, therefore, that the Governor would rather send a Hindu.

As to the problem why the Tibetans were suspicious of Englishmen, Younghusband attributed it to this:

> Naturally, therefore, the Tibetans would assume that it would only be a matter of time before the English Governor of Bengal would attack

Tibet. He had the power to subdue that country; he would therefore subdue it. In the first instance he would, of course, send up an agent to spy out the land, to see what it was worth, and to find out the best way into it; and such an agent doubtless Bogle was, in their opinion. It was inevitable, therefore, that Bogle should be viewed with suspicion.

The statements showed clearly why Bogle was sent to Tibet and how, in contact with Bogle, the Sixth Panchen viewed China's sovereignty and the relationship between Tibet and inner China.

The Tibetan biography of the Sixth Panchen also has an account of the interview between the Panchen and Bogle.

On the third day of the eleventh month of the forty-first year of the Qianlong reign period (1776), the Eighth Dalai and Regent Demo Hutuktu sent letters to the Sixth Panchen to ask him to ordain the Dalai into full monkhood at Lhasa in the following year, when the Dalai would be eighteen years old. The Panchen acceded to their request.

In the first month of the forty-second year of the Qianlong reign period (1777), the Sixth Panchen was informed by the Eighth Dalai, Amban Liu Baozhu and all the Kalons that the Regent had died on the twenty-second day of the first month. The Panchen was asked by them to chant sutras and pray for the deceased Regent. The Panchen sent Yelpa Lozang Gedun to hold a memorial ceremony at Lhasa for the Regent.

On the sixth day of the second month, the Kashag sent Dronyer Shelu Khenpo, Tsepon Jakhawa, and the *Kyiso* of the Drepung to invite the Panchen to give *gelong* vows to the Dalai at Lhasa. The Panchen left the Tashilhunpo on the seventh day and arrived at Lhasa on the twentieth day. The Panchen met the Dalai at the Potala's Sunlight Hall and they exchanged *katags*. The next day the Kashag held celebrations to welcome the Panchen at the Sunlight Hall in the presence of resident officials Liu Baozhu and Heng Rui.

On the fifth day of the fourth month an edict from Emperor Gaozong reached Lhasa, by which Ganden Sherathu Nomihan Ngawang Tsultrim (Tsemonling) succeeded Regent Demo. Panchen sent his representatives to congratulate the new Regent.

The fifteenth day of the fourth month was chosen as the day for the Eighth Dalai Lama Jampel Gyatso to take his *gelong* vows. On that day the new Regent, Ganden Sherathu Nomihan, accompanied the Eighth Dalai and the Sixth Panchen to Jokhang Temple. The ceremony was held in front of Sakyamuni's image. The Sixth Panchen, acting as the ordination *khenpo*, was assisted by Ngawang Chosdrak, Dalai's sutra tutor and ex-abbot of the Ganden, who performed the duty of *lelob* (assistant ordination lecturer); by the Panchen's sutra tutor, Lozang Chosphel, who acted as *sangton* (ordination tutor who saw to it that the Dalai Lama understood the commandments); by Ganden Tripa Lozang Tenpa, who served as *dukhorwa* (time keeper and manager of the ordination procedures), and by Charhan Nomihan Lozang Thubten Geleg Gyaltsen, who served as *tsebabao* (the one who presented the Dalai with containers of food at the prescribed time).

After he took the vows, the Eighth Dalai presented a *mandral* to the Sixth Panchen to express thanks, and the Panchen also gave the Dalai a *mandral* to express congratulations. Then the Dalai and the Panchen received *katags* and gifts from the Regent, Amban, Kalons and the representatives of the Three Major Monasteries. The Sixth Panchen submitted a memorial about the ordination to Emperor Gaozong through the Amban.

The Dalai and Panchen, after spending nine days in Jokhang Temple, went to offer sacrifices to Sakyamuni's image and then went back to the Potala on the twenty-fourth day of the fourth month. The Sixth Panchen took up one year's residence in the Potala and was said to be teaching the Dalai scriptures of exoteric and esoteric Buddhism and Tsongkhapa's works every day. The Panchen took farewell of the Dalai on the twenty-fourth day of the second month of the forty-third year of Emperor Gaozong's reign (1778), arriving at the Tashilhunpo on the twelfth day on the third month.

On the ninth day of the second month of the forty-fourth year of Emperor Gaozong's reign, Regent Ganden Sherathu Nomihan, Amban Liu Baozhu and Kalon Pandita Odser Namgyal and their party paid a visit to the Panchen and told him that Emperor Gaozong invited him to Beijing. The Emperor had instructed the Regent and Amban to make all preparations for his journey. The Panchen was very glad to hear the news and submitted a memorial to the Emperor through the Amban, saying he was willing to accept the invitation.

# 5. The Sixth Panchen's Audience with Emperor Gaozong at Chengde

To invite the Panchen to Beijing for an audience with the Emperor had long before been decided by the Qing Emperor Shengzu, who had invited the Fifth Panchen time and again. The Panchen was willing to go to Beijing, but failed to go because of Depa Sangye Gyatso's interference. At that time the Qing central government had been engaged in a decisive war with Galdan of the Dzungar tribes in Mongolia. Emperor Shengzu himself had led the military expedition. The Emperor had hoped to derive advantage out of the Mongols' support for the Panchen. If the Panchen came to Beijing by way of areas inhabited by the Mongols, it would have been very conducive for the Qing government's intended pacification of the Mongols. But his hope had not been realized.

However, things were quite different with the Sixth Panchen. By then the areas to the north and south of the Gobi had submitted themselves to the rule of the Qing Dynasty and had become a part of the Qing territory. The Dzungars were totally defeated by the Qing troops in 1754-1755 and Xinjiang was brought into the Qing Empire's territory. So by now it was not due to the problems of the Mongols and the Dzungars but due to other political problems that Emperor Gaozong invited the Sixth Panchen to Beijing.

In view of the incidents in which the Chief Kalon Khangchennas was killed in the seventh year of the Yongzheng reign period (1729) and resident officials Fu Qing and Labdon were killed in the fifteenth year of the Qianlong reign period (1750), Emperor Gaozong keenly felt it necessary to reduce the existing aristocratic ruling power by way of patronizing religious power so as to facilitate the Qing court's jurisdiction over Tibet through the resident officials. Therefore, the Emperor tried to raise the status of both the Dalai Lama and the Panchen, so that a second Gyumey Namgyal would not be able to emerge from among the aristocrats.

As the Dalai Lama had had an audience with the Emperor in Beijing, the Panchen's visiting Beijing would surely make the Panchen group favourably incline towards the Qing court and raise the Panchen's political status in Tibet. On his way to Beijing, the Panchen surely would pass Qinghai and Inner Mongolia, pastoral areas inhabited by Mongols and Tibetans. His great influence among them would be of great use for the Qing Dynasty to consolidate its rule over Qinghai as well as Outer and Inner Mongolia. So the Emperor's invitation had been planned elaborately for several years. He chose his seventieth birthday as a pretext of inviting the Sixth Panchen and decided the Imperial Summer Resort at Chengde would be the place for the audience. He also ordered that the Rehe Tashilhunpo Temple (officially known as the Temple of Sumeru Happiness and Longevity in Chinese) be built for the Panchen's residence.

The *Imperial Records of the Qing Dynasty* has the following accounts of the Sixth Panchen's visit to Beijing:

On the *yi-chou* day of the twelfth month of the forty-third year of the Qianlong reign period, in a decree to the Grand Ministers of State, the Emperor said: "I learned yesterday from the memorial submitted by Changkya Hutuktu that Panchen Erdeni asked to come to congratulate me on my seventieth birthday in the *geng-zi* year [the forty-fifth year of the Qianlong reign period, or 1780]. I have long desired to meet him, but as the distance is too far, I did not order him to come. Now since he is willing to come, it is a good omen, and so I approved his coming. I will spend my birthday in Rehe. All the envoys from vassal kingdoms will gather there. So it will be most convenient for Panchen Erdeni to go to Rehe. I have ordered that a temple be built in Rehe for his residence. The Board for National Minority Affairs should be responsible for the preparation of his journey. There is plenty of time, so the preparations can be made unhurriedly."

In the forty-fourth year of the Qianlong reign period (1779), the Emperor said to the Grand Ministers of State:

In the seventh month of the next year Panchen Erdeni will come to the Imperial Summer Resort in Rehe for an audience with me. I will send my sixth son to welcome him in the company of a minister, who should be familiar with foreign affairs. I think Yonggui is qualified to accompany the prince.

So Yonggui was called back from Xinjiang, and he was, by the Emperor's order, made responsible for the affairs of receiving the Sixth Panchen.

Considering that the Sixth Panchen would go to Rehe by way

of Gansu, Shaanxi, Shanxi and Chahar (Qahar), Emperor Gaozong ordered the governors of those provinces, such as Lerjing, Biyuan and Ba Yansan, to make appropriate preparations, which should be neither perfunctory nor extravagant. Lerjing, Governor-General of Shaanxi and Gansu, being alarmed by the Emperor's order, prepared to set up tents for the Panchen and his party to spend the night and repair all civil houses and roads along the route the Panchen would take in the areas under his administration. But the Emperor criticized Lerjing for his inability to handle the affair. The Emperor said that the Panchen and his party would bring tents for themselves on the journey, so it was not necessary to set up tents at places they would spend the night on the road. As to the roads, he said that only steep mountain roads should be repaired.

The Emperor also decided to invite the chieftains of the Outer and Inner Mongolian tribes, the Uygur chieftains from Xinjiang who had submitted themselves recently to the Qing Dynasty and the Turgut chieftains who had come back from Russia to Rehe to attend his birthday celebration for the purpose of consolidating his rule over Mongolia and Xinjiang by taking advantage of the Panchen's prestige and influence among them.

According to the Tibetan biography of the Sixth Panchen, the Panchen, after accepting the invitation from the Emperor, immediately began to prepare for his journey. First of all, he decided on the route. He planned to start off in the sixth month of the forty-fourth year of the Qianlong reign period (1779) and reach the Kumbum Monastery of Qinghai in the tenth month. After spending the winter there, he would leave the monastery in the third month of the following year (1780) and continue his journey by way of Ningxia, Suiyuan and Chahar, and finally arrive at Rehe in the seventh month. He planned to come back to the Tashilhunpo in the forty-sixth year of the Qianlong reign period (1781). He would spend altogether three years on the journey.

Next the Panchen had to decide on the problem of the retinue. Following the former practice of Sakya ruling lama Phagspa and the Fifth Dalai Lama, the party of two thousand would include the *Solpon Khenpo, Zimpon Khenpo, Chopon Khenpo, Dronyer, Dechongpa, Nechangpa, Gyupa Dorje Lopon, Chachapa, Lamangpa, Dapon, Garpa, Machin, Zopon,* etc., and a great number of servants and grooms.

After the Panchen left for Beijing, all affairs of the Tashilhunpo were to be put under the administration of Dechongpa Geleg Jungne.

On the seventeenth day of the sixth month of the forty-fourth year of Emperor Gaozong's reign (1779), the Sixth Panchen left the Tashilhunpo. The Kashag sent ex-Kalon Darhan Khenpo, Dzasa Teji, Tenpa Dondrup (the Eighth Dalai's representative) and others to escort the Panchen to the border of Tibet. On the twenty-seventh day of the sixth month the Sixth Panchen arrived at Trashitongmon of Yangpachen, where Eighth Dalai Lama Jampel Gyatso, Regent Ganden Sherathu Nomihan, resident officials Heng Rui and Suo Ling, and the Kalons and *dapons* came to see him off. On arriving, the Panchen exchanged *katags* with the Eighth Dalai, the Regent and the resident officials in Tibet. The Kashag held a farewell ceremony for him there. The Eighth Dalai accompanied the Panchen from Yangpachen to Drashitang of Upper Dam, a journey of eight days, and then went back to Lhasa on the sixth day of the seventh month. The Kashag sent Kalon Dorkhawa to escort the Panchen to the Tongtian River in Qinghai.

The Sixth Panchen arrived at Nagchu on the thirteenth day of the seventh month and spent five days there exchanging horses. He left Nagchu on the eighteenth day of the seventh month. He crossed the Tangula Mountains on the twenty-eighth day of the seventh month, then meeting with the *khenpo* of Tashilhunpo Monastery, Jampal Lozang, who was coming back from Beijing. The *Khenpo* brought the Panchen a decree and an image of Emperor Gaozong from the Emperor.

The Emperor said in the decree:

> How is Panchen Erdeni? How is the Dalai Lama? You are always on my mind. Now I am sending men to welcoming you. I will hold the same grand welcoming ceremony for you as that my ancestors accorded to the Fifth Dalai Lama. I have had a temple built in the Imperial Summer Resort for your residence, in the same style as that of Tashilhunpo Monastery. I am now studying Tibetan for the convenience of our talk. I will send ministers to welcome you when you near the Imperial Summer Resort.

The Sixth Panchen entered Qinghai on the eighth day of the eighth month. There the Grand Minister Superintendent of Qinghai took over responsibility for the supplies of the Panchen—providing the group with one thousand pack oxen, four hundred camels and four hundred tents, as well as fuel, forage grass, etc.

When the Panchen arrived at the Tongtian River, Kalon Dorkhawa, whose duty it was to escort the Panchen to the border of Tibet, went back to Lhasa. The Panchen arrived at the headwaters of the Yellow River on the twenty-eighth day of the eighth month. Envoys from the Emperor brought him an edict from Emperor Gaozong, which read:

> I was glad to know that you had arrived at Nomgen Wubaxidaba and the weather on your journey was warm and without much snow. I allow you, Grand Living Buddha in the West, not to kowtow to my portrait as a preferential treatment to you.

On the twenty-seventh day of the ninth month the Panchen and his party passed Mt. Shiaorola, where he was welcomed by over two hundred representatives of Mongolian and Tibetan monks and laymen in Qinghai. Among them were some religious leaders, such as Chosang Hutuktu and Jiye of Kumbum Monastery. Besides, over ten thousand Mongols and Tibetans of Qinghai also went to welcome him.

On the tenth day of the tenth month the Panchen and his party arrived at Kukutoloha and were welcomed by the Commander of Xining and the intendant of the circuit of Lanzhou and 140 Manchu, Han and Tibetan officials sent by Governor-General of Shaanxi and Gansu Lerjing and Grand Minister Superintendent of Qinghai Fu Li.

On the twelfth day of the tenth month the Panchen and his party were greeted by more than a hundred Manchu and Han officials headed by Governor-General Lerjing and Grand Minister Superintendent Fu Li, who brought with them over one thousand soldiers and servants. Lerjing inquired after the Panchen's health and told him that, by the Emperor's order, all the expenses of the Panchen and his party on the journey would be funded by the state treasury.

On the fifteenth day of the tenth month, the Panchen arrived at Kumbum Monastery. Buddhist flags were flying as lamas beat drums and blew bugles on the roofs, while about three thousand monks lined up before the entrance to welcome the Panchen. The Panchen took his temporary residence in the hall where the Third, Fourth and Fifth Dalais had lived. (Kumbum is one of the six main monasteries of the Yellow Hat sect [Gelug sect]. The other five are the Three Major Monasteries at Lhasa, the Tashilhunpo in the Tsang region and the Labrang in Gansu.)

Meanwhile, envoys from the Emperor, Sula and Wanfu, and Asahan Butai of Mongolia came to the monastery with an edict from the Emperor to him, which said: "I hope you will come a little earlier than scheduled to the Imperial Summer Resort to attend the celebrations of my seventieth birthday next year." The edict was accompanied with a present of a pearl rosary, a gold saddle and harness, a spirited horse, silver teapots, satin, etc. The envoys presented *katags* to the Panchen at the Kumbum's Great Chanting Prayer Hall and gave alms and sweet buttered-tea to all the monks of the monastery. The Panchen presented a memorial to the Emperor to express his gratitude through the envoys.

The Panchen spent the five winter months in Kumbum Monastery. During that time the Panchen blessed tens of thousands of Mongols and Tibetans by touching their heads and spent over 6,700 taels of silver on giving alms and sweet buttered-tea to all monks of the monastery.

On the tenth day of the third month of the forty-fifth year of the Qianlong reign period (1780), the Panchen left the Kumbum for the Imperial Summer Resort at Chengde via Ningxia, Ihju League in Inner Mongolia and Chahar. When he came to Gulang County of Gansu en route, Governor-General Lerjing and other Manchu and Han officials gave him a rousing welcome and held a farewell banquet for him.

On the tenth day of the fourth month the Panchen went through Ningxia City and Alxa Banner to Ihju League. On the way Mongolian chieftains and people and Manchu and Han officials held grand welcoming and farewell ceremonies for him and tens of thousands of Mongols were blessed by having their heads touched by the leader of Lamaism.

On the first day of the sixth month when the Panchen came to Otog Banner of Inner Mongolia, envoys from the Emperor, Kamrin Oto Namsun and Ranke Hutuktu, brought him a yellow sedan chair with a golden roof, four canopies, two red and two yellow, four sets of flags and forty articles to be carried by a detachment of guards of honour. So from then on the Panchen was carried on a sedan. When he arrived at Daihai (in modern Liangchen County of Inner Mongolia Autonomous Region), the Sixth Prince and Changkya Hutuktu, sent by the Emperor, met him and delivered an imperial edict, in which the Emperor said: "I went to the Imperial Summer Resort on the seventh day of the fifth month and had the temple built there for your residence." The edict was accompanied with a pearl hat for summer, a monk's robe made with gold silk threads and a crystal rosary as gifts to the Panchen. When he kowtowed to thank the Emperor, the prince stopped him, saying: "By the order of His Majesty, you are exempted from kowtowing."

On the twenty-first day of the seventh month in the forty-fifth year of the Qianlong reign period (1780), when the Panchen arrived at Chengde, the Emperor sent ministers Aiaipugong, Hu Daxing and Gongping Xiqilun as his representatives to welcome him. Meanwhile, the local Living Buddhas, *khenpos*, lamas and Mongol chieftains lined up on both sides of the road to welcome him. Aiaipugong, on behalf of the Emperor, presented the Panchen a *katag* and delivered a welcoming speech. Then the Panchen went to the Temple of Sumeru Happiness and Longevity (or the Rehe Tashilhunpo Temple).

After taking a short rest in the temple, the Panchen went by sedan to the Imperial Summer Resort to pay respects to Emperor Gaozong, his *khenpos* accompanying him on foot. The Panchen alighted from the sedan before the Emperor's residence, Emperor Gaozong standing at the gate of the house and several hundred princes, ministers and officials standing in the corridors on both sides to welcome his coming. The Panchen presented the Emperor a *Langzuo katag*, an image of *Zhuma Buddha* and a pearl rosary. Then when he was just about to kowtow, the Emperor stopped him saying in Tibetan: "Lama, don't kowtow."

In response, the Emperor also gave the Panchen a *Langzuo katag*. Holding his hand, the Emperor led the Panchen into the house. When the Emperor and the Panchen took their seats, Changkya Hutuktu presented each of them a *katag*, and the

Panchen's *khenpos*, in turn, presented *katags* to the Emperor. Then tea was served. Emperor Gaozong asked the Panchen in Tibetan: "How is your health? Lama, you must have had a tiring journey."

"I am very well, thank you." the Panchen answered.

"How is the Dalai Lama?"

"He is very well."

"How old are you, Lama? I am seventy now. I am very glad to meet you in my old age. With your coming, Buddhism in inner China will enjoy development and all worldly beings will sing the praise of peace and security."

The Panchen stood up to answer all questions raised by the Emperor. After showing the Panchen the chapel in the palace, the Emperor asked the Panchen to go back and take a good rest in the Temple of Sumeru Happiness and Longevity.

The *Imperial Records of the Qing Dynasty* has a brief account of the audience:

> On the *ding-you* day of the seventh month of the forty-fifth year of the Qianlong reign period, Panchen Erdeni came from Tsang and was received in audience by the Emperor in Yiqingkuang Hall. The Emperor granted him a seat, greetings and tea.

The next day (the twenty-second of the seventh month), the Sixth Panchen presented the Emperor many gifts for his birthday. These comprised a *Langzuo katag*, a silver *mandral*, a gold statue of Tsongkhapa, eight gold images of Sakyamuni, a set of satin cushions, one thousand taels of gold, a coral rosary, one thousand spirited horses, Tibetan incense, felt blankets, sugar, dried fruit, etc. The Emperor gave the Panchen the following gifts in return: a *Langzuo katag*, a gold *mandral* weighing thirty taels, a silver *mandral*, three images of Buddha, two sets of jade tea-cups, a set of gold Buddhist instruments, a gold box for Tibetan barley, a set of white jade tea-cups, ten glass bowls, a set of glass bottles and dishes, four glass pots, three table sets, five hundred taels of gold, twenty-nine bolts of satin in various colours, skins of otters, panthers and foxes, nine skins each, and one thousand lynx skins.

On the twenty-third day of the seventh month Emperor Gaozong paid a visit to the Sixth Panchen at the Temple of Sumeru Happiness and Longevity. The Emperor said in Tibetan:

"I sent my sixth son to welcome you. Was he attentive to you?"
"I am very grateful that the crown prince came to accompany me," replied the Panchen.

"When the Fifth Dalai came to pay respects to the court, my ancestor built the Yellow Temple for his residence," the Emperor continued. "Now I have built the Rehe Tashilhunpo Temple for you and I have studied Tibetan so that I could talk with you in Tibetan. But I can speak only a little of Tibetan. As to the Tibetan scriptures, I still have to ask Changkya Hutuktu to translate them for me."

After some time had passed, the Emperor went back to the Imperial Summer Resort.

On the twenty-sixth day of the seventh month the Panchen went to worship the Buddha and chant sutras at the Temple of the Potaraka Doctrine at Chengde. The temple, also called the Rehe Potala Palace, was built in the thirty-third year of the Qianlong reign period (1768) in the style of the Potala at Lhasa by Emperor Gaozong to commemorate his mother's eightieth birthday. When the temple had just been built, hundreds of thousands of Mongolian Turguts who had wandered in search of pastureland from Xinjiang to the lower reaches of the Volga River in the late Ming Dynasty, after extricating themselves from a fight spot Russian troops had backed them into, returned to their motherland. Also, the Qings had just suppressed the Dzungar rebellion in Xinjiang. The central government of the Qing Dynasty therefore had permitted the chieftain of the Turguts to pay his respects to the Emperor at Chengde. Wubashi, the Turgut chieftain, had at that time presented Emperor Gaozong the jade seal that was bestowed on his ancestor by the Emperor of the Ming Dynasty.

On the fourth day of the eighth month, Emperor Gaozong said in an edict to the Panchen that the Panchen was authorized to appoint the monk officials in charge of the Rehe Tashilhunpo Monastery, as it was built for his residence, and to set up the same institutions for it as those in the Tashilhunpo in Tsang. So the Panchen appointed Gangjian Shartse Lama Goching Lozang Dondrup as the *khenpo* of the temple, Danchingpa Goching Lozang Dorje as *woser* and Lozang Drashi as *gegu*, and left some twenty resident monks in the temple.

On the seventh day of the eighth month, the Panchen, together with the envoys from Korea, Mongol and Tibetan chieftains, and Manchu and Han ministers, celebrated Emperor Gaozong's seventieth birthday. The Panchen presented the Emperor eighty-one images of the Longevity Buddha as his birthday gift. The Emperor had yurts set up in the Garden of Ten Thousand Trees in the Imperial Summer Resort, where he

> held a banquet for the Panchen and his high-ranking attendant officials, Mongol chieftains, princes, *beiles*, *efus* and *tejis*, Durbat Prince Chelin Wubash, Turgut Beizi Salakoukeng, and Uygur Achim Bek and Beizi Setibardi, in addition to the three sons of Gezanachi Bek Aikar, a Kashgar official of the fourth rank, and Jialechan Langkang from the Muping Pacification Commissioner's Office in Jinchuan, and gave them official robes, gold and silver, silk and satin.

Another two banquets of the same scale were given to these people at the Juan-ah Garden in the Imperial Summer Resort (from the *Imperial Records of the Qing Dynasty*).

After the celebrations Emperor Gaozong was to hold sacrificial ceremonies at the East and West Imperial Mausoleums. By his order the Sixth Prince and the Sixth Panchen left Chengde for Beijing on the twenty-fourth day of the eighth month. They arrived at Beijing on the second day of the ninth month. There the Panchen Lama took up his residence at the Yellow Temple, where the Fifth Dalai Lama had lived.

During his stay at Beijing, the Panchen, accompanied by the prince, visited Yuanmingyuan Palace, the Zhao Temple on Fragrant Hill and the Deshou Temple at Nanyuan. He also gave sermons in Yonghegong Lamasery and other temples. On the ninth day of the ninth month Emperor Gaozong returned to Beijing and was greeted by the Panchen and princes and ministers. Emperor Gaozong paid a visit to the Panchen on the twenty-fifth day of the ninth month and held a banquet in honour of him at the Hall of Preserving Harmony in the Forbidden City on the first day of the tenth month. The *Imperial Records of the Qing Dynasty* has an account of the banquet:

> On the *wu-shen* day of the tenth month of the forty-fifth year of the Qianlong reign period, the Emperor held a banquet for Panchen Erdeni and others at the Hall of Preserving Harmony and granted them various gifts.

# 6. The Sixth Panchen Dies in Beijing

On the twenty-sixth day of the tenth month of that year, the Sixth Panchen fell ill in Beijing. When red spots appeared on his legs, his attendants, *solpons* and *khenpos* suspected them to be smallpox. They were very alarmed and told Changkya Hutuktu about the Panchen's illness. Meanwhile they spent 3,024 taels of silver on offering sacrifices, chanting sutras, praying and giving alms to the poor in Beijing. But the Panchen's health turned from bad to worse. The Emperor went and saw the Panchen on the twenty-ninth day of the tenth month, and then ordered his own physicians to treat the Panchen. The physicians diagnosed the illness as smallpox.

The Sixth Panchen Palden Yeshe died on the afternoon of the second day of the eleventh month of the forty-fifth year of Qing Emperor Gaozong's reign (1780) at the age of forty-two at the Yellow Temple in Beijing. The Tashilhunpo's Dzasa Lama, Drunpa Hutuktu, reported the Sixth Panchen Lama's death to Emperor Gaozong through Changkya Hutuktu. The Emperor sent the Sixth Prince and ministers to offer sacrifices to the Panchen. The Dzasa Lama immediately sent men back to Tibet to report the unfortunate news to the Eighth Dalai, the Regent and the Kashag, and to ask the Dalai to pray for the Panchen's early reincarnation. They spent altogether 93,178 taels of silver on giving alms and sweet buttered-tea to monks of all the great monasteries in Tibet, including the Three Major Monasteries at Lhasa.

The body of the Panchen was placed in the Yellow Temple for six days for the ministers and three thousand followers to offer sacrifices and pay their last respects. Then, after being treated with antiseptic, it was put into a stupa built of pure gold weighing seven thousand taels given by Emperor Gaozong.

After the Sixth Panchen had died, Emperor Gaozong issued an edict to Eighth Dalai Lama Jampel Gyatso:

Panchen Erdeni came to Beijing to celebrate my seventieth birthday. I sent ministers and commanders to give him a rosary and horses and hold banquets for him on the journey. I sent also the Sixth Prince and Changkya Hutuktu to welcome him. On the twenty-first day of the seventh month Panchen Erdeni arrived at Rehe. He led *hutuktus* to chant sutras for my birthday. He came to Beijing on the second day of the ninth month. I bestowed gifts upon him. He was happy to be received in audience by me. He did not say a word about going back to Tibet. He fell ill on the twenty-ninth day of the tenth month. I immediately sent physicians to treat him. His illness was diagnosed as smallpox. I went and saw him. He died on the second day of the eleventh month. I am sad at his death. It is a regret that he could not go back to Tibet as he had thought he could when he came to Beijing. I grant the Panchen's elder brother Drotpa Tsonkpa Hutuktu the title of Erdemtu Nomihan, and his younger brother Dasuipeng the post of Dzasa Lama and the title of Morgen Khenpo. When the funeral ceremony of chanting sutras for one hundred days is accomplished on the thirteenth day of the second month, his coffin will start off. The minister of the Board for National Minority Affairs, Bo Qing'e, and the Guard of Qianqing Gate, Yiluletu, and others will be sent to escort it to Tashilhunpo Monastery. Now Tashilhunpo Monastery is put under your administration for the time being. I hope you will understand my feelings and train the Tashilhunpo's monks well. This is also a philanthropic act (see the *Imperial Records of the Qing Dynasty*).

On the thirteenth day of the second month of the forty-sixth year of the Qianlong reign period (1781), all attendants of the Sixth Panchen left Beijing for the Tashilhunpo, escorting the Panchen's stupa by the same way as they came. Bo Qing'e and other envoys from the Emperor also escorted the stupa to the Tashilhunpo.

The escort party with the stupa reached the Tongtian River on the sixteenth day of the sixth month and met Kalon Tonpa and other officials sent by the Eighth Dalai, the Regent and the Kashag. On the third day of the eighth month they arrived at Dam in the north of Tibet, where the Regent, Amban Heng Rui and Kalon Dorkhawa came to offer sacrifices. The gold stupa was carried from Dam to Tsang. It arrived at Tashilhunpo Monastery on the twenty-first day of the eighth month and was placed at Tsejia Hall. A large silver stupa was built to contain it. After offering sacrifices to the stupa, Bo Qing'e, who came from Beijing to escort it, went to Lhasa. Drungpa Hutuktu, on behalf of Tashilhunpo Monastery, presented a memorial to express gratitude to the Emperor through Bo Qing'e.

To commemorate the Sixth Panchen, Emperor Gaozong had a temple built to the west of the Yellow Temple in the forty-ninth year of the Qianlong reign period (1784), four years after the death of the Panchen. The temple contained a magnificent pagoda, called the Pagoda of Purification. People called this temple the West Yellow Temple and the former one the East Yellow Temple.

The following is an inscription Emperor Gaozong wrote for the pagoda:

> On the *ding-you* day of the seventh month of the *geng-zi* year (1780), the Holy Monk Panchen Erdeni came from Tsang, travelling twenty thousand *li* to pay respects to me. I had the Rehe Tashilhunpo Temple built in the Imperial Summer Resort for his residence. After he had spent a month there he was escorted to Beijing, where he lived in the Yellow Temple. On the *bing-zi* day of the eleventh month he died there. On the *bing-chen* day of the second month of the *xin-chou* year (1781), his remains were escorted back to Tsang. It was a hundred days from his coming for an audience with me to his death, and another hundred days from his death to his relics being escorted back to Tibet. The reasons for his coming and going are too mysterious to know. I ordered to have the Pagoda of Purification built to the west of the Yellow Temple to contain his clothes and shoes.

The East Yellow Temple has now long been reduced to ruins. On its site are office and apartment buildings. But the West Yellow Temple still exists. In particular, the Pagoda of Purification has been well kept as an important cultural relic for protection by Beijing Municipality. The tablet with Qing Emperor Gaozong's inscription in Han, Manchu, Mongolian and Tibetan scripts is kept in the temple. It is a symbol of the friendship of all nationalities in China.

# Chapter Five
# Tenpai Nyima, the Seventh Panchen Lama

## 1. The Enthronement of the Seventh Panchen

The Seventh Panchen (1782-1853), given the religious name Tenpai Nyima, was born on the eighth day of the fourth month of the Water-Tiger year in the thirteenth Tibetan calendrical cycle (the forty-seventh year of the Qianlong reign period, or 1782). His father was called Palden Dondrup and his mother Jigme Jiamu. His was a minor aristocratic family in Jishong Shika of Bainang Dzong in Tsang. Four candidate soul boys of the Sixth Panchen were found. The *Solpon Khenpo* sent by the Tashilhunpo abbot conducted a secret investigation of the four boys' families. He placed in front of the boys a number of articles, among which were some teacups, bells, rosaries, etc., that had been used by the Sixth Panchen, for them to pick. This was one of the examinations. It was said that only the boy from Bainang Dzong picked out the objects of the Sixth Panchen. So the *Solpon Khenpo* confirmed that he was the reincarnation of the Sixth Panchen.

The *Solpon Khenpo* then made a report to the Dzasa Lama and other chief monk-officials of the Tashilhunpo. The Dzasa Lama decided to ask Lhamo Chosgyong, a professional oracle, for divine revelation of information on this candidate soul boy. He also sent men to report to the Eighth Dalai Lama. The answer given by the divine revelation was said to support the instructions of the Eighth Dalai. Both said that the boy of Bainang Dzong was the reincarnation of the Sixth Panchen.

So the abbot of the Tashilhunpo asked through Amban Bo Qing'e for the Emperor's approval. On the twentieth day of the twelfth month of that year (1782), the Emperor approved the confirmation of the reincarnation and bestowed a *katag* and a precious-stone rosary on the boy. Amban Bo Qing'e read the imperial edict to the Tashilhunpo monk and lay officials and passed to them the gifts from the Emperor. Thus, the procedure of confirmation of the Seventh Panchen Lama was completed.

On the fifth day of the eighth month of the forty-eighth year of the Qianlong reign period (1783), the several hundred monk and lay officials of the Tashilhunpo went to Jishong Shika of Bainang Dzong to invite the Panchen reincarnate to Ganden Leshad Chol-ing Monastery, thirty *li* south of the Tashilhunpo, to take up temporary residence. Then they chose an auspicious day for the Seventh Panchen's enthronement in the Tashilhunpo. The Eighth Dalai Lama sent Darhan Shalu Khensu as his representative to attend the enthronement.

According to the Tibetan-language biography of Seventh Panch-en Tenpai Nyima, Warren Hastings, British governor in India, sent Turner, a British officer aged thirty-three, to salute the Seventh Panchen on his enthronement at the Tashilhunpo.

Francis Younghusband also has an account of Turner's visit to the Tashilhunpo in his *India and Tibet*:

> Turner himself was very favourably received at Shigatse, and at his first interview informed the Regent [here a reference to the Tashilhunpo Dzasa Lama Drungpa Hutuktu] that Warren Hastings had an earnest solicitude to preserve and cultivate the amicable intercourse that had so happily commenced between them.... To this the Regent replied that the present and the late Tashi Lama were one and the same, and that there was no manner of difference between them, only that, as he was yet merely an infant, and his spirit had just returned to the human world, he was at present incapable of action....

Turner spent "nearly a year" in Shigatse. He felt "the power and influence of these Chinese officials in Tibet was evidently very great...." And though he was unable to visit Lhasa owing to the antipathy of the lamas,

> he was able to obtain some substantial concessions from the Regent of the Tashi Lama at Shigatse. He obtained his promise of encouragement

to all merchants, natives of India, that may be sent to traffic in Tibet, on behalf of the Government of Bengal.

Turner returned to India in March 1784. Hastings expressed enthusiastic appreciation of Turner's work in Tibet.

On the eleventh day of the eighth month of the forty-ninth year of Emperor Gaozong's reign (1784), the chief monk and lay officials of the Tashilhunpo went to the Ganden Leshad Choling and invited the Panchen Lama reincarnate to reside in the Tashilhunpo's Yige Chungchen Hall. The next day was chosen as the auspicious day for the Seventh Panchen's enthronement. The ceremony was presided over by Amban Bo Qing'e in the Tashilhunpo's Sunlight Hall.

Qing Emperor Gaozong sent envoys Dzasa Lama Gomang Hutuktu and Yidashing Ali to witness the ceremony and give to the Seventh Panchen a *katag* and a *ru-yi* (a double-curved scepter), in addition to a stone rosary, Buddhist ceremonial objects, glass articles, silk and satin and other gifts.

Later the imperial envoys, Dzasa Kalon Tunshe Wangdu, on behalf of the Eighth Dalai, presented to the Panchen a *katag*, a *mandral*, a picture of old pines (a symbol of longevity), a suit of monastic robes and a set of religious objects. The Regent, Kalons and the monk and lay officials of the Tashilhunpo also presented gifts to the Seventh Panchen. Afterwards, a celebration was held in Tashilhunpo's Sunlight Hall.

Eighth Dalai Lama Jampel Gyatso came to the Tashilhunpo Monastery on the twenty-first day of the eighth month. He was warmly greeted by the Tashilhunpo monks. The Eighth Dalai met with the Seventh Panchen in the Sunlight Hall. The Seventh Panchen kowtowed to the Eighth Dalai and acknowledged him as his tutor. Thus the tutor-disciple relationship was officially established between them. The Dalai resided with the Panchen at the Great Lharang in the Tashilhunpo for the time being.

The tonsure and name-giving ceremony was held in the Tashilhunpo's Yige Chungchen Hall on the seventh day of the ninth month. The Eighth Dalai presided over the ceremony. After chanting sutras, the Dalai shaved the Panchen's hair, put on him a monk robe and gave him the religious name of Jetsun Lozang Palden Tenpai Nyima Chole Namgyal Palzangpo (Tenpai Nyima for short).

The Dalai taught the Panchen commandments against sins. The Eighth Dalai left for Lhasa via Gyantse on the first day of the tenth month.

According to the Tibetan-language biography of Tenpai Nyima, in the first month of the fiftieth year of the Qianlong regin period (1785), the British governor in India sent Atsarsur Gandhi (probably an Indian) to attend the Seventh Panchen Lama's enthronement ceremony at Shigatse.

The *Imperial Records of the Qing Dynasty* has an account of the enthronement as follows:

> On the *ding-you* day of the first month of the forty-ninth year of Emperor Gaozong's reign [1784], the Emperor instructed: "I had intended to send men to take gifts to the Panchen Erdeni reincarnate, as I was originally notified that his residence would be moved to Tashilhunpo Monastery on the fourth day of the sixth month of this year at the invitation of Drungpa Hutuktu. But now Bo Qing'e has reported to me that Drungpa Hutuktu and Solpon Khenpo asked me for approval of the postponement of his moving to the Tashilhunpo to the thirteenth day of the eighth month, an auspicious day, as they said, chosen by the Dalai Lama. I found it feasible. The former Panchen Erdeni had devoted himself to the development of the Yellow sect and enjoyed my benevolence. He was immediately reincarnated. The day chosen by the Dalai is also my birthday. So it is an auspicious day. I approve their request. The envoys will be sent at that time. This edict will be issued to the Dalai and be made known to Drungpa Hutuktu and Solpon Khenpo.

The Emperor granted the Seventh Panchen's father the title of duke in the first month of the fifty-third year of the Qianlong reign period (1788) and an official cap of high rank.

The first half of the Seventh Panchen's life was the time when the Qing's rule over Tibet reached its zenith. It was in that time that the *Twenty-nine-Article Ordinance for More Effective Governing of Tibet* and important features of Tibet's political and religious systems were produced. Thus, when the Gurkhas invaded Tibet and Tashilhunpo Monastery was ransacked by the invaders, the Qing government was able to send troops into Tibet. The Qing force drove all the Gurkha invaders out of Tibet.

# 2. The Gurkhas Invade Tibet Twice

The Gurkhas invaded Tibet twice. The first invasion was from the fifty-third year to the fifty-fourth year of the Qianlong reign (1788-1789), and the second from the fifty-sixth year to the fifty-seventh year of that reign (1791-1792). The two wars lasted a total of five years.

The land of the Gurkha was originally called Balebu. After the Gurkha tribe unified and gained control of the Balebu kingdom, the kingdom was renamed Gurkha. The chieftain, Ratna Bahadur, claimed himself to be the king. On the pretext that a Tibetan local official laid a duty on goods imported from Gurkha, the Gurkha king dispatched a force of two thousand men to invade Tsang. The invaders occupied Kyirong, Nyelam and Dzongga, and surrounded Shegar. The Qing Emperor, upon the urgent request of Eighth Dalai Lama Jampel Gyatso and Amban Qinglin for troops to be sent to Tibet, dispatched three thousand Manchu and Han Chinese troops to Tibet under the joint command of Bazhong, Vice-Minister of the Board for National Minority Affairs, Cheng De, the Sichuan Governor-General, and General Ehui of Chengdu.

But Bazhong and his party acted in an irresponsible way after they arrived in Tibet. They sent Kalon Tenzin Paljor to negotiate peace with the Gurkhas. It was secretly agreed that the Gurkhas should leave the territories they had occupied and they were to be guaranteed with a payment of three hundred silver ingots (weighing 9,600 taels) each year. In a report to Emperor Gaozong, Bazhong and his party said: "Nyelam, Dzongga and Kyirong have been recovered successively." He then asked to be allowed to "return with the victorious troops."

The Dalai Lama did not give his consent to the compensation. Later, in a memorial to the Emperor, Fu Kang'an said:

> When Bazhong reached Tibet, the Dalai Lama suggested to him that the invaders should be wiped out. But Bazhong secretly purchased peace by giving silver to the Gurkhas without the Dalai's consent. The Dalai said the problem was settled so abruptly and unreasonably that it would come back again. Obviously, the Dalai was keeping in mind the overall interests. It is Bazhong and Tenzin Paljor who should be responsible for the mistakes.

When the Gurkhas invaded Tsang for the first time in the fifty-third year of Emperor Gaozong's reign (1788), the Seventh Panchen was six years old. He was at the age to take *getsul* vows. Amban Qinglin went to the Tashilhunpo on the twenty-eighth day of the seventh month to invite the Seventh Panchen to Lhasa to take his *getsul* vows before the Eighth Dalai and to take refuge there. The Seventh Panchen arrived at Lhasa on the eleventh day of the eighth month. The Panchen met with the Dalai at Norbulingka, the Dalai's Summer Palace, and resided in the Kelzang Phodrang Mansion there. On the third day of the ninth month, the Eighth Dalai and the Seventh Panchen moved from Norbulingka to the Potala to make preparations for the *getsul*-vow ceremony, especially for the Seventh Panchen's studying of scriptures under the guidance of the Eighth Dalai.

The Eighth Dalai and the Seventh Panchen went to Jokhang Temple on the fourth day of the sixth month of the fifty-fourth year of the Qianlong reign period (1789). The Seventh Panchen took his *getsul* vows from the Eighth Dalai in front of the image of Sakyamuni. After the ceremony they went back to the Potala. The Seventh Panchen then lived in the Potala for about two years.

In the eighth month of the fifty-fourth year of the Qianlong reign period, "the Dalai Lama and Panchen Erdeni sent *khenpos* to Beijing to express thanks to the court for calming down the Balebu Incident," and "Balebu chieftains Balabadur Khawas and Halisaye and other men, twenty-three in all, arrived at the Tashilhunpo on the fifteenth day of the seventh month... to accompany them to Beijing." (Cited from *Imperial Records of the Qing Dynasty*.)

Superficially, the conflicts between Tibet and Gurkha had come to an end. So the Amban permitted the Seventh Panchen to return to the Tashilhunpo on the eleventh day of the second month of the fifty-fifth year of the Qianlong reign period (1790). The Seventh Panchen bid farewell to the Eighth Dalai Lama, the Regent and the Amban. He arrived at the Tashilhunpo on the twenty-third day of the second month.

In the fifty-sixth year of the Qianlong reign period (1791), when the Gurkhas asked Tibet to honour the compensation agreement, that is, to give the three hundred silver ingots, the Tibetan local government refused. This triggered the second invasion of the

Gurkhas, who occupied many places of Tsang as far as the Tashil-hunpo. As they were advancing towards the Tashilhunpo, Amban Baotai, alarmed, hurriedly moved the Seventh Panchen Tenpai Nyima from the Tashilhunpo to Lhasa. He thereby narrowly escaped being captured.

At that time the Eighth Dalai's brother Lozang Gedun Drakpa happened to be in Beijing. Emperor Gaozong was informed by him of the bribed peace and the compensation agreement made by Bazhong. When Bazhong, who was then keeping the Emperor company in the Imperial Summer Resort at Chengde, learnt about it, he committed suicide by drowning himself in the lake. The Emperor said that if he had been alive, certainly he should have been executed.

What really brought about the second invasion was the unequal division of the deceased Sixth Panchen's inheritance. The former Panchen had several brothers. One was Drungpa Hutuktu, the Dzasa Lama of the Tashilhunpo, who was in charge of the Tashil-hunpo during the Panchen's absence. Another, Shamarpa, was the tenth Red Hat Living Buddha of the Karma Kagyu sect, whose religious name was Chosdrak Gyatso (1738-1791).

During his journey from Tibet via Qinghai and Inner Mongolia to the Imperial Summer Resort at Chengde and his stay in Beijing in the forty-second to forty-third year of the Qianlong reign period (1777-1778), the Sixth Panchen received innumerable gifts and offerings of gold, silver and cattle from Mongolian and Tibetan chieftains and the masses, aristocrats and high-ranking officials. When he died in Beijing, the gifts were carried back to the Tashilhunpo by Drungpa Hutuktu, who took possession of the gold, silver and all the valuables, leaving only a part of the cattle to the Tashilhunpo. But Shamarpa was not entitled to any share of the wealth, because he was of a different religious sect. Embittered, he went to Katmandu secretly in 1784 and informed the Gurkha ruler that, as Tibet had been drained of its military strength and Tashilhunpo Monastery, which possessed enormous wealth, was defenseless, it was the best time for them to take possession of the wealth in the monastery (see *Imperial Records of the Qing Dynasty*).

In their first invasion of Tibet in 1788, the Gurkhas found that the Tibetans were incapable of effectively guarding against invasion. The bribed peace made by Bazhong only encouraged the Gurkhas' intention to loot Tashilhunpo Monastery.

When the Gurkhas were marching on the Tashilhunpo in their second invasion in 1791, Drungpa Hutuktu fled with his valuables, and Amban Baotai, on the sixteenth day of the eighth month, moved the Seventh Panchen from the Tashilhunpo to Lhasa. The monks and lay inhabitants, who were frightened by a divine oracle obtained by the Tashilhunpo's Jetsun Lama and *dratsang khenpos*, who warned against any resistance against the invaders, had scattered about and gone into hiding. The only resistance came from eighty Han garrison troops under the command of Dusi Xu Nanpeng (*dusi*, "major"), who held out in the Shigatse fort.

On the twentieth of the eighth month, one thousand Gurkha troops reached Shigatse. After occupying the Tashilhunpo they began to attack the Shigatse fort, but were defeated by Xu Nanpeng and his men, who killed one enemy officer and a dozen soldiers. Being unable to seize the fort, the Gurkhas pulled back to Nyelam and other places on the Tibetan-Nepalese border.

Resident officials Baotai and Yamantai, panic-stricken by the Gurkha invasion, reported in a memorial to the Emperor that they would move the Dalai Lama and Panchen Erdeni to Taining. Emperor Gaozong criticized them with the following instructions:

> Baotai and Yamantai were so frightened by the invasion that they lost their senses. They proved themselves to be useless. Fortunately, the Dalai Lama did not listen to them. It would be disgraceful if Dalai fled from the Potala.... Baotai and Yamantai were too weak to be worthy of my trust. For the time being Baotai and Yamantai shall be removed from office. They should atone for their mistakes.

Upon reports of invasion, the Emperor ordered Ehui, General of Chengdu, and Governor-General Cheng De of Sichuan to lead troops into Tibet. But the two officials acted slowly, "going only a station each day," and so they "lost the opportunity to wipe out the Gurkhas." On the Emperor's order, Ehui and Cheng De were sacked for their inaction—though they were kept in the force, they were both reduced to the post of a petty officer under the command of Shu Lian and Fu Kang'an respectively (see *Imperial Records of the Qing Dynasty*).

After punishing Ehui and Cheng De, the Emperor dispatched a

crack army of one hundred officers and one thousand Solong and
Dahur soldiers from Heilongjiang into Tibet by way of Xining and '
the Qinghai grasslands. He appointed Fu Kang'an as General-in-
Chief and Hai Lancha the Grand Minister Consultant. They all were
ordered to reach Lhasa within forty days. Sun Shiyi, Governor-
General of Sichuan, was assigned by the Emperor the task of
collecting and transporting food supplies for the logistical support
of the troops.

When they arrived at Lhasa, Fu Kang'an and Hai Lancha consulted with the Dalai, the Panchen and the Kalons. With its 17,000
troops, 70,000 *dan* (piculs) of grain, over 10,000 head of cattle and
sheep and 5,000,000 taels of silver for soldier's pay and provisions,
the Qing army was dominant over the Gurkha invaders, who
numbered only 4,000 or 5,000 in all. By the order of the Emperor,
Fu Kang'an and Hai Lancha were not to grant the Gurkhas peace
until they marched into Yambu (Katmandu) after driving the
Gurkha invaders out of Tibet.

So Fu Kang'an and Hai Lancha recovered Nyelam, Kyirong and
Dzongga in the fifth month of the fifty-seventh year of the
Qianlong reign period (1792). By that time all the Gurkha invaders
had been driven out of Tibet. In the seventh month of that year,
after the Qing troops had marched over seven hundred *li* into
Gurkha territory and were only twenty *li* from Yambu, the Gurkha
ruler, Ratna Bahadur, released Wang Gang, a Han soldier, and
Kalon Tenzin Paljor and other prisoners of war and sent a chieftain
to ask the Qing troops to halt their advance. Besides, the Gurkha
ruler returned his certification of the bribed peace agreement as
well as the Tashilhunpo treasures (including the gold album granted to the Sixth Panchen by Qing Emperor Gaozong) they had
looted. Since Shamarpa had committed suicide by taking poison,
his body and his family were placed at the Qing army's disposal.
Because of the Emperor's instruction that the army had to be
withdrawn before heavy snows set in, Fu Kang'an granted the
Gurkha ruler's appeal for peace. According to Fu's demand, the
Gurkha ruler pledged never to invade Tibet again in a written
statement and sent his chieftain Kache Dewu and Dat Tabar and
others to Beijing to offer a humble apology and to pay a tribute.

The tribute included thirteen musicians, five tamed elephants, five spirited horses with saddles, three pairs of peacocks, an Indian open palanquin, a palanquin, a pearl ornament (made of sixty-four pearls, a precious stone, eight pieces of emerald, a diamond and fourteen red beads), five large coral beads, a string of 108 coral beads, a string of 152 coral beads, fifty bolts of satin—among which five were embroidered with golden thread, five with silver thread and the rest were in various colours—fifteen bolts of woolen cloth, five bolts of felt cloth, ten elephant tusks, six rhinoceros horns, two bundles of peacock tail feathers, ten Gurkha guns, eight Gurkha knives (five gold-plated and three silver-plated), five scimitars, two bottles of perfume, four baskets of betel nuts, ten boxes of cloves, and a box of round cardamon.

Emperor Gaozong ordered that the thirteen musicians should be brought to Beijing before the Spring Festival of the fifty-eighth year of his reign (1793) to play at the festival banquets for envoys from various kingdoms. Of the five tamed elephants, one was given by the Emperor to the Dalai Lama, one to the Panchen Erdeni and the remaining three, together with the other objects, were brought to Beijing via the Qinghai grasslands.

By now the newly-appointed Amban Helin had arrived at Lhasa. In view of the victory over the Gurkha invaders, he suggested to the Emperor that the Panchen be moved back to the Tashilhunpo. With the Emperor's approval, the Seventh Panchen left Lhasa on the ninth day of the tenth month of the fifty-seventh year of the Qianlong reign period (1792) and arrived at the Tashilhunpo on the twenty-first day of the same month.

On the twenty-fourth day of the tenth month, Fu Kang'an, en route from the front, met with the Panchen at the Tashilhunpo's Sunlight Hall. They exchanged *katags*. The Seventh Panchen gave numerous gifts to Fu Kang'an to express his thanks for the recovery of all the lost territory.

In his memorial to the Emperor, Fu Kang'an had a vivid description of the interview. He said:

> When I learnt on my way back that the Panchen Erdeni had returned to Tashilhunpo Monastery, I sent men to offer my greetings to him. Before that, the Panchen had sent his *khenpo* with food and greetings to me, and I gave him gifts in return.... When I brought the victorious troops back, the Panchen had intended to go out to await my arrival,

but I declined with thanks, saying that I really did not deserve that.... I reached Shigatse on the fifth day of the tenth month.... I met with him at the Great Prayer Hall on the fifth day after my arrival and exchanged *katags* with him.... The Panchen Erdeni is very wise, though he is only eleven years old. With nobody speaking for him in our conversation, he talked to me just like an adult.... On the following day when I left Shigatse, the Panchen Erdeni had a tent set up ten *li* away from the Tashilhunpo and waited there to see me off. As soon as I appeared before him, he kowtowed and respectfully offered his good wishes to Your Majesty. He made a present of a Longevity Buddha's image and a large *katag* to Your Majesty. We praised him for his grateful feelings to Your Majesty and his courtesy. Then I sent Batulu and a number of my guards to escort him back to the Tashilhunpo. The Panchen Erdeni has always put his hands together in front of his breast and bowed to the upper direction to pay respects to Your Majesty, but this time he kowtowed to express his deep gratitude to Your Majesty for protecting the Yellow Hat sect. So we did not stop him from kowtowing to the gold album granted by Your Majesty and to pay respects to Your Majesty (from *A General History of U-Tsang*).

After leaving Tashilhunpo Monastery, Fu Kang'an arrived at Lhasa on the fifteenth day of the tenth month of the fifty-seventh year of the Qianlong reign period (1792). He was greeted by the Eighth Dalai himself over ten *li* from Lhasa. This had never happened before. In a memorial to the Emperor, Fu Kang'an reported:

When we left Shigatse on the sixth day of this month, we sent men to offer our greetings to the Dalai Lama. By this time the Dalai had already sent his Khenpo Lama to meet us on the way. The *khenpo* said that the Dalai Lama, in order to express his gratitude to Your Majesty for protecting the Tibetans, had been waiting to greet the victorious army at Jamchen Rabten Monastery over ten *li* from the Potala. I sent men to persuade him to go back, but the Dalai insisted on waiting to greet us. We arrived at Lhasa on the fifteenth day of the month and met with the Dalai at Jamchen Rabten Monastery and had an hour's talk with him. He sincerely expressed the gratitude he felt for Your Majesty. As to the important articles of the ordinance, I only told a little about them to the Dalai. Since the Dalai Lama is grateful to Your Majesty for what you have done for Tibet and is absolutely obedient to us, he is expected to respect the ordinance and will not disagree with us.

In the process of dealing with the incident of the Gurkhas'

invasion, Gaozong created a profound impression that he was strict and fair in meting out rewards and punishment. The following are some important examples:

(1) The former Ambans Pu Fu, Fu Xihun (or Baotai, who was renamed by the order of the Emperor), and Yamantai and the Chengdu General, Ehui, were put in fetters before the public for their dereliction of duty. The Emperor instructed:

> I am informed today [the fourteenth of the eighth month] by Sun Shiyi that the Gurkhas had sent men to Pu Fu and requested him to give them the territory of Fenglu. [This happened before the second Gurkha invasion, but it had not been reported to the Emperor until it was found out by Sun Shiyi.] Pu Fu refused the request. He then told Yamantai about it and Yamantai made it known to Fu Xihun. But none of them reported it to me. If they did, I should have praised them and taken proper measures against the Gurkhas beforehand. When he came to Beijing, Pu Fu did not say a word about it to the Grand Ministers of State. This is unimaginable. I cannot forgive them, for they did not inform me of such an important matter happening on the borderland. I order that Pu Fu be deposed and tried by the Ministry of Punishments. As to Fu Xihun and Yamantai, they should have sent in a memorial about the fact after they had learnt of it. I can not imagine why they were so dull in mind. I order that they each be given forty blows with a cane and be put under Sun Shiyi's supervision.

In the fifty-fifth year of the Qianlong reign period (1790), Ehui did not report to the Emperor that the Gurkhas had sent an official letter and tribute to the imperial court. When Fu Kang'an inquired of him about it, Ehui could not but confess the fact. Fu Kang'an asked for the Emperor's permission to send Ehui, Yamantai and Fu Xihun under escort to Beijing to be punished by the Council of State. But the Emperor did not agree. Instead, he ordered that, if they were on the way to Beijing, the three be sent back to Tibet and there be imprisoned by Amban Helin. It was not until the fifty-eighth year of the Qianlong reign period (1793), when the Gurkha invaders had been driven out of Tibet, that the three prisoners were permitted to be sent back to Beijing. Ehui and Yamantai had only been too timid in that matter, the Emperor pointed out, and thus were forgivable. They were to be punished by being demoted to lower official ranks. But Fu Xihun, the

Emperor said, was so dull in mind that he even intended to give the whole of Tibet to the invaders. Because of his serious crime, Fu Xihun should be executed. However, considering his grandfather's merits, the Emperor said, he would be punished with exile to Heilongjiang.

(2) Kalon Sonam Wangyal was punished because he had conspired with Amban Qinglin in Qinglin's decision not to report the fact that the Gurkhas had sent a memorial and tribute to the Emperor. When the news reached Lhasa that Amban Qinglin had been removed from office and had had a severe punishment meted out to him for the crime, Sonam Wangyal committed suicide, taking poison to escape punishment.

The Emperor ordered that Sonam Wangyal be punished by a posthumous confiscation of his property and revocation of his title of Dzasa Teji. Sonam Wangyal was the prime culprit, the Emperor pointed out, and his crime was more serious than that of Tenzin Paljor, so his descendants should not be allowed to inherit the title. The Emperor ordered Fu Kang'an to confiscate Sonam Wangyal's property and turn it over to the Kashag, directing that the confiscated property of Sonam Wangyal and Shamarpa should be used to support financially the three thousand newly-recruited Tibetan soldiers.

(3) The Emperor punished Shamarpa heavily for his illicit relations with the Gurkhas, terminating the succession of reincarnation of the Red Hat Living Buddha and confiscating his property.

On the eighth day of the seventh month of the fifty-seventh year of Emperor Gaozong's reign (1792), in a letter to Fu Kang'an, the surrendering Gurkha ruler, Ratna Bahadur, said:

Shamarpa was a bad man sowing discord. If he were alive, he should be executed. But he has gone to the nether world. His body was cremated after being shown to the Kalon and the Han soldiers. We shall send you his body, together with his disciples, servants and property.

By order of Emperor Gaozong, Amban Helin went to Yangpachen, where Shamarpa's monastery was located, to confiscate Shamarpa's property and arrest his steward, Yeshe Jamchen, on the eighth day of the eighth month. Helin reported in a memorial:

Shamarpa had been away from his home for a long time. He left over one hundred monks of the monastery of the Red Hat line, cattle and sheep, villages and residents to the care of the steward. His property consisted of large amounts of silk and satin, cloth, precious stones, coral, silver, gold and metal articles, 20 silver ingots amounting to 1,500 taels of silver, 3,842 silver coins equal to 480 taels of silver, 2.4 taels of gold ore, women's adornments.... Besides, he has the gilded copper seal granted to the Initiation State Tutor by the Yuan Dynasty. It should be sent to the ministry and destroyed. There is also a suit of clothes, on which images of the Buddha and some Tibetan words have appeared naturally, said to have been worn in ancient times by a monk practising Buddhism in a mountain cave. According to Tibetans, it would be good to worship it in front of a statue of the Buddha. It is so rare that I send it in a small wooden box with my memorial to Your Majesty.... As to the steward, I shall send him and Punte Dondrup under escort to Beijing.

On the fourteenth day of the eighth month, Helin reported to the Emperor:

The Red Hat line is Lamaism's heterodoxy.... Shamarpa is the chief culprit. The succession by Shamarpa's reincarnation as the Red Hat Living Buddha should be terminated.... The 103 Red Hat Lamaist monks of Shamarpa's monastery should be forcibly converted to the Yellow sect faith and placed under the authority of the main monasteries in the U region. As to his property, I think it is good to confiscate it. His villages and fields should be put in the charge of another Tibetan chief, who will be responsible to collect grain taxes (over 2,300 taels of silver a year) and hand in the taxes to the Kalons. Besides, I ask Your Majesty for the favour of giving Shamarpa's two monasteries, a big one with 1,135 rooms (including 357 in the monks' quarters) at Yangpachen, and a small one with only three rooms at the foot of the hill, as well as the 271 Tibetan residents on the estates in the possession of his monastery, as rewards to Kyirong Hutuktu.

All these suggestions were approved by the Emperor. Again, Helin reported:

Shamarpa's property has been sold for over 64,000 taels of silver. The yearly grain tax collected from the estates is over 7,100 taels of silver. By Your Majesty's order, I have given them to the Dalai Lama as the financial support to the Tibetan army under *rupons* and *gyapons*.

Obviously, the Emperor severely punished Shamarpa, the chief culprit, for his illicit relations with the Gurkhas, not taking into consideration that he was the Sixth Panchen's brother.

(4) Drungpa Hutuktu, who instead of defending the monastery fled with any portable valuables when the Gurkhas were approaching the Tashilhunpo, was sent by order of the Emperor to Beijing. For the serious crime he committed, he should have been executed. But, considering that he was the Sixth Panchen's brother, the Emperor forgave him and had him settled in the temple where the Sixth Panchen Erdeni had lived in Beijing.

(5) The Jedrung Lama, who with the alleged oracular warning against resistance caused the monks to flee in panic, leaving the monastery wide open to the plunderers, was brought to U, defrocked and executed by order of the Emperor. Of the other five Khenpo lamas who had assisted the Jedrung Lama in committing the crime, Lozang Tenpa was executed and the rest were sent to Beijing for punishment.

(6) The gold album Emperor Gaozong had granted to the Sixth Panchen had been stolen, but was later returned by the plunderers. The Emperor was angry that the Eighth Dalai and the Seventh Panchen did not keep the album safe in Tashilhunpo Monastery. He said that the Dalai and Panchen should have been punished. Considering their young age, however, the Emperor forgave them. The album, after being returned by the plunderers, was given by order of the Emperor to the Panchen again to be kept well in the monastery.

Fu Kang'an suggested that the property of the Tashilhunpo returned by the plunderers should go to the Qing army, but his suggestion was turned down by the Emperor. By the Emperor's order, the returned property was given back to the Tashilhunpo to show the Emperor's concern for the Panchen, although only one-tenth of the Tashilhunpo's property was recovered and returned by the plunderers.

On the other hand, Emperor Gaozong gave rewards or posthumous compensations to those who had earned merit or died in action in the war against the invasion.

(1) Large rewards were given to Fu Kang'an and Hai Lancha for their great military merits and to Sun Shiyi for his rear service. Fu Kang'an was promoted to the post of Grand Secretary and concurrently Minister of Personnel. Sun Shiyi was appointed Grand

Secretary and concurrently Minister of Rites. Hai Lancha was promoted from *gong* (duke) of the second grade to the first grade. Besides, Fu Kang'an was granted a title of general that could be inherited by his descendants and an honorific title for his bravery on the battlefield.

(2) Amban Helin and other meritorious officials were also rewarded. Helin was promoted from Vice-Minister of War to Minister of Works and his title of general was to be inherited by his son. Officers such as Zhang Zhankui, Hu Shangxian, Shi Ge, Zhang Zhilin and Xu Nanpeng were promoted to higher-ranking posts.

(3) To those who died on the battlefield, different forms of consolation and pension were afforded according to their merits.

# 3. The Twenty-Nine-Article Ordinance of the Qing Government and the Institution of the "Drawing of Lots from the Golden Urn"

For more effective governing of Tibet after the war, Qing Emperor Gaozong ordered Fu Kang'an, commander of the expeditionary army, to lay down a proper ordinance for Tibet to abide by at all times. So, returning to Lhasa after defeating the Gurkhas, Fu Kang'an, Sun Shiyi, Helin and Hui Ling, together with relevant Tibetan dignitaries, lay and monk, began to work out the ordinance. Their efforts, which had the support of the Eighth Dalai and the Seventh Panchen, resulted in the production of the "Twenty-Nine-Article Imperial Ordinance." For the following two hundred years, the ordinance became the basic law for the Qing court in its rule over Tibet. This was another achievement of the Qing court's administration of Tibet.

My book *The Biographies of the Dalai Lamas* has already cited the "Twenty-Nine-Article Imperial Ordinance" from Tibetan documents, so here I would like only to make a detailed record of the "Institution of the Golden Urn" established by Emperor Gaozong.

The "Institution of the Golden Urn," or more completely, the "Drawing of Lots from the Golden Urn During the Reincarnation

Ceremony," was an important innovation of the Qing court in the Tibetan religious system. The innovation was caused by Shamarpa's treason. The instance that the Sixth Panchen, Drungpa Hutuktu and Shamarpa were all born of the same family showed Emperor Gaozong there was malpractice in the way of deciding the reincarnation by way of Lamo's oracle. So the Emperor decided on the "Institution of the Golden Urn."

In an edict dated the *ren-zi* day in the eleventh month of the fifty-seventh year of Emperor Gaozong's reign, the Emperor said to the Grand Ministers of State:

> According to a long-standing practice in Tibet, whenever a reincarnation is to be found, Lamo Chosgyong is first asked to invoke his oracle god to point out the locality and family where he may be found. More than one candidate is pointed out on such occasions. The searching parties then record the date of birth for each candidate they find with the full names of his father and mother and ask Lamo Chosgyong once more to invoke the divinity for revelation in identifying the true reincarnation. This has been the practice of long standing. But I think it is absurd and can not be trusted. Lamo Chosgyong was often bribed to give "divine" advice, and he has fooled the Tibetans into believing it. Lamo Chosgyong in Tibet is similar to the witches of the hinterlands. Both of them fool people with magic. Since the Chosgyongs are allegedly immune even to sword cuts once they go into a trance, let each of them be asked to prove in turn how true this is. It is common witchcraft. Even if it is effective magic, it is of low taste. How can we believe in such ridiculous things?

> Fu Kang'an and others are now in Tibet in charge of Tibetan affairs. We should take this opportunity to shed some light on the matter. Fu Kang'an should order Lamo Chosgyong to perform his magic in his presence. In the case that the magic works, we may leave the matter alone, as it has already been a long tradition in Tibet. Otherwise, Fu Kang'an should exhort the public, both clerical and lay, not to have further faith in such an manifest deception.

> In the future the practice of finding the reincarnation through the Chosgyong oracle should be prohibited and the option of the Golden Urn be instituted instead. Names of candidates born about the same year and month should be put in it and the Dalai Lama should be instructed on drawing lots for fairness.

Fu Kang'an and his associates twice memorialized the court

arguing for maintaining the practice of oracle divination on the ground that "if the Chosgyongs were banned, it would be impossible to test all the young children in U and Tsang alleged to be of superior intelligence," and so on. But the Emperor persisted and ordered an official test of the Chosgyongs by Fu Kang'an. None of the Chosgyongs, however, would dare to cut himself with a sword or lick it with his tongue. In a royal rescript dated the *xin-chou* day of the third month in the fifty-eighth year of the Qianlong reign period (1793), the Emperor refuted the arguments put forth by Fu Kang'an and his associates and ordered that Lamo Chosgyong be deprived of the role in identifying the reincarnation, and that this be left to be decided by putting all the selected names in the Golden Urn for a drawing of lots.

The Emperor ordered that two Golden Urns be made for the drawing of lots: one to be kept in the Yonghegong Lamasery at Beijing for the reincarnations of the Living Buddhas of Outer and of Inner Mongolia and the other kept in the Jokhang Temple of Lhasa for those of Qinghai, Kham and Tibet. In an edict the Emperor instructed:

> I have sent a Golden Urn to Jokhang Temple for the reincarnations of the Dalai Lama, Panchen Erdeni, Jetsun Dampa, Ganden Sherabtu, Demos, Kyirong and senior Hutuktus who serve in Beijing and Tibet. Consultation with the Chosgyong oracle for finding the reincarnation is hereby banned. I have ordered the Ambans and the Dalai Lama and Panchen Erdeni to have the names of candidates recorded for the drawing of lots from the Golden Urn. Only an intelligent and benevolent-looking boy can be selected as the reincarnation. Only by this way can Buddhism be developed. The thing is too serious even for me to decide alone, let alone the Chosgyongs. Their fraudulent practices are not to be allowed in any case. Thus, people will submit willingly.

Thus, in the ninth month of the fifty-seventh year of the Qianlong reign period (1792), a Golden Urn designed for the drawing of lots was sent to Lhasa in the custody of Palace Guardsman Hui Lun and his assistant, Altashi, and it was kept in Jokhang Temple upon their arrival at Lhasa on the twentieth day of the eleventh month of the same year. Fu Kang'an, in a memorial to the court, reported how, together with the Dalai Lama, Kyirongs,

Hutuktus and Kalons went respectfully to receive the Golden Urn and put it in front of Tsongkhapa's image in Jokhang Temple. To his memorial the Emperor gave the remarks: "This is good. I have taken notice of it."

How should we evaluate the Institution of the Golden Urn? With respect to the overall outlook, the Institution was not essentially different from the Chosgyong oracle, because Emperor Gaozong and Chosgyong both believed in the religious doctrine of reincarnation, that is, the soul enters, after death, into another body.

But in politics, they were quite different from each other. Lamo Chosgyong was often bribed to give advice about the reincarnation of the Dalai Lama, and the selected boy was usually a family member of a relative of a great aristocrat. When several aristocrats contended for the reincarnation of the Dalai, the only way to settle the strife was to have it found outside of Tibet. Thus, Ninth Dalai Lungtok Gyatso, Tenth Dalai Tsultrim Gyatso, and Eleventh Dalai Khedrup Gyatso were reincarnated respectively at Dengke, Litang and Kangding in Kham, but the Twelfth Dalai in Tibet. They all died young. The Ninth Dalai died at age eleven, the Tenth Dalai at twenty-two, the Eleventh Dalai at eighteen and the Twelfth Dalai at twenty. Nevertheless, things were somewhat different with the Panchen. In religion, the Panchens and Dalais were equal, but in politics the politico-religious power was in the hands of the Dalais. So the Panchens generally lived longer. The successive Ambans were aware of this, as was Emperor Gaozong.

Politically, the Institution of the Golden Urn meant to take away from the Lamo Chosgyong oracle the authority for identifying the reincarnation, leaving it to the Institution of the Golden Urn established by Emperor Gaozong. In fact, the authority was taken away from the Tibetan local administration by the central government of the Qing Dynasty. The Institution represented the height of the Qing's supervision of the appointment of the Dalais and Panchens, the highest religious and political rulers in Tibet, showing clearly the subordinate status of Tibet to the central government of the Qing Dynasty.

There were cases that the reincarnation of the Dalai or Panchen was selected through the old practice instead of drawing lots from the Golden Urn. But that was done with the approval of the Qing

Emperor, who would always play a decisive role in identifying the reincarnation. The Tibetan local administration had no right to make the decision. What it could do on the matter was to appeal to the Qing court for approval.

In coping with the aftermath of the war in Tibet, Emperor Gaozong gave relief to the victims of the Gurkhas' two invasions. Knowing that the area west of Shigatse had suffered much from the Gurkha invaders, the Emperor gave the Dalai thirty thousand taels of silver and the Panchen ten thousand taels of silver as relief funds to be distributed to the needy there. Those who were recruited for the service to transport the grain the Qing court bought for military supplies in the war were all paid by the Qing government.

In 1796, Emperor Gaozong retired. Emperor Renzong succeeded him, taking the reign title Jiaqing. The Eighth Dalai and the Seventh Panchen sent their *balyar khenpos* to Beijing to offer their congratulations to the Emperor. In turn, Emperor Gaozong wrote letters to the Dalai and Panchen. In the letter to the Panchen, the Emperor said:

> I afford consolation to my subjects and wish Tibetan aborigines peace, prosperity and civilization. The preceding Panchen Erdeni, who understood my intentions, devoted himself to the protection and development of the Yellow sect, studying Buddhist scriptures diligently. He deserved my awards. Now I am very glad that you, the reincarnation of the former Panchen, sent Balyar Khenpo Lozang Drashi to congratulate me on the sixtieth anniversary of my enthronement. Thanks to Heaven, I am healthy. I hope you are also healthy. The *Kalons'* wrongdoings led to the Gurkhas' invasion. So I sent an army under the command of General-in-Chief Fu Kang'an to drive the Gurkha invaders out of Tibet. Since then the Gurkhas have submitted themselves to us. Then I ordered Minister Helin to lay down a proper ordinance for more effective administration of Tibet to get rid of the drawbacks of its old institutions. With the ordinance, all affairs in Tibet are in good order. I ordered Song Yun to station in Tsang to keep everything there in order and do good things for the people's well-being. You are young. You should devote yourself to the study of Buddhist scriptures instead of paying much attention to civil affairs, as the preceding Panchen did. Now I have passed the throne to my successor Emperor. This year is the first year of the Jiaqing reign period. Yet I still indefatigably work,

dealing with state affairs. You should know that I and my successor Emperor always care about Tibet and give favours to Tibetan inhabitants. I order the *balyar khenpo* to deliver you the letter accompanied with some gifts.

When the Seventh Panchen received the letter, he ordered the four thousand monks of Tashilhunpo Monastery to chant sutras for the longevity of former Emperor Gaozong and the enthronement of Emperor Renzong.

## 4. The Relations Between the Seventh Panchen and the Eighth, Ninth, Tenth and Eleventh Dalais

In the sixth year of Renzong's reign (1801), the Seventh Panchen Tenpai Nyima reached nineteen. He was old enough to be ordained as a *gelong*. As his tutor, the Eighth Dalai should give him the ordination. On the fifteenth day of the third month the Seventh Panchen and his attendant *khenpos* left for Lhasa, arriving there on the twenty-eighth day of that month. The Seventh Panchen met the Eighth Dalai in the Potala's Sunlight Hall. On the fifteenth day of the fourth month, the day for the Seventh Panchen to take his *gelong* vows, the Eighth Dalai and the Seventh Panchen moved to Jokhang Temple. The ordination ceremony was held in front of the image of Sakyamuni. The Eighth Dalai Jampel Gyatso, acting as the Ordination Khenpo, was assisted by the Panchen's sutra teacher, Lozang Tenzin, who performed the duty of *lelob* (assistant ordination lecturer); by Choskyi Thubten Gyatso of the Ganden's Jangtse Dratsang, who acted as *sangton* (ordination tutor who saw to it that the Panchen Lama understood the commandments); by Ngawang Drashi, who served as *dukhorwa* (time-keeper and manager of the ordination procedures), and by Kelzang Dondrup, the *lopon* of Namgyal Dratsang, who worked as *tsebabao* (who presented the Dalai with food containers at the prescribed time). Prayers were said by twenty chanting monks throughout the ceremony. After the ceremony the Eighth Dalai and the Seventh Panchen stayed for thirteen days in Jokhang Temple. They returned to the Potala on the twenty-eighth day of the fourth month. After residing in the Potala for twenty days, on the eighteenth day of the fifth month the Panchen bid farewell to the Dalai and left for the Tashilhunpo. He arrived there on the first day of the sixth month. Eighth Dalai Jampel Gyatso fell seriously ill in the eighth month of the ninth year of Emperor Renzong's reign (1804). Having been informed about it, the Seventh Panchen ordered all monks of the Tashilhunpo Monastery to chant prayers for the Eighth Dalai's health. Unfortunately, the Eighth Dalai's condition turned from bad to worse and he died in the Potala on the eighteenth day of the eighth month of that year at the age of forty-seven. Regent Kundeling Hutuktu sent men to inform the Seventh Panchen of the death of the Eighth Dalai and ask the Panchen to write a prayer-obituary and pray for the Eighth Dalai's early reincarnation. The Panchen immediately wrote a prayer-obituary and sent men to take it to Lhasa. He gave alms and sweet buttered-tea to the monks of the Three Major Monasteries, who chanted prayers for the Dalai's early reincarnation.

After the Dalai's death, the search for his reincarnation began at once. The search party consisted of representatives sent by the Kashag and the Three Major Monasteries. The reincarnation was found at Dengke in Kham. He had been born on the first day of the twelfth month of the Wood-Ox year in the thirteenth Tibetan calendrical cycle (the tenth year of Emperor Renzong's reign, or 1805). His father was the *tusi* of Chunko, in Dengke of Kham. (Some years later after the Ninth Dalai died, his father returned to Kham, having found it difficult for his family to remain in Tibet. His estates in Tibet were captured by Surkhang, a big Tibetan aristocrat.)

According to the Institution of the Golden Urn, the identification of the Ninth Dalai Lama should be subject to the process of drawing lots from the Golden Urn. In a joint memorial to the Emperor, the Seventh Panchen, Regent Kyirong Hutuktu, the representatives of the Three Major Monasteries of Lhasa and all the *Kalons* said that, as the reincarnation was the genuine re-embodiment of the Eighth Dalai Lama, they asked the Emperor to dispense with the drawing of lots from the Golden Urn. Amban Yu Ning, in a memorial to Emperor Renzong, also said that the boy had been amply proved by various tests to be the genuine reincarnation of the Eighth Dalai, and the Amban also asked for imperial permission to waive the procedure of drawing lots from the Golden Urn as a matter of expediency. Emperor Renzong approved the petition. Thus the son of the Dengke *tusi* was recognized as the Ninth Dalai Lama. In an edict dated the twelfth year of the Jiaqing reign period (1807), the Emperor said:

> The old tests for identifying the reincarnation were absurd and unreliable. The purpose of Emperor Gaozong's institution of drawing lots from the Golden Urn was to prevent possible fraudulence and misconduct. It has never been heard before that a child barely two years old could already know his own previous incarnation. The authenticity of his being the reincarnation is proved beyond doubt. If it had happened at the time of Emperor Gaozong himself, he would no doubt have also gracefully agreed to the petition on the basis of such reports without insisting on the rule of drawing lots. But this is a unique matter and should not be taken as a precedent. From now on, any infant boy discovered as a reincarnation should still be subject to the process of drawing lots from the Golden Urn.

When the Ninth Dalai was approved by Emperor Renzong, the Kashag and Amban invited the Seventh Panchen to Lhasa to shave the Dalai's hair, ordain him into monkhood and give him a religious name. At their invitation the Panchen left the Tashilhunpo on the tenth day of the eleventh month and arrived at Lhasa on the twenty-ninth day. He lived in Jokhang Temple.

At that time the Eighth Dalai reincarnate was moved to Tselgungtang Monastery in the vicinity of Lhasa. The Kashag selected the fourteenth day of the second month in the thirteenth year of Emperor Renzong's reign (1808) as the auspicious day for that ceremony. On that day the Seventh Panchen went to the monastery and shaved the Ninth Dalai's hair and gave him the religious name of Lozang Tenpai Jungne Ngawang Lungtok Gyatso (Lungtok Gyatso for short). The next ceremony was the enthronement, for which some preparations had to be made. Therefore, the Seventh Panchen went on a pilgrimage to Radreng Monastery on the twenty-fifth day of the third month and then went to worship Tsongkhapa's stupa in the Ganden Monastery on the sixth day of the fourth month. He arrived back at the Tashilhunpo on the eighteenth day of the fourth month.

The Ninth Dalai's enthronement took place in the Potala in the ninth month of that year. The Seventh Panchen sent two of his brothers, Tsewang and Dronyer Rabten, to Lhasa to offer his gifts and congratulations to the Dalai. Emperor Renzong sent Prince Tuleng, Ganden Sherabtu Hutuktu, vice-ministers and officers of the Imperial Guards to Lhasa to supervise the coronation. The Emperor gave the Dalai ten thousand taels of silver and granted him the privilege of using the yellow palanquin and the seals of the preceding Dalai.

During the Ninth Dalai's reign Britain sent a man into Tibet who lived for a long time in Lhasa. It was the first British intrusion into Tibet. According to the *Imperial Records of the Qing Dynasty*, Manning, an Englishman, and his interpreter, Zhao Jingxiu, on the pretext of pilgrimage, came to Lhasa in the sixteenth year of Emperor Renzong's reign (1811). Having discovered the Englishman, Amban Yang Chun reported the incident to Emperor Renzong. The Emperor ordered that all Europeans who came into Tibet on the pretext of pilgrimage be driven out and that Zhao Jingxiu be arrested for punishment.

The Englishman Manning referred to in the *Imperial Records of the Qing Dynasty* was Thomas Manning, about whom Francis Younghusband has written in his book *India and Tibet*. Before coming into Tibet, Thomas Manning had studied Chinese in Britain and France and spent three years in Guangzhou, where he employed Zhao Jingxiu as his interpreter. With the Kashag's consent, Manning, attended by his interpreter, came to Lhasa from India by way of Phari and Gyantse. Younghusband writes in his *India and Tibet*:

> The answer from the Lhasa magistrate to his request to be permitted to proceed to Lhasa arrived a few days after his arrival at Gyantse. A passport was given him, transport and supplies furnished, and as he neared Lhasa, he was met by a respectable person on horseback, who dismounted and saluted and who had been sent out by the Tibetan authorities to welcome him and conduct him to Lhasa.

On the seventeenth of the twelfth month in the sixteenth year of Emperor Renzong's reign (1811) Manning went to the Potala to salute the Ninth Dalai Lama Lungtok Gyatso. He brought with him as an offering some broadcloth, two pairs of China ewers, a pair of brass candlesticks, thirty new bright dollars, some genuine Smith's lavender-water and a good store of Nanjing tea.

Arriving in the great hall, he made due obeisance, touching the ground three times with his head to the Grand Lama. This ceremony over, he sat on a cushion, not far from the Lama's throne. "The Lama was at that time, he thought, about seven years old, and had the simple and unaffected manners of a well-educated, princely child."

Manning also had a good knowledge of Western medicine:

> He practised medicine in Lhasa and gave many people medical treatment. Soon afterwards he was followed.... He was not maltreated, however. Still he was allowed to stay in Lhasa for several months, during which time he paid several visits to the Grand Lama. Finally, the authorities in Beijing ordered him to go back by the way he took on coming. He left Lhasa on April 19 and arrived at Kutsihar on June 10, 1812.

On this incident, some people in China hold the opinion that Manning was not a spy but a scholar who came to Tibet to gather materials of Tibetan folklore. According to the materials available at present, although Manning was employed by the British East India Company, he was not sent to Tibet by the British government. The Kashag granted his request because he said he was an inhabitant of Calcutta going on a pilgrimage to Tibet. (Indians were not prohibited to make pilgrimages to Tibet.) In Lhasa he paid a visit to Amban Hutuli. From his features and the colour of his eyes and beard, the Amban found he was a European, not an Indian, and thus suspected him to be a British spy. Upon the Amban's report, the Emperor ordered that he be driven out of Tibet. On this, Manning left Lhasa for India, but his interpreter, Zhao Jingxiu, a native of Guangdong, was arrested and escorted to Sichuan and then exiled to Ili of Xinjiang.

In the eighteenth year of Emperor Renzong's reign (1813) the Ninth Dalai was nine years old, and by Buddhist tradition he was to take his *getsul* vows. The ceremony was to be administered by the Seventh Panchen, because he was the Dalai's tutor. The Kashag therefore sent Dronyer Chongsha Jetsun and Khenche Kashopa to the Tashilhunpo to invite the Seventh Panchen to Lhasa.

The Seventh Panchen left the Tashilhunpo on the third day of the ninth month and arrived at Lhasa on the seventeenth day of the ninth month. He lived in Jokhang Temple. The Ninth Dalai moved from the Potala to the Jokhang on the twenty-second day of the ninth month. The ceremony was held before the image of Sakyamuni in the Jokhang, and the Ninth Dalai took his *getsul* vows from the Seventh Panchen. On the fourteenth day of the tenth month, the Seventh Panchen gave a sermon in Drepung Monastery and administered ceremonies of *getsul* and *gelong* ordination for many monks there. He left the Drepung for the Tashilhunpo on the twelfth day of the eleventh month.

In the second month of the twentieth year of Emperor Renzong's reign (1815) the Kashag sent men to inform the Seventh Panchen that Ninth Dalai Lungtok Gyatso had died in the Potala Palace on the sixteenth day of the first month that year at the age of eleven. The Kashag asked the Panchen to write a prayer-obituary for the deceased Dalai and pray for his early reincarnation. The Seventh Panchen ordered all monks of the Tashilhunpo to chant prayers in memory of the Ninth Dalai and wrote a prayer-obituary as requested by the Kashag. He sent Dronyer Lozang Rabten with the prayer to Lhasa to hold a memorial ceremony before the Dalai's body and to give alms and sweet buttered-tea to the monks of the Three Major Monasteries, who were chanting sutras for the deceased Dalai.

Emperor Renzong was shocked at the death of the Ninth Dalai. He gave five thousand taels of silver for lighting lamps and chanting sutras before the dead, and appointed Demo Hutuktu the Regent. In an imperial edict the Emperor pointed out that in the case of the Ninth Dalai's enthronement, sanction was given for his exemption from the procedure of drawing lots on the basis of his prodigious qualities as reported by Amban Yu Ning, who had claimed that he was beyond doubt the rebirth of the Eighth Dalai Lama. "If the testimonies as alleged had been true," continued the edict,

he should have lived a longer life in the world to propagate the doctrines of the Yellow sect of Buddhism instead of dying a premature death. This shows what Yu Ning reported in his memorial was mainly exaggerated, and I regret even now that I should have been so easily prevailed upon.

Therefore, the petition for another exemption in the case of the Tenth Dalai was not granted. Ambans Yu Ning and Keshike were reprimanded for the mistake of transmitting the petition instead of having it repudiated. In addition, it was decided that the Tenth Dalai should be identified according to prescribed procedures of the Institution of the Golden Urn.

In 1820 Qing Emperor Renzong died and Emperor Xuanzong ascended the throne. The year following was the first year of the Daoguang reign period. The Seventh Panchen sent a *balyar khenpo* to Beijing to offer sacrifices to the late Emperor and to congratulate the new Emperor. Meanwhile the Panchen gave alms and sweet buttered-tea to the monks of the Tashilhunpo and the Three Major Monasteries for their chanting prayers for the late Emperor and the newly-enthroned Emperor. For this Emperor Xuanzong issued an edict to the Panchen, saying:

> I was notified by Yu Ning and others that you, Panchen Erdeni, sent men to offer a Buddha *katag* to express condolences over the death of Emperor Renzong. You deserve my awards. Now I give you, Panchen Erdeni, a rosary, a plate of coconut beads, a pair of big pouches and two small pouches.

After the death of the Ninth Dalai, the representatives of the Kashag and the Three Major Monasteries began the search for the reincarnation of the Ninth Dalai. Three infant boys who were believed to be his reincarnate were found in Kham.

In the first year of Emperor Xuanzong's reign (1821), the Emperor issued an edict, which read in part:

> This is my instruction to the Grand Ministers of State: .... Wen Gan and others memorialized that, besides the boy of Litang as already reported by Yu Ning, two more boys had been found blessed with auspicious omens which were verified on investigation. But in order to make clear whether the local reports exaggerated the facts, the Amban should order that the three boys mentioned above be brought to U along with their parents and tutors for a joint examination with Ganden Sherabtu, Sama Depa Keshi and others. Only after the reports have been 'proved true, should their names be put in the Golden Urn for the drawing of lots according to the standing rule. Otherwise, there would be no need to do so, and an order should be issued for continuing the search in earnest until three other boys with really prodigious endowments are

found for the final test.

Thus the institution of drawing lots from the Golden Urn for determining the Dalai's reincarnation, which was initiated by Emperor Gaozong, was for the first time put into effect. The following is a description of the usual order of ceremonies in the drawing of lots from the Golden Urn as recorded in *An Account of Eminent Tibetan Monks*:

All those who took part in the ceremony took seats in accordance with their status, and tea and buttered-tea were served. The full names of the three boys were written on the tallies in Manchu, Mongolian and Tibetan scripts accordingly, all of which were subject to the inspection and verification of the Dalai and Panchen and all those present, including the parents of the three boys. Then the inscribed tallies were respectfully wrapped up in yellow paper and put before the Golden Urn.

All monks of the choir chanted the holy mantra three times over. Then, waiting till the due time in the recitation of the scripture, with the Dalai's invitation, the Assistant Amban advanced to make obeisance three times before the Urn, and while kneeling, raised the tallies over his head, put them into the Urn, stirred them twice around with his hand and covered it with a lid. While the Assistant Amban did all this, the Amban stood by. After the rite the two Ambans went back to their seats and waited till the end of the recitation of the scripture.

Then, at the lama's invitation, the Amban performed full obeisance before the Golden Urn, and while kneeling respectfully, picked out one tally from the Urn on the altar—on this was to be found the name of the true reincarnation. The Assistant Amban stood on his left. The Amban unwrapped the tally and showed it to all present. Then he summoned the father of the reincarnation and also showed him the tally, upon which the father performed the prostrations before the Amban in obedience to the instructions. After the tally was inspected by the Dalai and Panchen, the Amban solemnly placed it before the Urn. The other two tallies were then also taken out and inspected before all, and then the names written on them were wiped out.

By order of Emperor Xuanzong, the Tenth Dalai's lot-drawing ceremony was to be administered by the Seventh Panchen. The Panchen left the Tashilhunpo on the second day of the first month of the second year of Emperor Xuanzong's reign (1822) and arrived at Lhasa on the thirteenth day of the first month that year.

He resided in the Dalai's Summer Palace, Norbulingka, and consulted with Amban Wen Gan and Assistant Amban Bao Chang. They decided that they would go to Netang Monastery, where the three boy candidates were living, and bring them to Lhasa. The ceremony was held on the fifteenth day of the first month in the Potala. In the ceremony Wen Gan and Bao Chang picked out the tally of the boy candidate born in Litang, and so he became the Tenth Dalai Lama. The Seventh Panchen shaved the boy's hair, put on him a suit of monk's clothes, gave him the religious name of Ngawang Lozang Tenzin Tsultrim Gyatso (Tsultrim Gyatso for short) and the vows of a layman. On the third day of the second month the Tenth Dalai took his *getsul* vows from the Seventh Panchen. On the third day of the third month the Panchen bid farewell to the Dalai and went on a pilgrimage to Samye Monastery in Lhoka. He returned to the Tashilhunpo on the eighteenth day of the fifth month.

On the eighth day of the eighth month of the second year of Emperor Xuanzong's reign (1822), the Tenth Dalai was enthroned in the Potala. The Seventh Panchen sent his brother Khangjam Khenpo and Dronyer Dorcho as his representatives to attend the ceremony and to salute the Tenth Dalai. Emperor Xuanzong sent Su Chong'a, Vice Commander-in-chief of Chengdu, and Changkya Hutuktu to witness the ceremony and granted the Dalai the privilege of using the yellow palanquin and saddle and the seals of the preceding Dalai.

The Emperor issued an edict in praise of the Seventh Panchen for his administration of the lot-drawing ceremony and gave the Panchen two bolts of satin embroidered with four-clawed dragons (the style worn by high officials), a piece of glittering satin, six pieces of quality satin, a piece of golden satin, five large *katags* and ten small *katags*.

In the sixth year of Emperor Xuanzong's reign (1826) the Panchen submitted a petition for building a summer palace by the Nyangchu River near Shigatse, taking the Dalai's Summer Palace, Norbulingka, as a precedent. The Emperor granted his petition. The palace is called Konchokling in Tibetan. Emperor Xuanzong bestowed upon it the name Guangyou Temple and a horizontal board inscribed with four Chinese characters *Fa Jie Zhuang Yan*, meaning "the solemnity of Buddhism." The palace, standing in a picturesque place by the Nyangchu River, is where the successive Panchens have thereafter spent the summer.

In the fourteenth year of Emperor Xuanzong's reign (1834), when Tenth Dalai Tsultrim Gyatso was eighteen years old, the Kashag sent men to invite the Seventh Panchen to ordain the Dalai into full monkhood. So the Panchen set off from the Tashilhunpo on the twenty-fourth day of the second month and arrived at Lhasa on the fifth day of the third month. He resided at the Norbulingka. On the eighth day of the third month he went to meet with the Dalai in the Potala's Sunlight Hall. Then he consulted with the resident officials and the Regent, and they selected the seventh day of the fourth month as the auspicious day for the Tenth Dalai to take his *gelong* vows. On that day the Panchen and the Dalai moved to Jokhang Temple. The following day the ceremony was held before the image of Sakyamuni in the Jokhang according to the rules of Lamaism. After the ceremony, on the twenty-second day of the fourth month, the Seventh Panchen bid farewell to the Tenth Dalai, returning to the Tashilhunpo on the thirteenth day of the fifth month.

The Tenth Dalai died suddenly in the Potala on the first day of the ninth month in the seventeenth year of Emperor Xuanzong's reign (1837). He was then only twenty-two years old. In the tenth month the Kashag sent men to inform the Seventh Panchen of the Dalai's death and to ask him to write a prayer for the late Dalai's early reincarnation. The Panchen was very sad at his early death. He wrote a prayer and ordered the Tashilhunpo monks to chant sutras for the late Tenth Dalai. He sent representatives to Lhasa to offer sacrifices to the Dalai and to give alms and sweet buttered-tea to the monks of the Three Major Monasteries. Emperor Xuanzong ordered Amban Guan Shengbao to offer sacrifices to the Dalai Lama and give alms to the monks accordingly.

About the Tenth Dalai's death, the *Imperial Records of the Qing Dynasty* has the following to say:

> The Dalai Lama was wounded in the neck and blood was running down. Nomihan knew this but did not try to help him. The case was very suspicious. The Emperor ordered that the Amban and the Panchen Erdeni and other officials interrogate all the suspects to get their

confession.

Emperor Xuanzong and Amban Qi Shan knew that the truth would be difficult to find out. After a time, the Emperor ordered that the case of the Dalai's death, concerning which no clues had been uncovered, need not be traced to its source.

# 5. The Seventh Panchen Is Twice Awarded by the Emperor and Made Acting Regent for Eight Months

In the eighteenth year of Emperor Xuanzong's reign (1838), the Emperor bestowed on the Seventh Panchen a gold album of thirteen sheets weighing 235 taels and bearing Manchu, Chinese, Mongolian and Tibetan inscriptions. According to the Tibetan biography of the Seventh Panchen, the inscription is to the effect that the Tashilhunpo estates and residents should be under the Panchen's administration forever and nobody was allowed to seize them. Receiving the album, the Panchen kowtowed to the east to express thanks to the Emperor and presented a memorial via the Amban.

Meanwhile, Amban Song Ting officially informed the Tashilhunpo abbots that, by order of the Emperor, from then on the appointment of clerical and lay officials of Tashilhunpo Monastery above the fifth rank should be submitted to the Emperor via the amban for approval, and they would be granted authoritative official hats. The first ones in the monastery to get official appointments from the Emperor were Dechongpa Nyima Dondrup and Nyertsangpa Dondrup Phelgye, upon whom were bestowed the hats of the fourth rank, and the official hat of the fifth rank was awarded to Dondrup Tsering, manager of the stable.

After the Tenth Dalai died, the Kashag and the Three Major Monasteries sent men to search for the Dalai's reincarnation. They found four boy candidates in Kham. Having received Meng Bao's memorial that the four boys had been found blessed with auspicious omens, the Emperor issued an edict in 1841:

The four boys are to be brought by Meng Bao and the Governor-General of Sichuan to Lhasa along with their parents and tutors for joint examination with Ganden Sherabtu Samadi Bagchi and the Panchen Erdeni. Only after the boys are tested with articles used by the late Dalai, can their names be put in the Golden Urn for lot-drawing according to the standing rules.

In the second month of the twenty-first year of Emperor Xuanzong's reign (1841), by the Emperor's order, the Kashag and Amban sent Khenpo Jamyang Tenpa to the Tashilhunpo to invite the Seventh Panchen to administer the lot-drawing, tonsuring and name-giving ceremonies. The Panchen started off on the third day of the same month and arrived at Lhasa on the twelfth day of the fifth month. He took up his residence in the Norbulingka. The Panchen, Regent and Amban decided to set the twenty-fourth day of the fifth month as the day for the lot-drawing ceremony. On that day the ceremony was held before the Qing Emperor's spirit tablet by Amban Meng Bao and Assistant Amban Hai Pu. The result of the lot-drawing was that the boy from Taining (Garthar in Tibetan), Kham, was chosen as the Eleventh Dalai.

The four candidates were still living at Tselgungtang Monastery near Lhasa at that time. On the first day of the sixth month the Seventh Panchen, Regent, Ambans, Kalons and the representatives of the Three Major Monasteries went to the Tselgungtang to declare the result of the lot-drawing to the public. The Seventh Panchen then shaved the hair of the boy who had been acknowledged as the true reincarnation, put on him a monk robe and gave him the religious name of Ngawang Kelzang Tenpai Drome Khedrup Gyatso (Khedrup Gyatso for short). Then the Eleventh Dalai was invited to the Potala. The coronation was to be held on an auspicious day afterwards.

On the sixth day of the ninth month the Seventh Panchen bid farewell to the Eleventh Dalai, Regent and Amban and left for the Tashilhunpo.

The Eleventh Dalai was enthroned in the Potala on the sixteenth day of the fourth month of the twenty-second year of the Daoguang reign period (1842). Emperor Xuanzong sent Shimeng'e, Vice Commander-in-Chief of Chengdu, and Changkya Hutuktu to Lhasa to attend the ceremony and gave the Dalai a gold album and ten thousand taels of silver for the expense of coronation. The Seventh Panchen also sent men to offer a *katag* and gifts to the Eleventh Dalai.

In the sixth month of the twenty-fourth year of Emperor Xuanzong's reign (1844), the Panchen unexpectedly got a letter from Amban Qi Shan asking him to go to Lhasa immediately for an important matter. The Kashag sent Popon Palong to take care of the Panchen on the journey. Arriving at Lhasa, the Panchen lived at the Kelzang Phodrang Hall of the Norbulingka. As soon as he arrived, Amban Qi Shan read an imperial edict to him, in which the Emperor ordered him to act as the Regent in charge of *shangshang* (i.e., the local government of Tibet) affairs. The Panchen, now at the advanced age of sixty-two, said that he could not accept the task. It was only after persistent urging by the Amban, who said that the imperial edict could not be rejected, that he agreed to take over the job for only a few months.

It turned out that Amban Qi Shan had impeached Ganden Sherabtu Samadi Bagchi, the previous Regent, before Emperor Xuanzong for greed and graft. In an edict the Emperor said:

> If the Nomihan Ganden Sherabtu Samadi Bagchi, now in charge of *shangshang*, has committed crimes of greed and graft, it will much affect the reputation of the Yellow sect. I order Qi Shan, together with the Panchen Erdeni, Demo Hutuktu, Kyirong Hutuktu and Radreng Nomihan, to investigate the case. The Panchen Erdeni is temporarily put concurrently in charge of *shangshang*, to be assisted by Demo, Kyirong and Radreng. In one or two years the Amban and Panchen Erdeni should recommend a Regent to take charge of *shangshang*.

The ex-Regent's property was confiscated, of which over 144,000 taels of silver went to monasteries, and 278 *dan* (1 *dan* = 50kg) of rice and 6,946 *dan* of wheat, barley and beans went to the Tibetan troops.

On the sixth day of the eighth month of the twenty-fourth year of Emperor Xuanzong's reign (1844), the Kashag held celebrations for the Seventh Panchen being appointed as the acting Regent. Shortly thereafter, on the twelfth day of the eighth month, the Panchen, in an interview with the Eleventh Dalai at the Potala, insisted on resigning and retiring to his monastery.

When Ganden Sherabtu Samadi Bagchi was removed from

office, Amban Qi Shan had him jailed. The monks of the Sera Me Dratsang raided the jail, rescuing the ex-Regent, who originally came from the Sera Me Dratsang, and brought him to the Sera. So the Amban asked the Panchen to deal with the case. The Panchen consulted with the *Chikyap Khenpo* and the representatives of the Three Major Monasteries. By their order, 210 criminals involved in the case were arrested, among whom 180 were held in custody by Sera Monastery and the rest punished by the Nangtseshag (police station of Lhasa) and Sholekhung.

When assistant Amban Rui Yuan passed by Tashilhunpo Monastery during an inspection tour of the Tsang region in the first month of the twenty-fifth year of Emperor Xuanzong's reign (1845), representatives of the monastery presented a written petition to him for the Panchen's early return to the Tashilhunpo to take charge of religious affairs. After coming back to Lhasa, Rui Yuan memorialized that the Panchen's long residence in Lhasa was causing a general feeling of unrest among the Tibetans in Tsang, and he recommended that Radreng Ngachithu Nomihan take over the regency from the Panchen. His proposal was soon granted by the Emperor.

On the twenty-sixth of the third month the Seventh Panchen resigned from the regency; he handed the seal of the Regent over to the new Regent, Ngachithu Nomihan, before the Eleventh Dalai at the Potala. It was less than eight months (from the sixth day of the eighth month of the twenty-fourth year of Emperor Xuanzong's reign, or 1844, to the twenty-sixth day of the third month of the twenty-fifth year of that reign, or 1845) that the Seventh Panchen acted as the Regent. On the third day of the fourth month he bid farewell to the Eleventh Dalai, the new Regent, the Ambans and others and returned to Tashilhunpo Monastery.

In the twenty-sixth year of Emperor Xuanzong's reign (1846), the Seventh Panchen was granted by the Emperor a gold album, a gold seal and many gifts.

In the twenty-sixth year of Emperor Xuanzong's reign (1846), the Eleventh Dalai was eight years old, the age at which he should take his *getsul* vows. At the invitation of the Regent and the Kashag, the Seventh Panchen left for Lhasa on the nineteenth day of the second month, arriving at the Potala on the eleventh day of the third month. He met with the Eleventh Dalai as soon as he arrived at Lhasa.

The seventh day of the fourth month was chosen as the auspicious day for the Eleventh Dalai to take the vows. On that day the Eleventh Dalai and the Seventh Panchen went to Jokhang Temple, where the Dalai took his *getsul* vows from the Panchen in front of the image of Sakyamuni.

The Panchen left for Ganden Monastery on the first day of the fifth month to worship Tsongkhapa's stupa and give sermons there. He came back to Lhasa on the twentieth day of the fifth month. He bid farewell to the Eleventh Dalai, the Regent and the Amban on the twenty-ninth day of the sixth month. The Eleventh Dalai held a farewell banquet for the Panchen in the Potala's Sunlight Hall. The Seventh Panchen returned to the Tashilhunpo on the thirtieth day of the sixth month.

In the third month of the thirtieth year of Emperor Xuanzong's reign (1850) Amban Mu Teng'e went to Tashilhunpo Monastery to inform the Seventh Panchen that Emperor Xuanzong had died in the first month of that year, and that Emperor Wenzong had ascended the throne. The Panchen immediately ordered all monks of the monastery to chant sutras and prayers and sent his *balyar khenpo* to Beijing to hold a memorial ceremony for the late Emperor Xuanzong and to congratulate the newly-enthroned Wenzong.

# 6. The Tibetans' Struggle Against British Invasion

During the first half of the nineteenth century, while invading China's coastal areas, the British also tried hard to invade Tibet. The Tibetans, together with other nationalities of China, began a protracted and bitter struggle against British aggression.

The British invaded Tibet step-by-step. The first step was to capture Gurkha (Nepal), Bhutan, Drenjong (Sikkim) and Ladakh, the countries and areas bordering on Tibet. Being subject to the Qing Dynasty, they had regularly presented tribute to the Qing court, as well as to the Dalai and Panchen. To capture the areas was in fact to destroy Tibet's barrier. (Britain was called *Phyiling* in historical documents of the Qing Dynasty and in Tibetan documents. It was not until the twenty-sixth year of Xuanzong's reign [1847] that an imperial edict dated the *ding-chou* day of the twelfth month pointed out that "Phyiling is none other than England.")

British aggression was at that time directed towards Gurkha (Nepal), not Tibet. Still, they had to consider the Qing Dynasty's reaction to their invasion of Gurkha, since the kingdom of Gurkha had good relations with the Qing court. Early in the seventh year of Emperor Renzong's reign (1802) Britain occupied six places in Gurkha. But the Qing government and Amban thought that "Phyiling is a country too small to cause trouble." When the Gurkha troops lost one battle after another, the Gurkha ruler appealed to the Qing court for help. Emperor Renzong said:

> Phyiling is to the southwest of Gurkha. Since Phyiling and Tangut [Tibet] have neither contacts with nor hold hostility towards each other, Phyiling has no reason to invade Tangut.... What they say is unbelievable.

In the twentieth year of Emperor Renzong's reign (1815), Gurkha troops were defeated by the British army. The king of Gurkha again appealed to the Qing court for material assistance in resisting the aggressors. Instead of giving the needed help, however, Emperor Renzong criticized the Gurkhas for their appeal, saying, "Gurkhas are to blame for their war with Phyiling. The Heavenly Dynasty should not help them. They have appealed to us more than once for gold and silver and to the Dalai and Panchen for grain. They are very greedy."

Having lost the war, Gurkha was obliged to sign the Treaty of Sagolie with Britain in the twenty-first year of Renzong's reign (1816). Under this treaty Gurkha ceded three places to Britain and had to let a British resident envoy stay in Katmandu.

After signing the treaty, the Gurkha government sent men to report to Amban Xi Ming that, "Until now we have been paying tribute to the Heavenly Dynasty. Since we have surrendered to

Phyiling, we shall no longer be allowed to pay tribute."

Emperor Renzong, who continued to believe that the Gurkhas were engaged in trickery, responded: "The Heavenly Dynasty does not care whether that country is at war or peace with Phyiling. It should pay tribute as usual, even if it has surrendered to Phyiling."

After conquering Gurkha, Britain occupied Kashmir (called Senpa by the Tibetans) in the north and then instigated the Senpa to invade Ladakh, which was then a vassal state of the Qing Dynasty. (Ladakh, originally one of the three regions of Ngari, belonged to Tibet. When Gushri Khan unified Tibet, Ladakh had been placed under the jurisdiction of the Dalai Lama.) In the eighth year of Xuanzong's reign (1828), the Emperor granted Ladakhi ruler Dunop Namtsar an official hat of the fifth rank and two bolts of brocade and granted Ladakhi chieftain Samo an official hat and two bolts of silk, for they had captured over one hundred Uygur rebels. In the ninth year of that reign (1829), the Ladakhi ruler presented to the Emperor a memorial along with a *katag* and a bolt of silk to express thanks to the Qing court. The Emperor, noting that Ladakh was not in a position to hand in a memorial to him directly, nonetheless allowed this as an exceptional favour.

Not long after occupying Kashmir, Britain occupied Ladakh. In the twenty-first year of Emperor Xuanzong's reign (1841), Kashmir and Ladakh, at Britain's instigation, sent three thousand troops to attack Ngari and penetrated 1,700 *li* deep into Tibet. They captured Rutog, Gartok, Dapa, Purang and Tsaparang. The Qing government, fighting the Opium War, could not spare any troops for Tibet. So Amban Meng Bao sent Kalon Tseten Dorje and Dapon Pelshi to Ngari with 1,300 Tibetan troops to mount an offensive. The Amban equipped the Tibetan army with twenty-two heavy guns from inner China. Soon afterwards the Amban sent five hundred Tibetan troops under the command of two *rupons*, four *gyapons* and twenty *dingpons* as reserve units.

In the twenty-second year of Xuanzong's reign (1842), Amban Meng Bao memorialized that the Tibetans, led by the Kalon and Dapon, had defeated the Senpas, killing two hundred, including their leader, Wazir, and forty other chieftains. It was pointed out in an edict that over 40 chieftains of the Senpas were captured and 836 Senpas surrendered; and by that time the Tibetan troops had recovered all the lost Ngari territory. Meng Bao and Hai Pu were praised for their merits in the campaign.

In this Ngari war the main forces were the Tibetan army. It was to their credit that they recovered all the lost Ngari territory. As to Ladakh, after it was occupied by Britain, its ruler no longer presented tribute to the Qing court.

After capturing Ladakh, Britain expanded its aggressive activities to Drenjong (Sikkim). In the seventeenth year of Renzong's reign (1812) when Drenjong was still subject to China, its king asked the Qing court to allow him to seek protection in Tibet from the British aggressors, but Amban Yang Chun repudiated his request. The *Imperial Records of the Qing Dynasty* has the following to say:

> The Emperor instructed the Grand Ministers of State: "Amban Yang Chun said the king of Drenjong sent a letter to request to give his people a Tangut village so that they could live there. Yang Chun categorically refused his request.... What Yang Chun did was quite right. The Drenjong Tribe does not belong to Tibet. They ask to live in Tangut just because they are afraid of the Gurkha invasion. At present they still have Rinito and Gando. It is not that they have lost all their land or have no place to live.... Send my words to Hutuli and other people concerned that after this repudiation, the Drenjong king might send men to come again to make another request for aid, for they are greedy.... All their requests should be refused.

In the fifteenth year of Xuanzong's reign (1835), when border disputes arose between Gurkha and Drenjong, both of them appealed to the Amban for mediation. To Amban Guan Shengbao, the Emperor gave the following order:

> If hostilities break out between them, the resident official shall order the Chinese and Tibetan officials to tighten security measures at all checkpoints. No one shall be allowed to go beyond the border and cause trouble. This is a matter of importance.

As the order amounted to a refusal to intervene in the disputes between Gurkha and Drenjong, they turned to Britain for mediation. The British government sent Grant to act as a mediator.

Britain, in exchange for the return of Sikkim's former territory, Tela and Monan, which Gurkha had taken over from the defeated Drenjong, asked for the cession of the scenic city of Darjeeling. Drenjong ceded Darjeeling and the mountainous areas in the near vicinity to Britain for use as a British "summer resort," and Britain promised to pay the king of Drenjong an annual stipend of three hundred pounds.

Upon the Amban's suggestion, the Emperor ordered that the Drenjong king be allowed to enter Tibet only every eight years.

Britain, following its piecemeal encroachment on the areas bordering on Tibet, began to reach out its evil hand for Tibet. The pretext they used was "to establish trade relations and define the border."

According to the *Imperial Records of the Qing Dynasty*, Amban Qi Shan reported to the Emperor that the "Phyilings" had come to the western border of Tibet to deliver a letter to the *gyapon* there. They said the Senpas had surrendered to them and Ladakh and Kashmir were now under their jurisdiction. They said they wanted to establish trade relations with Tibet and to define the border and hoped to meet with Tibetan representatives. The Emperor ordered Qi Shan to inform the British that all foreign affairs could be conducted only by the imperial envoy, Qi Ying, and therefore the British businessmen should talk to Qi Ying at Guangzhou in order to begin trade.

At first the Qing government tried to turn a deaf ear to the British request. But later, when Britain informed Qi Ying, the Governor-General of Guangdong, that they had sent a commissioner to Tsang and had asked Tibet to send officials to meet him, Emperor Xuanzong had to instruct the resident officials: "Qi Shan, Bing Liang and Mu Teng'e should send reliable officials to Tsang. If the said foreign official has really come to Tsang, everything should be dealt with very carefully."

This was only a British exploratory action before their armed invasion. By this time the Qing government had become very corrupt and incompetent. After the Opium Wars, it carried out a policy of capitulation. Tibet being a part of China, this foreign policy was also carried out in Tibet.

# 7. The Seventh Panchen's Contributions to the Unification of the Country and the Solidarity of All Its Nationalities

By this time the Seventh Panchen was old and in poor health. The Tashilhunpo clerical and lay officials were taking good care of him; physicians were sent for to treat him for his illness and monks chanted prayers continually for his health.

Emperor Wenzong and the resident officials were very worried about his health. In the first year of Emperor Wenzong's reign (1851), Amban Mu Teng'e delivered an imperial edict to the Panchen which contained the following words: "I am distressed to learn from Mu Teng'e that the Panchen Erdeni is suffering an illness in the legs. The Panchen Erdeni, now at an advanced age, must set his mind at ease and have good treatment. Mu Teng'e shall pass my regards to the Panchen Erdeni" (from the *Imperial Records of the Qing Dynasty*).

The Seventh Panchen died at Tashilhunpo Monastery at dawn on the fourteenth day of the first month of the third year of Emperor Wenzong's reign (1853). All the monks of the Tashilhunpo prayed for the Panchen's early reincarnation. Men were sent to Lhasa to inform the Eleventh Dalai, Regent and Amban, and through them the Qing court, about the death of the Seventh Panchen. The Dalai was asked to write an announcement about the Panchen's death. Alms were given to all monks of the Three Major Monasteries at Lhasa for chanting sutras for the Panchen. Upon receiving the report of the Panchen's death, Emperor Wenzong ordered the Assistant Amban, Zhun Ling, to make offerings to the spirit of the dead and give five thousand taels of silver for the funeral expenses. The Emperor ordered Dzasa Lama Namgyal Chosphel to administer political and monastic affairs in Tsang for the time being. As the Panchen died in Tsang, not in Beijing as the previous Panchen had, the Emperor ordered Amban Mu Teng'e to report to him immediately all the details about the funerals of the previous Panchen Lamas who died in Tsang—who were appointed to preside over the funerals and what imperial edicts had been issued.

The Eleventh Dalai, the Regent, all the Kalons, and the Three Major Monasteries sent representatives to offer sacrifices to the late Panchen. The people of U and Tsang, clerical and lay, were asked to offer gold and silver to build a stupa. When the stupa, which was in the Great Chanting Hall along with those of the previous Panchens, was completed, the Panchen's body was put in it.

In summary, we can say that the Seventh Panchen made three major contributions which deserve to be mentioned.

(1) The Seventh Panchen witnessed the two Gurkha invasions, which were the cause of large disasters to Tashilhunpo Monastery and the people under its jurisdiction. As the Panchen was good at exercising leadership in the administration of Tsang and worked very hard, and the central government provided financial aid and other support to the monastery, it was restored to its former prosperity in his late years.

(2) The Seventh Panchen witnessed the reigns of four Qing emperors: Gaozong, Renzong, Xuanzong and Wenzong. He had worked with altogether thirty-seven Ambans and thirty-nine Assistant Ambans. He always granted that Tibet, as a part of China, was subject to the central government of the Qing Dynasty. He was always obedient to the Qing emperors and respectful to all the Ambans. He reported all major events of the Tashilhunpo to the emperors, via the Ambans, for instructions, and did his best to accomplish the tasks the emperors put on his shoulders. So all the four Qing emperors and Ambans trusted him for his contribution to the unification of the country and the unity of the nationalities in China.

(3) The Seventh Panchen, as a disciple of the Eighth Dalai and a tutor of the Ninth, Tenth and Eleventh Dalais, was on good terms with those Dalais. He attached great importance to his good relations with them. In the twenty-fourth year of Emperor Xuanzong's reign (1844), when the Emperor ordered him to act for the Regent, he dared not disobey the imperial edict and thus reluctantly took the responsibility. He then resigned after eight months. With his ability and political integrity, he was certainly qualified to hold the post of Regent. But considering his relations with the Dalai, he did not like to interfere in the internal affairs of the Dalai clique. He was wise

to do so. Thus, the Dalais and their groups were always friendly with the Seventh Panchen. This was his major contribution to the internal unity of Tibet.

# Chapter Six
# Tenpai Wangchuk, the Eighth Panchen Lama

## 1. The Short Life of the Eighth Panchen

The Eighth Panchen (1855-1882), whose religious name was Tenpai Wangchuk, was a native of Zhucang Village of the Thobgyal Shika in Tsang. He was born on the eighth day of the eighth month in the Wood-Hare year of the fourteenth Tibetan calendrical cycle (the fifth year of Qing Emperor Wenzong's reign, or 1855, the year when the Eleventh Dalai Lama died.) to Tenzin Wangyal, his father, and Drashi Lhamo, his mother, of a local petty aristocratic family.

After the Eleventh Dalai's death, Amban Man Qing proposed in a memorial to the Emperor that Radreng Hutuktu be put in charge of *shangshang* (the Tibet local government) affairs for the time being. His proposal was granted by Emperor Wenzong in the sixth year of his reign (1856).

Then, the Kashag, the Regent and the Three Major Monasteries sent representatives to search for the reincarnation of the Eleventh Dalai, and at the same time the Tashilhunpo also sent its representatives to search for the reincarnation of the Seventh Panchen.

According to the Tibetan biography of Eighth Panchen Tenpai Wangchuk, the Seventh Panchen's reincarnation was found in the sixth year of Wenzong's reign (1856). There had been three boys in Tsang who were eligible to be the reincarnation of the Panchen. Solpon Khenpo Palden Sherab went to Lhasa to report to Assistant Amban He Tehe, who then presented a memorial to Emperor Wenzong.

An imperial edict dated the twentieth of the twelfth month of the sixth year of Wenzong's reign pointed out:

> I am glad to know from He Tehe that two soul boys have been found.
> This is an auspicious omen. Their names should be put in the Golden
> Urn for lot-drawing according to the standing rule. The reincarnation
> should be chosen in this way and the result should be reported to me
> immediately.

Originally there were three candidates, but the parents of one
candidate decided that their child would not take part in the
selection, so there were only two candidates. Amban Man Qing and
Assistant Amban He Tehe ordered Tashilhunpo Monastery's representatives to bring the two boys, along with their parents, to Lhasa
for the lot-drawing.

Tenzin Wangyal with his wife and son from Zhucang of
Thobgyal Shika and Drugu Shaphel with his wife and son arrived
at Lhasa on the fourth day of the eighth month of the seventh year
of Wenzong's reign (1857). At the same time Dzasa Lama Nomihan
from the Tashilhunpo, the three high *khenpos* of the late Panchen
—the *Solpon, Zimpon* and *Chopon*—and a party of several hundred
lay and clerical officials of the Tashilhunpo also arrived at Lhasa to
attend the ceremony.

The lot-drawing took place in front of the Emperor's spirit tablet
in the Potala. It began, as prescribed, with the writing of the names
of the two candidates on two ivory tallies, which were then placed
in the Golden Urn. Monks from the Tashilhunpo and the Three
Major Monasteries then devoted seven days to praying and reading
the *Golden Urn Sutra*. The twenty-fourth day of the ninth month
was chosen as the day for the ceremony. On that day the Regent
and Kalons, together with lay and clerical officials, came to the
Potala. Resident officials Man Qing and He Tehe presided over the
ceremony. One of the two ivory tallies was picked out. The name
inscribed on the tally was the name of the boy from Thobgyal
Shika. Thus, Tenzin Wangyal's son was chosen as the Eighth
Panchen Lama.

A Tashilhunpo *dronyer* in white clothes and on a white horse,
according to the rules, was sent to inform the successful candidate
and his parents, who were at that time temporarily living at the
Kundeling Lharang in Lhasa, of the happy news. He then went to
the Tashilhunpo to inform all monks there of the result of the

lot-drawing. The Kashag gave a *gadro* party in celebration of
the successful conclusion of the ceremony. After that the Eighth
Panchen was invited from the Kundeling Lharang to the Norbulingka, the Dalai's Summer Palace. The next day the Eighth Panch-
en had his tonsuring ceremony, which was performed by Regent
Radreng Ngachithu Hutuktu as the ceremonial *khenpo*. The latter
shaved the Eighth Panchen's hair, put a monk's robe on him and
gave him the religious name Choskyi Drakpa Tenpai Wangchuk
Palzangpo (Tenpai Wangchuk for short). On the twenty-ninth day
of the ninth month the Eighth Panchen left Lhasa for the Tashilhunpo in the company of several hundred lay and clerical staff of
the Tashilhunpo. The Regent and all the Kalons put up tents at
Kidtsel Luding to bid farewell to the Panchen. The Eighth Panchen
lived, as decided by all monks of the Tashilhunpo, in Jamjun
Monastery in Rinpung Dzong before he was invited to the Tashilhunpo for the coronation on an auspicious day.

A royal edict about the lot-drawing for the Eighth Panchen,
according as the *Imperial Records of the Qing Dynasty* says:

> He Tehe and others presented a memorial about the drawing of lots in
> selecting the boy reincarnating the Panchen Erdeni. On the twenty-
> third day of the eleventh month of this year [1857], the Amban, in the
> company of Radreng Ngachithu Hutuktu, Sherab Nomihan and a party
> of monks and laymen chanting sutras, went to the Potala and took out
> one of the inscribed tallies from the Golden Urn, on which was the
> name of Namgyal Wangdu Jamchen [the Eighth Panchen's pet name],
> Tenzin Wangyal's child, who was chosen as the reincarnation.... This
> was an auspicious event. I am very happy at it. I order that the
> reincarnation be given a big *katag*, a coral rosary and a jade *ruyi* [an
> ornamental piece] to express my sincerity to the Yellow Hat sect.

On the fourteenth day of the first month of the eighth year of
Wenzong's reign (1858), Assistant Amban He Tehe went to the
Tashilhunpo. He was to conduct the enthronement ceremony
together with the Regent and Kalons. The Panchen Lama left
Jamjun Monastery on the fifteenth day of the first month and
arrived at the Tashilhunpo on the eighteenth day of that month.
He was warmly received by four thousand monks of the Tashilhunpo and invited to his Summer Palace, Konchokling, where he
took up temporary residence before he was enthroned.

After the death of the Eleventh Dalai, the Kashag and the Three Major Monasteries sent representatives to search for his reincarnation and they found in U three boys who were eligible to be the reincarnation of the Eleventh Dalai. It was reported to the Emperor via Amban Man Qing. Qing Emperor Wenzong instructed:

Man Qing memorialized that three soul boys were eligible to be the Dalai Lama's reincarnation. It is two years since the Dalai Lama died. Now three soul boys have been found who have special endowments. This is a good omen. I am very glad to hear of this. I approve the petition and order that the three boys' names be written on tallies and the tallies be put in the Golden Urn for drawing lots according to the standing rule for reincarnation selection.

On the thirteenth day of the first month in the eighth year of Wenzong's reign (1858), Phuntsok Tsewang's son, one of the three candidates, was chosen as the Twelfth Dalai Lama by lot-drawing conducted by Amban Man Qing in the Potala. (When the Twelfth Dalai died at the young age of twenty, his family merged with that of the Lhalu, a big aristocrat.) He then had his hair shaven and was given the religious name Ngawang Lozang Tenpai Gyaltsen Trinley Gyatso (Trinley Gyatso for short) by Regent Radreng.

In order to formalize the lot-drawing, Emperor Wenzong issued an edict:

Man Qing presented a memorial about the selection of the reincarnation of the Dalai Lama. On the thirteenth day of the first month, in the company of Radreng Ngachithu Hutuktu and Khenpo Lama, together with a party of monks who chanted sutras, the Amban took out one of the inscribed tallies, on which was the name of Phuntsok Tsewang's son, who was then chosen as the reincarnation. As the Panchen's reincarnation was too young to perform the ceremony, Radreng Ngachithu Hutuktu, acting as the Dalai's tutor, gave him the religious name Ngawang Lozang Tenpai Gyaltsen Trinley Gyatso. It was auspicious. I was happy to learn about this. Now the reincarnation is only three years old. He lives in a monastery near the Potala. Radreng should take good care of him. The coronation should be administered by Man Qing.

When the Twelfth Dalai was enthroned in the Potala on the third day of the seventh month in the tenth year of Wenzong's reign (1860), Emperor Wenzong sent two officials from the Board

for National Minority Affairs with an edict and gifts to the Dalai
Lama, in addition to ten thousand taels of silver for the expense of
his coronation. The Emperor ordered resident officials Man Qing
and En Qing to witness the ceremony. The Eighth Panchen also
sent representatives to Lhasa to offer a *katag* and gifts to the
Twelfth Dalai Lama to express his congratulations.

On the second day of the tenth month of that year the Eighth
Panchen was enthroned. Regent Radreng Ngachithu Hutuktu and
Assistant Amban En Qing performed the ceremony. Emperor Wen-
zong sent also two officials from the Board for National Minority
Affairs with an edict and gifts to the Panchen, in addition to ten
thousand taels of silver for the expense on the coronation.

At that time the Eighth Panchen was five years old and he was
to take the *getsul* vows. Emperor Wenzong instructed:

> The Panchen Erdeni is to be enthroned and to take vows, but the Dalai
> Lama is too young to preside over the ceremony. The Panchen had his
> head shaven and was given his religious name by Radreng Hutuktu.
> Now I order the Hutuktu to perform the coronation and vows-taking
> ceremony for the Panchen at the Tashilhunpo to express my sincerity
> to the Yellow sect.

The Eighth Panchen was enthroned and took his *getsul* vows on
the third day of the tenth month. On that auspicious day all monk
and lay officials of Tashilhunpo Monastery went to the Summer
Palace to invite the Panchen to the monastery. The coronation was
held in the Tashilhunpo's Sunlight Hall in the presence of the
Regent, Assistant Amban, Kalons, and more than one thousand lay
and clerical officials.

Before ascending the throne, the Panchen, kneeling, received
the Qing Emperor's edict and gifts, and performed full obeisance
to the east to express thanks to the Emperor. Then he took a high
seat in the hall, and the Regent, Assistant Amban, Kalons and the
Tashilhunpo's monk and lay officials presented him with *katags*
and gifts. A party was given in the Sunlight Hall in the Tashilhunpo
to celebrate the conclusion of the coronation.

On the seventh day of the tenth month the Eighth Panchen took
*getsul* vows in front of the Tashilhunpo's image of Sakyamuni
under the guidance of Radreng Hutuktu in accordance with the
lamaist customs. On the nineteenth day of the tenth lunar month

the Regent, Assistant Amban and Kalons bid farewell to the Panchen and left Shigatse for Lhasa. Shortly thereafter, the Assistant Amban requested Emperor Wenzong to endorse the appointment of Gechen Lozang Tenpa Gyaltsen as the Eighth Panchen's sutra tutor. The Emperor approved the request, granting him the title of Nomihan and instructing him to pay attention to his teaching work.

All this happened in the Second Opium War—at which time the British and French allied troops captured Beijing and set the Yuanmingyuan Palace on fire, and Emperor Wenzong fled away, not long afterwards dying at the Imperial Summer Resort in Chengde. The *Imperial Records of the Qing Dynasty* cites a royal edict:

> Man Qing and others memorialized that the Dalai Lama, Panchen Erdeni and Huilen Radreng Ngachithu Hutuktu, being sad at the death of the Grand Emperor, all offered their condolences and presented images of the Buddha and *katags*. They collected a party of monks to read sutras and pray for the late Emperor. They deserve rewards.... The Dalai Lama is granted a coral rosary, a coconut rosary, a pair of big wallets and four small ones, and the Panchen Erdeni a string of glass beads, a Bodhi rosary, a pair of big wallets and four small ones.

Qing Emperor Muzong succeeded to the throne, and his reign was called Tongzhi. However, the power was in fact in the hands of Empress Dowager Ci Xi, who attended to state affairs "from behind the screen." All the royal edicts since then were issued in compliance with Ci Xi's wishes. When the Dalai and Panchen, following old traditions, were preparing to send their *balyar khenpos* to Beijing to offer their congratulations to the new Emperor, a royal edict was issued ordering the messengers to come to Beijing after twenty-seven months.

In the third year of Emperor Muzong's reign (1864), when he was eight years old, the Twelfth Dalai Lama took his *getsul* vows from Lozang Khenrab Wangchuk, the abbot of the Ganden, as the Eighth Panchen was still in his minority. This was decided by the Regent and Kashag. The ceremony was held on the thirteenth day of the fourth month. The Eighth Panchen sent representatives to Lhasa to offer his congratulations. A royal rescript was issued extending congratulations on the vows-taking ceremony. It said:

Man Qing and others memorialized that the Dalai Lama took his *getsul* vows from his tutor, Lozang Khenrab Wangchuk, and presented images of the Buddha and *katags* to me on the thirteenth day of the fourth month of this year. This was an auspicious event. I was happy at hearing this.... I order that the Dalai Lama be granted a yellow *katag*, a coconut rosary, a jade bowl, a pair of big wallets and a pair of small ones. On receiving this edict, Man Qing should inform the Dalai Lama to take the gifts.

In the fourth month of the first year of Emperor Dezong's reign (1875), the Amban and Kashag sent men to the Tashilhunpo to inform the Eighth Panchen that Emperor Muzong had died and Emperor Dezong had succeeded to the throne. At the same time the Panchen was informed that the Twelfth Dalai had died at the age of twenty in the Potala on the twentieth day of the third lunar month. The Kashag asked the Panchen to write an obituary notice praying for the late Dalai's early reincarnation.

The *Imperial Records of the Qing Dynasty* makes no mention of the Twelfth Dalai's death. There are only two edicts concerning this matter. One, dated the eleventh month of the first year of Dezong's reign (1875), gave approval to Assistant Amban Xi Kai's proposal that Kyirong Hutuktu be put in charge of *shangshang* affairs, and the other, dated the third year of that reign (1877), granted the Kyirong Hutuktu the title of *Dashan*, but refused Amban Song Gui's proposal to grant him imperial certification. This, the edict said, would not be done until the late Dalai's remains were placed in the stupa.

In the first year of Emperor Dezong's reign (1875), when he was twenty-one years old, the Eighth Panchen was, as decided by the abbot of Tashilhunpo Monastery, ordained into full monkhood by Phurchok Rimpoche. The ordination ceremony was held in the Tashilhunpo's Yige Chungchen Hall in the presence of the representatives of the Kashag and Amban, who offered gifts to the Panchen to express congratulations.

After being ordained, the Eighth Panchen did not pay much attention to study of the doctrines of the Gelug sect. He showed much greater interest to the doctrines of the Red Hat sect. This aroused the displeasure of the Tashilhunpo monks, especially those of Tsosamling Dratsang. Owing to Dzasa Lama's painstaking mediation, as the Tibetan biography of the Eighth Panchen goes, the trouble ceased. The *Imperial Records of the Qing Dynasty* has the following to say:

> In the second year of Dezong's reign [1876] Amban Song Gui memorialized that the Panchen Erdeni, having been fascinated by the Red Hat sect, now has corrected his mistakes. The Emperor ordered the Amban to pay attention to the matter and handle it carefully.

After the death of Twelfth Dalai Trinley Gyatso, the Kashag and the Three Major Monasteries sent representatives to search for the boy reincarnating the late Dalai. The reincarnation was found in Dakpo of U in the third year of Dezong's reign (1877). The representatives of the Kashag and the Three Major Monasteries, unanimously confirming the authenticity of the reincarnation, requested the Qing court for the omission of the lot-drawing ceremony. According to the *Imperial Records of the Qing Dynasty*, in the sixth month of the third year of Dezong's reign,

> Amban Song Gui asked the Emperor in a memorial for permission to recognize the soul boy as the Dalai's reincarnation without resorting to the lot-drawing process. Emperor Dezong wrote at the end of the petition: "Lozang Thubtan Gyatso, the son of Kunga Rinchen, may be proclaimed the reincarnation of the Dalai Lama without resorting to the drawing of lots from the Golden Urn."

On the seventeenth day of the twelfth month of the third year of Dezong's reign (1877), the Kashag sent Kachopowa to the Tashilhunpo to invite the Eighth Panchen to conduct the tonsuring and name-giving ceremony for the Thirteenth Dalai. The Panchen accepted the invitation and left for Lhasa on the twenty-first day of the twelfth month of that year and arrived at Lhasa on the fourth day of the first month of the fourth year of Dezong's reign (1878). He lived in the Kelzang Phodrang Hall of the Norbulingka. At that time the Thirteenth Dalai was living in Tselgungtang Monastery. On the eleventh day of the first month the Eighth Panchen, in the company of the Regent, Amban, Kalons and representatives of the Three Major Monasteries, came to meet with the Thirteenth Dalai in Tselgungtang Monastery. The Panchen then cut his hair, clothed him in a monk's robe and officially gave him the religious name Jetsun Ngawang Lozang Thubten Gyatso Jigrab

Wangchuk Chogle Nampal Gyalwa Palzangpo (Thubten Gyatso for short). The conclusion of the ceremony was then celebrated by the Kashag in the Great Chanting Hall of the Tselgungtang.

On the ninth day of the third month the Eighth Panchen left Lhasa and went on a pilgrimage to the Radreng, Lhamo and Ganden monasteries to give sermons. On the twenty-eighth day of the third month he went back to Lhasa. On the fifteenth day of the fourth month he bid farewell to the thirteenth Dalai, Regent and Amban and left for the Tashilhunpo. He went back in the company of Kachopowa, who was sent by the Kashag.

After the ceremony the Dalai moved from the Tselgungtang to the Rekya Samtanling Monastery. He could not move into the Potala, as he was not yet enthroned, his coronation needing first to be reported to the Qing court for approval. According to the *Imperial Records of the Qing Dynasty*, in the fifth year of Dezong's reign (1879), an imperial edict was issued to approve the coronation, in which the Emperor said:

> I am sending the Dalai Lama a yellow *katag*, a statue of the Buddha, a rosary and a *vajra* with the matching bell. The Dalai Lama, after being enthroned, shall be entitled to the use of his predecessor's gold seal of authority. The request for the use of the yellow palanquin and the yellow saddle is granted. Kunga Rinchen, the Dalai Lama's father, shall be given the rank of duke and the privilege to wear a precious stone bead and peacock feathers on his hat.

With the approval of the Emperor, Dongshan Kyirong Hutuktu Ngawang Palden Choskyi Gyaltsen was made the Dalai's preceptor and Phurchok Shabdrung Lozang Tsultrim Jampa Gyatso, assistant preceptor. The Emperor ordered Ding Baozhen, the Governor-General of Sichuan, to allocate ten thousand taels of silver from the state treasury and send the silver to Se Leng'e in Tibet to cover the expenses of the Dalai's coronation.

On the thirteenth day of the sixth month in the fifth year of Dezong's reign (1879) the Thirteenth Dalai was invited from the Rekya Samtanling to the Potala. The coronation was held in the Potala's Sunlight Hall. The Eighth Panchen sent Tsedrung Namgyal Dondrup and others as his representatives to attend the Thirteenth Dalai's coronation and give him gifts to express his congratulations.

The Dalai celebrated his sixth birthday in the eighth year of

Emperor Dezong's reign (1882), and by Buddhist custom he should take his *getsul* vows. As the Eighth Panchen was too ill at the time to make the trip to Lhasa, the Kashag determined to ask the Dalai's preceptor, Dongshan Kyirong Hutuktu, to give the vows instead. The Kashag sent a request for this through the Amban to the Emperor for approval. The request was granted by the Emperor. The Dalai was initiated into monkhood in front of the image of Sakyamuni in the Jokhang on the thirteenth day of the first month in the eighth year of Emperor Dezong's reign. In the fourth month of that year the Emperor issued an edict, which, according to the *Imperial Records of the Qing Dynasty*, says:

> On the thirteenth day of the first month this year, the Dalai Lama took his *gelong* vows from his preceptor. I was happy to learn about the auspicious event. The Dalai Lama should devote himself to the study of the doctrines and the development of the Yellow Hat sect. In this way he will enjoy my favour. Now I bestow on him a yellow *katag*, a coconut rosary, a jade bowl, a jade box, a pair of big wallets and two pairs of small ones. Se Leng'e should read the edict and deliver the gifts to the Dalai.

# 2. The Struggle Between Monks and Big Serf-Owners

Eighth Panchen Tenpai Wangchuk lived in the period when the Taiping Heavenly Kingdom waged a revolutionary war, the national minorities in the southwest and northwest rebelled and the Second Opium War broke out. During this period disputes between monks and big serf-owners broke out over their scrambles for power and profits. The Amban also became involved.

In the first year of Emperor Muzong's reign (1862) a conflict flared up between Regent Radreng Ngachithu Hutuktu and the *khenpo* of Loseling Dratsang under Drepung Monastery. The Regent sacked the *khenpo* on the pretext that the latter was "pocketing part of the donations" to the monastery. This angered the *khenpo* and monks of the Drepung. Both sides resorted to force. The monks of the Drepung, uniting with monks of the Ganden, appealed to Amban Man Qing to dismiss the Regent from his post, and the Regent asked the Amban to punish the monks of Loseling Dratsang. The Amban attempted to mediate between them, but neither of them paid attention to his advice. The monks of the Drepung, with the help of Tibetan soldiers and residents of U, Tsang and Gyantse, shelled Shide Dratsang—the Regent's residence in Lhasa—with guns they had seized from the armoury in the Potala. The Tibetans, clerical and lay, fought with one another, but the Han Chinese officials were by now unable to keep a tight rein on them. Amban Man Qing asked Dzasa Lama and Wangchuk Gyatso, a retired Kalon, to mediate. But the two sides acted without restraint, knowing that the resident troops in Tibet sent by the Qing court were not large in number. The Qing troops and Han Chinese residents were all in fear of being accidentally killed by the Tibetans.

In order to deal with the matter, Amban Man Qing had sent Grain Commissioner Li Yupu, Lieutenant Colonel Tang Huaiwu and Sergeant Ma Tengjiao to make an investigation and mete out due punishments. But, owing to Li Yupu siding with the Drepung monks, the anti-Regent force was encouraged. The fighting lasted a whole day, with the Regent fleeing that night with his official seals.

The Qing Emperor, upon the Amban's impeachment, issued an edict, stripping Radreng of his title of Ngawang Yeshe Tsultrim Jamchen Huilen and declaring invalid the seals of authority of Ngachithu Hutuktu and the power bestowed on him by the Emperor. Regent Radreng Ngachithu, who had been in charge of *shangshang* affairs since the eighth year of Wenzong, said the edict, should be arrested and called to account and Wangchuk Gyatso be appointed to assist in the administration of *shangshang* affairs.

In the second year of Muzong's reign (1863), Radreng Ngachithu came to Beijing and accused Man Qing of taking bribes from Wangchuk Gyalpo and siding with the Drepung monks. Meanwhile, Luo Bingzhang, the Governor-General of Sichuan, memorialized the court that soldiers and people in Tibet had all called for reversing the verdict passed on Radreng and that Wangchuk Gyalpo had colluded with the Grain Commissioner Li Yupu in trying to murder Radreng. Accordingly, the Emperor issued an edict reprimanding Man Qing and Wangchuk Gyalpo, ordering Li

Yupu to come to Beijing to confront Radreng and sending Fu Ji and Jing Wen to Tibet to investigate the case.

But the above two imperial edicts were not carried out. Man Qing did not send Li Yupu back to Beijing and Fu Ji and Jing Wen delayed their departure to Tibet once and again. In the end, Fu Ji did not go to Tibet and Jing Wen arrived in Tibet only in the fourth year of Muzong's reign (1865) to relieve Man Qing. When Man Qing reached Beijing, Radreng had already died there. So it was needless to send Li Yupu back to confront Radreng. Man Qing was not punished. Wangchuk Gyalpo was praised for his skill at calming things down so that peace could be made in Tibet. When Wangchuk Gyalpo died in the third year of Muzong's reign (1864) Lozang Khenrab Wangchuk was appointed his successor by the Emperor and granted the title of Nomihan.

Around this time Tibet was rocked by an outburst of violence in which the chief *khenpo* of the Sera, who had been removed from office and was waiting a court trial, was rescued by monks of Sera Monastery. In the third year of Emperor Muzong's reign (1864), Thuthop Jampa, a lama of the Sera, with a party of several thousand monks of the Sera's Me, Je and Ngagpa *dratsangs*, broke into the jail and rescued the chief *khenpo*. Amban Man Qing, being at his wit's end, requested the Kashag to deal with it. The Kashag handed over the chief criminal, Thuthop Jampa, to the Amban. The Qing Emperor ordered Man Qing to have him imprisoned and then wait for imperial instructions until Fu Ji and Jing Wen arrived in Tibet.

In the twelfth month of the fourth year of Muzong's reign (1865), when Jing Wen and En Qing arrived at Lhasa, they interrogated Thuthop Jampa and announced him guilty. The written judgment said:

> When monks of the Me, Je and Ngagpa *dratsangs*, assembled to rescue the removed Khenpo Lozang Trinley Namgyal, Thuthop Jampa, instead of dissuading them from the riot, brought the Khenpo back to Sera Monastery. The next night he gathered seven hundred monks and organized them into an armed robbery gang. The Dalai Lama and Man Qing ordered him once and again to hand in the removed chief *khenpo* and chief rioters, but he refused to carry out the orders, and, in addition, sent troops to block the roads. He confessed his crimes. Thuthop Jampa

is guilty of the most heinous crimes and should be executed immediately.

In the tenth year of Emperor Muzong's reign (1871), the Ganden once again was the site of a disturbance. This time the

Ganden monastery Darhan Chief Khenpo Palden Dondrup, collaborating with Lama Ngadan and Dzasa Lama Drakpa Shelen and Lama Tsering Sangye of Ganden Chokor Ling, plotted to force Nomihan Hutuktu to resign his position as the deputy chief of *shangshang* [the Tibetan local government], and to send monk-assassins to murder the deposed Kalon, Phuntsok Tsewang Dorje, and his son, as well as Tsemon Dache Jigme Dorje, Jokhang Changzodpa Gyalo Lhawang Phuntsok, Tongpa Dapon Namgyal Dondrup and Kalon Mima Tsering. Afterwards, Palden Dondrup fled to the Ganden in dread of punishment for his crime. Kalon Tsering Wangchuk, who had been convinced of Palden Dondrup's cause, left his post without permission and, together with Palden Dondrup, took up resistance from Ganden Monastery.

En Qing and his deputy De Tai reported the riot to the Qing court. The Emperor ordered them to send Tibetan troops to arrest the criminals and, jointly with the Dalai Lama, to interrogate them.

By order of the Emperor, En Qing and De Tai sent Tibetan troops to surround the Ganden. The riot ended with

twenty-five rioters arrested, including Lama Ngadan and the deposed Kalon, Tsering Wangchuk. Palden Dondrup was fatally shot. Those fleeing away were being hunted and those who gave in were put under the strict control of the abbots of their monasteries.

The three events mentioned above took place in the Three Major Monasteries of Lhasa, one after another, in a period of ten years. Superficially, they seemed to be disputes among monks, but in fact they were handled by big clerical and lay serf-owners. In short, they were disputes among big serf-owners scrambling for power and benefits.

# 3. Britain Steps Up Aggression

The Eighth Panchen witnessed the period in which Britain stepped up its aggression in Tibet. Britain first of all tried to open the gate to Tibet on the pretext of establishing trade with Tibet. For this purpose Britain had to subdue Bhutan and Sikkim, since the traditional trade routes between India and Tibet passed through Phari of Tibet, Kalimpong of Drukpa (Bhutan) or Darjeeling of Drenjong (Sikkim).

In the fourth year of Muzong's reign (1865) British troops occupied Jiashe, Basang and Katonsang of Bhutan. The king of Bhutan appealed to the Amban for help "with Tangut soldiers, financial aid or materiel support to prevent the Phyilings [Britain] from seeking a way into Tibet by way of Bhutan." Amban Man Qing reported to the Qing court for instructions. The Emperor said: "Phyiling is Britain.... The Tanguts do not hope to do business with the Phyilings or let them do missionary work in Tibet. Drukpa's request for help and Phyiling's seeking a way into Tibet are two matters difficult to deal with." Not knowing what it should do, the Qing government only ordered the resident officials to handle the matter carefully and report to the government what measures they were to take.

At first, Bhutanese troops fought bravely with the British army. Jing Wen memorialized to the Emperor:

> Bhutanese troops killed several thousand British soldiers. By now they have become bitter enemies of each other. Phyiling has sent a big army allegedly of hundreds of thousands to take revenge, and they are expected to reach the pass on the Bhutanese border in the middle of the third lunar month [1866].

The Qing government could do nothing but ask Jing Wen to "send men to the pass to mediate a peace between the Drukpa and Phyiling."

The war ended up with Bhutan's defeat. Bhutan was forced to sign the ten-article New Treaty of Chula, by which Bhutan ceded to Britain many places, including Kalimpong, a place along the route into Tibet from India. In addition, Britain agreed to give fifty thousand rupees each year to Bhutan, while Bhutan was to remit the taxes of Indian traders in Bhutan.

Before the war against Bhutan, Britain had exerted pressure upon Drenjong. After seizing Darjeeling from Drenjong in the fifteenth year of Xuanzong's reign (1835), Britain turned Darjeeling into a county and posted a county magistrate there. This angered the king and the people of Drenjong. In the twenty-ninth year of Xuanzong's reign (1849) Drenjong jailed the British magistrate for a period of time before putting him to death along with a British tourist. Because of this, Britain stopped the payment of the annual stipend of three hundred pounds to the Drenjong king. In the tenth year of Emperor Wenzong's reign (1860), Ashley Eden, leading an expeditionary army sent by Britain, stormed the capital city of Toomling. When Britain defeated Drenjong, it dictated the following terms of peace: free trade by British subjects in Sikkim (Drenjong), construction of roads, Sikkim to act as British agent in handling communication affairs with Tibet and to receive from Britain an increased annual stipend of 1,200 pounds instead of 300 pounds, and Darjeeling to be directly administered by Britain.

British imperialists then constructed roads in Kalimpong and Darjeeling for its future military aggression against Tibet. This caused panic among the Tibetans. In the fifth year of Dezong's reign (1879), a petition signed by Dongshan Kyirong Hutuktu, who was in charge of *shangshang*, and others was sent to Amban Song Gui to be forwarded to the Emperor. In the petition they objected to the British trade and, much more vigorously, to the travelling by the British in Tibet. From what the Qing government did with the matter concerning foreign relations it was evident that there were big differences in politics between the Tibetan hierarchy and common people on the one hand and the Qing government on the other: the former struggling against the British aggression, while the latter giving no support to the struggle. An imperial edict said: "Dongshan Kyirong Hutuktu, who should have been punished severely, will be given clemency. Amban Song Gui is to be punished for his faulty handling."

While achieving domination over Bhutan and Drenjong, British imperialists instigated the Gurkhas (Nepalese) to make their third war against Tibet. In the fifty-seventh year of Gaozong's reign (1792), being defeated by the Qing army, the Gurkhas had surrendered to the Qing government, pledging that they would not invade Tibet again. Since then Tibet had coexisted peacefully with Gurkha for fifty-two years. However, when the First Opium War (from the twentieth year to the twenty-second year of Xuanzong's reign, or 1840-1842) ended up with the defeat of China and the

Qing government was forced to cede territory and pay indemnities and opening five trading ports, the Gurkhas changed their attitude. They began to make unjustifiable demands to Tibet (i.e., to China), trying to sound out the matter.

In the twenty-fourth year of Xuanzong's reign (1844) Amban Meng Bao memorialized that the Gurkha ruler demanded that "Nyelam and Kyirong be administered alternately by Tibet for ten years and by Gurkha for three years." By order of Xuanzong, the Amban refused with "sharp reproof."

In the second year of Wenzong's reign (1852) Gurkha, in a request to the Qing government to define the boundary between Tibet and Gurkha, claimed Jierpa and Jiayu to be under Gurkha's administration. The Qing government yielded. The Grand Ministers of State and the Board for National Minority Affairs memorialized:

> Amban Mu Teng'e memorialized that, according to tradition, the boundary between Gurkha and Tangut is the iron-chain bridge at Zhangmu. Not far from the path by the bridge, on the other side of the Dramchu River are Jierpa and Jiayu. The two places have been under Tangut jurisdiction. In order to calm down the dispute, we propose to put the two places under Gurkha administration, have stone walls built up on all the paths and have Gurkha and Tibet give written guarantees.

The memorial was approved by the Emperor. But the purpose of Gurkha was not only to get the two places but also to clarify China's defenses and the Ambans' attitudes. After annexing the two places, Gurkha, in the fifth year of Wenzong's reign (1855), sent an invading army of tens of thousands of men into Tibet. Kyirong, Nyelam and Dzongga fell to the invading Gurkhas on the sixth of the second lunar month, the nineteenth of the second month, and the fourteenth of the third month, respectively. Soon afterwards the Gurkhas occupied Rongshar in Tsang and Purang in Ngari. Thus, the third aggressive war of Gurkha against Tibet broke out.

Upon Amban He Tehe's urgent report, the Qing government, which at that time was facing the Taiping Rebellion, ordered him to go to Shekhar in Tsang to make an investigation of the matter. At the same time the Qings ordered the Sichuan authorities to provide military support by sending three thousand local troops into Tibet. But Le Bin, the General of Chengdu, did not carry out the order on the pretext that "Tibet was too cold to have a campaign conducted at that time."

After receiving the Emperor's order, Amban He Tehe asked Kashag to send a Kalon to go in his company to Tsang. The Kashag sent Kalon Tseten to go with the Amban, and at the same time dispatched seven or eight thousand Tibetan militiamen to resist the Gurkha invasion at Shigatse. After arriving at Shekhar, Amban He Tehe and Kalon Tseten sent some representatives to meet Gurkha chief Khache. They told the Gurkha chief Tibet would pay them fifteen thousand taels of Chinese silver for compensation in exchange for the five *dzongs* seized by the Gurkhas. The Gurkhas refused the terms. So the Tibetan army, under the command of Kalon Tseten, mounted an offensive on the Gurkhas and recovered Nyelam. However, the Gurkhas, not disheartened by their initial setbacks, raised a crack army of seven to eight thousand men. They descended on Nyelam from the cliffs at Yumukhala and captured the place again.

In the third month of the sixth year of Wenzong's reign (1856) He Tehe and Tseten were forced to make peace with Gurkha, signing a treaty of ten articles with them. The main terms of the treaty were the following: the Tibetan government was to pay a sum of ten thousand rupees (a monetary unit in Nepal as well as India) annually to the Gurkha government; henceforth Tibet was not to levy taxes on trade on Gurkha merchants; henceforth the Gurkha government was to have a resident envoy in Lhasa; Gurkha merchants were to be permitted to open shops in Lhasa and engage in free trade; the Tibetan government was not to be allowed to try any case arising among Gurkha merchants residing in Lhasa. This was the first unequal treaty Tibet signed with foreign countries. After that, Gurkha troops retreated from Nyelam and four other *dzongs*.

In his memorial to the Emperor, Amban He Tehe lied about the result of the war, saying that the Gurkhas had been defeated and requested to make peace with Tibet. Learning a lesson from the case of Ba Zhong, he did not say a word about the indemnity of ten thousand rupees Tibet had to pay annually to Gurkha. Instead, he said: "Tangut will annually pay ten thousand silver dollars to Gurkha as taxes it owed it. The sum will be delivered by *shang-*

*shang.* So it will not be detrimental to the fame of the state." Thus, the Qing government approved the unequal treaty and granted Amban He Tehe the brevet title of commander-in-chief and permission to wear peacock feathers on his hat. Man Qing was also praised by being granted feathers to be worn on his hat. All those who worked for the case of Gurkha had their official rank raised.

The war had lasted for two years, from the fifth through the sixth year of Wenzong's reign (1855-1856).

After taking his *gelong* vows, the Eighth Panchen was in poor health. Since the sixth year of Qing Emperor Dezong's reign (1880) he often took baths in the hot spring at Jiatso in northern Tibet to treat his illness. In the eighth year of Dezong's reign (1882), when he became worse in health, the Tashilhunpo's monk officials asked him to come back from the hot spring to the monastery, but he refused. On the sixth of the fifth lunar month of that year, he moved from the hot spring to his hometown in Thobgyal Shika to take rest and nourishment to regain his health. But his health worsened. On the fifteenth of the seventh lunar month he died at the age of twenty-seven. When he died, only the *Solpon, Zimpon* and *Chopon*—the three grand *khenpos* of the Tashilhunpo—were by his side. They immediately sent men to the Tashilhunpo to inform the Dzasa Lama of the Eighth Panchen's death. The Dzasa Lama immediately led several hundred clerical and lay officials of the monastery to Thobgyal Shika and had the Panchen's body carried in a yellow sedan back to the Tashilhunpo. After being treated with antiseptic, it was placed in Tsegyal Hall, where the monks and residents under the jurisdiction of the Tashilhunpo then offered sacrifices. At the same time messengers were sent to report the death to the Thirteenth Dalai Lama, Regent and Amban, and to request the Amban to report to the Emperor. The Dalai Lama was asked to compose a prayer for the late Panchen's early reincarnation. The Tashilhunpo Dzasa Lama ordered that alms of a tael of Tibetan silver be given to all monks of the Tashilhunpo and the Three Major Monasteries of Lhasa, and alms of five *gian* (1 *qian* = 5 grams) of silver be given to the 48,342 monks of the 977 monasteries in Tibet, Kham and Qinghai.

When the Thirteenth Dalai Lama, Regent and Amban learned about the Eighth Panchen's death, the Kashag sent Lhacha Teji,

Gashi Teji, Khenpo Gedun Datan and others to the Tashilhunpo to offer a thousand lamps as sacrifice to the Panchen's body.

In the eleventh month of the eighth year of Qing Emperor Dezong's reign (1882), the Qing government sent Amban Se Leng'e to "offer sacrifices to the late Panchen and give five thousand taels of silver for the funeral expenses, in addition to brocade, *katags*, an imperial rosary, a plate of court beads made of agalloch eagle-wood, and a volume of scripture." The Emperor then "ordered that all affairs in Tibet be put under the charge of Dzasa Lama Lozang Dondrup" (from the *Imperial Records of the Qing Dynasty*). Kalon Dokharwa was among those who accompanied the Amban to the Tashilhunpo.

According to protocol, a golden stupa was to be built to contain the Panchen's body. The stupa was built up in the eleventh year of Dezong's reign (1885) and the Panchen's body was placed in it. The stupa was placed in the Tashilhunpo's Lingtse Hall. The Emperor issued an edict on the occasion:

> The Panchen Erdeni set an example of hard study of scriptures and development of the Yellow sect for all monks in Tsang. I am relieved to learn that his disciples have had his stupa built and I miss him very much. To praise the diligent lama, I order that he be given a *katag* and a rosary, which are to be delivered by Se Leng'e to his disciples and placed before the golden stupa of the Panchen Erdeni (from the *Imperial Records of the Qing Dynasty*).

# Chapter Seven
# Choskyi Nyima, the Ninth Panchen Lama

## 1. The Enthronement and Vows-Taking

The Ninth Panchen (1883-1937), given the religious name Choskyi Nyima, was born in Kashe Village of Dakpo in Tsang on the twelfth day of the first month of the Water-Sheep year in the fifteenth Tibetan calendrical cycle (the ninth year of Qing Emperor Dezong's reign, or 1883) to his mother, Damchong Tsemo, a poor dumb woman who tended cattle and sheep for an aristocratic family. His father was unknown, though it was said that his father's name was Tenzin. The Ninth Panchen was brought up in the family of his grandfather on his mother's side. He had a younger brother, who became a monk and afterwards became the Tsechokling Hutuktu. After he was recognized as the Panchen, his mother became a nun.

Following the death of the Eighth Panchen, Tenpai Wangchuk, the Tashilhunpo began the search for his reincarnation. The search parties returned with reports that three boys had been discovered, one of whom was Tsangdrup Gyatso (who was afterwards recognized as the Ninth Panchen). As required by the Qing court, lots were to be drawn from the Golden Urn to determine which of the three candidates was to be established as the Ninth Panchen. Amban Wen Shuo reported to the Emperor about the case. In the eleventh month of the thirteenth year of Emperor Dezong's reign (1887), the Amban received an imperial edict:

Wen Shuo memorialized that three soul boys had been found. It is already five years since the Panchen Erdeni died.... I granted his memorial. The three boys' names should be placed in the Golden Urn for lot-drawing, the result of which must be reported to me through the post stations (from the *Imperial Records of the Qing Dynasty*).

Amban Wen Shuo ordered Tashilhunpo Monastery to send the three boy candidates to Lhasa. The date for the lot-drawing was fixed on the fifteenth day of the first month of the following year (1888). The ceremony was held before the spirit tablet of the Qing Emperor in the Potala. At the beginning of the ceremony Regent Ganden Tripa Demo Hutuktu, the Tashilhunpo Dzasa Lama and others came to chant the *Golden Urn Sutra* in the Potala. The lot-drawing began with the writing of the three boys' names on three ivory tallies, which were to be placed in the Golden Urn. Then the Amban picked one of the tallies. The name on the tally then was revealed. It was the name of the boy from Dakpo, Tsangdrup Gyatso. He was therefore recognized as the Ninth Panchen.

On the same day the Thirteenth Dalai, Thubten Gyatso, shaved the new Panchen's head and named him Jetsun Lozang Choskyi Nyima Geleg Namgyal, or Choskyi Nyima for short, in the Potala's Sunlight Hall. Afterwards, the Panchen left for the Tashilhunpo in the company of officials sent by that monastery. He took temporary residence in the Konchokling Summer Palace, waiting for an auspicious day for coronation. Amban Wen Shuo reported the proceedings of the ceremony to the Emperor.

On the twenty-fifth day of the fourth month of the fourteenth year of Dezong's reign (1888) Wen Shuo received an imperial edict:

> On the fifteenth day of the first month this year, the Amban went to the Potala, where Demo Hutuktu, Sule Nomihan Lozang Dondrup and others were chanting sutras. The name of Tsangdrup Gyatso was picked out of the Golden Urn. He was chosen as the reincarnation. On that day the weather was fine and everything was auspicious. All monks in Tibet were overjoyed.... I feel happy about it. I grant the reincarnation a *katag*, a string of coral beads and a jade *ruyi*.... I order that the Demo Hutuktu and all lamas of Tibet take good care of the reincarnation to fulfill my hopes to develop the Yellow sect (from the *Imperial Records of the Qing Dynasty*).

The date for coronation was fixed on the third day of the first month in the eighteenth year of Emperor Dezong's reign (1892).

The Qing government sent new Amban Sheng Tai to preside over the ceremony. The Thirteenth Dalai and the Kashag sent Regent Demo Hutuktu as their representative to offer congratulations. After coronation, the Ninth Panchen took his *getsul* vows from Regent Demo Hutuktu, as the Thirteenth Dalai, who had not yet taken *gelong* vows, was not qualified to give *getsul* vows to the Panchen.

Before the coronation, Amban Sheng Tai requested the Qing government to grant an imperial edict and gifts to the reincarnation of the Panchen Erdeni on his coronation and to have them sent speedily under the escort of local officials on the way to Tibet. He also reported to the government that the Dzasa Lama of the Tashilhunpo had requested, according to Buddhist customs, that Demo Hutuktu go to the Tashilhunpo to preside over the enthronement, vows-taking and scripture-reading ceremonies for the reincarnation. The request was granted.

As the Ninth Panchen had grown up in his maternal grandfather's family, Amban Sheng Tai requested the Emperor to grant his grandfather, Jigme Wangpo, the title of duke. His grandfather was granted the title of *Fu Guo Gong* (Counsellor Duke), which could not be inherited.

To congratulate the Ninth Panchen upon his enthronement, the Qing government ordered Liu Bingzhang, the Governor-General of Sichuan, to allocate ten thousand taels of silver from the state treasury to the Panchen and send men to deliver the silver to Tibet.

After the enthronement, the Ninth Panchen sent Khenpo Lozang Rondan to Beijing to express gratitude to Empress Dowager Ci Xi and Emperor Dezong.

In the twenty-eighth year of Dezong's reign (1902) the Ninth Panchen was nineteen years old, and by Buddhist custom he was to take his *gelong* vows. At that time the Thirteenth Dalai, at the age of twenty-six, had taken his *gelong* vows. Tashilhunpo Monastery thus invited the Thirteenth Dalai to give the vows to the Panchen. With the approval of the Dalai, Regent Demo Hutuktu and the Amban, the Ninth Panchen came to Lhasa in the company of Tashilhunpo monk officials and took his *gelong* vows from the Thirteenth Dalai in front of the image of Sakyamuni in the Jokhang on the fifteenth day of the fourth month that year. He went back to the Tashilhunpo on the tenth day of the fifth month.

## 2. The Ninth Panchen Takes an Active Part in the First Anti-British War

The period from the birth of the Ninth Panchen to the time he took his *gelong* vows was a time in which the British intensified their military invasion of Tibet and the Tibetan people, clerical and secular, staged a heroic anti-British war. The first anti-British war took place in the fourteenth year of Dezong's reign (1888), when Britain had occupied Drenjong. In order to resist British entry into Tibet, the Kashag built blockhouses at Lengtu, a place in Tibet bordering on Drenjong. The British imperialists falsely accused Tibet of crossing the boundary and made January 1, 1888, a deadline for the evacuation of the Tibetan troops. The Kashag strongly opposed this. In a petition to Amban Wen Shuo, signed in the thirteenth year of Dezong's reign (1887) by representatives from the Three Major Monasteries and the Tashilhunpo and all the officials of the Kashag above the seventh rank, their resolution to resist British invasion was given as follows: "The entire secular and clerical populace of Tibet is resolved to resist their intrusion even if it means the extermination of every one of us."

Amban Wen Shuo sympathized with the Tibetan people in their struggle against the British intrusion. But the Qing government, which submitted to British pressure, via Wen Shuo, ordered the Kashag, the Three Major Monasteries and the Tashilhunpo to pull down the blockhouses at Lengtu as Britain required.

The Tibetans ignored the order of the Qing government to evacuate, while Amban Wen Shuo disapproved of the Qing government's submission to British pressure. In the second month of the fourteenth year of Dezong's reign (1888) Wen Shuo was reprimanded by the Qing government as follows: "Wen Shuo, out of stupidity, acted in disregard to the interests of the country." Wen Shuo was dismissed as Amban in the following month. The decision to remove him from that post said: "Wen Shuo ignored imperial instructions.... As such outrages can never be tolerated,

Wen Shuo is hereby dismissed from his post." Chang Geng was appointed as the Amban to succeed him. However, the Tibetan people's struggle against the British invasion did not cease. On the twentieth day of the third month in the fourteenth year of Dezong's reign, British troops launched an attack on the Lengtu defense line held by the Tibetan forces. The British troops fought with modern weapons, while all that the Tibetans had for weapons were flame ropes, bows and arrows, small firearms and stones. As the British troops had the advantage in weapons, for all their brave resistance the Tibetans were completely defeated. The Lengtu defense line fell to the hands of British troops.

In the sixth month of that year three thousand Tibetan troops mounted a counteroffensive on Lengtu in an attempt to recapture it, but the attack was repulsed. So Tibetan troops had to give up Lengtu. It was the first anti-British war in the modern history of Tibet.

The Dalai's and the Panchen's groups maintained the same attitude on the war. The Three Major Monasteries on the Dalai's side and the Tashilhunpo on the Panchen's side all sent militiamen to the battlefield.

After the failure of the war, the Qing government ordered the new Amban, Sheng Tai, who succeeded Chang Geng, to make peace with his British counterpart on the Tibetan-Indian border. The Dalai Lama provided him with an entourage made up of Kalon Yeshe Norbu Wangchuk, Kalon Drashi Darje, acting-Kalon Lozang Yeshe Chumbi and Changzod Tepa Tseten Wangchuk. The Panchen also sent Changzod Tepa Sonam Wangyal from the Tashilhunpo to join in his entourage. But Sheng Tai was faithful to the Qing policy of capitulation to foreign powers. For that he was praised by the Qing government. At the same time, the Qing court ordered him to meet with the British representative as soon as possible.

Sheng Tai arrived at Rinchen Gang on the Tibetan-Indian border on the tenth day of the eleventh month. As requested by Charles Bell, Britain's representative, Sheng Tai met with him at Nathang in Drenjong while the Kalons and other Tibetan officials remained at Rinchen Gang waiting for the news of the meeting. Bell said to Sheng Tai that Britain had been given a protectorate over Drenjong. Then the British representative demanded war reparations from Tibet. On the question of trade, the British said they wanted to carry it as far as Gyantse.

After much argument, the British backed down. They allowed Drenjong to continue traditional expressions of respect (i.e., to send tribute) to China and Tibet and to waive the war reparations. He said that if the trade in Gyantse was out of the question, it should be carried out at Phari. Sheng Tai reported the meeting to the Qing government and asked the Kashag to discuss the questions of evacuating troops, delimiting the boundary and opening trade.

After a year's discussion, the Kashag replied that they agreed to pull back their troops and delimit the boundary. But, the reply continued, "We Tibetans are in an extremely difficult position on the question of trade. If there must be trade as the orders say, the Dzaleb must be made off limits for foreigners"— meaning that the British trade was to be allowed to be carried on only in the Tibetan-Indian borderland.

Sheng Tai, as the plenipotentiary of China, left for Calcutta on the twentieth day of the second month of the sixteenth year of Dezong's reign (1890). There he met with Lord Lansdowne, the Governor-General of India. The Anglo-Chinese Convention was signed on the twenty-seventh day of the second month of the same year. The treaty consisted of eight articles, of which the one on trade said, "The question ... will hereafter be discussed with a view to a mutually satisfactory arrangement..." —that is, the question of trade was not solved. Nevertheless, the treaty admitted the British protectorate over Drenjong. Afterwards, Drenjong was not allowed by Britain to continue its traditional expression of respect to China.

According to the treaty, the questions of pasturage on both sides of the border and official communication between the British authorities in India and the authorities in Tibet were reserved for further examination and adjustment. This left a chance for a further British invasion of Tibet.

In the eleventh month of the seventeenth year of Dezong's reign (1891) the British representative asked Sheng Tai to go to Calcutta to continue the talks on trade, pasturage and communication. In the eighteenth year of Dezong's reign (1892) Sheng Tai first went to the Tashilhunpo to officiate at the Ninth Panchen's *getsul* ceremony, and then left for Rinchen Gang on the twelfth day of the first month. The British put forward in written form the articles to be negotiated on trade, pasturage and communication; Sheng Tai passed them to the Dalai and Panchen for discussion. On the twentieth day of the second month, Demo Hutuktu forwarded to the Amban a petition from the Three Major Monasteries and the Tashilhunpo, which said that many of these articles were unacceptable. As the British insisted on the acceptance of these articles as they were, the meeting came to a deadlock.

In the ninth month of that year Sheng Tai died of illness at Rinchen Gang, leaving his successor, Kui Huan, to continue the negotiations with the British. On the twenty-eighth day of the tenth month in the nineteenth year of Dezong's reign (1893) the Regulations Regarding Trade, Communication and Pasturage To Be Appended to the Sikkim-Tibet Convention of 1890, a slightly modified version of a text drawn up by the British consisting of nine articles and three general articles, were signed in Darjeeling by Assistant Regional Commander of the Sichuan Yuejun Garrison He Changrong and James Hart (a Briton) of the Tax Bureau representing China, and Charles Bell, British Political Representative in Drenjong, representing Britain.

For the Qing government the regulations meant the loss of another important diplomatic battle with Britain, because these regulations allowed British merchants to trade in Tibet. The conclusion of the subsequent regulations was negotiated exclusively by Amban Kui Huan, and the Dalai and Panchen did not give their full consent to it beforehand.

The twenty-first year of Dezong's reign (1895) saw a serious political incident in Tibet—the murder of the Regent Demo Hutuktu and the Thirteenth Dalai Lama's assumption of temporal power. As required by lamaist customs, a Dalai Lama took charge of Tibet's religious and administrative affairs at the age of eighteen, until which time the power was in the hands of the Regent. In the tenth month of the twenty-first year of Dezong's reign Demo Hutuktu tendered his resignation on reason of illness. Amban Kui Huan reported this to the Qing government. The government approved Demo's resignation and ordered the Dalai to assume the religious and administrative power in Tibet. In the tenth month of the twenty-second year of that reign (1896) Assistant Amban Ne Qing memorialized: "The Dalai Lama has assumed Tibetan temporal power and taken his *gelong* vows. As a rule, he can be exempted from paying tribute."

Why did the Dalai Lama assume temporal power a year later than the Qing government's approval? Because there had been a life-and-death struggle between the Thirteenth Dalai and Demo Hutuktu. According to the Tibetan biography of the Thirteenth Dalai Lama, the former Regent Demo Hutuktu, after resigning from his office, continued to hold power and was plotting against the Dalai's life. Norbu Tsering, Demo's younger brother, gave the Dalai Lama a pair of boots with fatal incantations sewn in the soles. When the Dalai wore the boots he became distraught. So the Nechung Chosgyong was consulted, and the oracle invoked traced the Dalai's sickness to the boots. When the boots were torn apart, the incantations were discovered. Thus the Thirteenth Dalai Lama had Norbu Tsering arrested and interrogated. That very night Demo Hutuktu died suddenly at the age of forty-five in his monastery, the Tengyeling. There were various versions about his death, but a full investigation could not be conducted.

After the death of Demo Hutuktu, the Thirteenth Dalai Lama took charge of Tibetan religious and temporal power. It was at that time that British imperialists threatened to invade Lhasa. The Thirteenth Dalai Lama was determined to lead the Tibetan people, clerical and secular, in the second struggle against the British invasion. Facing British aggression, the Ninth Panchen maintained the same attitude as that of the Dalai, leading all monks and residents under the Tashilhunpo in the second anti-British war.

Tibetans rose again in arms against British invaders in the twenty-ninth year of Dezong's reign (1903). The Panchen was the first to be affected by the invasion. On April 16, the British-Indian government proposed a Sino-British meeting in Khamba Dzong on the problems of the boundary and pasturage. The British government sent envoy Francis Younghusband and deputy envoy Claude White with an escort of two hundred men to the place of negotiation. Meanwhile, "Reinforcements were held in reserve in Sikkim, and, should the Chinese and Tibetan representatives fail to appear, or should the former come without the latter, our representative should move forward to Shigatse or Gyantse" (from *India and Tibet*).

Khamba Dzong, a *dzong* under the Panchen's administration, is a place in Tibet bordering on Sikkim. The proposal aimed at exerting pressure on the Panchen and undermining the Panchen and Dalai's unity. But Britain did not succeed. The Panchen did not waver in his resolution to struggle against the British invaders and unite with the Dalai Lama in the struggle.

When Britain proposed Khamba Dzong as the place of negotiation, the Qing government, which was weak and incompetent in facing the British military invasion, agreed to the proposal without consulting with the Dalai and Panchen, and ordered the Kashag to send deputies to attend the meeting. Thus the relations between the Kashag and Qing government worsened. In the seventh month of the twenty-ninth year of Dezong's reign (1903), Amban You Tai dispatched a special delegate, He Guangxie, to Khamba Dzong and the Kashag sent two junior officials there. Two hundred British troops under the command of deputy envoy White and Captain O'Connor occupied Khamba Dzong on July 7, 1903. Envoy Younghusband arrived there on July 18.

When White came to Khamba Dzong, the two junior officers, representatives from the Kashag, protested regarding British violation of the frontier and asked him to go back to the Tibetan-Indian frontier and wait there for the meeting. He Guangxie also asked White to go back to Giagang on the border. But White did not yield and insisted that the meeting should be held in Khamba Dzong. Both sides refused to give in for a while. The two officials from the Kashag raised objections to the size of the British envoy's escort. Younghusband writes in his *India and Tibet*, "These so-called delegates never came near us again at Khamba Dzong, but shut themselves up in the fort and sulked...." He reported to the British government that the talks might drag on for a long time and that the British government should prepare to resort to arms.

The Panchen knew that war was coming in the near future and would cause great disaster to his people, so he sent his representative to Khamba Dzong to persuade British troops to go back to the Tibetan-Indian frontier. Younghusband continues in his book:

A deputation came to meet me on behalf of the Tashi Lama [the Panchen Lama], who is of equal spiritual importance with the Dalai Lama, though of less political authority. They said that they had been sent to represent to us that the Tashi Lama was put to great trouble with the Lhasa authorities by our presence at Khamba Jong [Dzong], that the Lhasa authorities held him responsible for permitting us to cross the frontier, and that he begged me to be so kind as to save him from the trouble by withdrawing across the frontier.

The Panchen's proposal was refused, and his representatives returned to the Tashilhunpo.

On August 21, the chief abbot of Tashilhunpo Monastery came to Younghusband to make another appeal on behalf of the Panchen. The abbot said that a council had been held by the Panchen and that it had been decided to send another representative to persuade the British representatives to withdraw to the frontier. Younghusband again refused the proposal. While they were staying in Khamba Dzong, the Panchen's representatives made close contacts with those from the Kashag.

On August 31, Younghusband and White were informed that some 2,600 Tibetan soldiers had occupied the heights and passes on a line between Phari and Shigatse. Younghusband thought:

> Their immediate policy was one of passive obstruction. They had made up their mind to have no negotiations with us inside Tibet, and they would simply leave us at Khamba Jong [Dzong], while if we tried to advance farther, they would oppose us by force. They were afraid that if they gave us an inch we would take an ell, and if they allowed us at Khamba Jong one year we should go to Shigatse the next, and Lhasa the year after. So they were determined to stop us at the start.

On October 11, Younghusband left Khamba Dzong for Simla to confer with the government of British India on a future military invasion of Tibet. Under the instructions of the British government, Earnest Satow, British Minister at Beijing, presented a note to the Qing government, stating that the Qing should take responsibility for the failure of the meeting in Khamba Dzong and that the British would attack Tibet as a last resort.

On November 6 the Qing government protested to the British government against an advance into Tibet. The Russian government also began to move in the matter. On November 7, the British government informed the Russian Ambassador:

> Owing to the outrageous conduct of the Tibetans, it had been decided to send our mission, with a suitable escort, farther into the Tibetan territory, but this step should not be taken as indicating any intention of annexing, or even of permanently occupying, Tibetan territory.

Soon afterwards, Younghusband ordered White to withdraw with his escort from Khamba Dzong and attack Phari by way of Chumbi Valley. Thus the second anti-British war broke out in the thirtieth year of Dezong's reign (1904).

The invading British troops consisted of more than one thousand men, with guns and modern weapons. In terms of military equipment, the British army was much better off. Having occupied Chumbi Valley and Phari by January 4 and 6, 1904, the British troops met a vigorous counterattack from the Tibetan troops, but the Tibetans were defeated. On April 11, 1904, after a fierce battle, the British invaders conquered Gyantse. The battle caused great losses on both sides and ended up with the defeat of the Tibetan troops. The heroic defense of Gyantse on that day is now famous. After the fall of Gyantse, the British army, having been reinforced, pressed towards Lhasa. Lhasa fell on August 3. On the eve of the fall of the city, the Thirteenth Dalai Lama fled from Lhasa via Qinghai to Outer Mongolia. Amban You Tai visited Younghusband and made a special present of food to the British troops to express sympathy and solicitude.

# 3. The Thirteenth Dalai Is Forced to Go to Outer Mongolia and the Ninth Panchen Is Forced to Go to India

When the British troops entered Lhasa, all high-ranking Tibetan officials, clerical and secular, had gone into hiding. Younghusband asked Amban You Tai to call them out for negotiations. With the Amban's mediation, the Kashag and representatives from the Three Major Monasteries signed the Treaty of Lhasa, consisting of ten articles, on September 7, 1904, in the Potala. The gist of the ten articles was that the Tibetan local government was to undertake to open trade marts at Gyantse, Gartok and Yadong and to pay a war indemnity of 7,500,000 rupees over a period of seventy-five years; and the British government would continue to occupy Chumbi until the indemnity had been paid. You Tai let the Tibetan representatives sign the treaty without getting the approval of the Qing government beforehand. Those who signed on behalf of Tibet were the Regent Ganden Tripa, all the Kalons and representatives from the Three Major Monasteries. What deserves attention is that the representatives from the Tashilhunpo were not forced to sign it, though the Panchen group had taken an active part in the two anti-British wars. This reveals a British conspiracy: to leave a way for the Panchen to be drawn over to the British side.

On September 22, 1904, after the Treaty of Lhasa had been signed, Younghusband and his troops pulled out of Lhasa. They took away large quantities of priceless cultural relics by pack animals—a total of over forty loads. When he reached Gyantse, Younghusband left Captain O'Connor there as trade agent with a party of sixty armed guards. In fact, O'Connor was left there to draw the Panchen in. Younghusband also left a part of his troops in Chumbi Valley in order to establish the occupation of it for the seventy-five years until Tibet paid all the indemnity.

The Qing government judged that the Treaty of Lhasa damaged China's sovereignty. On the fourth day of the eighth month in the thirtieth year of Dezong's reign (1904) the Qing government cabled its reply to You Tai. It pointed out Tibet was a part of China and then it said:

> As the two treaties of the sixteenth and nineteenth year of the reign of His Majesty were negotiated and concluded by Chinese and British officials deputed by their respective governments, it follows that the present one should be concluded in the same manner, with the Tibetans signing it only as a secondary party; Britain should not be allowed to conclude it with the Tibetans directly.

Therefore, in the first month of the thirty-first year of Dezong's reign (1905), the Qing government sent Tang Shaoyi to Calcutta as Chinese plenipotentiary to negotiate with the government of British India. The talks dragged on for more than a year without producing any results because of the intransigence of the British Viceroy in India. Tang, in ill health, returned to Beijing. He was replaced by Zhang Yintang in 1906. The talks went on in Calcutta and then in Beijing. According to the Treaty of Lhasa, Tibet was to pay Britain a reparation of 7,500,000 rupees in seventy-five annual installments. Now the British representative offered to reduce the sum to 2,500,000 rupees, but it was to be paid in twenty-five annual installments. Zhang Yintang, on behalf of the Qing government, said that the Chinese government would pay the reparations for Tibet in three years. The British negotiators, however, continued to argue over the length of the indemnity payment period. Finally the British made concessions on this issue. Thus, a second treaty relating to Tibet was concluded between China and Britain and was signed on April 27, 1906, the Treaty of Lhasa being attached to it as an annex. The treaty, called the Sino-British Convention, consisted of eight articles. In 1908, three years after the signing of the convention, the Qing government had paid the total sum of the indemnity of 2,500,000 rupees, and the British troops therefore had to evacuate Chumbi Valley.

When Britain and China were holding the second negotiations, a new plot against Tibet was hatched by the British imperialists. They planned to get the Ninth Panchen to India, arrange for him to meet with the British Crown Prince (who was then in India), bribe him into their service and send him back to Tibet to run the regime, acting as a deputy of the British government. The conspiracy failed because the Panchen objected.

In the second anti-British war the Ninth Panchen had stood on the Dalai's side and had sent his *Solpon Khenpo* to the battlefield. In the Tuna battle the *khenpo* had been killed by British troops.

When the British army conquered Lhasa, the Thirteenth Dalai had to escape for fear of being arrested by the British. You Tai denounced the Dalai Lama in a memorial to the Qing government:

> He acted contrary to the imperial instructions and gave no heed to advice, and when his army was defeated and a grave situation was threatening, he did nothing to avert it but took flight to some remote region.... Please inform the court of my request that the Dalai Lama be removed of his titles temporarily.... The court is also requested to order the Panchen Erdeni to head the Yellow sect in U for the time being and to handle matters related to the negotiations.

The Qing government telegraphed the following reply to You Tai:

"The Dalai Lama is to be removed of his titles temporarily, and the Panchen Erdeni is to act in his capacity for the time being." All the telegraphs were transmitted and received by Younghusband in India, as requested by You Tai.

The Ninth Panchen was farsighted in politics and kept the overall interests in mind. He thought that to take over the Dalai's office at a time when the Dalai was absent would do harm to the good relations between them and the Tibetan internal unity, and so he wrote a letter to You Tai, explaining that

> Tsang is a vitally important region, and the local public affairs require my management. Besides, with the British lurking in Gyantse, which is a two-day journey away, Tsang must be closely guarded. If I were in U, I am afraid I would not be able to look after things in Tsang.

Thus he refused to carry out the order. You Tai, in a report to the Qing government, requested the government to permit the Panchen to stay in Tsang—which You Tai called "a vitally important region"—to look after things there (see the *Imperial Records of the Qing Dynasty*).

Taking advantage of the Dalai's absence, British imperialists ordered Captain O'Connor, who was at Gyantse at that time, to induce the Panchen to go to India. According to the instructions, O'Connor, accompanied by an escort of over fifty soldiers, came to Shigatse on the twenty-fourth day of the ninth month in the thirty-first year of Dezong's reign (1905) to pay the Ninth Panchen a farewell visit. The Panchen received him politely. During the audience O'Connor told the Panchen that the British Prince of Wales would come to India for an important gathering and that the Prince would like to meet with the Panchen while he was there. O'Connor asked the Panchen to start in the tenth month. The Panchen replied that, while he did not object personally to going to India, he could not do so without the signed approval of the Qing Emperor given through the Amban. But the Englishman insisted on his going, saying that Britain was acting in good faith and asking him to give serious thought to the invitation.

Under such circumstances the Panchen, through Grain Commissioner Fan Qirong and Commander Ma Youlong, asked Amban You Tai to decide for him. You Tai did not know what to do except to tell the Panchen to persist in his refusal. At the same time You Tai asked Zhang Yintang, who was attending negotiations in India, to prevent the British envoy from causing trouble in Tsang. O'Connor insisted on the Panchen's going to India and threatened with British military might. He implied that not going would mean the British army would be used to subjugate Shigatse and Tashilhunpo Monastery.

Under the pressure of the British, the Panchen, in a letter to You Tai, explained:

> If I refuse to go to India, I would cause trouble to Tsang and the Tashilhunpo. If I go without the signed approval of His Majesty, I would be punished by His Majesty. Still, I cannot help being deeply concerned about the safety of the Tashilhunpo, its monks and the entire Tibetan populace. I cannot but risk my life and go to India as they insist. I beg Your Excellency to explain to His Majesty as soon as possible that, as my decision to go is made under great pressure, it should not be taken as an intended offense. If I act against His Majesty's favour, may I be thrown into hell after my death.

On September 29, O'Connor, in an overbearing manner, said to the Panchen that he would deliver to the Panchen the letter from the British King's representative and the Panchen should act as required, for Britain was an unusual, great country.

On the eve of his departure for India, the Panchen asked You Tai in a letter to send a resident official in Tsang to accompany him. The Panchen started off from Shigatse on the twelfth day of the tenth month in the thirty-first year of Dezong's reign (1905). Fan Qirong, the Grain Commissioner in Tsang, accompanied him to Gyantse and then returned to Shigatse. When the Ninth Panchen went through Qingxi, as the local officials reported, O'Connor and his calvary followed him as if escorting him.

In India the Panchen paid a courtesy call on the Prince of Wales. O'Connor asked the Panchen to kowtow to the Prince. The Panchen refused to do so, saying that he kowtowed to the Chinese Emperor only. He instead shook hands with the Prince.

The Panchen sent the Dzasa Lama to visit Zhang Yintang, the Qing envoy in India. Zhang upbraided the Lama for coming to India and said that if the Panchen had been able to wait ten days, the affair would never have come about. The Dzasa Lama explained that the Panchen had risked his life and had come to India under the pressure of O'Connor out of fear of British military might after reporting to the Amban twice. The Lama asked Zhang for help. Zhang urged the Panchen to leave on the seventeenth day of the month, so that the British could not cause more trouble to him. If the British did not let the Panchen go, Zhang said, he would come to protect the Panchen. Zhang would provide the money the Panchen needed for the expense of the journey back to Tsang. Unless the Panchen did this, Zhang said, he would be brought to account.

The Ministry of Foreign Affairs of the Qing government then telegraphed to its envoy, Zhang Yintang, and the British Governor in India. Said the telegram: "The Panchen is now in India for a visit. If he is forced to interfere in Tibetan affairs, the Chinese government will not recognize any document signed and sealed by him in India."

Since the Prince of Wales and the Governor of British India were thereafter unable to touch upon official business in their conversation with the Panchen, the British India government had to send the Panchen back politely.

The Ninth Panchen arrived at Gyantse under the escort of seventy-odd British soldiers on the tenth day of the twelfth month of that year. After a two-day rest there, he started for Tashilhunpo Monastery under the escort of another group of about thirty British soldiers.

On the twelfth day of the first month of the thirty-second year of Dezong's reign (1906) the Qing government instructed:

> It was wrong for the Panchen to go to India without our approval. Now that he has come back and considering the sincerity he expressed in his report to us, we approve that he can return to Tibet and take his office as before.

The Ninth Panchen expressed thanks to the Emperor in a memorial to the Qing government.

In a memorial Zhang Yintang said:

> The Panchen went to India under the pressure of O'Connor, who hoped to get a reward with the matter. On the journey O'Connor kept guard on the Panchen. On the visit to the Prince of Wales, O'Connor

asked the Panchen to kowtow to the Prince, but the Panchen refused to yield. The British had no alternative. The Panchen's conversations with the Prince and the Indian Governor were limited to polite inquiries into each other's health and never touched on Tibetan affairs. With no opportunity to take, the British had to send the Panchen back. The press has reported how O'Connor put pressure on the Panchen. It is informed that the British government also disapproved of it.

Not long after the Panchen came back to Tashilhunpo Monastery, on the sixth day of the ninth month in the thirty-second year of Emperor Dezong's reign (1906), Charles Bell, the British Resident in Sikkim, in a further attempt to establish connections with the Panchen, visited him at the Tashilhunpo. Afterwards, Bell paid him several visits. After spending two months in Shigatse, Bell, on the sixth day of the eleventh month, left for India. Bell treats the visit in a special chapter in his book *Tibet: Past and Present*. He reports that he found out that the area under the Panchen's jurisdiction had only three counties in addition to Shigatse, much smaller than the territory under the Dalai Lama, the lord of Tibet. He also found out that Lhasa and the Tashilhunpo (the Dalai and Panchen's groups) were bitterly jealous of each other, though it was said that the two grand lamas were in good relations and only the subordinates of both sides were hostile to each other. Bell came to the conclusion that the subordinates showed more hostility to each other than their lords, the two lamas. Bell gained nothing from his visit to the Panchen.

Knowing that Tibetan affairs were complex and Amban You Tai was not good at handling them, the Qing government authorized Zhang Yintang, a brevet Vice Commander-in-Chief of the fifth rank, to "investigate conditions and put things in order in Tibet" in the thirty-second year of Dezong's reign (1906). Zhang Yintang went to Tibet via India. He reached Lhasa on the twelfth day of the tenth month. The first thing Zhang did was to expose the misconduct of You Tai, including the latter's fawning on foreign powers and selling out of his own country to obtain power and wealth. Upon Zhang's charges against You Tai, the Qing government announced the dismissal of You Tai and then punished him by sending him to serve in the army. Assistant Amban Lian Yu was made Amban and Wen Zongyao, Assistant Amban. The other corrupt officials were also punished. This measure won the support of all Tibetans, clerical and lay.

After making an investigation and putting things in order in Tibet, Zhang Yintang left for Beijing via India for debriefing in the sixth month of the thirty-third year in Dezong's reign (1907). Zhang arrived at Gyantse and met with the Ninth Panchen, who had been waiting for an audience in Gyantse Kumbum. The Panchen requested permission for him to go to Beijing to report on Tibetan affairs in person to Empress Dowager Ci Xi and Emperor Dezong. Zhang Yintang promised to relay his request to the court. Then the Qing government instructed: "The Panchen Erdeni's request is sincere.... He may have an audience with the Emperor after the situation in Tibet gets better."

After the Thirteenth Dalai Lama arrived in Outer Mongolia, he requested the Qing government via De Ling, the Qing resident official in Urga, for help in the anti-British struggle. In the eleventh month of the thirtieth year of Dezong's reign (1904), the Qing court instructed De Ling by telegram to invite the Dalai to Urga. At the same time Yan Zhi was sent from Beijing to Urga to arrange for the Dalai to come to Urga. Though stripped of his titles, the Dalai still enjoyed very high prestige among the Mongolian people. And, as Mongolian princes and ministers had a grievance against the removal of the Dalai's titles, the Qing government therefore still had to show respect to the Dalai.

The Tibetan people, both lay and monk, also raised their objections to the decision of the Qing government on the removal of the Dalai's titles. Knowing that the matter had not been well-handled, Amban You Tai reminded the Qing government of the advisability of satisfying the Tibetans by restoring the titles to the Dalai Lama. The government's reply came: A decision will be made on this matter when the Dalai Lama leaves Urga.

In the thirty-first year of Dezong's reign (1905) the Qing government instructed:

> The British army entered Tibet but did not occupy a place. The Dalai Lama should not have fled with his seals and left his post.... Now all has become calm as usual in Tibet. The Dalai Lama is expected to go back as early as possible to enjoy the favour of the Qing court.

Here the Qing government publicly absolved Britain from guilt and, on the other hand, took the Dalai's refuge in Outer Mongolia as an intentional leaving of his post to justify its own wrong policy.

In the fourth month of the thirty-second year in Dezong's reign (1906) the Thirteenth Dalai left Urga for Tibet. When he reached Kumbum Monastery in Qinghai, an imperial edict was brought to him through the Governor-General of Shaanxi and Gansu, ordering him to stay at the Kumbum until further instructions from the Emperor. So the Dalai Lama stayed in the Kumbum.

In the thirty-third year of Dezong's reign (1907) the Qing government extended to the Dalai Lama an invitation to visit Wutai Mountain as a pilgrim before going to Beijing for an audience with the Emperor. In the eleventh month of that year the Dalai left the Kumbum. He arrived at the foot of Wutai Mountain on the eighteenth day of the first month in the thirty-fourth year of Dezong's reign (1908). He stayed there for half a year. On the twenty-seventh day of the seventh month, a Grand Minister of State and the Governor of Shanxi, sent by the Qing government, arrived at Wutai Mountain and asked the Dalai Lama to start immediately for Beijing for an audience with the Emperor. When he arrived at Beijing on the fourth day of the eighth month, he was well-received. Preparations were made for him to stay at Huang Si (Yellow Temple), where the Fifth Dalai and the Sixth Panchen had lived. Emperor Dezong gave a handsome banquet in honour of the Dalai Lama at the Purple Light Hall in Zhongnanhai, the imperial garden. Restoring the Dalai's previous titles, the Emperor conferred on him an additional title of "The Loyally Submissive Vice-Regent, Great, Good, Self-Existent Buddha of Western Heaven." In addition, the Dalai was entitled to an annual allowance of ten thousand taels of silver, to be paid from the National Minorities Treasury of Sichuan Province.

During his stay in Beijing, the Dalai Lama was received in audience several times by the Empress Dowager Ci Xi and the Emperor. The Dalai, according to the Tibetan biography of the Thirteenth Dalai Lama, requested permission to communicate with the Empress Dowager and the Emperor directly instead of going through the Amban. This request was rejected and the Dalai had to continue to follow the established rules of reporting to the resident officials in Tibet on all matters and waiting for imperial instructions.

Not long afterwards, Emperor Dezong and Empress Dowager Ci Xi died suddenly within a short time of each other, and Emperor Xuantong (whose personal name was Pu Yi), ascended the throne. With the government's approval, the Thirteenth Dalai left Beijing on the twenty-eighth day of the eleventh month. He arrived at the Kumbum on the twenty-ninth day of the twelfth month. The Dalai left the Kumbum on the fifteenth day of the fourth month in the first year of Emperor Xuantong's reign (1909). He arrived at Nagchukha, an important town in northern Tibet, on the second day of the eighth month. The Ninth Panchen travelled all the way from the Tashilhunpo to Nagchukha to greet him when he arrived there.

The Thirteenth Dalai returned to Lhasa on the thirtieth day of the tenth month in the first year of Emperor Xuantong's reign and was greeted by Amban Lian Yu in Trashi Town. On the first day of the eleventh month a grand ceremony for his return to the Potala was held.

# 4. The Thirteenth Dalai's Flight to India and the Ninth Panchen's Refusal To Be Regent

After returning to Tibet, the Thirteenth Dalai Lama came into a bitter conflict with Amban Lian Yu. The point of the conflict was that the Sichuan troops had entered Tibet. Lian Yu had requested the Qing government to send two thousand Sichuan troops into Tibet. The government approved his request and dispatched a brigade of two thousand Sichuan troops under the command of Zhong Ying.

According to reason, it was justifiable that the Qing government approved Lian Yu's request for sending Sichuan troops into Tibet, because the central government was responsible to send armies to protect Tibet, a part of the Qing Empire's territory, from British aggression. Nevertheless, the troops sent to Tibet were supposed to be of good discipline and well-trained and the commander should be a general who had received regular training and enjoyed high prestige in military circles. It was in this respect that the Qing government made mistakes. The commander was a civil official rather than a military officer. It was said that Zhong Ying was a deputy *daotai* (circuit intendant) and was ignorant of military affairs. He recruited the two thousand Sichuan soldiers from among the local riffraff, rascals, unemployed and secret society members and organized them into five battalions: three of infantry, one of cavalry and one of artillery. The Sichuan soldiers did not observe discipline and their commander was not good at controlling them. This caused the rebellion of the troops in Lhasa in the first year of the Republic of China (1912).

*A Sixty-Year Chronicle of Major Events in Tibet* by Zhu Xiu recounts what happened on the third day of the first month in the second year of Emperor Xuantong's reign (1910):

> Lian Yu sent his guards to meet the advance party of the Sichuan army upon its arrival in Lhasa. On their way back, the guards opened fire on the policemen, killing one of them; the Tsedron Lama of Jokhang Temple was also shot to death at the Glazed Bridge. Then the guards wantonly fired at the Potala, wounding a number of its monks. The shooting created great alarm in Lhasa and frightened its residents. Worried about his personal safety, the Dalai left Lhasa for India with his aides.

The Thirteenth Dalai had led his people, clerical and secular, in two bitter anti-British wars, and when the second war failed he made nothing of hardships to seek refuge in Urga of Outer Mongolia to escape from being captured by the British. The Dalai, an enemy of the British, now made a 180-degree turn to submit himself to the British. Such a thing could not have been done by any man of unyielding integrity, much less the Dalai as a leader of the Tibetan people. Such a matter cannot be explained in the light of common sense. In fact, that the Dalai fled to India and sought refuge with the British was what he had to do under the pressure of the circumstances.

It was unthinkable to the Dalai that Sichuan troops were so bad in discipline. This threatened the Dalai's personal safety. So he hurriedly fled. Obviously his flight was a decision made in a hurry. When he left the Potala, where to go was the problem he had to solve—one he had not thought of beforehand. Here is a passage of Lian Yu's memorial to the Qing government:

After he learned that the army was approaching, the deposed Dalai, frightened, took the unexpected step of fleeing from the Potala the following night. He had intended to go to Tsang, but before he reached there, he changed his mind, as a result of instigation, and went to India instead.

Here "Tsang" refers to the Tashilhunpo. It was reasonable for the Thirteenth Dalai to seek protection in Tashilhunpo Monastery, for he was the Ninth Panchen's tutor. But he thought of what would happen to him there if Lian Yu sent troops to Shigatse. The Panchen was weak in power in spite of being the equal of the Dalai in religious affairs and politics. As he was not sure if the Panchen was powerful enough to guarantee his personal safety in case Lian Yu sent troops to Shigatse, he changed his mind and fled to India.

Where could he go if he could not go to Tsang? Perhaps he could go to Beijing to lodge a complaint against Amban Lian Yu and the Sichuan troops with the Qing government, and perhaps he might win the lawsuit or at least find a place in Beijing in which to settle himself.

Amban Lian Yu, in a memorial to the Qing court, said that Luo Changqi, the First Counselor sent by the Amban to Darjeeling to ask the Thirteenth Dalai to return to Tibet, reported that the Dalai had replied that he had gone to Darjeeling because he had intended to go to Beijing.

If the Dalai had intended to go to Beijing, he had to go by sea. This was the only way he could take with a party of six officials and about a dozen guards. As to the expenses of the journey, this was not a problem to the Dalai. But the problem was that he had to go through India, Singapore and Hong Kong—British colonies. Would Britain —his enemy—permit him to pass through? Would he be arrested in India? These problems could not be solved beforehand. So the Dalai stayed at Yadong, testing the attitude of Britain towards him and waiting for a change of conditions in Tibet. He might have remained in Yadong if Lian Yu had not sent Sichuan troops to chase after him. But Lian Yu did this and the British in Phari informed the Dalai of it by telephone, so the Dalai left Yadong for Darjeeling in India, where he was "warmly greeted" by British officials.

When he came to India, the Dalai intended to go to Beijing. But at that time Amban Lian Yu's memorial denouncing the Dalai for his flight reached Beijing. The Qing government, disregarding the true facts, ordered that he be stripped of the title of Dalai Lama for a second time. This was a big blow to the Dalai and prevented him from going to Beijing, because he knew that after being stripped of the title of Dalai Lama, he was but an ordinary monk and was likely to be thrown into jail if he went to Beijing. So he coldly said to Luo Changqi that he had not gone to Beijing because the removal of his titles made him too ashamed to present himself there. It is evident that the blame for the Dalai's self-exile to India should be placed on the flawed policy of the Qing government towards Tibet.

After the Dalai took his flight, the Qing government approved Lian Yu's proposal and announced:

> The Amban is to seek some candidates for the reincarnation of the previous Dalai Lama and to select one of them by drawing tallies bearing their names from the Golden Urn as the true reincarnation of the previous Dalai Lama, who, with the approval of the court, will carry on with the propagation of Buddhism.

The announcement of the decision to depose the Dalai Lama was greeted by a wave of protests from Buddhists not only in Tibet but also in Outer and Inner Mongolia, Qinghai, Sichuan, Yunnan, Gansu and other provinces.

Facing the widespread protests, the Qing government did not countermand the order concerning the Dalai's title. It only ordered Lian Yu to send men to India to persuade the Dalai to come back. Lian Yu sent Luo Changqi to Darjeeling in the second year of Emperor Xuantong's reign (1910). Here is a passage from Luo Changqi's report:

> The deposed Dalai had his residence at a place called Balunpo behind a mountain in Darjeeling.... I met with him on the afternoon of the eighth day of the ninth month.... The deposed Dalai was cunning when he talked to me. He claimed that it was he who had stopped the Tibetans from trying to fight the Sichuan army and had prevented them from joining the British. He explained that he had come to Darjeeling because he had planned to go to Beijing by sea, but when he learnt he had had his title removed, he was too ashamed to present himself in the capital. He said he would very much like to return to

Tibet as he was being asked to do, but that his return was subject to the condition that there should be no changes in Tibet's religion and administration unless they were discussed one by one and officially recorded as measures to remedy the situation in Tibet.

At the same time Lian Yu requested that the Qing court install the Panchen on the Dalai's throne and put him in charge of Tibetan affairs. His request was approved by the government. At Lian Yu's invitation, the Ninth Panchen went to Lhasa. Lian Yu read to the Panchen the imperial edict which ordered him to administer all Tibetan affairs. The Panchen refused politely and meanwhile asked the Qing government to restore the Dalai's titles so that he might return sooner. Lian Yu reported this to the Qing government for instruction. On the sixteenth day of the second month in the third year of Xuantong's reign (1911) the Qing court ordered the Grand Ministers of State to send a telegram to Lian Yu, which said,

> We know that the Panchen has come to Lhasa to visit you, Lian Yu, and has asked that the Dalai's title be restored. Has the Dalai repented of his wrongdoing and does he intend to come back to Tibet? If the misunderstanding between the Panchen and the Dalai has been removed and the Panchen sincerely speaks for the Dalai, Lian Yu is expected to take the opportunity to look into the matter and act at his discretion.... As to the problem whether the Panchen is to take the Dalai's place in Lhasa, this depends on whether the Kalons under the deposed Dalai view it favourably. So the Amban is expected to make the matter clear and then report to the court for further instruction.

The Panchen declined the offer of the Dalai's position and returned to the Tashilhunpo after he had stayed several months in Lhasa. Then the Panchen sent men with many gifts to the Dalai Lama at Darjeeling.

# 5. The Sichuan Troops' Mutiny and the Tibetan Troops' Encirclement of Lhasa

At that time a rebellion broke out at Bomi in Tibet. Lian Yu sent two battalions of Sichuan troops under the command of Zhong Ying to suppress the rebellion, and another battalion to garrison Gyantse and Shigatse. Only eighty guards and over one hundred cavalrymen and artillerymen remained in Lhasa. Sichuan also was suffering a severe crisis caused by the problem of railway-building. Soon afterwards the Revolution of 1911 broke out. Most of the Sichuan soldiers in Tibet were members of a secret society, Gelaohui (Society of Brothers). They colluded with one another and, on the twenty-third day of the ninth month in the third year of Xuantong's reign (1911), the Sichuan soldiers rebelled.

The mutiny of the Sichuan troops stationed in Lhasa was launched by Yan Buyun, a Gelaohui leader and a guard of Qian Xibao, the Second Counselor, for the purpose of robbing the Amban's Office for the soldiers' pay and demanding money from the merchants in Lhasa for the trip back to Sichuan. On the evening of the mutiny the mutineers robbed the Amban's Office of 180,000 taels of silver, the soldiers' pay, and demanded from the Tibetan local government 80,000 taels of silver and conscription of them for labour service to earn money for the trip to Sichuan. The Tibetan local government paid the silver they asked for. On the twenty-fifth day of the ninth month the mutineers kidnaped Lian Yu and sent him to the Trashi Town military camp. Li Zhiping (a secretary of the Military Supply Section of the Amban's Office) and Fan Jin (a regiment secretary) were chosen as the heads of the mutineers. When he was called back from Bomi to Lhasa, Zhong Ying put Li Zhiping and Fan Jin to death and the mutiny was suppressed for the time being. Amban Lian Yu was released. This was the first mutiny of the Sichuan troops.

By now the Revolution of 1911 had succeeded and the Qing Emperor had been forced to give up the throne. The government of the Republic of China had been established with Dr. Sun Yat-sen as the acting president in Nanjing. Revolution also broke out in Sichuan, the province closest to Tibet. Zhao Erfeng, the Governor-General of Sichuan appointed by the Qing court, was killed, and Yin Changheng was chosen to be the Sichuan military governor. When they were informed of the news from Sichuan via India, the Sichuan troops launched the second mutiny in October 1911.

Lian Yu had appealed to the Panchen for protection, and the Panchen had asked the abbot of the Drepung in Lhasa to provide protection for Lian Yu in case he needed it. In the second mutiny, when taking refuge in the Drepung, Lian Yu gave Zhong Ying his seal of authority, making him the acting Amban. The mutineers chose He Guangxie (Lian Yu's secretary) as deputy military governor and established a Public Discussion Board with Wang Wenming (commander of the cavalrymen) as its head. The Gelaohui also established its office, called Datong Baozhang Zhonggongkou (Federation of Harmony and Protection), with Guo Yuanzhen (Lian Yu's guard-in-chief) as its head. Thus, He Guangxie, Wang Wenming and Guo Yuanzhen took the place of the Amban.

At the same time the two battalions of Sichuan troops sent to suppress the rebellion in Bomi also mutinied. At the beginning, they were sent by Lian Yu under the command of Zhong Ying to suppress the rebellion in Bomi. Incapable of military command, Zhong Ying was defeated once and again. Lian Yu called Zhong Ying back and sent Luo Changqi, First Counselor, to be the commander there. The rebellion in Bomi was soon suppressed by Luo Changqi. When they were informed of the mutiny of the Sichuan troops in Lhasa, the Sichuan troops in Bomi killed Luo Changqi. A small part of them went back to their homes in Sichuan via Chamdo, but most of them went to Lhasa, joining the Sichuan troops there.

Originally, a battalion under the command of Xie Guoliang, an officer from Hunan Province, was also sent by Lian Yu to Bomi. When Zhong Ying led the Sichuan troops into Tibet, this battalion was put under the command of Zhong Ying. Nevertheless, the battalion did not take part in the mutiny at Bomi and was again led by Xie Guoliang into Lhasa. In his *A Brief Account of Tibetan Affairs*, Xie said,

> In January of the first year of the Republic of China [1912], I resigned and left Tibet. Zhong Ying sent troops to block my way in Dalang, killing my guards and attendants and kidnapping my family and robbing my luggage. I took refuge at Dam.... In March Drungyig Chenmo, Commander-General of the Tibetan army, sent troops to attack Dam and killed the head of Dam, Gushanda, who was trying hard to protect me. He brought me by force to Lhasa and pressured me to be the commander-in-chief of the Tibetan army. Having no heart to kill my fellow countrymen, I flatly refused and asked him to cease the war.... In November when the Dalai returned to Lhasa, I paid him a visit at the Potala. The Dalai held my hands to his forehead to show

greetings to me.... I told the Dalai that he had better send men to Beijing to report the truth to the government of the Republic of China, since the five major nationalities [Han, Manchu, Mongol, Hui and Tibetan] were now equal in political status and the system of government was changed into a republic, which I expected the Living Buddha to support. All this, I said, was to be done to consolidate the foundation of his government. The Dalai said that what I said was a good idea.... In February of the second year of the Republic [1913] when I left Tibet, the Dalai saw me off. At Gyantse, I received a telegram from Lu Xingqi.... As President Yuan Shikai had sent the Panchen a telegram and as nobody was available to forward it to the Panchen, I made a detour and reached the Tashilhunpo. The Panchen held a welcoming ceremony for me to read him the telegram. In it the president expressed his appreciation to him.... The Panchen asked me to send his greetings to the President.... I stayed for several days and then left for inner China.... The British Resident in Drenjong, who had been asked by the Dalai to protect me...sent soldiers to escort me all the way. In October I came back to Beijing and reported all this to the government.

But *A Sixty-Year Chronicle of Major Events in Tibet* has a different account. It says:

By then the Tibetan local government had recruited more than ten thousand soldiers to make up for the heavy casualties inflicted on the Tibetans by the Sichuan army. For many days on end these soldiers, under the command of Xie Guoliang, engaged Zhong Ying's troops in fierce battle.

Another book, *Records Written with Tears and Blood*, says:

Xie, having been defeated, submitted to the Tibetans and persuaded them to attack the Sichuan troops, and the Sichuan army was almost completely annihilated by the Tibetans under Xie's command after a year.

According to his own account, Xie paid much attention to the unity between the Han Chinese and Tibetans, and thus refused to be the commander of the Tibetan army in fighting with the Sichuan troops. He also says that he had good relations with the Dalai and Panchen. At the same time, his *Brief Account of Tibetan Affairs* cannot help being a little one-sided and self-justifying. Nevertheless, from what he did to defend the unity between the Han Chinese and Tibetans and to restore the submission of Tibet to the central regime after he had come back to Beijing, we can consider him as a man of integrity, whose merits were more than his mistakes.

When the Sichuan army in Bomi mutinied, those in Gyantse and Shigatse declared their response to the call of the former and sent dozens of men to Lhasa to demand soldiers' pay from Lian Yu.

"Deputy Military Governor" He Guangxie was chosen as their representative to persuade Lian Yu back to the office from the Drepung. On the twenty-sixth day of the twelfth month in the third year of Xuantong's reign (1911) the silver from Sichuan for the soldiers' pay reached Lhasa. The following day Lian Yu came back to Lhasa. After he gave the pay to the Sichuan troops stationed in Bomi, Gyantse and Shigatse, things calmed down.

Nevertheless, the Sichuan troops did not change their bad habits. They spent their pay on eating, drinking, whoring and gambling. They stopped at nothing in doing evil, exposing their true colours —that they were rascals. Zhong Ying did not know how to control them. Second Counselor Qian Xibao saw something bad would happen soon. He resigned and went back to inner China by way of India.

According to Xie Guoliang's *Brief Account of Tibetan Affairs*, at that time "there were over twenty groups of Paoge (Robed Brothers) [a secret society], whose leader was a man surnamed Guo. Lhasa was in bad order. Law and discipline was not enforced there." Under such circumstances big aristocrats of Lhasa moved their valuables and families to Sera Monastery for protection (the Sera was the closest monastery to Lhasa). The Sichuan soldiers surrounded the Sera on February 5, in the first year of the Republic (1912) in an attempt to loot its wealth. This caused serious trouble. The Sera had 5,500 monks, and most of them had weapons. The Sichuan army attacked the Sera, firing on it from all sides for two days. But the monastery did not fall. The Sichuan army retreated to Lhasa, while Tibetan troops of all routes built long fences and pressed on them. The sound of firing did not cease day and night.

No textual research can prove that Zhong Ying gave the order to surround the Sera. But as the chief commander of the Sichuan army he was at least guilty of the crime of neglecting his duty.

Things became worse after the Sera's monks and the Tibetan

troops surrounded Lhasa. Being unable to cope with the situation, the Public Discussion Board and Datong Baozhang Zhonggongkou asked Lian Yu and Zhong Ying to come out to deal with the situation. Zhong Ying ordered that the organizations of the "Public Discussion Board" and "Datong Baozhang Zhonggongkou" be dissolved and that Wang Wenming and Guo Yuanzhen be put to death, and Lian Yu ordered that He Guangxie be executed, hoping to assuage popular indignation in this way. But this did not change the situation in Lhasa for the better. The most serious event was that the Kashag had prohibited Tibetan residents in the suburbs of Lhasa from selling grain to the Sichuan troops. Hunger threatened the army. It was rumoured that Sichuan Military Governor Yin Changheng and Yunnan Military Governor Cai E were to lead a big army to support the Sichuan army stationed in Tibet. But the distant water could not quench the present thirst. In a period of four months while Lhasa was surrounded from February 8 to June 19 in the first year of the Republic (1912), the city ran out of food. According to an article in *Four Versions of Details of Riots in Tibet,*

> At the beginning of the war, the Han Chinese troops thought they had enough money to maintain themselves. They did not know there would be no place to buy food. When the oxen, horses, mules, asses and other animals they had were all eaten up, they fell into great disaster.

On June 19, Galdan, the Nepalese Resident in Lhasa, by order of his king, became the mediator between the two conflicting parties. Soon an agreement was reached. The Sichuan army gave its firearms and ammunition to the Tibetans. For their part, the Tibetans permitted the Han Chinese to go back by way of India and promised to provide them with free transport and rations. The Chinese resident officials might remain in Lhasa, but their guards were allowed to have only twenty rifles. Thus the problem was eventually solved. The Sichuan army moved to Yadong and left Tibet for inner China by way of India.

In August President Yuan Shikai appointed Zhong Ying the Resident Commissioner in Tibet. Lian Yu was called back to Beijing to report to the President. Lian Yu left Lhasa on August 4 and returned by way of India. The Kashag did not deliberately make things difficult for him and provided him free transport.

Zhong Ying stayed in Lhasa with only a few dozen guards. The Kashag then declared that they recognized only the Amban but not the Commissioner and asked Zhong Ying to leave Tibet. The Northern Government in Beijing ordered him to stick to his post. Thus, conflicts sharpened between Zhong Ying and the Kashag. On August 11 Tibetan troops surrounded Lhasa again. The surrounding lasted for only about two months because Zhong Ying had only a few guards and Lhasa was still short of food. The Nepalese Resident in Lhasa, Galdan, at the end of September, again started to mediate between them. An agreement was reached on October 6 by which Zhong Ying and his guards should give out firearms and the Tibetans permit them to go back by way of India.

On April 2 of the second year of the Republic (1913) Yuan Shikai dismissed Zhong Ying from the post of Resident Commissioner in Tibet and appointed Lu Xingqi as Acting Resident Commissioner.

Lu Xingqi was a patriotic overseas Chinese in India. He was a businessman and had established a commercial company called Tian Yi there. He was much concerned about Tibet and often reported news about Tibet to the Foreign Ministry in Beijing and provided economic help to the Chinese officers and men who went back home from Tibet by way of India. So Sichuan Military Governor Yin Changheng and the former Customs Supervisors in Gyantse, Ma Shizhou and Shi Youming, recommended Lu Xingqi to the Northern Government in Beijing. Nevertheless, the Kashag refused to recognize the appointment of Resident Commissioner Lu Xingqi, and the Indian government also put up obstacles to it. The Northern Government in Beijing ordered Lu to rent a house in India for the "Office of the Acting Resident Commissioner in Tibet." This was not permitted by the Indian government. Thus, Lu Xingqi was never able to go to Tibet during his tenure of office of more than ten years.

When the problem of the second surrounding of Lhasa was solved, Zhong Ying arrived at Chumbi Valley on his way to India. In Chumbi he found that over four hundred Sichuan troops with their over three hundred families could not go back for lack of money for their trip. A similar problem in Gyantse and Shigatse had been solved by the Tibetans paying eighty rupees in exchange for a rifle from the Sichuan troops, and thereby most of them had left Tibet. However, those who came from Lhasa had given up their weapons through Zhong Ying to the Tibetans, for which the Tibetans had not had paid them. In addition, they had spent all their money in Lhasa. Facing this problem, Zhong Ying had to stay at Yadong and request the Northern Government to remit them money for their homeward trip. Having difficulties in finance, the government did not give them any money.

Their home journey was delayed from November 1912 to April 1913. It was not until the Tibetans, through MacDonald, the British Commercial Commissioner in Gyantse, warned that they would expel the Sichuan troops by force if they did not leave in fifteen days, that Zhong Ying could not but lead the Sichuan army to leave Chumbi on April 21, 1913. Four days later when they arrived at Kalimpong in India, Lu Xingqi, the Acting Resident Commissioner in Tibet, sent them back in groups. In 1915 the last group was sent back, and Zhong Ying arrived in Beijing in the same year. The son of the First Counselor Luo Changqi lodged a complaint against Zhong Ying with President Yuan Shikai, accusing him of causing trouble in Tibet. Zhong Ying was prosecuted and executed.

# 6. The Ninth Panchen Welcomes the Thirteenth Dalai Lama Back to Tibet

Before the problem of the Sichuan army in Lhasa was solved, the Thirteenth Dalai Lama left Darjeeling for Tibet on the fifth day of the fifth month of the Tibetan calendar in the first year of the Republic of China (1912). The Ninth Panchen went to welcome the Dalai at Gyantse. The Dalai informed him from Phari by a British official's telephone that he would not go to Gyantse and asked the Panchen to meet him at Ralung Monastery. No detailed records of the meeting can be found. *A Sixty-Year Chronicle of Major Events in Tibet* has a record of the event as follows:

The Panchen greeted the Dalai at Gyantse. The Dalai imposed a fine of

forty thousand taels of silver on the Panchen for aiding the Han
Chinese. The Panchen paid the fine with money borrowed from
MacDonald, a British official. From then on, the relations between the
two began to deteriorate.

Similar records could not be found in the Tibetan biography of the
Dalai nor in that of the Panchen. MacDonald's *Twenty Years in Tibet*
has not a word about the Panchen borrowing his money, either.
So the record in the *Chronicle* is not reliable.

Then the Thirteenth Dalai Lama moved from Ralung to Samding
Monastery. The Dalai remained there for about two months, because the war in Lhasa had not yet ended. He left Samding for
Lhasa on the twenty-ninth day of the eighth month and arrived
there on the sixteenth day of the twelfth month. A grand ceremony was held for his coming back.

At this time Dr. Sun Yat-sen (1866-1925, a great Chinese revolutionary pioneer who led the Revolution of 1911 to overthrow the
Qing Dynasty) resigned, and Yuan Shikai became the president of
China. On July 19 of the first year of the Republic of China (1912)
the Northern Government established the Bureau for Mongolian
and Tibetan Affairs (renamed the Mongolian and Tibetan Affairs
Office under the State Council in May of the third year of the
Republic) with the Mongolian prince of Karashin, Gongsang Nor-
bu, as its head. The Thirteenth Dalai sent a Mongolian lama named
Lozang Dondup to deliver his letter to the Mongolian prince at
Beijing. In the letter the Dalai said:

> When I came back from Beijing to Tibet, I did my best to develop
> Buddhism. Then I took temporary residence in Darjeeling because the
> title of Dalai Lama was removed from me. Since Sichuan troops caused
> trouble in Tibet, order has not yet been restored. I will do my best to
> develop Buddhism. Please report my case to the government.

The letter bore no date. As it was published in the Chinese
magazine *Orient Review*, No. 5, Vol. 9, of the first year of the
Republic of China (1912), perhaps it was written during July or
August of that year.

After reading the letter from the Thirteenth Dalai Lama, Yuan
Shikai gave an order to restore to him the title of Dalai Lama on
October 28, 1912. Said the order:

Now the republic of five nationalities has been founded. Since the Dalai Lama has shown his sincerity to the inland, the former misunderstanding is dismissed. The Dalai Lama is regranted the title of the Loyally Submissive Vicegerent, Great, Good, Self-Existent Buddha of Western Heaven. He is expected to develop the Yellow sect and support the Republic of China and enjoy peace with us.

Meanwhile Yuan Shikai issued a decree to grant an honorable title to the Ninth Panchen on April 1, 1913. It reads:

This is an order from the Grand President. The Panchen Erdeni said in his telegram that he has long admired the inland and enjoyed the favour and that he has done everything in his power to help the Han Chinese soldiers and residents, including providing them with food and lending them money. The Panchen Erdeni supports the Republic of China, is loyal to the government of the Republic, and works hard to handle Tibetan affairs. I, the Grand President, am glad at this. I order that he be granted the honorific title the Most Loyal Propagator to praise him for his loyalty to the Republic and to express my respect to the Yellow sect.

After receiving the title, the Panchen wrote a letter to Yuan Shikai to express his thanks. The whole text is as follows:

On the twenty-fifth day of the third month in the *kui-chou* year, Commissioner Lu Xingqi sent men to hand over the decree to me, in which the Grand President granted me the title of The Most Loyal Propagator. I humbly set up a sacrificial table in the Tashilhunpo and kowtowed with respect and gratitude to receive the decree from the President. Written by The Most Loyal Propagator Panchen Erdeni.

When the restoration of the title of the Dalai Lama was decreed, the Thirteenth Dalai sent a telegram through Lu Xingqi, the Acting Resident Commissioner, to Yuan Shikai. It said:

Mr. President of Boundless Happiness, thank you for your telegram. Britain has agreed to arrange the negotiations between the Han Chinese and Tibetans in Darjeeling. Representatives are going to be sent there. Your order is being waited. I hope to get your reply as soon as possible. Sincerely, Dalai Lama.

That the Dalai Lama asked the Northern Government to send representatives to negotiate with the Tibetans in Darjeeling reflected the urgent demands of the Tibetan situation. When the muti-

neers of the Sichuan army were surrounded in Lhasa by the
Tibetan army after being defeated in the battle with the Sera
monks, Ma Shizhou, the subprefectural magistrate of Qingxi in
Tibet, sent an express telegram to report the emergency to Sichuan
Military Governor Yin Changheng, and Lu Xingqi also sent express
telegrams from India to ask the Northern Government, Sichuan
Military Governor Yin Changheng and Yunnan Military Governor
Cai E for urgent military help.

Yin Changheng recommended himself to the Northern Government
to lead a crack army to Tibet. In a telegram to Yuan Shikai
dated May 12, 1912, he said,

> If Tibet falls, the frontiers will be hard to defend, and if the frontiers
> fall, the whole country will be in danger.... The only way out is to send
> crack troops from Sichuan and Yunnan to Tibet for emergency aid.

In a telegram to Yuan Shikai dated May 6 of the same year, Cai
E said:

> U and Tsang of Tibet concern the interest of the whole country. Should
> Tibet split off, Sichuan and Yunnan will be in the danger of being
> conquered.... I am anxious about the dangerous situation on the fron-
> tiers. You are urgently requested to arrange to save the frontiers from
> danger.

Shi Youming, the Gyantse Customs Supervisor, also sent a
telegram to the same effect from India to the Northern Government. Under such circumstances, the Northern Government was
forced to send an army under the command of Yin Changheng
to Tibet and ordered Hu Jingyi to act for the Sichuan Military
Governor. Meanwhile the government ordered Yunnan Military
Governor Cai E to send troops from Zhongdian of Yunnan to
Kham in coordination with Yin Changheng. Yin Changheng and
Cai E took actions according to the orders at once. Yin Chang-
heng and his Sichuan army crossed the Jinsha River and reached
Chamdo in order to attack Lhasa by the middle route, while Cai
E and his Yunnan troops occupied Xiangcheng and reached
Kham, planning to attack Lhasa through Bomi by the south
route.

# 7. The British Imperialists Intervene in the Internal Administration of Tibet and the Simla Conference

When the Sichuan and Yunnan troops were moving smoothly to Tibet, British imperialists came out to interfere with Tibetan affairs. On August 17, 1912, the British Minister in Beijing, John Jordan, lodged a strong "protest" in a note to the Foreign Ministry of the Northern Government. The note contained five points, the gist of which was as follows:

(1) China must not intervene in the internal administration of Tibet;

(2) Chinese officials are not allowed to hold the same administrative power in Tibet as in the inland;

(3) Except the Chinese Amban's guards, Chinese troops must not station in Tibet;

(4) The British government demands that a new treaty regarding Tibet be concluded;

(5) The British government declares that if China does not accept its demands, it will not recognize the government of the Republic of China and will block the communication between India and Tibet for the time being.

The British demands that openly interfered with the internal affairs of China were refused by the Northern Government in a reply, which pointed out: "It is China's internal affair that China sends troops into Tibet and Britain has no right to interfere with it.... The recognition of the Chinese Republic is a matter not to be connected with the Tibetan issue."

The British government demanded that the Northern Government send representatives to Darjeeling to attend a conference on the issue of Tibet and that Tibet be represented at the same conference. Under the pressure of the British imperialists, the Northern Government agreed to send representatives to the conference and had to order Sichuan Military Governor Yin Changheng and Yunnan Military Governor Cai E to halt the troops on their march into Tibet. The Chinese representatives were Chen Yifan (also called Ivan Chen) and Wang Haiping. (Owing to opposition from the British, Hu Hanmin had been replaced by Wang Haiping.) Tibet was represented by Lonchen Shatra and others. Representing Britain was Arthur Henry McMahon, secretary in the India Foreign Office, who was assisted by Charles Bell, British Political Representative in Sikkim. The Ninth Panchen had also hoped to send his representatives to attend the conference. He requested the Northern Government for approval through Commissioner Lu Xingqi, but the government refused his request.

The conference was originally scheduled to be held in Darjeeling but later it was held in Simla. It lasted for eight months and twenty days, beginning on October 13, 1913, and ending on July 3, 1914. The British representative presented a draft treaty, based on a "compromise." Under the draft treaty, Tibet was recognized as a part of China, but the areas inhabited by the Tibetans were divided into Outer Tibet and Inner Tibet. The former was Tibet and Kham, and the latter consisted of areas inhabited by Tibetans in Qinghai, Gansu, Sichuan, Yunnan and other provinces. Outer Tibet was to be detached from China, that is, China should not "interfere in its administration, which was to rest with the Tibetans themselves," but "a Chinese resident official [Amban] was to be reestablished at Lhasa with a military escort limited to three hundred men." Chinese representative Chen Yifan signed the draft treaty without the approval of the government. When the provisions of the draft treaty and Chen Yifan's signing of the treaty were reported in the newspapers in China, the whole nation was outraged. Facing the nationwide protest, the Northern Government ordered Chen not to sign the final instrument. Britain declared that since China had refused to sign the treaty, it would not be entitled to the benefits the treaty provided.

Not long afterwards, the First World War broke out, and the problem of Tibet was put aside.

Here we would like to discuss the relations between Tibet and the Northern Government headed by Yuan Shikai during the time of the Simla Conference. On the one hand, since Yuan Shikai restored the title of the Dalai Lama, the Thirteenth Dalai had returned to Tibet and come into power again. The Northern Government of the Republic of China appointed Lu Xingqi Commissioner for Tibet to replace Amban Lian Yu, who had left Tibet, but Tibet refused to recognize the appointment and Britain refused to permit Lu Xingqi to go to Tibet by way of India.

On the other hand, Tibet recognized itself as a part of China's territory. For example, in the second year of the Republic of China (1913) Yuan Shikai organized the Senate and the House of Representatives in the style of Western governments, among the members of which were the Dalai's and the Panchen's representatives. On May 15 in the same year the Office of Election Affairs of Tibet under the Northern Government published the list of Tibetan senators and members of the House of Representatives. Two lists were announced. On the first list there were five senators from U (the Dalai's group), including Dondrup Norbu and others, and another five senators from Tsang (the Panchen's group), including Gyaltsen Sangpo and others; besides, there were five alternate senators from U (Padma Rinchen and others) and another five from Tsang (Ngawang Chosdrak and others). On the second list there were ten representatives: five from U (Yeshe Togme and others), and five from Tsang (Ngawang Gedun and others); and ten alternate representatives, five from U (Ulegi and others) and five from Tsang (Lozang Konchok and others). The fact that the Chinese Senate and the House of Representatives had members from Tibet (from both the Dalai's and Panchen's group) showed that the Dalai and Panchen recognized Tibet's submission to the Northern Government of the Republic of China, and therefore had sent representatives to be members of the Chinese Parliament.

Here I would like to make some additional remarks. Since the Qing Dynasty there had always been three important resident monk officials sent by the Dalai Lama to the inland: the abbot of the Yonghegong Lamasery in Beijing, the abbot of the lamasery on Mt. Wutai in Shanxi, and the abbot of the Temple of Potaraka Doctrine in Chengde. The three abbots were high-ranking monk officials of the fourth rank or above and all had brought with them a retinue of interpreters and secretaries. They were installed at these posts by turn. The appointment and dismissal of the three officials were decided by the Dalai, but needed to be approved by the central government. They were paid monthly by the departments concerned of the central government. In the Temple of Sumeru Happiness and Longevity in Chengde, three high-ranking

monk officials—a *khenpo*, a *woser*, and a *gegu*—and twenty monks
for chanting sutras from Tibet were to be appointed or dismissed
by the Panchen and paid by the central government. Most of the
Tibetan representatives in the Parliament as mentioned above were
selected from Tibetan residents in inner China. At that time the
only way for the journey from Tibet to inner China was to go via
India, but the British imperialists were carrying out a policy of
breaking the relations between Tibet and inner China, so it was
difficult for the Tibetan local government to send representatives
from Tibet to attend the Parliament.

According to archives now available, alterations were made in
the groups of Tibetan Senators and Representatives several times.
In 1917, among the Tibetan Senators who attended the Provisional
Senate called by the Northern Government of China were Lozang
Palden, Shadrung Ngawang Yeshe, Lozang Tsedrul and Wuhuai-
qing. Shadrung Ngawang Yeshe was appointed by the Dalai and
his name was on the second list. Lozang Tsedrul was the Dalai's
resident official in Beijing appointed in 1913.

As shown by the historical documents cited above, the relations
between the Tibetan local government and the Northern Government after the Revolution of 1911 were not so normal as they were
during the Qing Dynasty. Even so, the British imperialists tried
hard to make them even worse.

On June 28, 1915, Gu Weijun, a councilor of the Foreign Ministry
of the Northern Government, was sent to make three suggestions
to the British minister Jordan:

(1) If the provision in the exchanged notes that Tibet was a part
of China's territory was put into the final instrument, China would
allocate Chamdo to the autonomous Outer Tibet. The rest would
be in accordance with the last proposal put forward by Chinese
representatives the year before. In such a case, China would
withdraw all Chinese officers and men from Chamdo in a year.

(2) China was to send Chinese agents into Chamdo, Gyantse,
Tashilhunpo, Yadong, Gartok and other places that were to be
opened as trading ports. The Chinese and British agents were to
be equal in official post and guard escort.

(3) The provision that the autonomous Outer Tibet recognized
China's suzerainty over the whole of Tibet should be added to the

final instrument.

Jordan flatly refused the three suggestions and warned that, as the World War was still on, there was no time to think it over. If the issues of Tibet were not solved, he continued, they would cause something unpleasant between Britain and China after the war. The discussion was thus ended.

Soon afterwards civil wars between the northern and southern warlords broke out, Yuan having claimed himself to be enthroned as emperor and people rising to protest against him. The wars forced the Tibetan question into the background. But the Tibetan local government took advantage of the chaos to attack Chamdo. In September 1917 Tibetan troops were sent to attack the Sichuan army stationed in Chamdo and some other places.

Records *A Sixty-Year Chronicle of Major Events in Tibet*:

> In September 1917 Yu Jinhai of the artillery troops stationed at Riwoche attacked the Tibetans in a squabble over grass. In the conflict two Tibetan soldiers were captured and sent to Chamdo. Peng Risheng, Commander of the Border Army, had them beheaded without any investigation into the cause of the conflict. The enraged Tibetans then resorted to arms.

In January of the following year Riwoche fell. On February 19 Enda County was lost. The counties of Derge, Dengke, Serxu, Baiyu, and Ningjing then also fell one after another. When Tibetan troops surrounded Chamdo on April 3, Peng Risheng, commander of the Chinese troops, wrote to the Kalon proposing a cease-fire. The Kalon replied: "All we want you to do now is to lay down your arms."

On April 16, Peng Risheng surrendered, but Zhang Nanshan, Magistrate of Chamdo, drowned himself in the river. At first the Tibetans allowed the surrendering Sichuan troops to go back to Sichuan directly, but then they changed their minds and instead escorted Peng Risheng and others to Lhasa and sent them back by way of India.

At that time Eric Teichman, a British deputy consul, came out to act as a mediator. After Teichman came to Chamdo, he invited Liu Zanting, Deputy Commander of the Border Army, to come to Chamdo to negotiate with Kalon Jampa Tenthar there. On October 17, 1918 a cease-fire agreement of four provisions was signed.

According to the agreement, neither army was to violate the temporary line of demarcation and the time set for the evacuation was one year. It was stipulated that the document was provisional, not final. From then on, the Sichuan army stationed in Garze and the Tibetan army in Derge. This was the Tibetan army's first eastern expansion.

In 1919 Britain sent the deputy consul in Sichuan to Beijing to urge British minister Jordan to suggest resuming the conference on the problem of Tibet to the Northern Government. When the meeting was resumed, the British minister, on May 30, put forward two alternatives for the revision of the treaty of the Simla Conference:

(1) The names of Inner and Outer Tibet would not be used, and the area of Inner Tibet as previously specified would now be divided into two parts, the one including Batang, Litang, Tachienlu (Dajianlu), Dawu, Luhuo, Nyagrong and Garze would be put under Chinese rule and the other, consisting of the area west of Derge, would go to Tibet;

(2) The names of Inner and Outer Tibet would be used as already specified, while Batang, Litang, Tachienlu, Nyagrong and Garze would be put under Chinese rule, and the land south of the Kunlun Mountains and north of the Dangla Range would go to Inner Tibet, where China would not station troops, and Derge would go to Outer Tibet.

The Northern Government replied that China could hardly accept either of the two alternatives. On December 3, the British minister urged the Northern Government to resume the meeting, but the latter paid no heed to it and the Sino-British talks on Tibet was suspended.

During that time, the Northern Government sent two missions to Tibet and made direct contact with the Dalai Lama. In 1919 Prince Elole Medrab was sent to Tibet. *An Outline History and Geography of Tibet* records:

> He asked the Thirteenth Dalai to allow Commissioner for Tibet Lu Xingqi to come to Lhasa, but the Dalai replied that Lu could not come to Lhasa until all problems between China and Britain were solved. The government could do nothing with the Dalai.

Also in 1919, the Northern Government asked Military Governor of Gansu Province Zhang Guangjian to send Zhu Xiu, Li Zhonglian, Lama Kulangtsang of the Red Hat sect and a small retinue by way of Qinghai to Lhasa to make friendly contact with the Dalai for the purpose of defusing the crisis. The envoys arrived at Lhasa in August 1919 and left Lhasa for Gansu in April 1920 after staying there for over eight months.

According to *A Sixty-Year Chronicle of Major Events in Tibet*, Zhu Xiu and the other envoys met with the Thirteenth Dalai at Lhasa. The Dalai called a conference attended by the representatives of the Dalai, the Panchen, the Three Major Monasteries and the four Kalons to discuss the important problem. At the same time, new soldiers were being recruited for attacking inner China again.

In March 1920, the conference of Lhasa decided to continue the previous cease-fire proposal concluded two years before, only making a few modifications on it and canceling the cease-fire time-limit. The Tibetan government declared that the Yalung River was the border between the Tibetan and Sichuan armies, that from then on the two armies should not move forward without orders from the Dalai or the President and that all issues should be solved on a tripartite conference attended by China's central government, Britain and Tibet to be held at Lhasa or Chamdo. This was what the mission headed by Zhu Xiu achieved in Lhasa.

At a farewell banquet he gave in honour of the departing mission headed by Zhu Xiu, the Dalai said that, first, he would not have turned to Britain had it not been for the high-handed treatment he received from the Amban. He thanked the envoys for their coming to Tibet and hoped that the President would soon appoint a plenipotentiary to settle the outstanding issues concerning Tibet. Second, he assured Zhu Xiu that he was all for the motherland and would work for the well-being of the five nationalities. Third, as to the Simla draft treaty, the Dalai said it could be revised. These three points show that the Dalai was friendly to the mission.

Before Zhu Xiu's departure, the Panchen sent a messenger from the Tashilhunpo to bring a formal letter in Tibetan and many gifts to him, an act showing that "the Panchen stood by the new Republic more firmly than the Dalai did." This comparison was made by Zhu Xiu. When he arrived at Gansu, Zhu Xiu presented the two lamas letters, gifts, and reports to the government. It was in the time of the civil war between the warlords of the Zhili clique and the Anhui clique, so the issue of Tibet was again put aside.

On January 15, 1921, British Minister Elston paid a visit to Chinese Foreign Minister Yan Huiqing and said that it was not proper for the Chinese government to instruct, as it had, the government of Gansu to carry a policy of control through conciliation towards Tibet and to suspend the conference on issues of Tibet. Yan replied:

> The so-called policy of control through conciliation towards Tibet was but a personal act based on the personal friendship of the Gansu governor. The government can do nothing about it, nor has Britain any reason to lay the blame on the Chinese government. The time is not ripe to solve the problem of Tibet. You are expected to suspend the negotiations for the present.

From the conversation cited above it can be seen that Britain paid much attention to the activities of Zhu Xiu's mission. Soon after Zhu Xiu left Lhasa, Britain sent Charles Bell, the former British political officer in Sikkim, on a mission to Lhasa. He arrived in Tibet in November 1920 and left Lhasa in November the next year after spending a whole year in Lhasa, accommodated in a villa not far from the Norbulingka. In *Tibet: Past and Present*, Bell gives a detailed account of his mission and activities in Lhasa.

What Bell tried to do in Lhasa was to make the already strained relations between the Han Chinese and Tibetans even worse, instigating Tibetans to make expansions into inner China. He said:

> My private conversations with the Dalai Lama, which were frequent, ranged over a wide variety of subjects. Sometimes the power of Tibet to defend itself came under discussion. During one of these conversations—which were entirely informal—being asked my opinion, I expressed my view that the Tibetan army was inadequate. It consisted only of some five thousand men. I thought that it should be increased gradually, as funds and equipment became available, till it reached about fifteen thousand.

An expanded Tibetan army would mean more taxes. So Bell proposed to the Dalai taxing the monasteries and the aristocrats. The proposed imposition of new taxes to meet the expenses of an expanded army immediately ran into the stiff opposition of lay and clerical Tibetans, especially those of the Three Major Monasteries. It nearly led to the expulsion of Bell out of Lhasa. Of the three monasteries the Drepung was the strongest opponent to Bell's proposal. As the Thirteenth Dalai had to be prudent in dealing with the matter, Bell was not able to carry his plot through.

According to *An Outline History and Geography of Tibet,* in January 1922 Dondrup Wangal was sent by the Thirteenth Dalai to Beijing to express the Dalai's hope to submit to the central government. In November of that year he was sent again by the Dalai to pay respects to President Li Yuanhong. At that time Tibetans and Han Chinese would have restored their good relations, but owing to Britain's instigations, the Tibetans failed to do so.

# 8. Discord Between the Ninth Panchen and the Thirteenth Dalai and the Panchen's Flight to the Interior

Since the Thirteenth Dalai came back from India to Lhasa, his relations with the Ninth Panchen became worse. In 1915 the Dalai set up a *kyidzong* (equal to the Prefecture Administrative Office in inner China) in Shigatse with a monk official, Lozang Dondrup, and a lay official, Musha, as its heads. The *kyidzong*, in charge of the four *dzongs* and all the *shikas* under the Panchen's jurisdiction as well as the Dalai's *dzongs* and *shikas* in Tsang, was an encroachment on the Panchen's status and power—in the Qing Dynasty the Panchen and Dalai were religious and political equals. In addition, they had both been under the leadership of the Qing Emperor, and the Panchen's areas were directly supervised by the Amban. Therefore, the Dalai's move depreciated the Panchen's status and functions. The Panchen, even on principle, could not endure it. To make matters worse, though, the *kyidzong* imposed levies of grain, free transportation and taxes in the Panchen's domain. In particular, when the Kashag imposed a quarter of the total levies of grain, or 10,000 *khal* (approximately 140,000 kilogrammes), in the Panchen's domain, the residents there, both clerical and lay, became more dismayed. They could not afford it. All this led to a serious deterioration of the relationship between the Panchen and the Dalai.

In 1916 the Panchen wrote a letter to the Dalai, asking for a meeting with the latter to cite the grievances of the Tashilhunpo. The Dalai replied that the meeting had to be postponed to the next year as he was very busy, though he would be glad to meet with the Panchen.

In 1917 the Dalai declared that he was to be secluded for practising meditation for three years, during which time he would not meet with anybody, with no exception of the Panchen.

In the spring of 1919 the Dalai permitted the Panchen to meet with him. When he arrived in Lhasa, the Panchen was received coldly. At Kidtsel Luding the Dalai sent only one representative to meet him, and only a few less important officials were sent by the Kashag to attend the welcoming ceremony. The Kalons and other important officials greeted the Panchen only by the gate of Jokhang Temple, the temporary dwelling of the Panchen. Having a meeting with the Dalai, the Panchen returned to the Tashilhunpo after only a short stay in Lhasa. The Tibetan biographies of the Dalai and Panchen do not have any records about the meeting.

According to the biography of the Ninth Panchen, the direct reason that led to his flight was that several of his ministers had been summoned urgently to Lhasa by the Dalai, and they were thrown into prison as soon as they arrived there. Their attendants fled back to the Tashilhunpo and reported to the Panchen. The Panchen knew this was an omen of disaster. If he stayed on, surely a dire calamity would befall him very soon. So he decided to flee to inland China.

On the night of November 15, 1923, the Panchen rode away secretly from the Tashilhunpo to the north, accompanied by fifteen monk attendants. Three days later, on the night of the eighteenth of that month, the Panchen's attendant officials, Solpon Khenpo Lozang Gyaltsen, Chopon Khenpo Wangdu Norbu, Zimpon Khenpo Galdan Rabgye, Phurchok Khenpo Lozang Palden, Drungyig Chenmo Wang Lejie, Dronyer Drungzurlo, Sengge Sangye Gyatso, Sol Thabpa Lozang Wangdan and a hundred or so attendant lamas left secretly to catch up with the Panchen. They left for Changtang in north Tibet. After crossing the Tanggula Range they came into Qinghai.

The Kashag's *kyidzong* in Shigatse, on learning that the Panchen had fled, sent men to Gyantse to inform the Dalai of the Panchen's flight by telephone through the British post office, because at that time Shigatse had no telephone or telegram service. The Dalai Lama immediately sent Tsepon Lungshar and Dapon Tsogo with a thousand troops to intercept the Panchen's party in the north. But the Panchen's party was not taking the ordinary northeastward route from Shigatse to Qinghai—via Nagchukha and the Tanggula Range—instead, turning north and passing through the unpopulated region of Changtang. As the pursuers did not know which route the Panchen was following, and because heavy snow was closing all the roads in the mountains, they soon had to give up the pursuit.

When the Panchen's party fled out of Tibet and went into Qinghai, they were sad to find that, though they had brought enough money, they could not buy food in the unpopulated region. Nor could they hunt—for Buddhist monks are not permitted to kill any living beings, and so the Panchen's party knew nothing about hunting. They had to kill some horses for food. But without horses they could not reach the end of the grasslands. They were in despair.

When they reached Tsitsun Tsathang grasslands, they came across the returning camel caravan of Shabdrung Khenpo, sutra preceptor of Outer Mongolia's Jetsun Dampa, and Lozang Thubten, Jetsun Dampa's Solpon Khenpo. They were going back to Outer Mongolia from Lhasa. As recorded by Liu Jiaju in *The Complete Works of the Panchen Lamas*, the caravan provided enough food to them and "accompanied the Buddha to interior China."

The Panchen's party reached Anxi, a county on the western border of Gansu Province, on March 20, 1924. The journey from the Tashilhunpo to Anxi had taken them four months and five days. At Anxi they bid farewell to the caravan of Shabdrung Khenpo, who continued his journey north to Outer Mongolia. The magistrate of Anxi warmly received the Panchen's party, meanwhile cabling the news to the Military Governor of Lanzhou, Lu Hongtao, who immediately reported to President Cao Kun.

The Northern Government decided to receive the Ninth Panchen in the same manner as Qing Emperor Gaozong had received the Sixth Panchen. As the Huangsi Temple in Beijing had decayed out of many years' neglect, Yingtai in Zhongnanhai was chosen as the residence for the Panchen. Kunsang Norbu, head of the Mongolian and Tibetan Affairs Council, was responsible for the preparation of entertainment. By order of the government, Lu Hongtao wired the magistrate of Anxi to escort the Panchen and his party to Lanzhou.

When the Panchen and his party reached Lanzhou on May 4, 1924, Lu Hongtao led officers and troops, a party of several thousand, to greet the Panchen in the outskirts of Lanzhou. Yellow cloth was used to cover the streets the Panchen was to pass, and yellow brocade to decorate walls of Leitan Temple, where the Panchen was to be accommodated. Archways were set up on streets. President Cao Kun appointed Li Naifen as the commissioner in charge of the Panchen's safety. Li Naifen, together with a hundred guards, as he was leaving Beijing for Lanzhou to greet the Panchen, declared that the President had bestowed upon the Ninth Panchen the title of The Most Loyal Buddhist Preacher.

By now a civil war between the Zhili (Hebei) and Fengtian (Liaoning) warlords broke out, with Feng Yuxiang capturing Beijing, and Cao Kun being forced to step down from the presidency. Duan Qirui became the Interim Governor. With Feng Yuxiang's invitation, Sun Yat-sen left Guangzhou for Beijing. The Panchen was going to Beijing by way of Shaanxi. At that time a civil war was also going on in Shaanxi. The National Army, under the command of Yang Hucheng and Li Huchen, was besieged in Xi'an by the troops of Liu Zhenhua under Wu Peifu. When he reached Xi'an in August 1924, the Panchen, prevented from going forward by the war, sent Dronyer Drungzurlo to consult with the heads of the belligerent sides of the war. They all agreed to escort the Panchen out of their lines of defence. Seeing bodies all over the battlefield, the Panchen prayed for the deceased (see *The Complete Works of the Panchen Lamas*).

While staying in Xi'an, the Ninth Panchen sent an open telegram to the heads of all sides of the country, appealing for ceasing the civil war and for unity in order to save the country. This was the first declaration in which he made clear his political inclination after coming to the inland. It is of historical significance. The whole text reads as follows:

> To Interim Governor Duan Qirui, the two chambers of the Parliament, Ministries and Commissions, Commander-in-Chief Zhang Zuolin, Commander-in-Chief Lu, Commander-in-Chief Feng Yuxiang, Deputy Commander-in-Chief Hu, Deputy Commander-in-Chief Sun, Mr. Wang Pingqing, Mr. Xiong Bingsan, Mr. Sun Muhan, Mr. Wang Botang, Mr. Zhao Cishan, Mr. Wang Youshan, Mr. Li Yuanhong, Mr. Xu Shichang, Mr. Liang Qichao, Mr. Yan Fansun, Mr. Zhang Jingyu, Mr. Sun Bolan, Mr. Sun Yat-sen, Mr. Wu Peifu, Mr. Kang Gengsheng, Mr. Qin Yunjie, Mr. Zhang Taiyan, Mr. Zhang Jizhi from Nantong, Mr. Hu Hanmin from Guangzhou, Mr. Chen Jingcun from Shantou, Inspector Qi from Nanjing, Inspector Xiao from Wuchang, Inspector Sun Chuanfang from Hangzhou, Commander-in-Chief Li of Tianjin, Governor Zheng of Jinan, Military Governor Yan of Taiyuan, Commander-in-Chief Wu of Jilin, Commander-in-Chief Zhang of Heilongjiang, Governor Wang of Anhui, Governor Cai of Jiangxi, Military Governor Liu Zhenhua of Xi'an, Military Governor Lu of Lanzhou, Military Governor Yang Zengxin of Xinjiang, Governor Zhao of Hunan, Commander-in-Chief Tang Jiyao of Yunnan, Commander-in-Chief Liu of Guizhou, General Mi in Rehe, General Zhang in Chahar, General Ma in Suiyuan, Governor Yang in Chongqing, Provincial Governor Deng, editors of all Chinese newspapers, all corporations, all military commanders, all provincial parliaments, Changkya Hutuktu, Hutuktus and princes in Inner and Outer Mongolia:
> Sirs:
> The five Chinese nationalities are now under the administration of the government of the Republic. Mt. Potala and the Lhasa River are also a part of China. I have experienced many hardships since I left Tibet for the inland. When I arrived in Xi'an after a journey of almost a year, I learned that the whole country was undergoing political changes. I was happy to know that His Highness Mr. Duan has come out to shoulder the important tasks of the head of the government and declared the beginning of reforms. Nevertheless, I have some suggestions to make. Our country is now swaying in the storm. At this critical moment of life and death it is an urgent thing to calm down the

internal strife. In the flames of war that flared up everywhere people are panic-stricken at the slightest breath of danger. If we fight against our own countrymen, it will provide an opportunity for foreigners to seek easy profits. When the lips are gone, the teeth will be exposed to the cold. I am deeply concerned about the safety of the beautiful land of the interior and the borderland. I have always stood together with the central government through thick and thin. On my journey I saw the country in desolation and economic depression. The war must be stopped. Let the strength of our country be recovered. To cease the war and safeguard the peace in our country is what we should do right now. I hope that the republic polity will be realized and the people may live in peace and prosperity.

Panchen Erdeni

In the original text only the month and year were given. According to *The Complete Works of the Panchen Lamas*, the telegram was issued from Xi'an on December 29, 1924.

When he arrived in Xi'an, the Ninth Panchen was greeted by the representatives of Military Governor of Shanxi Yan Xishan. Then he was escorted by troops sent by Liu Zhenhua to Tongguan Pass; he crossed the Yellow River at Fenglingdu Ferry and went by car to Taiyuan. When he arrived at Taiyuan, Yan Xishan led a party of several thousand troops to welcome him and saluted him with a salvo of guns. He was accommodated in a new hotel. Interim Governor Duan Qirui sent his son Duan Hongye, accompanied by Lozang Norbu from the Mongolian and Tibetan Affairs Council, Mongolian Prince Yang Sangqiao, Changkya Hutuktu and others, to Taiyuan to invite the Panchen to Beijing. Yan Xishan persuaded the Panchen to stay till the end of the Spring Festival.

On February 2, 1925, the Panchen and his party left Taiyuan for Beijing by a special train. While arriving at Beijing, he was welcomed by the representatives of Interim Governor Duan, officials of the Mongolian and Tibetan Affairs Council, monks from Yonghegong Lamasery and tens of thousands of people. In Beijing the Panchen was accommodated at Yingtai in Zhongnanhai. On the day following his arrival, the Panchen visited Duan Qirui and reported the situation in Tibet and his mission. Duan replied the problems of Tibet would be solved as soon as the country was in peace.

After the Panchen came to Beijing, tens of thousands of Mongols, clerical and lay, including Mongolian princes, came to worship him. He had to receive at least one or two groups and sometimes five or six groups of the worshippers every day, an unprecedented pomp in Beijing. A total of tens of thousands of Mongols came to Beijing to seek an audience with him.

On February 1, 1925, the Northern Government called a conference which was to cope with the aftermath of war, and the Tibetan local government was asked to send representatives. Dondrup Wangyal (on behalf of the Dalai), Lozang Gyaltsen (on behalf of the Panchen) and Zhu Qinghua (on behalf of Lu Xingqi, the Commissioner for Tibet) attended the conference. The Panchen wrote a letter to the conference, hoping the representatives would solve all the problems fairly and give consideration to the overall situation. But the Tibet issue was not raised or discussed at the conference. During the conference Dr. Sun Yat-sen died of illness in Beijing on March 12.

Seeing that it would be a long time before a solution of the Tibet issue was reached, the Panchen accepted the invitation of Sun Chuanfang, Inspector of Zhejiang, and travelled to the south on April 5, 1925, in the company of Da Shou, Qi Chengwu and Xi Yu (sent by Governor Duan), and eight men from the Mongolian and Tibetan Affairs Council. A special train carried the Panchen and his party through Nanjing and Shanghai to Hangzhou, where the Panchen worshipped the Buddha in Lingyin Temple and initiated many Buddhists.

They left Hangzhou for Shanghai on April 16. Then he went on a pilgrimage to Mt. Putuo of the Zhoushan Archipelago on May 9, travelling there by ship. On Mt. Putuo, where there were fourteen hundred monks in the temples, the Panchen touched each monk on the head as a blessing and gave them alms—for each, two silver dollars. In addition, he gave three thousand silver dollars to Putuo Temple for burning joss sticks and candles. He went back to Shanghai on May 15. Then he left Shanghai for Beijing by train.

On a pilgrimage to Mt. Wutai, he first went by train to Datong and then by car to the mountain. He spent over three months in temples in Mt. Wutai, during which time he practised meditation in seclusion for twenty-one days. He also gave alms to all monks on Mt. Wutai.

In late July Duan Qirui sent Mindrol Hutuktu and Don Shi'en as special envoys to Mt. Wutai to invite the Panchen back to Beijing. He was again accommodated at Yingtai in Zhongnanhai when he came back to Beijing. On August 1 Interim Governor Duan Qirui bestowed on the Ninth Panchen a title of *Xuancheng Jishi* (Propagator of Honesty, Saviour of the World) along with a gold album and a gold seal of authority. These honours were brought to Yingtai and granted to the Panchen by Gong Xinzan, Minister of Internal Affairs, and Kunsang Norbu, head of the Mongolian and Tibetan Affairs Council, by order of Duan.

The next day the Panchen paid a visit to Duan at his office to express his gratitude for the title and album and seal granted to him. That evening Duan held a banquet in honour of the Panchen in Huairentang Hall.

Meanwhile, the Interim Governor approved the application for setting up the Panchen's Office in Beijing. It was located in Fuyou Temple. The Panchen appointed Lozang Tsultrim as its head. By order of the Panchen, Wangdu Norbu went to Xining to set up the Panchen's Office in Qinghai, Ngawang Jingpa went to Chengdu to set up the Panchen's Office in Sichuan, and Fukang'an went to India to set up the Panchen's Office in India. These three offices were set up over the following year.

By now the civil war between the warlords had broken out again, with Zhang Zuolin and Wu Peifu expelling Feng Yuxiang and his troops from Beijing. Feng moved to Chahar, Suiyuan and Gansu. Then Duan Qirui stepped down from the post of Interim Governor, and Zhang Zuolin proclaimed himself "Generalissimo," acting as the head of the state. He arrested and killed Li Dazhao, one of the founders of the Communist Party of China. In Guangdong, with Dr. Sun Yat-sen's death, Chiang Kai-shek came to power. Chiang claimed himself the Commander-in-Chief of the Northern Expeditionary Army and united Feng Yuxiang, Yan Xishan and Li Zongren to fight against the northern warlords. Not long afterwards, under the pretext of "clearing up the Kuomintang Party," Chiang began to wipe out Chinese Communists, and the first Kuomintang-Communist cooperation collapsed.

# 9. The Ninth Panchen's Activities in the Interior and the Relations Between the Kuomintang Government and Tibet

Facing such an unfavourable political situation, the Panchen felt that it was not good for him to live in Beijing. So at the invitation of Mongolian princes in East Mongolia, the Panchen moved to Shenyang. Zhang Zuolin was polite to the Panchen: agreeing to his moving and assigning the Huangsi Temple in Shenyang as his residence. On October 10, 1926, the Panchen arrived at Shenyang and was warmly greeted by Provincial Governor Mo Dehui, Mongolian princes and several thousand people.

On May 13, 1927, at the invitation of Mongolian Prince Yang, the Panchen went to Dalahan Banner to bless the worshippers by touching their heads. Tens of thousands came to worship him. In September he was invited by Mongolian Turkic Prince Tu to Keshesoma Monastery to preach Buddhist doctrines, and he was warmly welcomed by the Mongolians there.

In March 1928 the Kuomintang nationalist government was founded in Nanjing, with Tan Yankai as its chairman. The Panchen sent Solpon Khenpo Lozang Gyaltsen and Zhu Fu'an to Nanjing to offer his congratulations to the new government. It was the beginning of official contact between the Panchen and the nationalist government. By now the Northern Expeditionary Army had moved to northern China. Zhang Zuolin claimed to step down on June 2 and to pull out of Beijing. On his way back to Shenyang he was killed, on June 4, in a bomb-explosion incident on the train at Huangutun, a murder schemed by the Japanese. The Northern Expeditionary Army marched into Beijing, and the nationalist government in Nanjing was reorganized, with Chiang Kai-shek being made chairman. Zhang Xueliang, Zhang Zuolin's son, was one of the commissioners of the government. The government established the Commission for Mongolian and Tibetan Affairs and granted the Panchen's request for opening an office in Nanjing. The Panchen appointed Lozang Gyaltsen and Zhu Fu'an as the director and vice-director, respectively, of the office.

That year the Panchen continued his Buddhist activities in East

Mongolia. In April the Panchen held the first Buddhist meeting of Kalachakra Dorje (lit., Thunderbolt of the Wheel of Time), which was financially supported by Prince Yang Sangqiao and attended by one hundred and seventy thousand Mongolian people in Xiwang Temple. In July the second Buddhist meeting of Kalachakra Dorje was held in Tsasatu-Abu Temple, financially supported by the princes of ten banners and attended by eighty-four thousand Mongolian people. That year Zhang Xueliang granted the Panchen's request for opening his Fengtian Office at Shenyang headed by Khenpo Pakshi.

In 1929 a civil war broke out between Chiang Kai-shek on one side and Feng Yuxiang, Yan Xishan and Li Zongren on the other side. The Panchen again appealed by wire for peace. The telegram reads:

> Since the nationalist government was established the whole country has become united and the civil war of over ten years has been put to an end. I hope that people will be saved from misery by those leaders who are merciful and patriotic.

On April 15, at the invitation and with the financial support of the head of the Xilingol League and princes of ten banners, the Panchen held the third Buddhist meeting of Kalachakra Dorje in the Beiji Temple of the Xilingol League, which was attended by seventy thousand Mongolian people. After the meeting, the Panchen gave sermons at temples of many banners of Inner Mongolia. In September Zhang Xueliang sent Li Shaobai with fifteen cars to invite the Panchen back to Shenyang, where he was again accommodated in Huangsi Temple. By now the war between Chiang Kai-shek on one side and Feng Yuxiang, Yan Xishan and Li Zongren on the other had come to an end. The whole country seemed to be united again. The Thirteenth Dalai at that time sent Konchok Jungnas, his resident *khenpo* at Yonghegong Lamasery in Beijing, and Khenpo Lozang Palzang, his resident representative at Mt. Wutai, to Nanjing, to tell Chiang Kai-shek that the Dalai had never entered into alliance with Britain, harboured no hostility towards the Chinese people and would welcome the Panchen's return to Tibet. Chiang Kai-shek wrote a letter to the Dalai and asked Konchok Jungnas to hand it to the Dalai in person.

Konchok Jungnas was an important figure. He had been received in audience by Chiang Kai-shek several times. He was sent by the Dalai to Beijing in 1924 to be the Dalai and Kashag's resident representative in Beijing, although ostensibly he was only the *khenpo* of the Yonghegong. When he came to Beijing from Tibet he brought with him about ten attendants. On January 16, 1924, he reported his arrival at Beijing to the Mongolian and Tibetan Affairs Council and handed in his résumé for the record.

The following is a letter written by Chiang Kai-shek on September 18, 1930, to the Thirteenth Dalai, which concerned Konchok Jungnas:

> To the Dalai Lama, State Tutor, Your Highness: I was pleased to know from Lozang Tsultrim Tenzin, who has come to Nanjing, that after Commissioner Konchok Jungnas arrived at Lhasa, you have frequently granted him audiences and expressed sincerity and respect to the central government. Following the instructions of the late Director-General Sun Yat-sen on supporting all nationalities in China, the government tries hard to work for the Tibetans' well-being. Now Commissioner Konchok has come to Beijing. I have ordered Chairman Ma of the Commission for Mongolian and Tibet Affairs to work out a programme for the settlement of the Tibetan issue. I offer my good wishes to you.

On September 22, the Dalai replied by wire to Chiang Kai-shek:

> To Chairman Chiang of the nationalist government in Nanjing, Your Highness: I was very glad to receive your telegram and your letter and gifts from Konchok Jungnas, who reported to me in detail in person. I am also praying for world peace. China and Tibet will have communications between them in the end. I pray for peace. I am glad to know that Ma Fuxiang, Commissioner of the Commission for Mongolian and Tibetan Affairs, is now dealing with the Tibetan issue for us. Yours humbly, Dalai Lama.

At the same time, the nationalist government sent Liu Manqing, a woman employee at the Office of Civil Personnel, to Lhasa by way of Xikang in July 1929. Liu Manqing was a Tibetan from Xikang. In Lhasa she had two interviews with the Dalai, who treated her well. At that time Tibetan troops were expanding eastwards for the second time. The Dalai told her:

> As for Xikang, I hope you would tell the government that it should

replace the sadistic army officers there, who subject my people to brutal treatment, with an honest civil official of clean reputation. I am ready to withdraw the Tibetan troops at any moment. As the place is Chinese territory, there is no need to argue which one of us owns it.

What he said was recorded in Liu's book *My Mission to Xikang and Tibet*.

In 1930 some disputes developed incidentally in the relations between Tibet and Nepal. The cause was said to be the Kashag government's imposition of taxes on Nepalese merchants in Lhasa. The Nepalese resisted openly. The Dalai had the protesters arrested. The Nepalese government gave orders for nationwide mobilization for a large-scale invasion of Tibet. The Dalai, being informed of the approaching invasion, asked the nationalist government for aid. The Commission for Mongolian and Tibetan Affairs, with the approval of the government, sent Ba Wenjun, a counselor of the commission, to Nepal to investigate the cause of the conflict between Nepal and Tibet. Records *An Outline History and Geography of Tibet*:

> Ba was very well received in Nepal. When the disputes ended, Ba returned to Nanjing with a number of gifts from Nepal for the Chinese government. The relations between China and Nepal are gradually turning for the better.

While Ba Wenjun was sent to Nepal, Xie Guoliang, a member of the Commission for Mongolian and Tibetan Affairs, left for Lhasa with his secretary, Tan Yunshan. He was sent by the commission to make further contact with the Dalai under the pretext of investigating the disputes between Nepal and Tibet. Xie, formerly a Qing resident official in Tibet, had intended to talk with the Dalai on the relations between the Tibetan local government and the nationalist central government.

Prior to Xie Guoliang's mission to Tibet, the 220th session of the Kuomintang Central Political Conference revised and approved the eleven-point proposal for solving the Tibet issue worked out by the Commission for Mongolian and Tibetan Affairs. The eleven-point proposal is as follows:

> (1) Tibet should continue to maintain close relations with China.
> (2) Tibet is not allowed to have any direct political relations with other

countries than China.

(3) The treaties that Tibet has concluded with foreign countries should be referred to the central government for final decisions to be made on them.

(4) The Dalai should welcome the Panchen's return to Tibet.

(5) The Dalai should return to the nationalist government all the counties in Xikang he has occupied.

(6) Important matters concerning Tibet's political, military and foreign affairs shall be administered by the central government.

(7) The nationalist government will grant Tibet autonomy.

(8) The political and religious powers of the Dalai and Panchen shall remain the same as before.

(9) The nationalist government will post its resident officials in Tibet. The Dalai and Panchen shall protect them and give them all conveniences available.

(10) Tibet may post its resident officials in the capital of the country. They will be funded by the nationalist government according to real conditions.

(11) The recent disputes between Tibet and Nepal will be handled impartially by the nationalist government.

Xie Guoliang left Nanjing in May 1930 and reached a place called Lang about a day's journey from Lhasa in November, where he suddenly died. His secretary, Tan Yunshan, came back to Nanjing and returned the eleven-point proposal to the Commission for Mongolian and Tibetan Affairs.

Hearing that Nepal was to invade Tibet, the Panchen prepared to go back for the defence of Tibet. He asked the central government to provide him with 5,000 rifles, 2,500,000 rounds of ammunition, 5,000 suits of uniforms and a monthly fund of 100,000 *yuan* for army pay. He said: "If these cannot be made available at the present moment, I ask to be allowed to raise them on my own."

The nationalist government ordered the ministries of foreign affairs, internal affairs and military-political affairs to have a discussion of the Panchen's request, and a three-point proposal for solving the problem was made. It is as follows:

(1) The central government is to install two high-ranking resident officials in Tibet—with one of them posted in U and the other in Tsang —for handling foreign affairs and important administrative matters and acting at the same time as commanders of the garrison troops in Tibet.

(2) In order to carry out a new policy in Tibet and to carry out all plans of the central government without meeting obstacles, the Panchen shall request the central government and announce that all Tibetan foreign and military affairs shall be administered by the central government. The resident officials shall be consulted on all the programmes concerning Tibetan political reforms.

(3) If the Panchen will make an announcement according to the above-mentioned second item, it is only natural that aid shall be given to him and soldiers will be sent to escort him to Tibet. As to his request for organizing his own guards, and for allocating guns to his soldiers or getting them with his own expenses, it is a question to be decided by the commanders of the army, navy and air force.

In the end, however, an armed conflict had developed between Tibet and Xikang. The Panchen's return to Tibet again came to a deadlock.

In 1930 the Tibetan troops stationed in Xikang, taking a dispute between Dargye Monastery and the headman of Beri as an excuse, attacked the Sichuan garrison troops at Garze. In 1931 the Dalai sent a mission of twenty men headed by Konchok Jungnas to Nanjing for setting up an office there, and at the same time asked Chiang Kai-shek to send an official to handle the conflict between Dargye and Beri. Chiang appointed Tang Kesan, an official of the Commission for Mongolian and Tibetan Affairs, to investigate the case in Garze. Tang was assisted by Liu Zanting, also an official of the commission. By order of the government the Sichuan garrison troops abandoned Garze and retreated to Luhuo. Tibetan troops captured Garze and Zhanhua.

In the same year there was a land dispute between the Qinghai Ganden Monastery and the Dudtsi Dil Monastery in Yushu (Jyekundo). Tibetan troops, taking the dispute as a pretext for attack, began their assault on the defence zones of Yushu. Soon Ma Bufang sent a great army of cavalrymen from Xining to Yushu. When the newly assembled Qinghai troops reached the battlefront, they mounted a counteroffensive, in which they defeated the Tibetan troops. With the whole of Qinghai now cleared of Tibetan troops, the victorious Qinghai army pressed on, penetrating into Xikang and recovering Serxu, Dengke and other county seats lost to the Tibetan army. The sweeping victory scored by Ma's troops brought about quick and dramatic changes in the war situation in Xikang. The Tibetan army in Garze, Zhanhua and Derge had to retreat to the west of the Jinsha River because its supply and communication lines could be cut off at any time and its flanks were now exposed to attack.

On October 8, 1932, a cease-fire agreement was reached at Gangtuo by Deng Jun, a negotiator authorized by the Sichuan army, and Dapon Khyungram, his Tibetan counterpart. It stipulated that both sides agreed to take the Jinsha River as their borderline.

On June 15 the next year, a truce was signed by representatives from Qinghai and Tibet. After the withdrawal, the troops of both sides are to be kept within their areas and are not to violate the other's territory.

The two wars mentioned above were the Tibetans' second eastward expansion. The weapons Tibetan troops used during the invasion of Xikang and Qinghai were all provided by British India. According to *An Outline History and Geography of Tibet*, "The weapons the Dalai's troops used during the invasion were all made by an ordnance factory in Bombay, and the troops fought under the command of British officers."

On the matter of Britain supplying arms and ammunition to the Tibetan army, the Chinese Ambassador to Britain asked the British Foreign Office for an explanation. The Foreign Office replied that the Indian government was acting in accordance with its treaty obligations, but, it said, future military supplies would be strictly for the purpose of self-defence and the maintenance of public order, and expressed the readiness of the British government to mediate and to help in finding a peaceful solution. In reply the Chinese Ambassador said, "The dispute between the central government and Tibet is China's internal affair; therefore, we decline any offer of mediation."

At the time the Ninth Panchen was continuing his religious activities in Inner Mongolia. In August 1930, he held the fourth Buddhist meeting of Kalachakra Dorje, financed by Prince So in West Ujimqin Banner and attended by fifty thousand people.

In February 1931, the central government invited the Panchen to attend the National Conference at Nanjing. On May 4, the

Panchen arrived in Nanjing and was warmly greeted by He Yaozu, representative of Chiang Kai-shek, officials from all ministries, councils and commissions, as well as several tens of thousands of citizens and students. Navy guns thundered a salute. The Panchen was accommodated in Chiang Kai-shek's headquarters at Sanyuanxiang in Nanjing.

On May 5, the Panchen, accompanied by Dai Chuanxian, the head of the Examination Yuan, was received by Chiang Kai-shek in audience. Then the Panchen visited Hu Hanmin and other high-ranking officials of the central government. On that day the Panchen made a short speech to the conference. He said:

> I come from the borderland and am well acquainted with the situation there. I sincerely support the central government. I trust the government will save the Tibetans from their miserable life in the near future. I have gone to the south and north, devoting all my energy to the cause. I wish all you gentlemen to have a good discussion on how to rectify the administration of the borderland. To follow the late Director-General Sun Yat-sen's instructions of helping the weak, to consolidate our country's sovereignty over territory, to raise the prestige of our country and not to give up the precious land in the west, is what I wish and pray for.

On May 10, the Panchen gave a lecture to the third session of the New Asia Society in Nanjing. His topic was "Tibet Is China's Territory." He said:

> Tibet is China's territory. Here I need not dwell on this subject, as you all know this well. I would like to cite some important historical events. During the time from Songtsen Gampo, who married Tang Princess Wencheng, to Tride Tsugtsen, who married Tang Princess Jincheng, Tibet was in harmonious relations with China, and blood was mixed between Tibetans and Chinese to a considerable extent. The Yuan Dynasty granted Phagspa the honorific title of State Tutor and trusted to him the administration of Tibet. The Ming Dynasty patronized Tibet. The Fifth Dalai and the Sixth Panchen came to the interior and were received by the Emperor in audience. The Qing Emperor sent troops to drive Dzungar invaders out of Tibet and installed Ambans in Lhasa with Chinese garrison troops for the protection of the Dalai and Panchen. This was done for the cause of defending our territory. These examples prove Tibet is a part of China. I would like to talk about what I think on this subject: (1) If Tibet, a part of China, is invaded by

imperialists, it means that our door is destroyed, in other words, when the lips are gone, the teeth will be exposed to the cold; (2) To make Mongols and Tibetans unite closely with the Chinese, the central government, as well as all the people, should make an effort.

# 10. The Ninth Panchen Is Granted an Honorific Title

Only July 1, 1931, the nationalist government officially conferred on the Panchen the title of "Great Master of Infinite Wisdom, Defender of the Nation and Propagator of the Doctrine," in addition to a jade seal and a jade album. At the same time he was made a recipient of an annual stipend of 120,000 yuan.

On July 8, the Panchen left Nanjing for the Hulunbuir League in Inner Mongolia. He was accommodated in the office of the governor of Hailar. He gave sermons to the local Mongols and blessed them by touching their heads. Soon afterwards, the September 18 Incident occurred, and the Japanese troops invaded and conquered northeast China. Chiang Kai-shek, making no resistance to the Japanese invaders, ordered Zhang Xueliang to retreat with his troops to south of the Shanhaiguan Pass. Fearing that he might be detained by the Japanese, the Panchen hurriedly went west via the wilderness in Outer Mongolia. After a rapid journey of twelve days, he arrived at the East Ujimqin Banner in Inner Mongolia. In October, at the invitation of Mongolian Prince De, he went to the Prince's mansion in Suiyuan Province. At that time a dispute broke out among the Tibetans in Jinchuan of Sichuan Province; he appointed Gedun Drashi as the head of the Panchen's Office in Kangding and ordered him to settle the dispute.

In March 1932, at the invitation of Prince Yun, head of the Ulangqab League, the Panchen went to Bailingmiao. He set up an office in Guisui (present-day Hohhot) headed by Dingwang Dorje. When he was in Bailingmiao, the Panchen sent a telegram to the people of the whole country to protest against the Japanese invasion. The telegram reads:

> I am angry to know that the vicious Japanese, neglecting justice and the treaty of alliance and relying on military power, invaded our

country to bring about the plot of conquering the mainland. Now the Chinese army and people beyond all bearing have thrown themselves into the hot fight against the Japanese invaders to save the country. For their bravery and patriotism, they are respected at home and abroad. Though I am a monk, I cannot lag behind others in the struggle to save the country. I have gathered more than one thousand Mongolian and Tibetan monks at Bailingmiao, and from March 1 we began to chant sutras, give alms and sermons and pray for peace and for those who have died on the battlefield, hoping to extinguish the war with the power of Buddhism.

In July 1932, patronized by Prince Yun and other chiefs of all banners, the Panchen held the fifth Buddhist meeting of Kalachakra Dorje, attended by over 37,000 Mongols. It was the last one the Panchen held in Inner Mongolia. In October, Duan Qirui invited him to Beijing. Patronized by Duan Qirui, Wu Peifu and Zhu Qinglan, he held the sixth Buddhist meeting of Kalachakra Dorje, attended by about 100,000 people, in the Hall of Supreme Harmony of the former Imperial Palace, on October 22.

On November 4, Shi Qingyang, chief of the Commission for Mongolian and Tibetan Affairs, sent commissioner Li Peitian to invite the Panchen to Nanjing. On December 12, the Panchen reached Pukou railway station and was greeted by Lin Sen, the newly-appointed president of the nationalist government, and heads of all departments of the government. He was accommodated in Lingyuan, Chiang Kai-shek's residence. Two days later he paid his respects to Dr. Sun Yat-sen's tomb and then paid visits to President Lin, Generalissimo Chiang Kai-shek and heads of all the departments. On December 24, the nationalist government officially announced the Panchen's appointment as Western Borderland Publicity Commissioner. The Panchen was inaugurated in the auditorium of the Nationalist Government Mansion. The inauguration ceremony was presided over by Zhang Ji, commissioner of the nationalist government. President Lin Sen said in his speech at the ceremony:

There are misunderstandings between the western borderland and the central government. So the Publicity Commissioner is expected to publicize the desires of the central government in the borderland, in order that joint efforts will be made to consolidate the security of our country. When the Publicity Commissioner goes west, he is expected to propagate, with the help of religious belief, the Three People's Principles, teachings of the late Director-General Sun Yat-sen.

The Panchen's speech in reply was translated and read by Liu Jiaju, his secretary-general. Briefly, it is as follows:

It is an honour to me to be appointed Western Borderland Publicity Commissioner, though I am embarrassed by undeserved praise. Still, the desire to save the world is always in my mind. I am grateful to you for your speech. I should try my best to preach the late Director-General's teachings for the cause of peace and the unity of the five nationalities, to repay the central government for its kindness.

# 11. The Ninth Panchen's Return to Tibet Is Obstructed

Chiang Kai-shek intended to settle the problem of the Panchen's return to Tibet, but he did not know the Dalai and Kashag's attitude. By his order, the Panchen sent Ngachen Hutuktu and Wang Lejie to Lhasa. The mission left Nanjing for Tibet via India on December 12. Chiang Kai-shek gave them twenty thousand yuan for the expenses of the journey.

At the invitation of Dai Chuanxian, Shi Qingyang, Ju Zheng, He Yaozu, Huang Musong and Ye Gongzhuo, the Panchen held a Buddhist ceremony of initiation on January 12, 1933, at Longchang Temple on Mt. Baohua east of Nanjing. The ceremony, lasting for three days, was attended by over three hundred people, excluding the two hundred monks. On February 17, the Panchen left for Bailingmiao of Suiyuan via Beijing.

As the Dalai's representatives—Konchok Jungnas, Ngawang Drakpa, Ngawang Gyaltsen, Chosphel Thubten and others—were now in Nanjing, the government considered it the proper time to call a meeting on the problem of Tibet. The Dalai and the Panchen were asked to make written proposals respectively. The Panchen made a sixteen-point proposal with three preconditions in March. The sixteen-point proposal is as follows:

(1) A pledge by Tibet of absolute obedience to the central authorities

is the principle to solve problems of Tibet.

(2) All the treaties that Tibet has concluded with foreign countries but are not recognized by the central government are null and void.

(3) A line of demarcation shall be made between U and Tsang and Xikang, and boundary markers shall be erected to make sure that the line is respected. The borderline between U and Tsang is Gampa La and the borderline between U and Xikang is Danta Mountain.

(4) Tibetan troops that have invaded Xikang shall be withdrawn immediately, and a Xikang provincial government shall be established without delay.

(5) The Dalai will be in charge of the administrative and religious affairs at U, and the Panchen in charge of those at Tsang.

(6) The central government is requested to station one resident official at U and one at Tsang.

(7) The central government will be in charge of Tibet's military and external affairs.

(8) The Chinese and Tibetans shall enjoy absolute freedom of communication and contact.

(9) Those officials and civilians from Tsang who have been captured by the troops of U shall be set free.

(10) U shall return the properties it has confiscated from the Tsang officials and civilians.

(11) Before the Panchen returns to Tibet, a proper title shall be conferred on him and some place in Qinghai or Xikang shall be made available for his residence and for his followers to settle in.

(12) The central government is requested to have the Panchen escorted by a high-ranking official and to ask the Hutuktus and the heads of all banners of Inner Mongolia to welcome him as they like when the Panchen travels to Qinghai or Xikang.

(13) The Panchen is to receive from the central government a yearly stipend of 100,000 yuan as previously determined.

(14) The Panchen is to receive from the central government 50,000 yuan for his office expenditures each month before he returns to Tibet.

(15) The central government is requested to give the Panchen permission to organize and train two guard regiments and provide them with weapons and pay before he returns to Tibet.

(16) The central government is requested to provide the Panchen with five radio transmitters and twenty long-distance buses to facilitate communications and improve transportation.

The three preconditions are as follows:

(1) All the commodities and materials needed by the Chinese and Tibetan people, as well as by Panchen, shall be free to go into and out of Tibet.

(2) No other duty than the justified one shall be imposed on the Tibetans in Tsang.

(3) Yeshe Konchok Gosul, a relative of the Panchen who has been imprisoned in Lhasa, shall be released and sent to Beijing immediately.

The Dalai's representatives were slow in giving any proposal. It was not until May that Konchok Jungnas and other representatives made public a "declaration of the clerical and secular officials of the Three Major Monasteries and the mass of the people"—it amounted to a condemnation of the Panchen. (For the whole text of the declaration, please refer to my book *The Biographies of the Dalai Lamas*.) At the same time they raised four demands with the nationalist government. Their demands were these:

(1) Withdraw from the Panchen the title, seal and title certificate and remove him from his new position;

(2) Confiscate immediately or declare a ban on the arms and ammunition the Panchen has purchased, and keep the Panchen in Beijing for the time being;

(3) Stop immediately the Panchen's stipends and the payment for his accommodations;

(4) Order an immediate shutdown of all the Panchen's offices in the interior.

Shortly after the declaration was made public, the Panchen's Office in Nanjing made a counter-statement, in which the Dalai was accused of ten crimes.

According to Liu Jiaju's *The Complete Works of the Panchen Lamas*, the counter-statement had not been approved by the Panchen beforehand. When he was told about it, the Panchen said that he did not approve it. Obviously, the Panchen was cool-minded and always kept the interests of the whole in mind.

In view of the fact that the two sides held quite different opinions, the nationalist government had to put the settlement of the Tibetan issue aside for the time being.

After going back to Bailingmiao in Suiyuan, the Panchen continued to give sermons in all the banners in Western Mongolia. He provided over ten thousand head of camels, horses, oxen and sheep, given as alms to him in Inner Mongolia, to the monasteries and temples of all banners in the support of the monks. Instigated by the Japanese, some Mongolian princes proposed autonomy of Inner Mongolia. The Panchen persuaded them to be cautious on the matter and meanwhile sent Lozang Gyaltsen and Liu Jiaju to report it to Chiang Kai-shek at Mt. Lushan. Chiang sent Huang Shaoxiong to Inner Mongolia to make an investigation. At that time some unfortunate news came: the Thirteenth Dalai Lama died unexpectedly in Lhasa on December 17, 1933. All felt surprised at this, for the Dalai was healthy and should not have died at the comparatively young age of fifty-eight.

## 12. The Thirteenth Dalai's Death. The Kunphela and Lungshar Incidents. Radreng Takes Up the Regency

When the Thirteenth Dalai died, the Kashag cabled the message to the Tibet Office in Nanjing. The telegram reads:

The Dalai Rimpoche passed away at 7:30 p.m. on the thirtieth day of the *Hai* month of the Tibetan calendar [December 17]. The Silon and Kashag are in charge of affairs in Tibet for the time being. Please inform the central government of this. The details will be cabled later.

According to the tradition in Tibet, during the time after the Dalai died and before his reincarnation assumed power, a Regent would act for the Dalai. Thus, the Three Major Monasteries, Silon, Kalons and other clerical and secular officials called a General Assembly, at which three candidates for Regent were recommended: (1) Minyang Yeshe Wangdu, the abbot of Ganden Monastery, (2) Radreng Hutuktu Thubten Yeshe Tenpa Gyaltsen, and (3) Phurchok Rimpoche Thubten Jampa Tsultrim, the late Dalai's sutra tutor. The selection was decided by oracles before an image of the Buddha in the Potala. The oracle commissioned by the General Assembly gave the most favourable omens to Radreng Hutuktu. The Assembly therefore decided that Radreng Hutuktu would be the Regent until the next Dalai assumed office. On January 26, 1934, it cabled a telegraphic message to the Tibet Office in Nanjing.

The telegram reads:

> The Assembly unanimously agreed to appoint Radreng Hutuktu to perform the duties of the supreme Dalai Lama before his rebirth and his coming of age after his rebirth. Radreng Hutuktu has been known since childhood for his extraordinary intelligence and wisdom, and is respected throughout Tibet for what he has achieved in his religious training and academic studies. The oracular message obtained before the Bodhisattva image in the Potala speaks highly of the selection. We have decided to ask Radreng Hutuktu to act during the transitional period as Tibet's administrative and religious leader, with the Silon and Kashag remaining in charge of political and military affairs. Please inform the central government of our decision.

On January 31, the Executive Yuan of the nationalist government cabled its approval of the decision to the Silon and Kashag through Konchok Jungnas, director of the Tibet Office in Nanjing. The telegram reads:

> The conference of the Executive Yuan on January 30 agreed to the appointment of Radreng Hutuktu as Regent to perform the duties of the Dalai Lama and submitted its decision for approval by the nationalist government. We believe Radreng Hutuktu will use his wisdom to strengthen the administration of Tibet and will support the central authorities in the cause of Buddhism and well-being of the Tibetans.

To the death of the Thirteenth Dalai Lama, the central government responded by calling a massive memorial meeting in Nanjing, sending a mission headed by Huang Musong, the deputy-chief of the General Staff, to Tibet to pay homage to his memory and to officiate at a ceremony to grant the Dalai the posthumous title of "Great Master of Patriotism, Magnanimity, Benevolence and Sagacity," in addition to a jade seal and a jade album, and allocating fifty thousand yuan to Kashag for the funeral expense.

When he learned about the death of the Dalai Lama, the Panchen immediately sent a telegram to all monasteries in the country. It reads:

> In December all were grieved to learn of the Dalai's death on the 17th, and I myself was overwhelmed by especially deep sorrow. When I sent Ngachen Hutuktu to Tibet I was still gladdened by the thought of one day following the Great Master. But I was shocked to hear of the unexpected death of the Master. Without him the world becomes

darkened. Looking at the west, I feel sad. I have requested the central government to generously award the Great Master Dalai with posthumous titles and to honour his memory with the highest possible form of respect. You are required to conduct religious services in memory of the Dalai Lama for seven days, stopping all banquets and recreation as soon as you receive the message. Please ask all monks of lamaseries through their rectification committees to chant sutras for the early reincarnation of the Dalai Rimpoche in the cause of maintaining peace and order in Tibet.

In addition, the Panchen funded the memorial activities in Tibet, Qinghai, Xikang and Inner Mongolia with 73,200 yuan.

Then the nationalist government invited the Panchen to Nanjing to attend all activities in memory of the Dalai Lama. Accordingly, the Panchen arrived at Nanjing on January 24, 1934, his residence being at No. 5, Shenjiaxiang Lane.

On February 14, a grand meeting in memory of the Thirteenth Dalai Lama was held in Nanjing, attended by over two thousand people from various circles and representatives from Beijing, Shandong, Shanxi, Henan, Shaanxi, Chahar, Anhui, Hubei, Guangdong, Yunnan, Qinghai and other provinces. The memorial meeting was presided over by Wang Zhaoming and Ye Chucang from the nationalist government and conducted by Lu Chao, representative of Lin Sen, Chairman of the nationalist government; Chu Minyi, Chairman of the Executive Yuan; Liang Hancao from the Legislative Yuan; Xie Guansheng from the Judicial Yuan; Dai Chuanxian from the Examination Yuan, and Zheng Luosheng from the Supervisory Yuan. It was held in the Examination Yuan from 8 a.m. to 5 p.m.

Wang Zhaoming made the memorial speech.

To those who paid homage to the memory of the Dalai, Konchok Jungnas, Ngawang Gyaltsen, and other representatives of the Tibet Office in Nanjing responded with thanks.

That day saw three meetings in memory of the Dalai in Nanjing. The Panchen with fifteen monks chanted sutras for the Dalai in Yuanminlou for ten days. Forty-eight Han Chinese monks also chanted sutras in Jiming Temple for three days.

When the memorial meetings were held in Nanjing, Konchok Jungnas, Ngawang Drakpa, Ngawang Gyaltsen, and Chosphel

Thubten—the Kashag's four resident representatives in the Tibet Office in Nanjing—jointly published an article entitled, "A Brief Account of the Dalai Lama," of which three paragraphs are as follows:

> In the fourteenth year of Qing Emperor Dezong's reign British troops invented an excuse to invade Tibet, but failed. In the thirtieth year of that reign British troops went all out to attack Tibet and pressed on to Lhasa. The Dalai could not bear Lhasa, the place of Buddhism, being destroyed by the enemy and the Tibetan people being plunged into great affliction, so he left Lhasa for the inland via Qinghai, Gansu, Mongolia and Shanxi. At that time he was twenty-nine years old.

This is a reference to the Dalai's leading of the Tibetan people in two anti-British wars:

> For twenty years since the Dalai returned from India, Tibet has become prosperous under his good administration. Tibet has become a place eagerly coveted by foreigners, and so Lhasa has been haunted by foreigners, who come to spy on Lhasa's wealth and to coerce the Dalai by sweet words. Being good at coping with them, the wise Dalai did not fall into their trap. Though Tibet did not continue its contact with the interior because of incidents in Sichuan, China's sovereignty over Tibet was kept well. Thus we can resume our relations with the central government.

This passage means that the Thirteenth Dalai protected China's sovereignty over Tibet from foreigners:

> The Dalai longed for the central government. Upon the founding of the Republic, the Dalai was glad to know that the new form of government was based on equality of the five nationalities [Han-Chinese, Manchu, Mongols, Hui and Tibetans]. But civil wars continued in the interior, so the central government could not direct its attention to Tibet at the time. The Dalai thought that the central government with its reformed administration would not be so decadent as the system in the reign of the Regent in the Qing Dynasty. He devoted himself to the political and religious administration of Tibet and still yearned for the central authorities. He tried to resume the former relations with the interior by way of following the principle of equality of the five nationalities.... In the seventeenth year of the Republic [1928], General-in-Chief Chiang Kai-shek accomplished the Northern Expedition. A visit of Yonghegong in the former capital made the General-in-Chief think of Tibet. He thought it would not be good to the country that relations between

Tibet and the interior had been broken for a long time. Thus, when he was still busy with military affairs, he sent representatives to Tibet to express sympathy and support for the Dalai. The Dalai was overjoyed at this, for what he had longed for would come true. The Tibetan people were overwhelmed by especially deep joy. So the representatives of the central government enjoyed a grand reception in Tibet. The Dalai also sent representatives to the capital to resume the former relations between Tibet and the interior. Despite all incidents in Sichuan, Tibet and the central authorities have become closer to each other ever since.

This passage means that the Thirteenth Dalai supported the nationalist government and stood for the restoration of Tibet's subordinate status to the central government.

In his "Records of Huang Musong's Errand to Tibet," Kong Qingzong, Chairman of the Office of the Commission for Mongolian and Tibetan Affairs in Tibet, made an analysis of the Thirteenth Dalai as follows:

The Thirteenth Dalai was a man of sagacity.... He consistently held the belief that to draw himself near to the central authorities to continue his feudalist rule by divine right was better than to fall under British colonialist control. In addition, he was influenced by the patriotism of the masses of the Tibetan people. Many events in his life showed that he was neither controlled by pro-emperor elements of the upper strata, nor under the influence of British imperialists. Over a long period of time he hesitated to get in close contact with the central government. This was also due to the fact that the Chinese reactionary government of that time carried out a policy of nationality discrimination and submitted itself to imperialism and it was not trusted by the Dalai.

This is an objective analysis—though the Thirteenth Dalai was not without fault, yet for all the serious mistakes he made, he can nonetheless be considered as an anti-imperialist patriotic Tibetan leader in modern Tibetan history.

During his stay in Nanjing, the Panchen took part in all memorial activities for the late Dalai, and he was appointed by the nationalist government a commissioner of the government. In the afternoon of January 24, 1934, when he had arrived in Nanjing, he received an official letter from the Civil Personnel Department of the nationalist government as follows:

According to the official letter No. 67 from the Central Executive Commission issued by the Chairman of the nationalist government, the fourth plenary session of the Fourth Central Executive Committee decided to appoint the Panchen Erdeni as commissioner of the nationalist government. This letter is to inform you of the decision.... Signed by the Chief Civil Official Wei Huai

On February 20, the Panchen was sworn in in the auditorium of the Nationalist Government Mansion. At the ceremony he made a speech as follows:

The Panchens through the ages have been treated preferentially by the central government and have taken it as a duty to follow the instructions of the Buddha, obey the central government ordinances and enlighten mortal beings.... During recent years I have enjoyed especially good treatment from the government. Now I have the honour to be appointed a commissioner of the nationalist government. I should endeavour to follow the late Director-General Sun's teachings that a public spirit and his Three People's Principles should rule everywhere under the sky, and to preach Buddhism for our country's unity, our people's well-being and world peace.

While the Panchen continued his stay at Nanjing, Ngachen Hutuktu, Wang Lejie and other emissaries, fifty-six persons in all, sent by the Panchen to Lhasa in 1932, returned to Nanjing. They reported to the Panchen that the Kashag expressed its wish for his early return to Tibet and promised to restore to him all the rights he previously had enjoyed in Tsang. Then the Panchen's emissaries left for Tibet again by sea, going back to do some preparation work for the Panchen's return to Tibet.

On March 8, the British Minister to China, Alexander Cadogan, an embassy official, Eric Teichman, and the British Consul paid a visit to the Panchen and proposed that he leave for Tibet via India by sea. To their proposal the Panchen made no reply.

On March 9 some public personages in Shanghai, such as Wang Yiting, Qu Yingguang, Feng Yangshan, Guan Jiongzhi, Du Yuesheng, Huang Jinrong and Zhang Xiaolin, planning to sponsor a Buddhist meeting of Kalachakra Dorje in Hangzhou, decided to invite the Panchen to preside over the meeting. For this, some monks—Quefei, Yuetao, Shengyi and Huizong—of the Lingyin Temple in Hangzhou, came to Nanjing on April 14 to invite the

Panchen on behalf of some five thousand Buddhist followers. The Panchen arrived at Hangzhou the next day to hold the seventh Buddhist meeting of Kalachakra Dorje, which was attended by more than seventy thousand people. When the Buddhist meeting was finished, the Panchen went to Shanghai on May 22 at the invitation of Wu Tiecheng, mayor of Shanghai. A grand meeting in honour of the Panchen was held in Shanghai on June 3, attended by 300,000 people. The Panchen made a speech entitled "Mongolia and Tibet are China's Important Frontiers" at the meeting. He said:

Mongolia and Tibet, China's northern and western frontiers, are wide in territory, sparse in population and rich in natural resources. Foreigners call them "secret treasures".... For eleven years I have travelled here and there, making nothing of hardships, to restore the friendship of the Hans and Tibetans. What I wish is to restore the original unity of China's five nationalities and achieve an extremely happy world for us all. The southwestern borderland is China's important frontier. I always sincerely hope that the government will pay much attention to it and put the region in good condition. The government has bestowed upon me every favour, granting me the title of "Great Master of Infinite Wisdom, Defender of the Nation and Propagator of the Doctrine," and appointing me as "Western Borderland Publicity Commissioner," and recently as a "commissioner of the nationalist government." This is evidence of the equality of China's five nationalities and of the government's support of religion.... Now when I am in Shanghai again, I am given a grand and warm reception that I will never forget. I will hereafter carry out more propagation for the nation . . . to repay the people's and the government's kindness.

The Panchen left Shanghai for Nanjing on July 3, arrived at Beijing on July 14 and Suiyuan on August 11. In order to prepare for his return to Tibet, the Panchen withdrew his subordinates and their families from Bailingmiao to Ningxia, and he himself with some attendant *khenpos* went to propagate Buddhist doctrines in the Ihju League and Alxa Banner.

He arrived at Dingyuanying in the Alxa Banner on January 26, 1935, where he set up the "Office of the Western Borderland Publicity Commissioner." On February 2, when his brother Tsechokling Hutuktu of U came to Ningxia, the Panchen went there to meet him. After their ten-year separation the two brothers felt very happy to meet again.

Now let us look into Huang Musong's mission to Tibet to pay homage to the Dalai's memory. The mission went to Tibet in two groups. Jiang Zhiyu, Wang Liangkun, Wu Mingyuan and others, members of the first group, went to Lhasa by sea to discuss with the Kashag matters concerning Huang Musong's mission of homage to the late Dalai. The second group, consisting of Liu Puchen, Chen Jingxiu, Lin Donghai, Li Guolin and Gao Changzhu and headed by Huang Musong, left Nanjing for Tibet in April 1934, bringing a 100-watt radio transmitter along. They left Chengdu on May 7 via Xikang. When Huang Musong and his party arrived at Lhasa on August 28, he was given a warm welcome by the Kashag as grand as if it were given to an Amban. The ceremony to grant the Dalai the posthumous title of "Great Master of Patriotism, Magnanimity, Benevolence and Sagacity" took place on September 23 in the Potala with the presentation to the portrait of the Dalai of a jade certificate bearing the title and a jade seal.

At another ceremony on October 1 at the Dalai's memorial hall in the Potala, Huang offered condolences for the Dalai. After the ceremonies the Kashag sent a telegram through the Tibet Office in Nanjing to express gratitude to the nationalist government. The Tibet Office sent a letter to the Chairman of the nationalist government, which reads as follows:

To Chairman Lin of the nationalist government,

We have just received a telegram from the Tibetan Kashag, which reads: "After the Dalai Rimpoche passed away, the central government sent its special envoy Huang to offer condolences. The special envoy arrived at Lhasa safely on the nineteenth of the seventh month of the Tibetan calendar. We all feel immense gratitude to the central government for its great kindness. Tibet is now taking measures to secure peace. This time the central government presented splendid gifts to Regent Radreng, Silon, Kalons and all the officials above the *lechen* level. Please forward our gratitude to the central authorities."

Therefore, we here present the Kashag's telegram to you, and please be graciously informed hereby.

Sent by Tibetan representatives Konchok Jungnas, Ggawang Gyaltsen and Chosphel Thubten.

According to tradition, Huang Musong offered monks of the Three Major Monasteries sweet buttered-tea and distributed alms of two silver dollars to each monk. It was said that Huang spent 400,000 silver dollars on his activities in Tibet.

Huang Musong stayed in Lhasa for about three months. During this time the negotiations between him and the Kashag went through many sessions. Huang, in his *My Mission to Tibet*, says:

> October 6 [1934] . . . at 8:30 a.m. I paid a visit to Kalon Tsemo. The following are the two main points I asked him and his answers:
> (1) Does Tibet want to cooperate with us sincerely in the republic of the five nationalities of China?
> Answer: Tibet will, if the Manchu and Mongolian nationalities take part in it.
> (2) What will be Tibet's political relationship with the central government?
> Answer: External affairs will be handled by the central government, but the internal affairs of Tibet must not be interfered in.
> The Kalon asked the central government to hold a discussion with Tibet on the problem of Xikang and expressed the hope that the central government would make a strict examination of local officials. I said that without settling the Chinese-Tibetan political relationship it would be impossible for the central government and the personages of the borderland to solve the problem of the borderland. The Kalon promised to give the matter further consideration.

Huang Musong telegrammed a report to the central government about what he had talked over with the Kalon. On October 20 the Executive Yuan sent him a telegram in reply, instructing him to come back if the problem could not be settled through negotiation.

The Kashag responded to Huang's proposal on November 6, putting forward a thirteen-point counterproposal. Among the points were the following:

> In dealing with external affairs, Tibet shall remain an integral part of the territory of China. But the Chinese government must promise that Tibet will not be reorganized into a province....
>
> One representative of the central government may be stationed in Tibet, but his retinue shall not exceed twenty-five....
>
> When a new representative is appointed to replace the old, the route he and his retinue take to and fro must be by sea and not through Xikang....

Huang's *My Mission to Tibet* says:

Consultant Wu passed the Kashag's thirteen-point counterproposal on to me and asked for my opinion. I said it was but one-sided demands and would do nothing positive for our territory and sovereignty. So I politely refused and said that it would be taken into further consideration.... On November 9, four Kalons came to persuade me to stay on in order to continue talks on the Chinese-Tibetan relationship. I said if Tibet did not grasp the importance of co-prosperity with the inland, there would not be any use for me to stay. I proposed the following points for talks:

—On foreign affairs there must be unified action with the central government.

—In the preservation of the traditional political system, Tibet shall be granted autonomy and the central government will not interfere with any administrative measures within the authority of an autonomous Tibet.

—All administrative matters of a national character shall be administered by the central government, such as foreign affairs, national defence, communications, the appointment and removal of important officials of Tibet, etc.

—The central government shall grant Tibet autonomy, but for the purpose of exercising full sovereignty in an integral part of its territory, the central government shall appoint a high commissioner to be stationed in Tibet as the representative of the central government, on the one hand to carry out national administrative measures, and on the other to guide the regional autonomy. This shall not be interpreted as interfering in Tibetan autonomy.

The four Kalons asked me to write down the proposed points so that they could present it to the Tibetan National Assembly for discussion. This I did, passing it to them on November 10. I asked them to give me a reply at their earliest convenience.

On November 13, by order of the Executive Yuan, Huang Musong cancelled the sessions on the Chinese-Tibetan relationship and prepared to go back to the capital of Nanjing.

On November 16, the Kashag put forward a ten-point counterproposal, fundamentally the same as the thirteen-point one. The mission, after much discussion, reported it to the central government. On November 22, the mission received a telegram from the Executive Yuan which ordered the group to go back to Nanjing, leaving behind Consultant Liu, who was to be stationed in the

Lhasa Office. His monthly expenditure was budgeted at three thousand yuan.

On November 25, Huang Musong paid his respects to the Dalai Lama in the Potala and then took leave of Regent Radreng and Silon Langdun. The Regent was satisfied with the fact that General Consultant Liu Puchen was to be stationed in Lhasa to appease the people. As to the Panchen's return to Tibet, Huang said that the Panchen would go by way of Qinghai and Xikang under the escort of a few men instead of by sea, and asked the Kashag to guarantee his security and to treat him better than before. The Regent and Silon said they would do as Huang asked.

Huang Musong left Lhasa for Nanjing on November 28, 1934. General Consultant Liu Puchen and Consultant Jiang Zhiyu were left behind as directors of the Lhasa Office. The office kept the 100-watt wireless transmitter that had been brought with the original group.

Liu Puchen died from a fall from a horse in Lhasa in January of the following year. Jiang Zhiyu did not leave Tibet until 1937. Afterwards he was replaced by Zhang Weibai, who arrived to run the radio station.

When Huang Musong and his party were sent to Lhasa, Britain also sent a mission, headed by F. Williamson, the British Political Officer in Sikkim, to Lhasa in August 1934 to express congratulations to the Regent. They brought a transmitter with them as well. The establishment of the Lhasa Office and the radio station of the nationalist government was taken by the British mission as an excuse to ask for the creation of a similar office of their own in Lhasa, and their request was granted by the Kashag. The British office had under it a hospital that gave medical treatment to Tibetans. The office was run by a Tibetan-Sikkimese by the name of Rai Bahadur Norbu Thondup.

After the Thirteenth Dalai's death the Kunphela and Lungshar incidents broke out in succession. These had great impact on Tibetan society. I have given a brief account of them in *The Biographies of the Dalai Lamas*. A more detailed account of them is given as follows.

The Kunphela Incident was related to the unexpected death of the Thirteenth Dalai, who had not been very old and had been in good health. According to some memoirs, the Thirteenth Dalai was suffering from influenza and had not recovered after his personal physician, Jampa, had treated him for seven or eight days. Kunphela, the Dalai's trusted attendant, and a prominent figure, then consulted Nechung, a professional divine oracle invoker. The oracle the Nechung invoked said that the Dalai needed to take fourteen medicines to treat his influenza. The physician did not agree to this treatment, but he dared not refute a divine oracle invoked by the Nechung. Instead, he said that he had no such medicines with him. Kunphela, declaring that he had them, hurried to take them and gave them to the Dalai. By then the Nechung had fled. No sooner had the Dalai taken the medicine than he died—from the beginning of his illness to his death only nine days had passed. It was only after the Dalai had died that Kunphela informed the Kashag of his death. The Silon and Kalons were shocked at the news, and they had Kunphela, the physician and the Nechung arrested. The Kashag intended to condemn Kunphela to death for not reporting the Dalai's illness to the Kashag and for deciding by himself to ask for a divine oracle and then offering the Dalai evil medicines. But owing to lack of evidence sufficient for punishment by death, the Kashag, on December 29, 1933, condemned him to be exiled to Tsona Dzong of Kongpo and had his property confiscated. The exile of the physician to Darang Dzong was his punishment for not having accomplished his duty. The Nechung, the divine oracle, was imprisoned for life in Drepung Monastery. In the end, whether this was a case of medical incompetency or a political conspiracy was difficult to decide. The incident happened between December 1933 and January 1934, when Radreng had not yet been appointed as the Regent.

The Lungshar Incident took place in the reign of Regent Radreng. Lungshar, born of a big aristocratic family, had been to Britain and had been appointed as Tsepon and commander-in-chief of the Tibetan army. He was a trusted advisor of the Thirteenth Dalai. When Radreng was appointed Regent, Lungshar organized a organization called "Kyijug-kunthun" (Alliance of Those Who Seek Happiness). It was said that over eighty officials, half of them lay and half monk, joined in it. After his arrest he admitted only that he had wanted to carry out some political reform in the election of Kalons—that the election should be held once every four years and the candidates should be selected from the Tibetan Assembly. In fact, he had acted against Kalon Trimon, attempting to oust him from the Kashag, as Kashopa, a member of the organization, admitted. When Silon Langdun interrogated Lungshar about it, Lungshar suddenly took a piece of paper from his boot and swallowed it. A search was made of his person, and another piece of paper was found, on which were incantations against Trimon Lozang Wangyal—incantations which the Tibetans believed could cause a person's death. The Kashag decided to throw Lungshar into prison and have his eyes gouged out and his property confiscated. Of those involved in the case, some were exiled and the majority were fined.

It is difficult to determine whether Lungshar was actually contending with Trimon for power and profit or he merely wanted to make some political reforms, as he claimed. The incident happened between May and June 1934.

On May 29, 1935, the nationalist government issued a decree to grant Radreng Hutuktu the honorary title of "Buddhist Master of Patriotism and Universal Doctrine." After being granted the title, Radreng, on June 22, 1935, sent a telegram in reply to the nationalist government, in which he expressed sincere thanks and loyalty to the central government and expressed his support for Consultant Jiang Zhiyu's work at Lhasa.

# 13. The Panchen's Return to Tibet Is Obstructed Again

With the Thirteenth Dalai's death the Ninth Panchen should have returned to Tibet without a hitch. On the contrary, however, his return was obstructed more seriously than before, because the youthful Regent Radreng lacked political experience and could not control the situation, and thus the pro-imperialist and separatist elements became arrogant. Radreng, born in 1914, died in 1947 at the age of thirty-three. In the year he became Regent he was only twenty years old.

On March 19, 1935, the Panchen sent Huang Musong, head of the Commission of Mongolian and Tibetan Affairs, a plan for his return to Tibet. Its main points are as follows:

(1) Regarding the latest developments in connection with the Tibetan issue: According to reports from Ngachen Rimpoche and Wang Lejie, who went to Tibet for the second time several months ago, the negotiations between U and Tsang may soon come to a satisfactory conclusion. In such circumstances I could even return to Tibet with a light escort. But I hear that concrete proposals for the settlement of the outstanding issues between the central government and Tibet are yet to be made. I have come to the interior to prove my loyalty to the motherland and to promote the unity of the five nationalities. It is my hope that the gentlemen at the helm of state will soon produce guidelines for the settlement of the Tibetan issue through pressure and persuasion.

(2) Regarding publicity for government policy: I have intended to go to the western borderland ever since I was appointed as the Publicity Commissioner. But as national calamity was impending and the borderland was in danger, so I went to Inner Mongolia to publicize government policy, my footsteps tracking across every league and banner, big and small. It is a comfort to know that the princes and *Beizi*, abbots and high-ranking lamas are all deeply conscious of the righteousness of our cause, support the leadership of the central government and are determined to resist foreign aggression, and that the society is becoming prosperous and the people live and work in peace and contentment. At present Qinghai and Xikang are still being ravaged by successive wars, and the masses live in dire poverty. So I don't think I should go back to Tibet right now, but I should go to Qinghai and Xikang instead. If I go back to Tibet directly, I shall fall short of the expectations of the government and the people. This does not conform to the Buddha's wish to save all beings. So I plan to go to Qinghai in the near future and then to Xikang. Wherever I go, I shall do my best to publicize government policy and work for the unity of the five nationalities. I shall seek financial assistance for the repair of damaged monasteries, make an effort to relieve the sufferings of the lamaist monks who have been forced to leave their monasteries, make inventories of monastic property and tighten monastic discipline and do all I can to help the people in distress. A relief fund of reasonable amount provided by the central government for the distressed may be necessary to convince the people in the frontier regions that the [Kuomintang] party and the government will always be there when needed.

(3) Regarding construction projects: In order to build up national defence and the harmonious relations among nationalities, it is necessary to do some work to maintain the national economy and the people's livelihood, to facilitate communications and transportation and to popularize education. As there have been no construction projects carried out in Qinghai, Xikang, U and Tsang, the roads between towns and villages are very poor and cultural and educational work is backward. Such a terrible situation makes one shiver all over, though not cold. After I return to Tibet, the first thing I plan to do is to build badly-needed highways connecting Qinghai, Xikang, U and Tsang. This will be followed by the establishment of telegraphic and postal offices in the major counties. I also plan to set up primary schools in the *dzongs* and *shikas*. The curriculum will begin with Tibetan language and then Chinese language and elementary science will be added. Students will be selected at regular intervals for further study in the interior. The initial cost of these undertakings is estimated at one million yuan, which the government is requested to make available at an early date. We shall be very glad if the government will send experts and technicians through the Ministry of Education and the Ministry of Communications to assist us in these undertakings.

(4) Regarding what is needed for my return journey: Last year when I came to Nanjing to ask for instructions on my return journey, it was decided that I should take the Qinghai route, and I wrote a report on what was needed for my journey. The report was handed to Generalissimo Chiang Kai-shek through the Commission for Mongolian and Tibetan Affairs, and it was promised that everything would be provided when the time comes. The following is what should be done without delay: (a) The central government is requested to appoint high-ranking and capable officials to escort me to Tibet, in order to be able to deal with international influence, assert the central government's authority and further publicize government policy. (b) As land travel is very difficult, the journey will take about two months and need several thousand horses and pack animals. The government is requested to make an early decision on the subsidy of the journey's expenditures as I asked for last time I went to Nanjing. (c) An armed escort of moderate size as a guard of honour and token of the might of the country is essential to my party, no matter how my journey back to Tibet is arranged. It is my hope that the government will see to it that the escort will have the best in equipment and discipline so that my party will be able to travel with dignity.

The Panchen and his attendants went to Lanzhou by air on April

20, 1935, and were welcomed at the airport by Governor of Gansu Province Zhu Shaoliang and others. Then the group headed by the Panchen went by air from Lanzhou to Xining and were welcomed by Governor of Qinghai Province Ma Bufang on May 20. After consulting with Ma about his return to Tibet, the Panchen left for Kumbum Monastery, where he gave alms and sweet buttered-tea to all the monks—some three thousand.

On June 18 the Executive Yuan of the nationalist government made a decision on the Panchen's return to Tibet. The full text is as follows.

> The Commission for Mongolian and Tibetan Affairs has made proper arrangements for the Panchen Erdeni's return to Tibet, with consideration of all things concerned. As the Panchen has already reached Qinghai, all the problems concerning his return to Tibet must be solved, so the 217th meeting of the Executive Yuan makes a decision as follows:
>
> (1) Regarding the expenses: The Panchen's Office in Nanjing has requested more than 1,600,000 yuan. The Commission for Mongolian and Tibetan Affairs has appraised this and decided on 800,000 yuan, with an additional 200,000 yuan in reserve. The Office is instructed to revise its accounting and send it through the Executive Yuan to the Chief Accountant Section.
>
> (2) Regarding the escort, according to the 210th meeting of this Yuan, the Panchen is permitted to be escorted back to Tibet, but the number of guards will be decided by the Commission for Mongolian and Tibetan Affairs. The Panchen's Office proposed five hundred guards. The number is considered proper in accordance with the actual need.
>
> (3) Regarding the officials in the escort: The Panchen asked the government to send some high officials to escort him back to Tibet. In view of the fact that the Fifth Dalai Lama was escorted by a prince to the capital in the ninth year of the Shunzhi reign period in the Qing Ddynasty and that when the Panchen came to the capital in the thirteenth year of the Republic [1924], Mindrol and Dong Shi'en were appointed as Special Escort Envoys and that the Panchen's return to Tibet will be concerned with international influences and the central government's authority, it is advisable that the central government send some high officials to escort the Panchen back to Tibet.

The Ngachen Rimpoche and Wang Lejie, the Panchen's mediators in Tibet, came back to Xining on August 16, 1935. They said to the Panchen:

> The Lhasa government is anxiously waiting to see you back in Tibet. A party of lay and clerical officials and *khenpos* of the Three Major Monasteries it has selected will arrive in Qinghai to welcome you. Representatives of Tsang have already left for Qinghai with three hundred of your servants. Please do not return with Mongolian or Han Chinese soldiers, but go straight back to Tsang so the U government will have no excuse to block your return.

This was a blow to the Panchen's plan for his return, because "do not return with Mongolian or Han Chinese soldiers" meant that he was not allowed to bring back any guards or be escorted by any central government officials. Without any escort from the inland the result of his return would surely be worse than anything imaginable.

In September 1935 the Dalai's Office in Nanjing also made a suggestion to the Commission for Mongolian and Tibetan Affairs: "The Panchen is welcome to go back to Tibet. But it is hoped he will return without any troops. If he needs an escort, an escort of Tibetan soldiers will be provided him when he reaches the Tibetan border."

In late December of that year the Kashag sent a telegram to the Commission for Mongolian and Tibetan Affairs. The telegram said: "No troops of the central government will be allowed into Tibet before the central government and Tibet reach an agreement in their negotiations."

On October 27, Khenchung Champa Chowang and the representatives of the Three Major Monasteries sent by the Kashag came to meet with the Panchen in Kumbum Monastery by way of Jyekundo. They repeated to the Panchen what the Kashag said, warning him that he was to "return with a light escort, unaccompanied by Mongolian or Han Chinese officers and men."

On November 9 in the same year, Cadogan, the British Minister to China, lodged a "protest" with the Foreign Ministry of the nationalist government, alleging that the dispatching of Chinese troops to Tibet would violate Article III of the Simla Convention. On December 23, a secretary of the British embassy went to the Foreign Ministry of the nationalist government to present a memorandum, objecting to the Chinese government's provision of guards to escort the Panchen, and said that he had been asked by the Kashag to warn against it.

The key point in the debate among the Panchen, the Kashag, the nationalist government and Britain was that the Panchen was not allowed to bring any Mongolian or Han Chinese soldiers to Tibet. Superficially, it seemed to be a matter of guards only, but in fact it was concerned with the relationship between Tibet and the central government, or the Chinese government's sovereignty over Tibet.

The Panchen made no concession as to the principle of the matter. The nationalist government did not recognize the Simla Convention and said it would be necessary for the Panchen to be escorted by guards into Tibet. The Kashag warned that if the Panchen brought Mongolian or Han Chinese soldiers into Tibet there would be military resistance and no transportation facilities would be provided. The Panchen said in a telegram to Huang Musong:

> What the Kashag says in this letter represents merely the opinion of a handful of those in power but not the opinion of all the people. I am not going to change my plan and will enter Tibet next spring. It is hoped that the central government will persist in its decisions and follow them through. We believe the central government knows what to do if the Tibetan side uses force to block the entry of Han Chinese soldiers into Tibet when they reach the Tibetan border next spring.

On September 21, Chiang Kai-shek sent a telegram through Zhu Shaoliang to the Panchen, saying: "Your Holiness is asked to enter Tibet according to your plan. The central government will arrange everything for you."

At the invitation of the abbot of Kumbum Monastery, the Panchen held the eighth Buddhist meeting of Kalachakra Dorje from August 13 through September 15, 1935, the meeting being attended by more than fifty thousand Mongolian and Tibetan people.

The Executive Yuan of the nationalist government appointed Cheng Yun the Special Escort Envoy to accompany the Panchen back to Tibet. The Office of the Special Escort Envoy was also set up, with Ma Hetian and Gao Changzhu as counselor and deputy-counselor, respectively. Cheng Yun then met with the Panchen and the officials of the Panchen's Council of *Khenpos* in the Kumbum to talk over the arrangements for the Panchen's return to Tibet. The Communication Ministry and the Surveying and Mapping Bureau of the General Staff also sent men to escort the Panchen.

On June 15, 1936, the Panchen went to the Labrang Monastery of Gansu at the invitation of its abbot, Jamyang Hutuktu. A grand welcoming ceremony was held for him. Among those attending the ceremony were Special Escort Envoy Cheng Yun, the staff of the Office of the Special Escort Envoy, Commander of Security Forces of the Labrang Huang Zhengqing, former abbot of Drepung Monastery Ngawang Khanckok, former abbot of Sera Monastery Lozang Genchok, former Gegu of Ganden Monastery Dondrup Gyatso, director of the Panchen's Office in India Fu Kang'an, as well as tens of thousands of people.

On July 4, 1936, the Panchen held the ninth Buddhist meeting of Kalachakra Dorje in the Labrang, the last one of his life. The meeting was sponsored by Jamyang Hutuktu and attended by more than sixty thousand Mongolian and Tibetan people.

On August 12, the Panchen was informed in a telegram from the Executive Yuan that Cheng Yun, upon his resignation, was succeeded by Zhao Shouyu. Zhao brought a guard of honour of three hundred men, armed with modern weapons. On August 21 the Panchen and the Special Escort Envoy Zhao Shouyu and others left the Labrang for Jyekundo (Yushu) in Qinghai, intending to leave for Tibet from there. On August 27 they arrived at the residence of the Prince of Huanghe-nan and were welcomed by the Prince and several thousand Mongolian people. More than twenty representatives of the Kashag , headed by Doring Teji, also came to welcome him and again warned him not to bring Mongolian or Han Chinese troops into Tibet.

At the same time the British Ambassador Cadogan again lodged a protest with the Foreign Ministry of the nationalist government, objecting to the dispatching of Chinese troops to Tibet. The Chinese official stationed in Lhasa, Jiang Zhiyu, said in a telegram to the central government: "I am afraid that some unfortunate incidents might happen in Tibet at the instigation of Britain."

The Panchen said in a telegram to Chiang Kai-shek: "My return to Tibet is China's internal affair. If the Kashag allows Britain to interfere in it, a bad precedent will be set for the future of Tibet. So Your Excellency is requested to stop that."

In view of the situation the nationalist government made two decisions:

(1) The Chinese-Tibetan relationship is China's internal affair. Britain is not qualified to speak for Tibet.

(2) The Chinese government is trying its best to facilitate the Panchen's negotiations with Lhasa for his peaceful return to Tibet. Surely this will not cause hostility from the Tibetan side.

The Chinese Foreign Ministry informed the new British Ambassador to China about the two points.

At the same time, the nationalist government instructed the Commission for Mongolian and Tibetan Affairs to inform the Kashag that the escort guard of honour would be withdrawn as soon as the Panchen arrived in Tibet.

On December 18, 1936, the Panchen and his retinue arrived at Jyekundo and were warmly welcomed by several thousand people. The Panchen's headquarters were at the Gyalha Phodrang Hall of Jyekundo Monastery.

On May 7 the following year, Keutsang Rimpoche and Kheme Sey, the heads of the search party to look for the Thirteenth Dalai's reincarnation, arrived at Jyekundo. They asked the Panchen, who was then stopping at Jyekundo on his journey to Tibet, to reveal to them the name of the place where the Dalai had been reborn and the name of the boy. The Great Master gave them the name of the boy and told them where he could be found, and sent Tsechokling Rimpoche and Ngachen Rimpoche to assist them in their search. On account of the war between Qinghai and Tibet in 1932, Keutsang Rimpoche and Kheme Sey were full of misgivings about travelling in Qinghai and thus asked the Panchen to write a letter to Ma Bufang. The Panchen wrote a letter to Ma Bufang to request him to give the search party all the assistance he could when they arrived.

On August 1, 1937, the Kashag again sent Khenchung Champa Chowang to Jyekundo to express their welcome, but also instructed him to repeat to the Panchen that "he was to return to Tibet without the escort of Mongolian or Han Chinese soldiers."

The Panchen referred the problem to the nationalist government. By then the domestic situation in China was deteriorating —after the July 7 Incident Japanese imperialism having begun to wage total war against China. With the outbreak of the Anti-Japanese War the nationalist government had to arrange itself for the second period of cooperation between the Kuomintang and the Communist Party—this being done in response to the request of all the Chinese people—and call the people to fight against the Japanese invasion. As to the Panchen's return to Tibet, the government initially ordered Zhao Shouyu to carry it out. The Panchen and his aides therefore left Jyekundo for the Lhashu Monastery on the border of Qinghai and Tibet on August 18 and waited for the transportation facilities that were to be provided by the Tibetan side. But the *qianhu* and *baihu* of the Thirty-Nine Tribes informed the Panchen that by order of the Kashag they were not allowed to provide him with any transportation facilities.

The Kashag also put forward nine points in a telegram to its representatives sent to welcome the Panchen, of which the most important one was that,

> if it is not convenient for the central government's escort to withdraw when it has come to the border of Tibet and the Great Master can not stay long in Jyekundo, they will be asked to go to Tsang directly by way of Nagchukha. But the escort will have to leave Tibet within five months as the central government has proposed, and they shall take the sea route. We request the Great Master to give his guarantee for this, and we want an international guarantee for this as well.... Please send us a telegram in reply at the earliest convenience, so that we can make preparations.... But if the Great Master enters Tibet along with the central government's troops before an agreement on the problem is reached, or if the central government's troops do not go directly to Tsang but intend to come to Lhasa, we shall resort to arms.

On August 19 the British Ambassador addressed a note to the Foreign Ministry of the nationalist government. In it he referred to a copy of a letter from the Tibetan Kashag to the British trade agent at Gyantse, in which the Kashag opposed the entry of Chinese officials and the guards of honour into Tibet and asked, in the name of peace, the British government to intervene. The British Ambassador said in the note that he hoped the letter would dispel the doubts of the Foreign Ministry about the request of the Lhasa government for mediation, and asked the Chinese government to stop what it was doing about the Panchen's return.

At that time the nationalist government, headed by Chiang Kai-shek, was relying on American and British financial and military support for the War of Resistance Against Japan. For fear of offending Britain, Chiang Kai-shek changed from his initial decision and instead suggested that the Panchen suspend his journey to Tibet. On August 19 the Executive Yuan of the nationalist government issued an order to the Special Escort Envoy Zhao Shouyu, the Military Committee and the Foreign Ministry that, owing to the Anti-Japanese War, the Panchen should suspend his return to Tibet.

By order of the Executive Yuan, the Commission for Mongolian and Tibetan Affairs telegrammed the following instructions to Special Escort Envoy Zhao Shouyu:

> In the time of the Anti-Japanese War, the Sino-British relations must be taken into consideration. The Panchen's return to Tibet will not be carried out until the Tibetan side agrees to it and sends troops to the border to welcome him.

Zhao was also instructed to persuade the Panchen to suspend his journey and keep the overall situation in mind.

Being very much surprised at the decision of the central government, the Panchen said to Zhao Shouyu that he would not in any case enter Tibet without the escort sent by the central government, nor would he be forced by the Kashag to estrange himself from the government after going back to Tibet.

But it was difficult for the Panchen to suspend the journey at a time when all arrangements had been made and he had already reached the border of Tibet. So he decided to try his best to have the decision withdrawn. Nevertheless, the key point was still that the Kashag would not allow the Panchen to enter Tibet under the escort of Han Chinese and Mongolian officers and soldiers.

In order to solve the problem, the Panchen's Council of *Khenpos*, the Office of the Special Escort Envoy, the representatives of the Kashag Doring Teji and Khenchung Champa Chowang and representatives of the Three Major Monasteries reached the following agreement on September 1:

(1) The Special Envoy and his retinue and the guards of honour sent by the central government to escort the Great Master on his journey back to Tibet, shall leave Tibet after a rest period of five months following the accomplishment of their mission.

(2) The settlement of the remaining differences between U and Tsang shall wait until the Great Master returns to Tibet.

(3) The Kashag shall provide transportation facilities for the Great Master and the escort party of the central government as soon as they have reached Tibet.

As the agreement showed, the representatives of the Kashag dropped the condition of an "international guarantee," but requested the Panchen to sign a written statement guaranteeing that the agreement would be observed. Afterwards, they agreed that the statement might be issued by the Panchen's Council of *Khenpos*.

The agreement was sent to the Kashag for approval. On September 25 the Kashag telegrammed its reply to the Council of *Khenpos*:

(1) The escort party accompanying the Great Master shall leave Tibet by sea after a two-month rest.

(2) The envoy and his retinue and the guards of honour must obey the orders of the Lhasa government while in Tibet.

(3) The Great Master is requested to sign the written guarantee.

The telegram was tantamount to a refusal to the Panchen's return; so the Panchen communicated to the Commission for Mongolian and Tibetan Affairs his agreement that his journey be suspended. In the communication the Panchen wrote:

Their telegram carries many implications, without any sign of a sincere welcome to my return. What they show is an attempt to pull me away from the central government and have me at their beck and call. During my stay in the east in the past fifteen years, I have been treated royally by the central government. I take it as my obligation to the party and the state to contribute my share to the unity of the five nationalities and peace on the frontiers. For the sake of national interests I would rather sacrifice everything I have than see any damage done to the prestige of the central government. I have now decided to stop my journey to the west for the time being as ordered by the Executive Yuan and will await new opportunities.

Thus the Panchen decided to delay the journey to Tibet for the duration of the Anti-Japanese War. At the same time the Panchen asked the central government (1) to have his headquarters settled in Garze of Xikang and protected by the Xikang authorities; (2) to maintain the annual fund of forty thousand yuan originally budgetted for the Panchen's Office; and (3) to have him escorted back to Tibet by peaceful means or by force in the following April (1938), or to permit him to try to go back by himself if the war had not come to an end in the next year and the government was still taking its international relationships into account.

Then the Panchen left Lhashu Monastery on October 8, 1937, and returned to Jyekundo on October 12. The Panchen's headquarters remained in the Gyalha Phodrang Hall of Jyekundo Monastery. The representatives of the Kashag and the Three Major Monasteries went back to Tibet.

At that time, Beijing, Tianjin and Shanghai had fallen to the Japanese aggressors. The Panchen donated thirty thousand yuan for the front, bought government bonds of twenty thousand yuan and encouraged his aides to make donations and extend their regards to the wounded soldiers and refugees. The Panchen prayed for the early victory of the War of Resistance Against Japan in Jyekundo Monastery.

## 14. The Panchen Dies in Jyekundo Monastery

Frustrated in his effort to return to Tibet, the Panchen fell seriously ill. On November 4, 1937, he could hardly eat anything, for food made him sick. And for a sharp pain on the left side of his chest, he could not sleep. His condition went from bad to worse. At 2:25 on the morning of December 1, the Ninth Panchen died at the age of fifty-four in the Gyalha Phodrang Hall of Jyekundo Monastery. Beginning on November 15, 1923, when he escaped to the interior, he had lived in various parts of the motherland for fourteen years and fifteen days until his death on December 1, 1937.

His death was not only a personal tragedy, but also a tragedy for the Tibetan (especially the Tsang) people. The tragedy was inevitable owing to the current conditions. When the Panchen tried to return to Tibet, Tibet's subordination to China had not been restored. So, even without the Anti-Japanese War, the Ninth Panchen would still have been unable to go back to Tibet—the Panchen's failure to return was caused not only by the open opposition of the pro-imperialist separatists, but also by the behind-the-scene manipulation of the British imperialists. The Kashag demanded that the Panchen obey the orders of the Lhasa government; in other words, it would not allow the restoration of the Panchen's original status but wished to put the Panchen and his people under its control. This was unacceptable to the Ninth Panchen. That was why the Panchen failed to return to Tibet even after a fifteen-year struggle.

It was hardly a month from the beginning of his illness to his death. On his deathbed he still retained clearness of mind. He left a will as follows:

My cherished ambition is to support the central government, preach Buddhism, promote solidarity of the five nationalities and secure the prosperity of the whole nation. During my stay in the inland in the past fifteen years, I have been treated royally by the central government. I am very glad to have seen that the government respects Buddhism and treats the Tibetans on an equal footing. By order of the government I have intended to propagate the government's policies in the western borderland and return to Tibet. But I have failed. Now I am dying. I leave the following things to be done after my death. Lozang Gyaltsen has been appointed Dzasa Lama in charge of Tsang affairs, and he will be responsible for propagation for the time being. Before he comes to the office, my seals of authority shall be put in the charge of Dinggye Rimpoche. He, together with the Council of *Khenpos* and the six Designing Commissioners for the Panchen's Return to Tibet [the Panchen had appointed Wangdu Norbu, Dinggye Rimpoche, Liu Jiaju, Rakshi Chagtsa, Min Su, and Lhamin Yeshe Tsultrim as Designing Commissioners] will be responsible for handling Tsang affairs. The weapons in the Office of the Publicity Commissioner, except those of the guards and for self-defence, will be offered to the central government to relieve our nation from distress, and the central government is requested to return them to me when I am reincarnated in the world some day. The rights enjoyed by the successive Panchens must be restored at the earliest convenience. Finally, I hope all Tibetan officials and common people, lay or monk, will promote good relations between the central government and Tibet. The Dzasa Lama and *khenpos* in particular should fulfill my will.

The Council of *Khenpos* informed the Commission for Mongolian and Tibetan Affairs of his death in the following telegram:

> During this period of national calamity, the Great Master Panchen intended to go back to Xikang by your order, as he found he was unable to go back to Tibet. He became heavy-hearted and thus fell ill. He failed to respond to any medical treatment, and at 2:25 on the morning of December 1, that is, the twenty-ninth of the tenth month by the Tibetan calendar, the Great Master died in the Gyalha Phodrang Hall of Jyekundo Monastery. We ask for your instruction on the measures to be taken in consequence of his death.

After receiving the telegram, the nationalist government, which had moved its capital from Nanjing to Chongqing of Sichuan, issued an order to grant the Ninth Panchen a posthumous title of "Great Master of Perfect Enlightment, Infinite Wisdom, Defender of the Nation and Propagator of the Doctrine." The order also said that the central government would send Dai Chuanxian, Chairman of the Examination Yuan, to Kangding (Tachienlu) to offer religious tribute and condolences for the late Panchen and give ten thousand yuan for funeral expenses.

By order of the government the entire staff of the Council of *Khenpos* moved the remains of the Panchen to Garze of Xikang, leaving Jyekundo on December 25, 1937. They lived in Garze Monastery, where monks read prayers for the late Panchen for forty-nine days.

On May 25, 1938, the Council of *Khenpos* received a letter from the Commission for Mongolian and Tibetan Affairs, which communicated the decisions of the Executive Yuan in regard to the Panchen's headquarters after the demise of the Panchen. These decisions were as follows:

(1) To dissolve the Office of the Western Borderland Publicity Commissioner;

(2) The Panchen's headquarters will remain in operation, and the central government will continue to fund it, but the expenses will be cut down;

(3) To stop the payment of the annual stipends of the Panchen;

(4) The Panchen's Office in the national capital will remain in operation, but the funds will be reduced accordingly;

(5) The Education Ministry and the Commission for Mongolian and Tibetan Affairs should make a plan on how to treat the continuation school under the Panchen's Office in the national capital and then submit a report to the government for approval;

(6) The Panchen's headquarters should make a plan on how to deal with its transmitters and then submit a report to the central government for approval, but those given by the Communication Ministry should be returned;

(7) To dissolve the Office of the Special Escort Envoy and withdraw the guard of honour after Chairman Dai Chuanxian offers religious tributes and condolences for the late Panchen;

(8) To deal with other items according to the original plan of the Commission for Mongolian and Tibetan Affairs;

(9) To give thirty thousand yuan to the Panchen's entourage as decided originally by the Executive Yuan.

At that time the nationalist government had decided to move the staff of the Council of *Khenpos* and their families to Kangding of Xikang, but the staff instead stayed at Garze, which was on their way, and would not proceed to Kangding. The nationalist government then agreed that they live temporarily in Garze.

On August 5, 1938, Chairman Dai Chuanxian, as a special envoy with a party of more than sixty officials, arrived in Garze. Dai Chuanxian (on behalf of the central government), the staff of the Examination Yuan and General Tang Ying (on behalf of the Reconstruction Commission of Xikang Province) paid their last respects to the late Panchen on August 8, 9 and 10, respectively. Dai brought the thirty thousand yuan given by the central government as well as greetings to the Council of *Khenpos*. After staying for eighteen days in Garze the party headed by Dai Chuanxian left Garze for Sichuan on August 23.

Special Escort Envoy Zhao Shouyu and two other officials, Ma Hetian and Gao Changzhu, as well as the guard of honour of three hundred men also left Garze together with Dai Chuanxian. Owing to the national calamity caused by the Japanese aggression, the funeral activities for the late Ninth Panchen were kept simple.

After the Panchen's death and the withdrawal of the guard of honour the Council of *Khenpos* still had a number of weapons. Though the late Panchen had ordered in his will to offer them to the central government, most of the weapons remained with the council for the sake of self-defence. Afterwards, this led to an armed conflict, known as "The Garze Incident," between the garrison troops, the 815th Regiment of the 136th Division and the Panchen's headquarters.

When Dai Chuanxian, as representative of the central government, came to pay his last respects to the late Panchen in Garze, Garze Living Buddha Shanggen Rimpoche and the former Garze *Tusi*, Dechen Wangmu (a woman), asked Dai Chuanxian to assign the six counties of Garze, Derge, Zhanhua, Dengke, Baiyu and Serxu for the residence of the Panchen's headquarters. Their request was refused because Dai considered the six counties to be under the jurisdiction of the Reconstruction Commission of Xikang Province.

When Dai was in Garze, former *Tusi* Dechen Wangmu fell in love with Yeshe Dorje, a captain of the guard of the Panchen's headquarters. Not long after Dai left there, the two lovers decided to get married, setting a date in December 1938. Their love affair caused opposition, and the accusations against them were laid before Liu Wenhui, the Governor of Xikang Province, who reported the accusations to the central government. On an allegation made by only one of the parties concerned, the government sentenced Dechen Wangmu to one year's imprisonment.

After being imprisoned for one year, in December 1939 Dechen Wangmu appealed to be released. Her appeal was supported by the Council of *Khenpos* under the Panchen's headquarters—it was acknowledged that the local authorities were wrong to have violated Dechen Wangmu's freedom of marriage. But this support met strong opposition. Those opposed would not set Dechen Wangmu free, much less allow her to marry the captain of the Panchen's guard.

Therefore, working hand in glove with one another, Dechen Wangmu, the Shanggen Living Buddha and Liu Jiaju, secretary-general of the Panchen's headquarters, secretly mobilized local inhabitants, monks and the guards of the headquarters, altogether about three thousand armed persons, and put them under the command of Luo Youren, the head of the Section for Military Affairs under the Panchen's headquarters. They besieged the Garze'

County government office and the headquarters of the 815th
Regiment, appealing the government to set Dechen Wangmu free
immediately and dismiss the magistrate of Garze County and the
commander of the 815th Regiment from their posts. A fierce battle
broke out on December 7, 1939. As there were only three compa-
nies of Sichuan garrison troops there, the county government
office was soon captured and the magistrate, Zhang Jialing, fled to
take refuge in a lamasery. Having been besieged for seven days and
nights, the commander of the 815th Regiment, Zhang Zhenzhong,
sent three men—Xu Bing, an officer, and Dong Zhiming and Guan
Yitang, two officials of the county government—to mediate with
the Panchen's headquarters for a peaceful settlement of the Garze
Incident. As a result, the following agreements were reached:

(1) To release Dechen Wangmu;

(2) The Panchen's headquarters will take measures to insure the
safety of the regimental commander and county magistrate after
they are disarmed;

(3) To escort the officers and soldiers of the regiment and the
staff of the county government office to Luhuo;

(4) To assign those who do not want to move to Luhuo to work
in a local peace preservation corps or in a new county government;

(5) To have the written guarantee signed by both sides.

Having reached the agreements, the regimental commander,
Zhang Zhenzhong, went to take refuge in the Panchen's headquarters. When he was on his way there, he was forced to swallow
some black medicine by someone from the headquarters and was
cruelly treated. This resulted in his sudden death (see *Xikang
Pioneer Monthly*, Vol. 2, No. 8).

After capturing Garze, the Panchen's headquarters appointed
Lhamin to be county magistrate and Liu Jiaju and Dechen Wangmu
to be commander and vice-commander, respectively, of the local
peace preservation corps.

At the same time Liu Jiaju and others, colluding with the
upper-class Tibetans of Zhanhua and Luhuo, occupied the two
counties. The Panchen's Council of *Khenpos* appointed two *khenpos*
to be magistrates of the two counties. Thus, Garze, Zhanhua and
Luhuo became a district under the council's administration.

Liu Wenhui reported the Garze Incident to the central government and at the same time sent Sichuan troops to attack Garze. The Council of *Khenpos* sent Lhamin Yeshe Tsultrim, Jigme, He Badun and others to Chongqing to report on the incident to the central government as well.

. On February 6, 1940, the Sichuan troops recovered Garze. The staff of the Panchen's headquarters had to leave Garze and brought the remains of the Panchen again to Jyekundo of Qinghai. Thus the Garze Incident, which had lasted two months, came to an end.

How to treat the Ninth Panchen's body was an urgent problem the Council of *Khenpos* faced when they reached Jyekundo. According to tradition, the Panchen's body should be enshrined in a gold stupa in Tashilhunpo Monastery. But since the Kashag had forbidden the Panchen to return to Tibet, the Council did not know what attitude the Kashag would hold towards the Panchen's body, so it requested the central government to deal with the Kashag on the problem, hoping the Kashag would let the Panchen's body be moved to the Tashilhunpo. That year, at the invitation of the Lhasa authorities, the nationalist government sent Wu Zhongxin, Chairman of the Commission for Mongolian and Tibetan Affairs, as its representative to preside over the confirmation and enthronement ceremonies of the Fourteenth Dalai. Upon Wu's mediation the Kashag promised to send officials to Jyekundo to consult with the Panchen's Council of *Khenpos* on the problem of moving the Ninth Panchen's remains back to the Tashilhunpo.

On April 18, 1940, the officials sent by the Kashag arrived in Jyekundo. By order of the Kashag they instructed that the Council of *Khenpos* must bring the Panchen's remains from Jyekundo to the Tashilhunpo directly, rather than going by way of Lhasa. On November 4, 1940, with the consent of the Kashag, Secretary-General Wang Lejie, Dronyer Jampa Langda, Letsanpa Lhi-ngor and more than four hundred others sent by the Council of *Khenpos*, left Jyekundo and brought the remains of the Panchen back to Tibet.

The nationalist government sent Zhao Shouyu to Xining to consult with Ma Bufang, and it was decided that Ma send a cavalry battalion from Qinghai to escort the Panchen's remains to the Qinghai-Tibet border. When they came to Gyelsangkha of Nagchukha on the border, the Qinghai escort guard halted, and the Tibetan officials and soldiers sent by the Kashag took over the duties of escorting the body directly to Tashilhunpo Monastery.

On February 4, 1941, or the eighth day of the first month of the Iron-Serpent year by the Tibetan calendar, the Panchen's remains arrived at Tashilhunpo Monastery, where they were enshrined.

The life of the Ninth Panchen was marked by vicissitudes. He was not only well-versed in the philosophy of Buddhism, but also politically mature. He, along with the Thirteenth Dalai, led the struggle against British imperialists in his early years and actively took part in anti-Japanese activities in his remaining years. He deserved the title of a brave anti-imperialist soldier. As to the cause of defending national unity, he contributed all his life to it. Among the members of Tibetan upper classes he was praiseworthy for his excellent conduct.

After the Panchen's body was taken back to Tibet, the members of the Council of *Khenpos*, along with their families, numbering more than four hundred, moved to Shangde, a pastoral area inhabited by Tibetans and Mongolians in central Qinghai, which had been granted to the Sixth Panchen by Qing Emperor Gaozong in the forty-fifth year of the Qianlong reign period (1780). A small lamasery had been founded there. Then the search began for the infant boy who was believed to be the new incarnation, the Tenth Panchen Erdeni.

# Chapter Eight
# Choskyi Gyaltsen, the Tenth Panchen Lama

## 1. The Search and Enthronement

Choskyi Gyaltsen (1938-1989), the Tenth Panchen, was born in a peasant family at Wendu of Xunhua County (modern Xunhua Salar Autonomous County) in Qinghai Province on the third day of the first month of the Earth-Tiger year of the sixteenth Tibetan calendrical cycle (1938, or the twenty-seventh year of the Republic of China). His father was Kongpo Tseten, and his mother, Sonam Drolma.

After the death of the Ninth Panchen in 1937, a search party was organized by the Council of *Khenpos* to look for his reincarnation. Meanwhile, the Kashag also instructed Tashilhunpo Monastery to do the same in Tibet.

The party of the Council of *Khenpos* found the reincarnation in Xunhua County in 1941. The boy's childhood name was Gonpo Tseten. He was three years old when he was found. Following the discovery, the Council of *Khenpos*, according to divine oracles and many religious rituals and judging by what the boy picked up among the articles used by the deceased Panchen, claimed that the boy was the Ninth Panchen's reincarnation. The boy was moved to Kumbum Monastery near Xining. The Council presented Chiang Kai-shek, the head of the Executive Yuan of the nationalist government, a written report in the name of Dzasa Lama Lozang Gyaltsen:

We have reported in a telegram to Commissioner Wu [Wu Zhongxin, Chairman of the Commission for Mongolian and Tibetan Affairs] about the ceremony for confirming the Panchen's reincarnation held in Kumbum Monastery on the fifteenth of the first month by the lunar calendar. At eleven in the morning of that day, the reborn person, Gonpo Tseten, accompanied by monks holding religious articles and playing religious musical instruments, was brought in to worship the Buddha before he was confirmed as the new Panchen. The ceremony was attended by more than 100,000 people, including representatives of the government of Qinghai Province, Living Buddhas, Mongolian and Tibetan princes, *qianhu, baihu*, and monks and lay people of Qinghai Province. The fortunate result is achieved because the Mongolian and Tibetan people have always sincerely supported their religious leader, and, in fact, the genuine reincarnation of the Panchen has been discovered. It is our duty to report the ceremony to you and ask you for approval.

Chiang Kai-shek did not give any response to the telegram, because the Kashag at that time was also looking for the reincarnation. According to the institution established by the Qing Dynasty the confirmation of the reincarnation of the Panchen or Dalai should be made by a lot-drawing ceremony under the supervision of representatives of the central government.

In 1947, the Kashag informed the Tashilhunpo that they had found two other boys who were also believed to be the reincarnation of the Panchen and said that the Qinghai boy should be brought to Tibet for the confirmation formalities. Wang Lejie, the secretary-general of the previous Panchen, was sent by the Tashilhunpo to discuss the matter of confirmation with the Council of *Khenpos*. The Council's decisions were: (1) the confirmation formalities would not be necessary because they were positive that the Qinghai boy was the genuine "reincarnation" of the Ninth Panchen and the decision had been reported to the Executive Yuan of the nationalist government; (2) it would be unwise for the prospective Panchen to go to Tibet before the relationship between Tibet and the central government was normalized.

In 1948 Wang Lejie went back to Tibet and informed the Kashag of the decisions of the Council of *Khenpos*.

On June 3, 1949, the acting president of the nationalist government issued a decree for official recognition of the Qinghai boy as the Panchen and the permission to omit the confirmation formalities. The decree reads:

The Qinghai boy, Gonpo Tseten, known for his profound wisdom and intelligence, has been proved as the reincarnation of the Ninth Panchen Erdeni and shall succeed as the Tenth Panchen Erdeni without the confirmation formalities.

With the ratification of the nationalist government the Tenth Panchen officially inherited the Ninth Panchen's authority. As Lamaism stipulates, he was to be tonsured, given a religious name and take *getsul* vows, so the Council of *Khenpos* invited the most eminent lama of Labrang Monastery at that time, Jigme Trinley Gyatso, to tonsure the Tenth Panchen, hold a ceremony for him to take the *getsul* vows and give him the religious name of Lozang Trinley Lhundrup Choskyi Gyaltsen (Choskyi Gyaltsen for short).

On August 10, 1949, the nationalist government sent Guan Jiyu, head of the Commission for Mongolian and Tibetan Affairs, and Ma Bufang, Governor of the Qinghai provincial government, as special envoys to attend the Tenth Panchen's enthronement in Kumbum Monastery. As Ma Bufang could not attend the ceremony in person for certain reasons, he appointed Ma Jirong as his representative. The enthronement held in the Kumbum was attended by more than four thousand people, including officials of the Qinghai provincial government, Mongolian and Tibetan Living Buddhas, *qianhu, baihu,* etc. Guan Jiyu, on behalf of Acting President Li Zongren, extended congratulations by granting the Tenth Panchen a large piece of gold, 390 taels in weight.

After enthronement the Tenth Panchen sent a telegram to Acting President Li Zongren to express his thanks and loyalty to the central government.

At this, the Tenth Panchen had gone through all the formalities needed to legally inherit the Ninth Panchen's political and religious status and authority. He thereafter applied himself to study of the Buddhist sutras under the guidance of Jamyang Rimpoche. During a period of eleven years—from 1938, the year of his birth, to 1949, the founding of the People's Republic of China—the political situation at home and abroad underwent great changes.

Internationally, the Second World War broke out. During the war Britain did not stop its aggressive activities in Tibet. After the war it instigated more openly the Tibetan pro-imperialist elements to engage in reactionary activities for "Tibetan Independence." The

American imperialists also had a hand in the affair.

In China, on the one hand, the Kuomintang reactionaries, headed by Chiang Kai-shek, after the finish of the Anti-Japanese War, once again launched the civil war; and, on the other hand, the Eighth Route Army and the New Fourth Army, under the leadership of the Chinese Communist Party, was becoming rapidly stronger by setting up many base areas behind enemy lines. Thus, the Chinese people's revolutionary movement became irresistible. It soon defeated the reactionaries' offensive launched after the Anti-Japanese War and had liberated most of China's territory by 1949.

In Tibet the pro-imperialist separatists clamoured for "Tibetan Independence," trying to split Tibet from its motherland. This could not be allowed by the liberated Chinese people, including the Tibetan people.

This was the general tendency of the situation at home and abroad when the Tenth Panchen was a child.

## 2. Wu Zhongxin Presides over the Enthronement of the Fourteenth Dalai Lama

After the death of the Thirteenth Dalai Lama, the Kashag sent a party headed by Keutsang Rimpoche to look for his reincarnation in Qinghai in 1937. It was not until 1938 that Keutsang Rimpoche's party found a promising candidate in a Tibetan peasant family at Qijiachuan of Huangzhong County, Qinghai Province. The boy, whose childhood name was Lhamo Dondrup, was four years old when he was found.

After the Qinghai boy was found, Regent Radreng sent a telegram to Wu Zhongxin, Chairman of the Commission for Mongolian and Tibetan Affairs. The full text is as follows:

Three promising candidates for the incarnate Thirteenth Dalai have been found. I am very glad to know that you have asked the Qinghai provincial government for permission to let the boy candidates be escorted to Lhasa by Keutsang Rimpoche. As to the lot-drawing ceremony, it has been decided after consulting with the Silon and Kashag that it will be held after the three boy candidates are moved to Lhasa.

According to the traditional institution, the central government should send a high-ranking official to Tibet to supervise the confirmation ceremony, so as to give its faith to the public and please the people far and near. Whether the central government will send Commissioner Zhang Weibai, its resident official in Tibet, or another high official to Tibet to attend the ceremony is to be consulted upon later. According to divine oracles, if the three boy candidates are not moved to Tibet this year, the matter will be a bad omen for the Dalai himself. It is such a crucial matter that I myself cannot take it on my shoulders. So I sincerely request you to ask the provincial government of Qinghai for permission to let Keutsang Rimpoche escort the boys to Tibet. I am waiting for your instructions.

In response to the request, the nationalist government sent Ma Bufang a telegram ordering him to provide the boy incarnation with an armed escort for his journey to Tibet, and funded the escort mission with 100,000 yuan. Ma, under orders, organized an escort of a cavalry battalion led by Divisional Commander Ma Yuanhai. They started from Xining on July 1, 1938. The escort guard returned when they escorted the boy to Nagchukha.

The Kashag sent a telegram through the Commission for Mongolian and Tibetan Affairs to Chiang Kai-shek, which said:

The boy incarnation from Qinghai and his party started from Qinghai on the first of the sixth month by the Tibetan calendar, reached Nagchukha on the seventh of the eighth month, and arrived at Lhasa on the twenty-fifth of that month. The boy is settled in the Kelzang Phodrang Hall of the Norbulingka. He has gone through the necessary ceremonies. As to his tonsure, ordination, name-giving and enthronement ceremonies, they will be held accordingly on auspicious days. We shall report to you on them later as they occur.

On December 28, 1938 (the twenty-seventh year of the Republic), the nationalist government decided that the Chairman of the Commission for Mongolian and Tibetan Affairs, Wu Zhongxin, should jointly be responsible with Regent Radreng in supervising the ceremony of the choice and installation of the Dalai Lama. To Wu Zhongxin's coming to Tibet, the Kashag extended its welcome. The nationalist government drew up eleven points as the guidelines for the coming talks between Wu Zhongxin and the Kashag. The fundamental points included the following:

Tibet is an integral part of China, but the central government promises that Tibet will not be reorganized into a province. Tibet shall be granted autonomy, with its traditional political and religious systems being preserved.

The central government shall appoint a high official to be stationed in Tibet as the representative of the central government; on the one hand to carry out national administrative measures; on the other to report to the central government about Tibetan affairs.

Tibet has the right to set up an office in the national capital to take charge of liaison duties. The Tibetan officials, to be chosen by the central government, shall be employed by the institutions under the Yuan, Ministry and Commission of the central government.

Tibet is responsible to maintain its local public order. In case of any foreign invasion or extraordinary incident, the central government, if Tibet so requests, shall provide support for it as far as possible.

Wu Zhongxin and his entourage started from Nanjing in March 1939, and arrived in Lhasa via India on December 15 of that year. Soon after his arrival in Lhasa, Wu found the situation had changed; instead of three candidates there was only one. The one was the boy from Qinghai, whose childhood name was Lhamo Dondrup. Before Wu's arrival the boy had acknowledged Regent Radreng Hutuktu as his tutor, had been tonsured, and had been given the religious name Tenzin Gyatso (this is the short form). It was declared that all this was the decision of the *Tsongdu* (Tibetan Assembly) and it was the final decision. Thus, Wu Zhongxin's supervision of the confirmation ceremony became empty of meaning. What the Kashag did on the matter did not conform to the traditional institution established by the Qing Dynasty. In the Qing Dynasty the omission of the lot-drawing ceremonies for the Ninth and Thirteenth Dalai Lamas was approved by the Qing Emperor. In the period of the Republic, such an omission should have been approved by the nationalist government.

Wu concluded that he must not yield himself to the matter because it concerned national sovereignty. After repeated consultations with Radreng, the Silon and Kalons, it was decided that the confirmation formalities would be omitted on the condition that Wu examine the boy personally to determine whether the boy was the reincarnated Dalai as was said; otherwise, all the representatives of the central government would leave Tibet immediately. As there was only one candidate left and he had already been tonsured and given his religious name, it was obvious that the Kashag wanted Wu to accept the established fact.

When the candidate was about to be examined, Radreng wrote a long letter to Wu Zhongxin, in which he repeated that the Qinghai boy had been proved to be the true reincarnation of the Thirteenth Dalai and said that by divine oracles the fourteenth of the first month of the *geng-chen* year had been chosen as an auspicious day for the enthronement. Radreng asked Wu at the end of his letter to forward their request to the central government for approval.

So Wu Zhongxin presented to the Commission for Mongolian and Tibetan Affairs the following report on January 28, 1940:

> According to the letter from Tibetan Regent Radreng Hutuktu, the Qinghai boy, Lhamo Dondrup, who had been passed by revelation and divine oracles, distinguishes himself by his extraordinary intellect and has been accepted by all in Tibet as the reincarnation of the Thirteenth Dalai Lama. In view of this, the *Tsongdu* [Tibetan Assembly] decided that the confirmation formalities would not be necessary and, citing precedents, asked the central government for permission to omit them. The boy was tonsured and ordained. The enthronement ceremony was proposed to be held on February 24 [the fourteenth of the first month by lunar calendar]. The Regent asked me to forward all this to the central government for approval. I examined the boy personally and found he possessed the extraordinary intellect as he was said to. So I ask the central government to issue orders for approving Lhamo Dondrup to succeed as the Fourteenth Dalai Lama, so that we might arrange for the enthronement in time. The Regent's letter is too long to be cited here. It will be presented later.

According to Wu's report, the nationalist government issued the following decrees on February 5, 1940:

> (1) Lhamo Dondrup, the boy candidate from Qinghai, being endowed with profound wisdom and extraordinary intellect and being the reincarnation of the Thirteenth Dalai Lama, shall be enthroned as the Fourteenth Dalai Lama without the confirmation formalities.

> (2) As a special favour, the Executive Yuan shall appropriate, through the Ministry of Finance, 400,000 yuan to meet the expenses of the enthronement of Lhamo Dondrup, who has been decreed to succeed as the Fourteenth Dalai Lama.

Thus, the Fourteenth Dalai Lama completed the legal procedures of the nationalist government in regard to the omission of the lot-drawing ceremony.

The seating of Wu Zhongxin at the enthronement ceremony then became a problem. The Kashag was to seat Wu together with Radreng, in a lower rank than the Dalai. Taking the seating as a matter concerning national sovereignty, Wu demanded that he should at least be given the same treatment as was due to the Qing's Amban on such an occasion; that is, a seat on the same elevation as the Dalai Lama. Wu's objection was so firm that the Kashag complied. Thus, the enthronement ceremony was set.

Following the enthronement, on March 8, 1940, the Kashag sent a telegram to Lin Sen, Chairman of the nationalist government, and Generalissimo Chiang Kai-shek to express thanks. The telegram reads:

The arrival of the reincarnation of the Thirteenth Dalai in Lhasa brought wild joy to the clerical and lay populace of Tibet. The Dalai was enthroned in the Potala on the fourteenth of the first month by the Tibetan calendar. We are very grateful for the fact that the central government sent Commissioner Wu as its representative to preside over the ceremony and grant the Dalai gifts. As to the war between China and Japan, monks of the Three Major Monasteries and others in Tibet are praying for China's victory.

Wu's other task in Tibet was the deferred granting of a gold seal and a second-rank medal to Regent Radreng Hutuktu. The title of "Buddhist Master of Patriotism and Universal Doctrine" had been granted to Radreng in November 1935. The gold album and gold seal should have been brought to Tibet and given to the Regent at that time, but owing to the Ninth Panchen's death, they were left in the Commission for Mongolian and Tibetan Affairs. Now they were brought and given to the Regent by Wu by way of a deferred granting. The granting ceremony was held in Radreng's mansion on February 15, 1940. Afterwards, Radreng sent a telegram to express his gratitude to Lin Sen, Chairman of the nationalist government.

Wu had intended to discuss some major political problems with the Kashag after the enthronement ceremony. But, as Wu's *Highlights of Tibet* describes, "The Tibetan side made no concession even on the communication problem, let alone other problems." Wu could not continue the discussions. He left Tibet for Chongqing via India on April 14, 1940.

Before leaving Tibet, Wu was instructed by the Executive Yuan to rename the Special Envoy Office in Lhasa, which was established by Huang Musong in 1934, as the Office of the Chinese Resident Official in Tibet. When Wu consulted with Radreng, the latter said, "Such an important matter should be presented to the Tsongdu for approval. I think the Tsongdu will not approve it. This will injure the central government's prestige. If so, I will be uneasy about it."

Wu reported to the Executive Yuan what Radreng had said and asked for instruction. The Executive Yuan instructed Wu:

It is decided that the Special Envoy Office in Lhasa be renamed as the Tibet Office under the Commission for Mongolian and Tibetan Affairs, with Kong Qingzong as its head and Zhang Weibai vice-head. You should inform the Kashag about the decision instead of consulting with them, so that there will be no deadlock caused by any refusal.

Wu did as the Executive Yuan instructed and informed the Kashag that the office was to be established on April 1, 1940. To this the Kashag did not make any response—expressing neither consent nor opposition. Later, however, the Kashag negotiated with the nationalist government only through its office in the national capital instead of the Commission's Tibet Office.

The Tibet Office did some work there. First, it installed a wireless transmitting station, which created the possibility of swift and regular communication between Lhasa and the inland. The Kashag could use the service to communicate with the inland free of charge. The service was also a convenience to the inland merchants in Tibet. Secondly, it set up a primary school in Lhasa, whose students were children of Han and Hui inhabitants in Lhasa. The students, numbering more than two hundred at the most, learned Chinese in the school. Thirdly, it established a meteorological observatory in Lhasa.

Though established by the office, the three units were under different higher authorities: the wireless transmitting station being under the Ministry of Communications, the primary school under the Ministry of Education and the meteorological observatory under the Central Meteorological Bureau.

# 3. American and British Imperialists Openly Support Tibetan Pro-Imperialist Separatists. Radreng Leaves Office, and Taktra Assumes Office

Simultaneously with Wu Zhongxin's arrival in Lhasa, in February 1940, Basil Gould, British Political Officer in Sikkim, was sent to the city by Britain. His pretext was to celebrate the Fourteenth Dalai's enthronement, but his object was to fulfill another task. According to H. E. Richarson's *Tibet and Its History*, this was not the first time Gould came to Lhasa. During his tenure in that office (1936-1944), he might come to Tibet at any time he liked. The first time he came to Lhasa was in 1936, not long after he assumed the office of the Political Officer in Sikkim. Gould came to Lhasa accompanied by two British officers, H. E. Richardson and P. Neame. They brought with them a wireless transmitter. When Gould left Lhasa for Sikkim after a five-month stay there he arranged for Richardson to stay on as the successor to head the British mission. The former head was called back. Richardson, an Englishman, had a good knowledge of Tibet and the Tibetan language. He was in close relationship with Tibetan pro-imperialist separatists. All the activities for the "Independence of Tibet" were plotted by Richardson according to the scheme of British imperialism.

Gould came to Lhasa under the pretext of extending congratulations to the Fourteenth Dalai on his enthronement, but as Tibet had never had a foreigner attending the Dalai's enthronement ceremony, the Kashag arranged a meeting on the day following the ceremony, at which time Gould met with the Dalai and extended his congratulations to him. So Gould did not meet with Wu Zhongxin in Lhasa.

As to his task in Lhasa, Richardson writes in unequivocal terms in his *Tibet and Its History*:

> By common talk the Regent was regularly in receipt of large sums of money from the Chinese which caused anxiety lest he should lend himself to some arrangement that might compromise the Tibetan

position.

In other words, the British were afraid the Tibetan local government would resume its normal relationship of subordination to the central government. After Wu Zhongxin left Tibet, Gould continued to stay in Lhasa, supporting the pro-imperialist separatists and plotting new political schemes behind the scenes. The next year (1941), Radreng was compelled to step down from the post of Regent.

About the "Radreng Incident," Richardson says in *Tibet and Its History*:

> Nevertheless, in February 1941...there was an event to which the Chinese attached a sinister significance—the resignation of the Regent, the Reting (Radreng) Rimpoche, on whom they had pinned great hopes. The Regent was highly-strung, somewhat immature, capricious, and with a pronounced liking for money. He was generally believed to favour the Chinese....

From the words "to favour the Chinese" we may know that the Regent was an anti-imperialist patriot.

When leaving office Radreng sent a telegram to Chiang Kai-shek on January 16, 1941, saying:

> Thanks to Your Excellency's support everything went smoothly in my seven-year tenure in the office of Regent. The only important thing I did was to search for the Dalai's reincarnation. Owing to my poor health and to my ability and knowledge being insufficient for the office, I offered my resignation to the Dalai Lama, the Three Major Monasteries and the Tsongdu, and my resignation has been accepted. My duty has been turned over to Taktra Rimpoche, the Dalai Lama's sutra tutor.

After he assumed office, Taktra Rimpoche sent a telegram to Wu Zhongxin, head of the Commission for Mongolian and Tibetan Affairs, on November 18, 1941. The gist of the telegram is as follows:

> I beg to inform you that the former Tibetan Regent Radreng Hutuktu has resigned his position. The Dalai Lama and the Tsongdu decided that I succeed to the post of the Tibetan Regent, and I assumed the office on the first day of the first month by the Tibetan calendar. Please transmit the telegram to Generalissimo Chiang and place it on file.

Richardson wrote in his *Tibet and Its History*: "The Regent resigned because of increasing unpopularity." In fact, he was "unpopular" among the pro-imperialist elements. Radreng, however, would not take his defeat lying down. As Shartse Yeshe Thubten said in his recollections (in *Selected Literary and Historical Materials About Tibet*, Vol. 2), in order to resume the regency, Radreng appealed to Chiang Kai-shek for help, but Chiang did not give him an explicit response.

According to Tibetan tradition, the candidate for the regency should be a senior Living Buddha of high status, such as the Kundeling Rimpoche, Tsemoling Rimpoche or Tengyeling Rimpoche. A minor Living Buddha of low status like Taktra Rimpoche should not have had the chance to be nominated. Although he had been Radreng's and then the Fourteenth Dalai's sutra tutor, he was low in political status and without political experience. The reason why the pro-imperialist separatists picked him to replace Radreng was that he could be controlled easily.

It was not long after Taktra Rimpoche assumed office that the political situation in Tibet took a sudden turn. At the instructions of Britain, the pro-imperialist separatists established a "Foreign Affairs Bureau" in 1942 to show that Tibet was "an independent country." The Kashag notified the British and Nepalese resident representatives in Lhasa and the Lhasa Office of the Commission for Mongolian and Tibetan Affairs that from then on all matters should be referred to the Foreign Affairs Bureau before they were forwarded to the Kashag.

On July 7, 1942, the Kashag sent a letter to Kong Qingzong, head of the Tibet Office of the Commission for Mongolian and Tibetan Affairs, saying:

> To Mr. Kong, the Chinese Chief Official:
> We are submitting for your attention the following information. The Tsongdu has approved the Regent's proposal to establish the Foreign Affairs Bureau of Tibet and put Dzasa Surkhang and Konchok Jungne Ta Lama in charge of the Bureau. The Foreign Affairs Bureau was established on the twenty-third of the fifth month by the Tibetan calendar. Please refer all matters between China and Tibet to the Foreign Affairs Bureau from now on.

After receiving the letter, Kong immediately made a report to the Commission for Mongolian and Tibetan Affairs, in which he said:

> As the Foreign Affairs Bureau is an institution dealing with foreign affairs, to refer all matters to the Bureau, as the Kashag asked us to do, means that Tibet is considered as an independent country and the central government a foreign country. If this situation is accepted, the provision that Tibet is a part of China concluded in the treaties between China and foreign states will virtually be of no avail, and, on the other hand, the treaties between Tibet and some foreign countries, disapproved by the central government, will, in fact, be valid. The matter is very serious. The central government is suggested to send a telegram to the Kashag to give them a flat refusal. The central government's resident officials in the Tibet Office should refer all matters directly to the Kashag as before.

The Commission for Mongolian and Tibetan Affairs, having received Kong's telegram, asked the Executive Yuan for instruction. For this, the Executive Yuan issued the following order on August 1, 1942:

> If the Tibetan authorities deem it necessary to establish an institution to deal with local affairs concerning foreign countries, Tibet should observe two points: (1) all matters concerning national interests, that is, all political problems, should be handled according to the wishes of the central government; (2) the Tibet Office should maintain the usual procedures in its communication with Tibetan authorities and not to have anything to do with the Foreign Affairs Bureau.

The nationalist government was so angry at the rampancy of Tibetan pro-imperialist separatists that Chiang Kai-shek himself called in Ngawang Gyaltsen, head of Tibet's Chongqing Office, for an interview on May 12, 1943. Zhou Kuntian, secretary of the Commission for Mongolian and Tibetan Affairs was also present. Chiang put forward five points:

(1) Tibet should help to build the China-India highway;

(2) Tibet should help to improve the post stations between Tibet and the inland;

(3) The Tibet Office under the Commission for Mongolian and Tibetan Affairs should directly contact the Kashag in dealing with Tibetan affairs and not have anything to do with the Foreign Affairs Bureau;

(4) Tibet should provide transportation facilities to the persons sent by the central government to Tibet who are holding passports issued by the Commission for Mongolian and Tibetan Affairs;

(5) The overseas Chinese in India will take the way of Tibet, if necessary, when they come back to the interior of China.

Chiang Kai-shek said that if Tibet did not fulfill the five tasks, the central government would send troops into Tibet to take care of the matter.

By that time Japanese imperialists had occupied all China's seaports and Burma and Viet Nam. The only way left between China and the outside world, the Yunnan-Burma highway, was in danger of being cut off by Japanese troops at any time. In order to guarantee transportation of foreign aid materiel, particularly weapons, the nationalist government in 1941 put forward the plan of building a China-India highway, which would go from the southwest of Sichuan through the southeast of Tibet along the Loshit valley to Assam. Britain agreed to the plan, but asked the nationalist government to seek the Kashag's consent in advance. The Kashag did not agree to it and informed Kong Qingzong that the Tsongdu had decided not to allow the highway survey team to enter Tibet. For this reason, Chiang Kai-shek put the building of the China-India highway as the first task among the five given to Ngawang Gyaltsen.

In response to the five points put forward by Chiang Kai-shek, the Kashag sent a telegram through Tibet's Chongqing Office to the Military Commission of the nationalist government on June 14, 1943, saying that to implement the five points in Tibet was one of the important matters to be decided by the Tsongdu, according to Tibetan institution. Nevertheless, after that the Kashag did not give any answer to Chiang's instructions, nor did it force the Tibet Office to contact the Foreign Affairs Bureau in dealing with Tibetan affairs. The Tibet Office maintained the usual procedures in its communication with the Kashag.

In order to carry out the five points, particularly the building of a China-India highway, Chiang Kai-shek reorganized the leading group of the Tibet Office, replacing Kong Qingzong with Shen Zonglian, one of Chiang's aides, on October 18, 1943.

Shen Zonglian had intended to bring fifteen officials to Tibet

when he went to assume office. Among them, two "commissioners" were engineers, who intended to make a survey for the
Tibetan part of the China-India highway. Thus, the Kashag did not
allow them to enter Tibet. In order to solve the problem, Shen went
to Gangtok to meet Gould, British resident official in Sikkim, on
July 1, 1944. Shen asked Gould for help.
Gould replied:

> I have tried my best to help you and your entourage to enter Tibet. But,
> as agreements between India and Tibet stipulate, without the Tibetan
> authorities' consent we shall not sign the visas for those who want to
> go to Tibet via India. Since Tibet allows you to bring only thirteen
> people into Tibet, no more visas will be signed for you.

Shen said:

> Tibet is a part of China. It is ridiculous that the central government
> should ask the Tibetan local government for approval when it wants
> to send officials into Tibet. It is unimaginable that your country has
> such complex procedures for signing visas.

Gould said: "I think the Simla Conference has laid a good basis
for solving Tibetan problems."
Shen: "The so-called Simla agreements, which have not been
signed by the Chinese government, cannot, of course, be taken as
the basis."
Then Shen Zonglian had a talk with Caroe, Foreign Minister of
the Indian government. In their discussion of Tibetan problems,
the Indian minister said China had only suzerainty over Tibet. As
to the difference between suzerainty and sovereignty, they consulted the *Encyclopaedia Britannica*, but did not find a distinctive
difference. On this Caroe said: "In a word, when the state is strong
and powerful, suzerainty is tantamount to sovereignty; otherwise,
it might not be so" (from "A Brief Account of My Political Career
in Tibet" by Chen Xizhang). Not long afterwards the Anti-Japanese
War ended in Japan's surrender, so the plan of the building of the
China-India highway was shelved.
While reorganizing its Tibet Office, the nationalist government
intensified spy activities in Tibet. The spies were members of the
Statistics Bureau under the Military Commission.
Dai Li had a group of spies trained in Lanzhou in 1942 and

selected five of them in March of that year. The five spies were organized into a special task group headed by Hu Mingchun and equipped with two radio transmitters, five pistols, cipher codes, etc. Disguised as traders, they went from Qinghai into Tibet. Their task was establishing secret radio stations in Lhasa, Shigatse, Gyantse, Shannan, Chamdo and other places. When Shen Zonglian came to Lhasa as the head of the Tibet Office, he sent a telegram to Dai Li, saying that it was not proper to let Hu Mingchun stay in Tibet. Thus Dai called Hu back in 1946.

In addition, there was in Tibet an Information Station of the National Defence Ministry headed by Xiao Chongqing. The station had three subgroups, one each in Shigatse, Shannan and Chamdo. But to the outside its members claimed themselves to be officials of the Tibet Office. Their task in Tibet was to collect information about the Kashag and the British Mission in Lhasa.

After he took office in Lhasa as the director of the Tibet Office under the Commission for Mongolian and Tibetan Affairs, Shen tried to take more matters under control and made such a proposal to Chiang Kai-shek. Chiang instructed Dai Chuanxian and Chen Bulei to inform Shen to maintain the status quo instead of playing up his authority.

In 1945, the year of the victory of the Anti-Japanese War, the Kuomintang decided to convene the Chinese National Assembly. Shen took the opportunity to persuade the Kashag to send representatives to attend it and to express congratulations to the central government. Taking the advantage of the chance, Shen left Tibet.

Having consulted with H. E. Richardson, head of the British Mission in Lhasa, the Kashag decided to send a "Mission to Convey Greetings and Appreciation to the Allied Nations." The mission consisted of five persons: monk official Dzasa Lama Ronpalhun Thubten Sangpel (head), lay official Khemey Sonam Wangdu (deputy head), Khemey Tsewang Dondrup, Yeshe Dargye (interpreter) and Jampa Dorje Ngodrup (interpreter).

As the nationalist government agreed that the Kashag might send ten representatives to attend the National Assembly, the Kashag added five more representatives to the mission. They were Jetsun Thubten Trinley, Khenchung Thubten Zangpo, Jetsun Thubten Tseten, Thubten Sengge (interpreter) and Jampa

Ngawang (interpreter).

The mission went to India to offer greetings and appreciation to the British and American governments before going to convey greetings to the nationalist government in Nanjing. Such an arrangement, elaborately worked out by Richardson and the Kashag, aimed at putting China on a par with Britain and the United States as nations allied with Tibet and thus showing that Tibet was an independent country. At that time Gould had retired. Hogginson, who succeeded Gould to be the British resident official in Sikkim, warmly welcomed the mission in Gangtok, and accompanied them to New Delhi, where they presented gifts and letters from the Dalai and Regent Taktra to the British Governor in India, Lord Wavell, and the American Ambassador to India. Then, together with Shen Zonglian, Gyalo Thondrup, Phuntsok Drashi and others—totalling some thirty in all—they went to Nanjing by air on April 4, 1946. To Chiang Kai-shek they also presented gifts and letters from the Dalai and Regent, expressing the same greetings. They had to stay and wait in Nanjing because the National Assembly was scheduled to be held in December 1946.

The Panchen's Council of *Khenpos* also sent six representatives —Tromche Noryun, Jigme, Lhamin Yeshe Tsultrim, Tsering Dondrup, He Badun and Song Zhishu—to attend the assembly.

The Kashag instructed its delegates that they should try to persuade the assembly not to mention Tibetan problems in its decisions. The Kashag sent a letter to the heads of its delegation through the Tibetan governor in Chamdo. Jampa Dorje Ngodrup says in his memoirs:

> By order of the Kashag, the Chamdo governor sent a man to take a report to the two heads of the Tibetan delegation, together with a report from the Tsongdu to the Nanjing National Assembly. Accidentally I read the report when Dai Xuelian and Secretary Liu were translating it. Its main idea was: the relationship between China and Tibet was that of alms-giver and alms-receiver; the Han Chinese and the Tibetans were different in spoken language, writing, clothes and customs; the areas in the upper reaches of the Yangtse River and west of Kangding should be assigned to Tibet; the central government should not interfere into the affairs of selecting and enthroning the reincarnation of the Dalai and Panchen, etc.

The "report" clearly showed that Tibetan pro-imperialist separatists were scheming for the independence of Tibet.

The report was presented through the Commission for Mongolian and Tibetan Affairs to the nationalist government. The answer was that the government had organized a special group headed by the Chairman of the Commission for Mongolian and Tibetan Affairs to solve the problem.

The "delegation" stayed in Nanjing for more than a year. On their departure Chiang Kai-shek received them and asked them to take his letters and gifts to the Dalai and Regent. Khenchung Thubten Zangpo, Jetsun Thubten Tseten and Jampa Ngawang were left behind to work in Tibet's Nanjing Office, and Gyalo Thondrup stayed on to study in Nanjing. The rest of the delegation left by air for India in early April 1947. After staying for three months in India they went back to Lhasa at the end of July.

Shen Zonglian did not go back to Tibet. Instead, Chen Xizhang went to act on behalf of Shen in Tibet. Afterwards, the nationalist government appointed Xiong Yaowen head of the Tibet Office. But Xiong also did not go to assume the office. So the Commission for Mongolian and Tibetan Affairs appointed Chen Xizhang deputy-head and, concurrently, acting head of the Tibet Office.

Instigated by Richardson, Tibetan pro-imperialist separatists tried another move. In March 1947 they sent a "Tibetan delegation" to attend the "Asian Relations Conference" which was called in New Delhi. At the conference they more wildly made an ugly performance of the "independence of Tibet." Zangpo Tenzin Dondrup and Kunga Gyaltsen describe this in their memoirs:

> In 1946 Richardson, the British commercial representative, instigated the chief of the Foreign Affairs Bureau, Surkhang Solpa Wangchen Tseten, to report to the Kashag that Mr. Richardson had received the invitation for Tibetan delegates to attend the "Asian Relations Conference" and Mr. Richardson said if Tibet would send delegates to attend the conference, it would show itself to be an independent country. He said that the current world situation was favourable to the scheme for realizing the independence of Tibet, so Tibet should send a delegation to attend the conference, and that the British government also said that it would try its best to support the activities for Tibet's independence.

Thus Regent Taktra immediately sent a delegation headed by

chief Zangpo Tsewang Rinchen and deputy chief Lozang Wangyal. It consisted of eight members, including Zangpo Tenzin Dondrup and others. The delegation left Lhasa on January 6, 1947.

After the departure of the delegation, Richardson made a proposal through the Foreign Affairs Bureau to Regent Taktra that Tibet, being a nation, should have a national flag brought by its delegation to the conference. So the Kashag hurriedly sent a flag usually used by the Tibetan troops, the "lion in the snow mountains" flag, to the delegation, who had arrived at Yadong.

The "Asian Relations Conference" was organized by the Congress Party of India. Nehru was its chairman. In the conference hall the "lion in the snow mountains" flag was deliberately put side by side with the national flags of other participating countries. What was more outrageous was a map of Asia hung in the conference hall showing Tibet outside the boundaries of China. The chief of China's delegation, Zheng Yanfen, made a protest to Nehru as soon as he found out about the map of Asia and the "national flag" of Tibet. According to the news report of the Central News Agency on March 24, 1947, Nehru said to Zheng that he had not till then learnt of the matter and promised to have it corrected. The correspondent of the Central News Agency said that the map was thereafter corrected to show Tibet within the boundaries of China. But he did not mention whether the "lion in the snow mountains" flag was taken down.

The conference was held for ten days (March 14-23, 1947). During the conference the British Governor in India warmly received the Tibetan delegation several times.

# 4. The "Radreng Incident" and the "Han Chinese, Go Home!" Incident

Not long after the Tibetan delegation returned to Lhasa, Tibet witnessed another serious political event, the Radreng Incident. The incident broke out between April and May (or the second and the third month by the Tibetan calendar), 1947. It was a sharp conflict mainly between Tibetan troops and monks of the Je

Dratsang of Sera Monastery. Both sides suffered many casualties. It ended up with the failure of the monks of Je Dratsang and the murder of Radreng. The thing that triggered off the battle was said to be a "box" given as a gift to Regent Taktra by Radreng. When Nyungnas Rimpoche, by order of Radreng, brought the box to Regent Taktra, the Regent was not at home and his attendant accepted it for him. But a little while later smoke was found coming out of the box, so it was thrown outside of the house and it exploded immediately. Afterwards it was found out that a bomb had been put in it. Fortunately, it did not cause any casualties.

Regent Taktra concluded that Radreng had tried to kill him. So he ordered that the chief officials of Radreng Lharang and other officials involved in the matter be arrested—Dzasa Lama of Radreng Monastery Jampal Jamchen, ex-Dzasa of Radreng Monastery Jamyang Deleg, Kartho Rimpoche Kelzang Thubten, Phunkhang Teji Drashi Dorje and Phunkhang-se Gompo Tsering. Nyungnas Rimpoche killed himself with a gun before the arrest. At the same time the Regent sent more than two hundred cavalrymen under the command of Kalon Surkhang Wangchen Geleg and Lhalu Tsewang Dorje to Radreng Monastery in northern Tsang to arrest Radreng. He was arrested and escorted to Lhasa on the twentieth of the second month by the Tibetan calendar and was locked up in the prison of the Potala. During imprisonment Radreng was subjected to questioning by more than ten monk officials sent by the Regent and the Kashag. They included Khenche Thubten Lozang, Khenche Bumthang Thubten Chosphel, Khenche Ngawang Namgyal, Tsepon Lukhangwa Tsewang Rabten and Tsepon Shakabpa Wangchuk Dedan, as well as abbots of the Three Major Monasteries. When he was interrogated about the "box," Radreng said he knew nothing about the bomb in it and that the bomb must have been made by someone else. At the third interrogation session, when the letter he wrote to Nyungnas Rimpoche was put before his eyes, Radreng said that, while he would admit that he could not tolerate what the Regent Taktra had done to harm the Radreng Lharang, he definately knew nothing about the bomb.

On May 8, 1947 (the twenty-eighth day of the third month

by the Tibetan calendar), Radreng fell ill in prison. Sholdron
Kelzang Ngawang and Khenchung Khenrab Norbu came to
examine him. They felt his pulse and said he was seized by
apoplexy. At about four o'clock in the afternoon Sholdron Kelzang Ngawang brought three pills of medicine to the prison and
made Radreng swallow them. After that the patient's condition
became worse. At about one o'clock after midnight Radreng died.
It was obvious that he had been poisoned by Tibetan pro-
imperialist separatists. The problem whether the bomb case was
also created by the separatists was not solved. As his consistent
attitude showed, Radreng was a patriotic anti-imperialist Tibetan
leader.

According to Chen Xizhang's "A Brief Account of My Political
Career in Tibet,"

> The Commission for Mongolian and Tibetan Affairs contacted the
> Kashag by wire after Radreng's arrest. The main point of the wire was
> that Radreng deserved leniency as he had performed meritorious
> service in maintaining good relations between Tibet and the central
> government. When I passed the telegram to the Kashag, Kalon Rampa
> Thubten Konchok promised that they would be lenient towards Rad-
> reng. Afterwards, the Commission sent two other telegrams to the same
> effect to the Kashag.

India declared independence on August 15, 1947. Nehru became the Indian prime minister. The British Mission at Lhasa
was renamed as the Indian Mission. Its staff remained the same;
only its flag was changed. Richardson, the chief of the British
Mission, remained as the chief of the Indian Mission. Hogginson,
the British resident official in Sikkim, was replaced by Harishwar
Dayal. The British officials continued to support Tibetan pro-
imperialist separatists' engagement in activities for the "independence of Tibet."

Instigated by Richardson, the Kashag organized a trade mission
to visit the United States and United Kingdom for "trade" surveys
on October 18, 1947. The mission, headed by Tsepon Shakabpa
Wangchuk Dedan, with Khenchung Drekhang and Pangda Yar-
phel as members and Dapon Surkhang as interpreter, represented
an illegitimate diplomatic effort to win the recognition of Tibet as
an "independent country" by the governments of Britain and the

U.S.

The Tibetan mission arrived at Calcutta, India, on December 17, 1947. On December 27 Shakabpa gave an interview to a journalist of the English newspaper *Statesman*. He said they had come by order of the Tibetan government to contact the Indian government on trade problems and would go to New Delhi to pay visits to Chinese and U.S. embassies, as well as the British resident official. Chinese Ambassador Luo Jialun called on Nehru on December 21. He asked the Indian government to stop the transportation of British weapons to Tibet and not to recognize the Tibetan mission's illegal passports issued by the Kashag. Nehru replied that the weapon transactions might be occurring, but he did not know the details. He noted that during the time when the Indian regime was replacing the British regime it was very easy to buy weapons in India. As to the passport and visa problem, Nehru said: "The Tibetans need no passports for entering India. The visas for Britain are given by the British resident official in India instead of the Indian government." He added that Tibet was an autonomous territory of China and that Britain recognized China's suzerainty over Tibet.

To this Luo Jialun said: "But autonomous territory is not an independent country. Tibet's autonomy is restricted within the limits given by the Chinese constitution." Nehru said the Indian government would not continue Britain's policies.

The Tibetan "trade mission" had to obtain visas from the American embassy in China before going to the United States. The problem took Shakabpa and his party to Nanjing in February 1948. The nationalist government tried to dissuade the mission from making their trips abroad and thus refused to issue passports to them. The mission contacted U.S. Ambassador John L. Stuart secretly. Through Stuart the mission obtained visas for the United States from the U.S. Consul-General in Hong Kong, with the illegal "passports" issued by the Kashag. On July 7, 1948, the mission arrived in San Francisco. In a statement issued to the press soon after they arrived there, the mission said:

> We have come to contact your country on barter trade. We hope your country will supply us with machinery in exchange for our yak tails. We also hope to pay a visit to your president....Tibet is surrounded

by three countries: China, the Soviet Union and India. We cannot possibly show favour to any one of them by granting it special privileges and ignoring the other two. That is why we deny them any such privileges. We hope to establish friendly relations with your country.

In his statement Shakabpa went so far as to put Tibet on a par with China, the Soviet Union and India, hoping to portray Tibet as an independent country.

The nationalist government criticized the U.S. Consul-General in Hong Kong for his violation of international law and encroachment upon China's sovereignty by visaing the illegal passports issued by the Kashag without China's consent. Deputy Foreign Minister Ye put forward the following oral statement to the U.S. Embassy on July 12:

(1) Tibetan authorities have no right to independently deal with foreign affairs. The passports Tibet has issued cannot be used to replace the passports issued by China;

(2) Shakabpa and his party have no right to contact directly the U.S. government on trade and other affairs in the United States;

(3) Why did the U.S. Consul-General in Hong Kong not inform Chinese resident official Guo in Hong Kong before visaing the illegal passports?

(4) On the Tibetan problem the U.S. government has always recognized China's sovereignty over Tibet and takes it as a principle in treating this problem. So the Chinese government is surprised to find that the U.S. government has accepted the illegal passports issued by the Tibetan local government. Whether it was the U.S. Consul-General's personal wrongdoing or it shows that the U.S. government has changed its attitude towards Tibet is a question to which it is hoped the U.S. government should give a reply.

In response to the four points, officials of the U.S. Embassy said: "The U.S. recognizes China's sovereignty over Tibet and does not intend to change its stand in treating the Tibetan problem. To your questions we will reply after consulting with the State Department."

The nationalist government ordered by wire the Chinese Ambassador in the U.S., Gu Weijun, to inform the U.S. government of the Chinese government's opinion on the Tibetan mission. When Gu informed Secretary of State Marshall of this, Marshall said that on the Tibetan problem, the U.S. government values absolutely China's opinion.

Thus, when Shakabpa requested permission to pay a visit to the U.S. president, Gu Weijun said that the thing could not be decided before the Chinese Ambassador negotiated with the U.S. government and that Shakabpa could not go to visit the president without Gu Weijun's company. Then Shakabpa told Gu that they had decided not to ask for an interview with the U.S. president, and that the documents the mission brought to the U.S. would be passed by the U.S. State Department to the president. Gu asked Shakabpa what the documents were about. Shakabpa said by order of the Dalai Lama the documents would be directly presented to the U.S. president, and refused to tell him the content of the documents.

Shakabpa and his party left for New York on August 9. After staying in the United States for about three months, on December 1 the Tibetan trade mission took the H.M.S. *Queen Elizabeth* to France, and after a week's stay there, went on to Britain.

After arriving at London they were warmly received by the British government. When Chinese Ambassador in Britain, Zheng Tianxi, heard of the mission's plans to meet with the British prime minister and king, he presented a protest to the British Foreign Minister. According to Zheng's report to China's Foreign Ministry, the undersecretary of the British Foreign Ministry said: "In view of the Lhasa agreements between Britain and Tibet, we have to receive them politely." He promised to consult with the British government on the problems Zheng raised, but said the mission's visit would not play any political role.

Counselor Duan of the Chinese Embassy in Britain went to the British Foreign Ministry to criticize the British Embassy in Nanjing for giving visas to the Tibetan trade mission. The reply was that, according to the British diplomatic tradition, if those whose nationality had not been identified requested visas, they could obtain visas on the condition that they took an oath, and in such a case there was no need for a local passport. Duan said that since Tibet was a part of China, the Tibetans were not among those whose nationality had not been identified. The British Foreign Ministry had to apologize for what had been done.

After staying for twenty days in Britain, the trade mission went to Switzerland via France, and after a short stay there, it went on to Rome and Bombay, and then it returned to Lhasa. The mission had intended to win the recognition of Tibet as an "independent country" by the British and U.S. governments. But at that time China was witnessing dramatic political and military changes on the eve of national liberation. Considering China's changes, the American and British imperialists did not dare to openly—though they did secretly—support Tibetan separatists' activities for independence of Tibet.

By 1949 the political scene in China had changed completely. In April, the People's Liberation Army swept across the Yangtse River and liberated Nanjing; the nationalist government fled to Canton (Guangzhou). Chiang Kai-shek declared his "resignation" and Vice-President Li Zongren became Acting President. Realizing the future conditions would be more unfavourable for them, the Tibetan separatists engineered the "Han Chinese, go home!" incident. Richardson wrote in *Tibet and Its History*:

> ...in July 1949 the Tibetan Government asked the whole of the Chinese official mission at Lhasa, and some Chinese traders also, to leave Tibet.... The Tibetans...feared that some if not all of the staff of the Chinese Mission would, if only for the sake of their bread and butter, transfer their allegiance to Mao Tse-tung and the Tibetan Government would thus be faced by an established Communist foothold in Lhasa.

According to Thubten Tenthar's memoirs, Richardson said to Dzasa Neushag Thubten Dapa and Dzasa Surkhang Wangchen Tseten (heads of the Foreign Affairs Bureau of the Kashag): "There are many communists in Lhasa. If they are allowed to remain here, they will surely help the Liberation Army to enter Lhasa." The two Dzasas reported their opinion to the Kashag. Soon after this, the "Han Chinese, go home!" incident happened.

Chen Xizhang says in his memoirs:

> On July 8, 1949, the Kashag invited me for an interview. When I went into the office I found three Kalons—Rampa, Surkhang, and Kashopa—and Chikyap Khenpo were there. Chief Kalon Rampa was the first to speak. He said the Communist Party and Kuomintang were engaged in a fierce civil war and Kuomintang troops and officials were being followed by Communists everywhere, so the Kashag could not

be responsible for the security of the personnel of the Tibet Office. The Tsongdu has made a decision to break off political relations with the nationalist government temporarily, but the religious relations would be maintained. They asked me to inform immediately all the organizations of the nationalist government in Lhasa to evacuate their personnel and their families to the interior by way of India within two weeks and said the Kashag would send a guide and an officer with troops to escort them to the border of India.... I said that I would give him a reply after wiring the Commission for Mongolian and Tibetan Affairs for instructions. Rampa said that the Kashag had already given notice to the Commission, that all communications and mail between Tibet and the interior had been cut off and that I would not be able to send any telegram to the Commission.... Towards evening I came back from the Kashag's office and found the Kashag had put the Tibet Office and my residence under armed surveillance and seized the Lhasa radio station and had had its transmitter dismantled.

On July 9, 1949, the Kashag sent a telegram to Acting President Li Zongren:

The Tsongdu asks the Chinese representative in Lhasa and his entourage, transmitter operators, teachers, medical workers and all suspicious persons to go back to their hometowns within a prescribed time-limit, so that the relations between China and Tibet as alms-giver and alms-receiver will not be obstructed.

The nationalist government refuted this by wire immediately:

It was unlawful, and it was unreasonable, for the Kashag, without reporting the matter to us, to press all resident personnel in Tibet to leave. It is very important that the Kashag should call them back to continue their work in Lhasa and give special protection to the Han Chinese in Tibet and maintain the traditional relationship between the central government and Tibet.

Ignoring the nationalist government's instruction, the Kashag continued to press the personnel of nationalist organizations to leave Tibet. So the personnel of the Lhasa Office and their families and the agents of the Information Bureau of the Ministry of National Defence, numbering over two hundred, left for home via India in three batches on July 11, 17 and 20. They were escorted by Tibetan troops to the border between India and Tibet.

# 5. The Xinhua News Agency's Editorial

The Xinhua News Agency, in an editorial on September 3, 1949, expressed China's just and solemn stand with regard to the "Han Chinese, go home" incident. The full text of the editorial, the title of which was "We Can Never Allow Foreign Aggressors to Annex China's Territory—Tibet," reads:

The expulsion from Tibet of the people of the Han nationality and of the Kuomintang personnel in Tibet by those in power in the Tibetan region was plotted by the British and U.S. imperialists and their follower, the Indian government of Nehru. This anti-Communist incident engineered by the British, American and Indian reactionaries in collusion with the local authorities of Tibet is aimed not only to prevent the Tibetan people from winning their liberation at a time when the liberation of the whole country by the People's Liberation Army is in sight, but also to turn them into colonial slaves of foreign imperialism by further depriving them of their freedom and independence. It is similar to the conspiracy that American imperialists embarked upon for swallowing up Taiwan. During the past hundred-odd years British and American imperialists have consistently schemed to invade and annex Tibet. The British imperialists occupied Drenjong, Tibet's vassal state, in 1860, and launched wars of aggression against Tibet in 1888 and 1904. After the Second World War American imperialists also schemed to invade Tibet by sending spies to Tibet and trying to obtain actual ruling power over the Tibetan people through some elements of the Tibetan upper class. To the aggressive activities of Britain, the United States and India, the Chinese people have paid close attention for a long time, and they shall never forget these offences against the Chinese people.

In their vain attempt to swallow up Tibet, the British and Indian reactionaries have the audacity to deny the fact that Tibet is part of Chinese territory. Such a denial is sheer nonsense uttered by the aggressors, for it is not supported by any maps published in China or in any foreign country, nor is it supported by any documents about China's internal and external affairs. Tibet is part of Chinese territory. There is a long history to the Tibetan nationality's membership in the Chinese multinational big family and brotherly relationship with the Han Chinese and other nationalities of China. The brotherly relationship has been injured by the British and Indian aggressors and reactionary elements of both the Han and Tibetan nationalities. Nevertheless, the patriotic Tibetan people have gradually realized that Mao

Zedong's policy of New Democracy, as well as Chinese Communist Party's and People's Liberation Army's policies of supporting and assisting Chinese national minorities, will save the Tibetan people from distress. Any Chinese minority nationality, if separated from the Han nationality, would be reduced to the status of a colony under the slavery of imperialist countries. The Tibetan people would never allow themselves to be enslaved by imperialist countries. The best evidence is that they fought bravely against the British aggression and invasion in 1888 and 1904.

It is a very silly and adventurist thing that the British and Indian aggressors have instigated the Tibetan authorities to make turmoil under the pretext of anti-communism in order to fish in the troubled waters. The Kuomintang reactionaries should be wiped out of Chinese territory. But the Chinese people's revolutionary struggle led by the Chinese Communist Party has nothing to do with any foreign country or anti-Communist elements. The Chinese people have already wiped the Kuomintang reactionary power out of most parts of Chinese territory and will surely mop up the remnants of the Kuomintang reactionaries in the near future. The Chinese Communist Party is the party of Chinese labourers and the leader of a Chinese people's republic. The leadership of the Chinese Communist Party enjoys the Chinese people's general acknowledgment and trust. Today, those who try to oppose the Chinese Communist Party and Chinese People's Liberation Army will face the same risk of being wiped out as the Kuomintang. The Chinese Communist Party advocates the autonomy of national minorities and respects their religious beliefs and cultural habits. Those who have acquainted themselves with the situation in the liberated regions of Inner Mongolia and among the Huis of Gansu do not suspect what was mentioned above. The foreign aggressors are trying to cheat and threaten Tibetan authorities by spreading anti-Communist rumours in order to reduce them to the most dangerous status. Surely this is plain to everybody.

The four-million-strong Chinese People's Liberation Army under the leadership of the Chinese Communist Party is determined to liberate all Chinese nationalities, not only the Han nationality but also all Chinese national minorities. The army has liberated the great majority of the Han Chinese and Inner Mongolian people, is liberating the Hui people and will liberate the Tibetan people and other nationalities of the northwest, southwest and south of China, to free them forever from the oppression of imperialism and the Kuomintang, and from poverty and a miserable life. The People's Liberation Army is determined to liberate the entire territory of China that includes Tibet, Xinjiang, Hainan Island and Taiwan; it will not stop until every single inch of the land of China is brought under the jurisdiction of the Chinese people's republic. Tibet is part of China's territory. No foreign country is allowed to invade it. The Tibetan people are an inseparable component part of the Chinese people. No foreign country is allowed to split them off. This is the unshakable policy of the Chinese people, the Chinese Communist Party and the Chinese People's Liberation Army. If the aggressors, ignoring this, dare to make provocation on Chinese territory and in their attempt to split off and invade Tibet and Taiwan, they will get their skulls cracked by the iron fists of the great People's Liberation Army. We warn the aggressors: You must stop your invasion of Tibet and Taiwan; otherwise, you shall be held responsible for what you have done.

# 6. The Tenth Panchen's Telegraphic Message to Mao Zedong and the Peaceful Liberation of Tibet

After the liberation of Qinghai in September 1949, Jigme, as the representative of the Tenth Panchen, came into contact with the People's Liberation Army and expressed his warm welcome and support. In a telegraphic message on October 1, 1949, the day the People's Republic of China was founded with Mao Zedong as Chairman of its Central People's Government, the Panchen paid his respects to Chairman Mao and Commander-in-Chief Zhu De. The message reads:

...For generations, the Panchen has been treated most generously and bestowed with many honours by the country. For more than twenty years, I have never slackened my efforts to defend the territorial integrity of Tibet, but nothing has been achieved, for which I feel most guilty. I am now staying in Qinghai, waiting for the order to return to Tibet. Thanks to the leadership of Your Excellencies, Northwest China has been liberated and the Central People's Government has been established—events that all the people who are proud of the country find highly inspiring. These accomplishments will surely bring happiness to the people and make it possible for the nation to stand on its feet again; and with these accomplishments the liberation of Tibet is only a matter of time. On behalf of all the Tibetan people, I pay Your

Excellencies the highest respects and pledge our whole-hearted support.

In a telegram of reply dated November 23, 1949, acknowledging the respects, Mao Zedong and Zhu De said:

> The Tibetan people love the motherland and oppose foreign aggression. They disagree with the policy of the reactionary Kuomintang government and desire to be a member of the big family of a united, strong and prosperous New China where all the nationalities are equal. The Central People's Government and the Chinese People's Liberation Army will certainly comply with this wish of the Tibeten people. We hope you and the patriotic personages throughout Tibet will make a concerted effort for the liberation of Tibet and the unity of the Han Chinese and Tibetan people.

The Central People's Government decided to use peaceful means to help the Tibetan people with their liberation. In line with this policy the government sent men from the northwest and southwest to Tibet to urge the Kashag to send its representatives to Beijing to negotiate a peaceful liberation. In 1950, the Headquarters of the Northwest Military Area Command organized a "Mediating Mission" with Taktser Rimpoche, the Fourteenth Dalai's brother, as its chief head, Sharichang Rimpoche and Shinnying Rimpoche as deputy heads and Chi Yurui as secretary. The mission brought along a fifteen-watt transmitter and three radio operators. The mission, consisting of eight persons, started from Xining in July 1950. They were detained by the Kashag in Nagchukha. Their transmitter and the pistols they were carrying for self-defence were seized. After staying there for about forty days, the Rimpoches were allowed to go to Lhasa, but Chi Yurui and the other three Han officials were sent under armed escort to Nedong of Shannan, where they were put under house arrest. Taktser, after an interview with the Fourteenth Dalai, went to India, but the other members remained in Lhasa.

It was not until February 2, 1951, that Chi Yurui and the other three Han officials were allowed to go to Lhasa. The transmitter and pistols were returned to them. At that time Chamdo had been liberated and the Fourteenth Dalai and the Kashag had sent a Tibetan delegation to Beijing to hold talks on the peaceful liberation of Tibet. Chi Yurui, who was sent by the Liaison Department of the Central Military Commission, and the other three Han Chinese were the first cadres of the People's Liberation Army sent to Lhasa before the liberation of Tibet. Later the Liaison Department awarded Chi Yurui a First-Class Citation for Merit for his outstanding service in the Mediating Mission.

The Headquarters of the Southwest Military Area Command sent Getag Rimpoche to Lhasa to mediate with the Kashag in June 1950, but he was held up in Chamdo on his way to Lhasa. Getag Rimpoche, whose religious name was Lozang Tenzin Drakpa, was born in a peasant family in Beri of Garze County, Xikang, in 1903. He was recognized as the reincarnation of the late Living Buddha of Beri Monastery at the age of three and was then taken to the monastery, where he was accommodated. At nineteen he went to study Buddhist philosophy in Lhasa, where he met with the Thirteenth Dalai Lama. In 1935, when the Red Army went northward to fight against Japanese invaders and the Second and Fourth Front Armies established the Bodpa government (the Tibetans call themselves Bodpa), Getag Rimpoche was elected as its vice-chairman. Influenced by Getag Rimpoche, Beri Monastery granted the Red Army 134 *dan* (picul) of highland barley, 22 *dan* of peas, 15 horses and 19 yaks. When the Red Army moved on to the north, Getag made arrangements for more than three thousand sick and wounded soldiers to settle down. When the People's Republic of China was founded on October 1, 1949, Getag Rimpoche, as well as Shak Daoten and Pangda Dorje, who had also participated in the Bodpa government, sent men to Beijing to pay respects to Chairman Mao. When the Southwest Military and Administrative Committee was founded in June 1950, Getag Rimpoche was appointed commissioner of the committee and concurrently Vice-Chairman of the Xikang Provincial People's Government. The Chinese People's Political Consultative Conference invited Getag to attend its meeting. Getag, however, refused the invitation, because he had decided to go to Lhasa to persuade the Fourteenth Dalai to dispatch a delegation to Beijing for talks on the peaceful liberation of Tibet.

Getag left Garze on July 10, 1950. No sooner had he arrived in Chamdo on July 24, on his way to Lhasa, than he was held up by Tibetan soldiers. He paid a visit to Robert Ford, "Chief of the British Radio Station in Chamdo," asking him to send a telegram to the

Kashag for him. Ford promised and gave Getag a cup of tea. After drinking tea Getag became ill. The Rimpoche was immediately put under house arrest by the Tibetan authorities. The Kashag's Chamdo governor, Lhalu, sent a physician to treat Getag. The physician came on August 21 to treat him, giving him some medicine; but after taking the medicine, Getag Rimpoche lost the ability to speak. He died the next day at the age of forty-seven. The Tibetan authorities immediately had his body cremated and his entourage sent under escort to Lhasa.

To mourn over Getag's death the Headquarters of the Southwest Military and Administrative Committee held a memorial meeting on November 25, 1950, which was attended by Deng Xiaoping, Wang Weizhou, Li Da, Zhang Jichun and Liang Juwu, as well as more than eight hundred people. *Xinhua Daily* published an editorial entitled, "We Are Determined to Liberate Tibet—In Memory of Getag Rimpoche." In his memorial speech, He Long, Commander of the Southwest Military Area Command, had the strongest praise for Getag Rimpoche. So did Liu Bocheng, Chairman of the Southwest Military and Administrative Committee. It was not until after the liberation of Tibet that Getag's ashes were sent back to Beri Monastery.

Such outrages of the separatists in Tibet prompted the Central People's Government to order the People's Liberation Army to march to liberate Tibet. In Chamdo the People's Liberation Army ran into the opposition of the Tibetan army, numbering about twenty to thirty thousand men, including about eight thousand troops under ten *dapons*. Thus, by order of the Central People's Government, troops from Sichuan, Yunnan, Qinghai and Xinjiang simultaneously marched to Tibet. Of the troops marching to liberate Tibet, the Eighteenth Corps, with Zhang Guohua as its commander and Tan Guansan as political commissar, was the main force. To annihilate the main forces of the Tibetan army in Chamdo was the first task the Eighteenth Corps had to accomplish before the peaceful liberation of Tibet could be achieved.

For this purpose the Eighteenth Corps drew up a well-conceived battle plan. The corps divided itself into three groups marching simultaneously along northern, central and southern routes to Chamdo. The northern route marched from Dengke across the

Jinsha River through Qinghai's Ba-thang grasslands, then southward through Riwoche to Enda after joining the cavalrymen sent by the Northwest Military Area Command, to cut off the enemy's western route of retreat. The southern route went from Kangding through Litang and Batang to seize Ningjing (modern Markam), then northwestward through Baxoi to join the northern route in Enda. The two routes formed a circle around Chamdo. Along the central route the main force of the corps went from Garze to Chamdo. The three military groups—northern, central and southern—arrived at the front line in September 1950. The northern route, consisting of a regiment of the 52nd Infantry Division and cavalrymen of the Northwest Military Area Command under the command of Yin Fatang, vice political commissar of the 52nd Division, and Xi Jinwu, commander of the 154th Regiment, marched on September 21 from Dengke across the Jinsha River through Qinghai's Ba-thang grasslands to Nangqian to join the cavalrymen of the Northwest Military Area Command headed by Sun Gong. They seized Enda on October 18, thus cutting off the enemy's route of retreat. They marched on to the west on November 10 and seized Jiayu Bridge on November 11 and Lhorong Dzong on November 12. The enemy troops were annihilated and Commander of the Seventh Dapon Phulung Drakpa Tseten was captured.

The southern route, consisting of the 157th Regiment, an artillery company and engineer company of the 53rd Division under the command of Miao Piyi, vice political commissar of the 53rd Division, arrived at Ningjing on October 11. The Ninth Dapon, under the leadership of Derge Kelzang Wangdu, came over to the side of the People's Liberation Army. In a telegraphic message on October 18 to Chairman Mao and Commander-in-Chief Zhu sent through Liu Bocheng, Chairman of the Southwest Military and Administrative Committee, he said:

> The Tibetan people are suffering much from the rule and oppression of imperialism and reactionary Tibetan authorities, but find no way to free themselves. The People's Liberation Army's march into Tibet, as we have known from our friends and relatives, aims at liberating the Tibetan people from the aggressive power of imperialism and bringing them back to the big family of the People's Republic of China.... So we

hereby decide to break away from the reactionary camp in order to return to our own big family and struggle side-by-side with the Liberation Army for the cause of Tibet's liberation. We hope that all Tibetan officers and soldiers will cooperate with the PLA as soon as possible . . . instead of going astray.

Liu Bocheng sent a reply by wire to Kelzang Wangdu on the same day:

I am very glad to learn that you know well the cardinal principles of right and wrong and have resolutely come over to us, so that Ningjing has been peacefully liberated and its people's life and property have been saved from meaningless casualties and loss. So I wire to express my best wishes to you. I hope you will make further progress in the cause, set yourself as an example to call more Tibetan soldiers and officers to come over to the big family of the People's Republic of China and help the People's Liberation Army to liberate Tibet.

The Ninth Dapon's uprising was a heavy blow to the Tibetan officers and soldiers stationed in Chamdo. In their desperation, they seemed to fall apart. Meanwhile, the troops of the southern route, marching victoriously on, came to Zogang, Tiantuo and Bangda on October 19, 1950.

The central route, the main force of the 52nd Division of the 18th Corps, consisting of the 155th and 156th regiments and an artillery battalion, under the command of Wu Zhong, commander of the 52nd Division, marched from Dengke across the river on October 5. At the same time, the 54th Division's scout battalion, engineer battalion and artillery company feigned an attack on Gangtuo, hoping to attract the enemy troops' main force to Gangtuo and thus leave Chamdo undefended. On October 7, the PLA troops tried to cross the Jinsha River at Gangtuo and immediately ran into fierce resistance from Tibetan troops. After a battle of two hours at Gangtuo the Tibetan troops fled back to Chamdo.

The main force of the 52nd Division along the central route came to Shengda on October 14 and wiped out the Third Dapon. In order to prevent the enemy troops in Chamdo from fleeing west, Xi Jinwu was ordered to lead his troops and cavalrymen of the Northwest Military Area Command to capture Enda, and the 9th Company of the 156th Regiment was sent to capture the hill to the east of Chamdo city. The company, by a forced march, reached Chamdo on October 19 and put the city under their control. Nothing could be done to save the situation, so the Tibetan troops in Chamdo had to surrender. Before the fall of the city, the Kashag's governor in Chamdo fled westward with 2,600 troops. At Enda they were blocked by PLA men. Turning to the south they fled to a mountain valley near Drugu Monastery to the east of Lagongla. They were found praying in the valley by the Chief of Staff of the 52nd Division Li Ming and his cavalrymen and the 2nd Battalion of the 154th Regiment on October 21. The PLA men immediately besieged them, then shouting in Tibetan at them, explaining the Party and the Army's policy towards enemy soldiers. The enemy soldiers, numbering about 2,600, including British and Indian spies, in the face of the powerful political offensive and military pressure of the PLA men, had to surrender.

The Chamdo campaign, with its more than twenty battles, lasted for eighteen days. It ended with the wiping out of the 2nd, 3rd, 4th, 7th, 8th and 10th Dapons (the 9th Dapon had staged an uprising)—a total of more than five thousand Tibetan troops—and the capture of more than twenty Tibetan officers of the fourth rank and over, in addition to two British and two Indians. Except the Tibetan officers and the British and Indians, who were taken into custody, all captured soldiers were set free on the spot. The PLA gave them money for travelling expenses—three silver dollars to each, and five dollars to those who offered a gun while surrendering. They got their personal belongings back. Those with families were allowed to take away their horses.

Following the liberation of Chamdo, the People's Liberation Commission was founded in the Chamdo region according to the Central People's Government's policy of regional autonomy in areas of minority nationalities. Being neither a Military Control Commission nor a government of regional autonomy, it was an embryonic form of Tibetan regional autonomy, a political regime under the leadership of the Chinese Communist Party, in which representatives of all Tibetan circles participated, with Wang Qimei as its chairman and Ngabo Ngawang Jigme, Phagpalha Geleg Namgyal, Pangda Dorje, Hutuktu Loton Sherab, Jamyang Phagmo, Phuntsok Wangyal, Kelzang Wangdu and Hui Yiran as vice-chairmen. Military representatives were dispatched to thirteen *dzongs*—Chamdo, Chagyab, Jomda, Lado, Gonjo, Lhorong, Sodu, Riwoche, Dengke, Baxoi, Sanyan, Zogang and Ningjing—to enlarge the patriotic anti-imperialist united front.

In coordination with the Chamdo campaign, the 125th and 126th regiments of the 42nd Division of the 14th Corps in Yunnan marched to Zayu and Yanjing in southern Xikang. The 125th Regiment, under the command of Wang Jiemin, vice-director of the Divisional Political Department, started from Lijiang on August 15, 1950, marching through Gongshan and Chawalong, and liberating Zayu on October 1. At the same time the 125th Regiment liberated Yanjing.

In order to liberate Tibet, the Headquarters of the Xinjiang Military Region Command organized a Special Cavalrymen Division. On August 1, 1950, the division sent advance troops from Hotan of southern Xinjiang to Ngari of western Tibet. The commander of the Xinjiang Military Area Command, Wang Zhen, went from Urumqi to Hotan to see the troops off.

The advance troops, consisting of 135 soldiers of seven nationalities—Han, Tibetan, Mongolian, Hui, Uygur, Kazak and Xibe—under the command of Company Commander Li Disan, reached Gerze Dzong of Ngari after a month's march. The Kashag's resident official in Ngari demanded in a haughty manner that the PLA men leave Ngari. Li Disan argued against him with the force of justice. The Tibetan official finally had to sign a four-point agreement raised by the PLA. Afterwards, the Xinjiang military headquarters cited the advance troops as a "Hero Company." Soon afterwards on May 21, 1951, the main force of the Special Cavalrymen Division, under the command of An Zhiming, came to Ngari to join forces with the advance troops. They marched together into Gartok of Ngari on May 29. Thus the whole of Ngari was liberated.

Following the liberation of Chamdo, Richardson, the chief of the former British, but now Indian, Mission in Lhasa, urged Tibetan separatists to appeal to the United Nations. Instead of shouting for independence, said Richardson, they should prepare a statement of appeal. The statement, according to Thubten Tenthar, was drawn up by the Kashag on Regent Taktra's orders, and then translated into English by Richardson. When all this was done, Gyalo Thondrup and Shakabpa Wangchuk Dedan were sent to the United Nations with the statement.

Hugh E. Richardson says in his *Tibet and Its History*:

....The Tibetan government, on 7 November, appealed to the United Nations. The case was simply and clearly put to the following effect: Chinese claims that Tibet is part of China conflict radically with the facts and with Tibetan feelings. Even if the Chinese wanted to press their claim against Tibetan opposition, there were other methods than the resort to force. The Tibetans described the Chinese attack as clear aggression.

According to Richardson, Britain and the United States did not have the courage to openly support the Tibetan appeal to the United Nations—only the Republic of El Salvador, instigated by them, proposed that the United Nations discuss the Tibetan problem.

The United Kingdom delegate, pleading ignorance of the exact course of events and uncertainty about the legal position of Tibet, proposed that the matter be deferred. That was supported by the delegate of India.... Both the Soviet and the Chinese Nationalist delegates opposed discussion on the ground that Tibet was an integral part of China. The United States delegate agreed to an adjournment solely because of the statement by the Indian representative. The debate was, accordingly, adjourned....

On December 21, 1950, Shakabpa Wangchuk Dedan asked the United Nations to send "a fact-finding commission" to Tibet. They received no answer.

After the fall of Chamdo, Tibetan separatists sought help from divine oracles to decide whether to make war or negotiate a peace. As Thubten Tenthar describes in his memoirs,

When the liberation of Chamdo was known to Lhasa, Taktra and other pro-imperialist splittists were seized with a great panic. They immediately convened the Tsongdu, which was attended by the Regent, Kalons, Chikyap Khenpo, *drungyig*, *tsepons* and representatives of the Three Major Monasteries. They discussed how to deal with the situation, but no practical and effective measures were conceived. So they appealed to divine oracles. Accordingly, divine revelations were asked from Nechung and Gatong, two professional divine oracle invokers. They were invited to the residence of the Dalai and Regent. Having performed a ritual, Nechung only superficially murmured that they should pray more for the people's safety, but gave no substantial reply to the Kashag's questions about the current situation, such as which would be better, war or peace, and who should hold the power over Tibet.... Gatong, performing his rituals . . . knelt down before the Dalai and said, as if he was almost ready to burst into tears, "You, Dalai Lama, are the wisdom and treasure of all the Tibetan people, lay or monk. If you hold political power you will bring happiness to all the Tibetans." Hearing that, Regent Taktra, who was on the spot, became pale.... About ten days later Taktra handed in his resignation.... So the Kashag again convened the Tsongdu to announce the divine oracles and Taktra's resignation and to ask the Dalai Lama to assume the temporal power of Tibet.... To the Kashag's request the Dalai Lama gave his consent.

On the eighth day of the tenth month by the Tibetan calendar [in 1950] a ceremony was held to mark the returning of temporal power to the Fourteenth Dalai. In a letter he wrote immediately to Chairman Mao, the Dalai said: "I was deeply pained at the conflicts between the Han Chinese and Tibetans that happened when I had not yet come of age. Now all the Tibetan people have asked me to hold temporal power. I was duty bound to accept their request. On the eighth of the tenth month I began to run Tibetan affairs personally. I hope Chairman Mao will show concern to me and all Tibetan people."

Surkhang Surpa Wangchen Tseten and Drungyig Khyungpo Chosphel Thubten, who had been sent by the Kashag to the United Nations, met with Yuan Zhongxian, Ambassador of the People's Republic of China in India, on their way back to Tibet. Yuan asked them to pass a letter of Chairman Mao to the Dalai Lama, in which Chairman Mao expressed congratulations to the Dalai. The letter set most Tibetan officials at ease. They realized that relying on foreign countries would be in vain and the only way out for Tibet was to rely on the motherland and to have Tibet peacefully liberated. After many discussions they agreed to send a negotiating team to Beijing.

The immediate exchange of letters between the Dalai and Chairman Mao after the temporal power was returned to the Dalai was a matter of great historical significance in the cause of peaceful liberation of Tibet.

Before the negotiating group had been sent out, the Dalai Lama, on the eleventh of the eleventh month by the Tibetan calendar, had appointed Chief Khenpo Lozang Drashi and Tsepon Lukhangwa Tsewang Rabten as Acting Regents in charge of the daily affairs of the Tibetan local government, while he himself had gone to Yadong. So it was in Yadong that the Dalai Lama made the decision to send a negotiating team to Beijing. The team was headed by Kalon Ngabo Ngawang Jigme, with Khenchung Thubten Lekmon and Second Dapon Zangpo Tenzin Dondrup as its members. They went via Sichuan to Beijing. At the same time Maji Khemey Sonam Wangdu and Thubten Tenthar were also appointed team members, with Phuntsok Drashi and Sadu Rinchen as interpreters, and they went via India by sea to Beijing. The Tibetan negotiating team arrived at Beijing on April 22, 1951. In Beijing the Tibetan delegation held talks with the delegation of the Central People's Government, which was headed by Li Weihan and had Zhang Jingwu, Zhang Guohua and Sun Zhiyuan as its members.

On April 27, 1951, the Tenth Panchen and the leading members of the Council of Khenpos came from Kumbum Monastery in Qinghai to Beijing to offer their suggestions on the Tibetan question. They were also warmly welcomed by the Central People's Government. The Panchen and his party took their residence in the Changguanlou Building in the western suburbs of Beijing.

Negotiations proceeded smoothly and it took the negotiators only a short time to reach agreement on all important issues. The agreements included such clauses as "the Tibetan people shall return to the big family of the motherland," "the local government of Tibet shall actively assist the People's Liberation Army to enter Tibet," "the Tibetan people have the right of exercising national regional autonomy," "the central authorities will not alter the existing political system in Tibet," "officials of various ranks shall hold office as usual," "the policy of freedom of religious belief shall be carried out," "lamaseries shall be protected," "in matters related to various reforms in Tibet, there will be no compulsion on the part of the central authorities," "the local government of Tibet should carry out reforms of its own accord," etc.

An agreement was also achieved on the question of the Panchen's return to Tibet. The agreement further stipulated that the established status, functions and powers of the Panchen Erdeni should be maintained—meaning the status, functions and powers of the Thirteenth Dalai Lama and of the Ninth Panchen Erdeni when they were in friendly and amicable relations with each other.

On May 23, 1951, The Agreement of the Central People's Government and the Local Government of Tibet on Measures for the Peaceful Liberation of Tibet was signed in the Hall of Industrious Government in Zhongnanhai. The ceremony was administered by Vice-Premier Chen Yun and attended by Dong Biwu, Guo Moruo, Huang Yanpei, Chen Shutong, Nie Rongzhen, Peng Zhen, Ma Xulun, Zhang Bojun, Tan Pingshan, Zhang Xiruo, Xu Deheng, Lan Gongwu, Zhang Zhirang, Long Yun, Shen Yanbing, Ulanfu, Fu Zuoyi, Li Shucheng, Li Siguang, Ye Jizhuang, Zhu Xuefan, Liu Geping, He Cheng and Seypidin, as well as Lhamin Yeshe Tsultrim, Jigme and Ngawang Jingpa, representatives of the Panchen's Council of Khenpos. The agreement was signed first by the representatives of the Central People's Government and then by those of the local government of Tibet. At the ceremony, Li Weihan and Ngabo Ngawang Jigme made speeches, and Vice-Chairman Zhu De made a speech as well.

At 4 p.m. on May 24, the Panchen Erdeni, with all the officials of the Council of Khenpos, paid respects to Chairman Mao. The Panchen offered to Chairman Mao more than ninety gifts, which included a red satin banner with "Great Liberator of All Chinese Nationalities" in Chinese and Tibetan writings, a gold shield inscribed with the characters "Long Live Chairman Mao," a copper image of the Buddha made in Tibet, a silver *Mandral*, satin ornamented with gold thread, pilose antler, musk, saffron, *phuru* (Tibetan woolen fabric), etc. At 4:30 p.m. of the same day the delegation of the local government of Tibet, headed by Ngabo Ngawang Jigme, also paid respects to Chairman Mao and Commander-in-Chief Zhu. They offered more than thirty gifts, including a photo of the Dalai Lama, Tibetan placer gold, Tibetan perfume, serge, *phuru*, etc. The two ceremonies for offering gifts were attended by Zhu De, Li Jishen, Dong Biwu, Chen Yun, Huang Yanpei, Chen Shutong and Li Weihan, as well as chief directors of the government departments, democratic parties and people's organizations — those in attendance numbering more than one hundred.

On the evening of May 24, Chairman Mao held a grand banquet for more than 180 persons in celebration of the signing of the agreement on the peaceful liberation of Tibet. Among the guests were Panchen Erdeni Choskyi Gyaltsen and Ngabo Ngawang

Jigme. Chairman Mao said:

> In the recent several hundred years, Chinese nationalities, including Hans and Tibetans, were not united, nor were the Tibetans among themselves. This was the result of the rule of the reactionary Qing government and the Chiang Kai-shek government, and of imperialists' instigation. Now the power under the Dalai Lama and the power under the Panchen Erdeni and the Central People's Government are united. This unity is achieved after the Chinese people wiped out imperialism and the reactionary rule of domestic enemies. This unity is the unity among brothers instead of that between the oppressors and the oppressed, a result of common effort from all sides. From now on, owing to the unity, Chinese nationalities will attain progress and development in politics, economy and culture.

The Panchen and his Council of Khenpos expressed support for the agreement in a statement on May 28, 1951, saying:

> The Central People's Government and the local government of Tibet have achieved an agreement on the peaceful liberation of Tibet. From now on the Tibetan nationality has freed itself from the fetters of imperialism and returned to the big family of the great motherland. Chinese nationalities all are rejoicing at the important event. Particularly we, the Tibetan people, feel indescribable excitement.... Facts prove that the solemn historical task could only be triumphantly fulfilled under the leadership of the Chinese Communist Party and Chairman Mao.... For the complete liberation and development of the Tibetan nationality as well as the consolidation and development of the Chinese people's victory, we shall resolutely support the leadership of Chairman Mao, the Central People's Government and the Chinese Communist Party, and shall make great efforts to carry out the agreement and struggle for the solidarity of all Chinese nationalities and of Tibetan nationality.

In a telegraphic message to the Fourteenth Dalai on May 30, 1951, the Tenth Panchen said:

> When you assumed the temporal power...you sent representatives to negotiate with the Central People's Government and achieved the Agreement on Measures for the Peaceful Liberation of Tibet. This was a great victory of the Tibetan people, lay and monk. I will do my bit towards our unity and, under the wise leadership of the Central People's Government and Chairman Mao, will help you and the local government of Tibet to carry out the agreement for the cause of the

peaceful liberation of Tibet. I tender my congratulations and best wishes to you.

In a reply by wire on the nineteenth of the seventh month (by the Tibetan calendar) of 1951 to the Tenth Panchen, the Fourteenth Dalai, who was then in Norbulingka, said:

I was very glad to receive your telegram of May 30, which reached here on the fourth day of the sixth month by the Tibetan calendar.... According to the favourable omens of the divine oracles I have consulted, you are indeed the true reincarnation of the previous Panchen. I have informed Tashilhunpo Monastery and Kalon Ngabo, the Tibetan delegate in Beijing, about this. I am looking forward to your early return to Tashilhunpo Monastery. Please inform us by wire which route you will take.

This was the first friendly contact between the Dalai and the Panchen after the Thirteenth Dalai came into discord with the Ninth Panchen. By Tibetan tradition a reincarnation of the Panchen could not be religiously legal without the Dalai's recognition, and the same was the case with the Dalai. Now through the telegram the Dalai declared his recognition of the Tenth Panchen's legal status by announcing the result of his consultation with divine oracles.

On the fifth of the ninth month (by the Tibetan calendar) of 1951, the Fourteenth Dalai sent another telegram to the Panchen to say that he was looking forward to the latter's early return and to tell him the local government of Tibet had decided to send Khenchung Medo Jangtsha, Rimshi Khala and representatives of the Three Major Monasteries to go to welcome the Panchen; in addition, an armed escort of one hundred Tibetan soldiers under Gyalthang (the Fifth Dapon) was waiting at Nagchukha for his arrival.

In December 1951 the Panchen's Council of Khenpos was informed by the representatives of the Dalai and the Three Major Monasteries, who had arrived at Kumbum Monastery, that the Panchen would be provided with transport facilities and *ula* service for his journey in Tibet. The Panchen at once wired back to express his thanks to the Dalai and said that he would leave Xining for Tibet on the seventeenth day of the tenth month of the Iron-Rabbit Year by the Tibetan calendar (December 19, 1951).

Following the signing of the peace accord, Tibetan representatives returned to Tibet in two groups. Ngabo Ngawang Jigme, Khenchung Thubten Lekmon and Zangpo Tenzin Dondrup went back by way of Sichuan and Xikang, together with Zhang Guohua, while Khemey Sonam Wangdu, Thubten Tenthar, Phuntsok Drashi and Sadu Rinchen again went by sea via India, together with Zhang Jingwu, the representative of the central government. The second group arrived at Yadong in Tibet on July 14, 1951. On July 16 Zhang met with the Dalai at Dongkar Monastery and passed on a letter from Chairman Mao to him. The Dalai expressed his good wishes to Chairman Mao and told Zhang the Kashag would discuss some problems after Ngabo, who was expected to come back to Lhasa on the fifteenth of the sixth month by the Tibetan calendar, brought back the original text of the agreement. He himself would go to Lhasa on the eighteenth of that month of the Tibetan calendar.

The Dalai left Yadong on July 21, 1951, and arrived in Lhasa on August 17. Zhang Jingwu and his party came to Lhasa on August 8 and received an enthusiastic welcome by representatives of the Acting Regents, Kalon Lhalu Tsewang Dorje and Khartsan Lozang Rinchen, five hundred soldiers from the Second Dapon, the Indian resident official in Tibet, the Nepalese Commercial Agent and Chi Yurui, secretary of the "mediating team" of the Northwest Military Area Command. To extend a warm welcome to him, the men and women of Lhasa were in their holiday best and the whole city had a festival atmosphere.

On October 26, 1951, the 18th Corps of the PLA, headed by Zhang Guohua and Tan Guansan, arrived in Lhasa to the welcome of the Kashag and the lay and monastic population. Leaving a battalion in Lhasa, the forces of the 18th Corps continued their march. They entered Gyantse and Shigatse on November 15. On November 25, Zhao Yanxiang, Chief of Staff of the 154th Regiment of the 52nd Division of the 18th Corps, with an infantry company and a scout cavalry company, escorted British spy Robert Ford and other foreign agents captured in Chamdo to the border of India and completed the procedure for expelling them from the country.

On September 11, 1951, Ngabo Ngawang Jigme, the chief delegate of the Tibetan negotiation team, and his party came back to

Lhasa and gave the Dalai and the Kashag an account of the signing of the peace accord. In a telegraphic message on October 24 to Chairman Mao, the Dalai said:

> The local government of Tibet and the Tibetan lay and monastic population support the agreement on the peaceful liberation of Tibet signed on May 23, 1951, and will, under the leadership of Chairman Mao and the Central People's Government, help the People's Liberation Army units in Tibet to consolidate national defence, wipe the power of imperialism out of Tibet and safeguard the territory and sovereignty of the motherland.

Two days later Chairman Mao sent a telegram in reply to the Dalai. The full text is as follows:

> To Mr. Dalai Lama:
> Thank you for your telegram of October 24, 1951. I am grateful to you for your efforts in the cause of peaceful liberation of Tibet. With congratulations!
>
> Sincerely,
> October 26, 1951                                         Mao Zedong

But Tibetan splittists did not resign themselves to their defeat. Behind the scenes, they secretly organized the so-called People's Conference with Lukhangwa Tsewang Rabten and Lozang Drashi, the Acting Regents. In March and April 1952 they went so far as to prevent the *dzongs* near Lhasa from selling vegetables, meat and firewood to the PLA units and urged a number of people who did not know the truth to encircle Zhang Jingwu's residence. They openly demanded that the PLA units get out of Tibet.

As Zhang Guohua describes in his "Records of the Actual Events of the Marching of the 18th Corps into Tibet,"

> In the face of danger we ordered the troops in Shannan to make a forced march to Lhasa and at the same time called together the chief administrators of the local government of Tibet, Lukhangwa Tsewang Rabten and Lozang Drashi, for a meeting.... The first thing Lukhangwa said to me as soon as he saw me was "Commander Zhang, to be hungry is more uncomfortable than to be defeated in a war, isn't it?" I asked him if he had read the agreement on the peaceful liberation of Tibet.... He did not answer.

But as Li Weihan points out in "The Road to the Liberation of the

Tibetan Nationality,"

March and April of 1952 witnessed the "People's Conference" incident. A part of the Tibetan troops, monks and hooligans were urged to make petitions and trouble in Lhasa. Being against the agreement, they encircled the residence of the representatives of the central government and of Ngabo Ngawang Jigme, attempting to drive the People's Liberation Army out of Tibet soon after the latter had entered Tibet and had not stood firmly. But they went too far to gain profit. Even the local government could not but admit that the People's Conference was illegal. After we argued with them on just grounds, to our advantage and with restraint, the Dalai Lama had to declare the dissolving of the "Conference" and the dismissal of the two Acting Regents who secretly instigated and supported it.

According to the policy of the Central Committee of the Chinese Communist Party that the PLA entering Tibet must not rely for food supply on the local people, the PLA troops in Tibet established the "July 1" and "August 1" farms in the west suburb of Lhasa. They opened up wasteland to grow grain and vegetables for self-sufficiency.

At the same time, in order to solve the problem of transportation, the main force of the 18th Corps was sent to build the Xikang-Tibet highway through Garze, Chamdo and Bomi. The Northwest Military Area Command sent engineering troops, along with civilian labourers, to build a highway from Shangde of Qinghai through Golmud and Nagchukha to Lhasa. The Xinjiang Military Area Command also sent engineering troops along with civilian labourers to build a highway from Yecheng in southern Xinjiang through the Kunlun mountains to Gartok of the Ngari area in Tibet.

The People's Liberation Army in Tibet did its best to win more people of the Tibetan upper classes over to the anti-imperialist patriotic front by explaining to them the seventeen-point agreement and the Chinese Communist Party's policy towards national minorities and their religious beliefs. In addition, the army sent men to serve the masses of Tibetan people by giving them free medical service, interest-free loans and other help. All this was done under the Central People's Government's strategic principle of "exercising prudence in making steady progress."

# 7. The Tenth Panchen Returns to Tibet

After the signing of the Agreement on Measures for the Peaceful Liberation of Tibet, the Panchen and the officials of the Council of Khenpos left Beijing for the Kumbum to prepare for his return to Tibet. The Northwest Military and Administrative Committee, by order of the Central People's Government, appointed Fan Ming its resident representative in the Panchen's administrative office, and me, Ya Hanzhang, his assistant. Fan Ming and I were responsible for escorting the Panchen and his entourage back to Tashilhunpo Monastery. In the spring of 1951 we came to Beijing to consult with Li Weihan, director of the United Front Work Department of the CPC Central Committee, on some important problems of the escort and asked Premier Zhou Enlai for instructions. Meanwhile, the local government of Tibet sent Khenchung Medo Jangtsha and Dapon Khala as representatives of the Dalai and the Kashag, along with representatives of the Three Major Monasteries, to the Kumbum to welcome the Panchen to return to Tibet.

After going back from Beijing to Qinghai, Fan Ming and I went to the Kumbum to consult with the Panchen and the chief officials of the Council of Khenpos, Jigme and Lhamin Yeshe Tsultrim, on the details of the return to Tibet. It was decided to leave in two groups. Fan Ming and Jigme would go first to Lhasa to arrange transportation facilities and other things with the Kashag for the Panchen on his journey in Tibet. Then I, together with some troops and government officials, would escort the Panchen, all the officials of the Council of Khenpos and their families, the Panchen's guard battalion, a medical team and a song and dance ensemble to the Tashilhunpo by way of Lhasa.

The first group, headed by Fan Ming and Jigme, and consisting of 560 troops and cadres, 570 workers and a part of the officials of the Council of Khenpos and their attendants, numbering about 100, with 1,130 horses, 1,700 mules, 1,300 camels and 7,000 yaks, started from Shangde. They left Xining on August 1, 1951, and arrived in Lhasa on December 1, where they met with the 18th Corps. The whole journey covered 2,500 kilometres and lasted 120 days.

The second group, consisting of the Panchen, all the remaining officials of the Council of Khenpos and their families, and escorting personnel, by order of the Central People's Government, left Xining via Shangde and Nagchukha for Lhasa in December 1951. Weather is always crucial for the journey to Tibet, as an old saying describes:

> In the first, second and third lunar months, mountains are buried deep under the snow; with the fourth, fifth and sixth months comes the rain; the seventh, eighth and ninth months are the best season for journeys, but in the winter you have to crawl like a dog.

The first group took their journey in August, the best season for a journey, but we, the second group, went in December, when the Tanggula Mountains were covered with heavy snow.

In view of the bad weather, we prepared ourselves for two eventualities—we planned to take the road through the "Thirtynine Tribes" region to Nagchukha if the weather was too bad for us to cross the mountains, though this route would take us a month longer. In order to cross the snow-covered mountains, we brought with us 3,000 camels, 7,000 yaks, and sufficient food, feed and firewood, in addition to horses, 200 mules and 100 stretchers.

Our journey started on December 19, 1951. On December 18 Xi Zhongxun, vice-chairman of the Northwest Military and Administrative Committee, on behalf of Chairman Mao and the committee, came from Xi'an to Xining to see the Panchen off. On December 19 the chairman and vice-chairmen of the People's Government of Qinghai Province, Zhao Shoushan, Zhang Zhongliang, Sherab Gyatso and Ma Fuchen, political commissar of Qinghai Military Region Liao Hansheng, monks of Kumbum Monastery and about ten thousand people of various nationalities gathered in the suburbs of Xining to see the Panchen off.

In February 1952 the second group reached the Tanggula Mountains, which were covered with snow about one foot deep. The officials of the Council of Khenpos said that it was possible for the group to cross the mountains. Mobilizing the group for action against the natural obstacles, we planned to pass over the mountains within six days. In the end we made our way across the mountains, only about a dozen people of the group and a few yaks and mules dying on the road, though a large number of camels met their death and their bodies covered the paths on the mountains. When we arrived at Nagchukha, only one-third of the three thousand camels remained alive.

After crossing the mountains we entered the pastoral area of the Maima tribe of Amdo, where a group of a dozen people headed by a *khenchung* and a *rimshi* were waiting for us. They offered *katags* to the Panchen and said they were an advance group of the party sent by the Dalai and the Kashag to welcome the Panchen. They said transportation facilities would be provided by the local government of Tibet for the rest of the journey in Tibet. At the same time, a large number of yaks and horses were brought to us. Thus, the transportation difficulties caused by the great loss of camels were overcome. The welcoming party said the Kashag had ordered the Fifth Dapon with a hundred men to be the Panchen's guards and they were waiting in Nagchukha.

In March 1952, the Panchen and his party arrived in Nagchukha to the welcome of two *chikyaps*, resident officials of the Kashag in Nagchukha, the Living Buddha of Nagchukha Monastery and several thousand lay people and monks. It was at that time that the "People's Conference" incident happened. For the Panchen's safety, Zhang Jingwu, the representative of the Central People's Government, sent a telegram to us from Lhasa, asking us to stay in Nagchukha and heighten vigilance against a pro-imperialist separatists' surprise attack. So we stayed in Nagchukha for more than a month under the pretext of taking a rest. Nothing special happened to us. It was not until the incident was put to an end that Zhang Jingwu asked us to leave for Lhasa.

The Panchen and his entourage safely arrived in Lhasa on April 28, 1952, to the enthusiastic welcome of all the inhabitants of the city. The doors in Lhasa were marked with lime symbols of good omen, religious banners were displayed atop all the buildings in the city and aromatic pine and cedar branches were burning in front of every house. This was the religious ceremony for paying the highest respect to the Panchen. The Kashag had welcoming tents set up in the eastern suburbs of the city. All *kalons* came to welcome the Panchen. The welcoming party consisted of all lay and monastic officials of the Kashag, several hundred in number, including Chief Kalon Rampa Thubten Gongchen, Kalon Surkhang

Wangchen Geleg, Dokhar Phuntsok Rabje, Ngabo Ngawang Jigme, Tashi Linpa Khenrab Wangchuk, Drungyig Chenpo, the Tsepon of the *Yigtsang* (monk council) and other officials, in addition to a Tibetan military band and a guard of honour from the Potala.

Zhang Jingwu, representative of the Central People's Government, Zhang Guohua, Commander, and Tan Guansan, Political Commissar, of the 18th Corps, and Fan Ming, representative of the Northwest Military and Administrative Committee in the Panchen's headquarters, all had their welcoming tents set up there.

After the welcoming ceremony, the Tenth Panchen went to the residence specially reserved for the Panchens, which was in a building over the gateway of Jokhang Temple. On the afternoon of the same day a meeting that made history took place between the Panchen and the Dalai. They exchanged *katags* and kowtowed to each other. This showed that they were not to take the roles of tutor and disciple.

The Panchen stayed in Lhasa for about a month, during which time officials representing the Dalai and the Panchen negotiated, on the basis of the peace agreement, the restoration of the Panchen's status, functions and powers—that is, those of the Ninth Panchen when he was in friendly and amicable relations with the Thirteenth Dalai. The relations, as both sides agreed according to their consulting with historical documents, were set before the Fire-Cock year of the fifteenth Tibetan calendrical cycle (the twenty-third year of Qing Emperor Guangxu's reign, or 1897), when the Thirteenth Dalai, at twenty-one, and the Ninth Panchen, at fourteen, were equal in status and were both under the direct leadership of the Emperor, and the daily affairs of the Kashag and the Tashilhunpo were supervised by the Qing imperial resident officials. After the time of the good relationship between the Dalai and Panchen was defined, all the officials sent by the Dalai to the Tashilhunpo and to its *dzongs* and *shikas* were to be drawn back and their power would be handed over to the Panchen and his Council of Khenpos.

As to the reduction or remission of the taxes and the *ula* service (unpaid transportation duty) of the Tashilhunpo, both sides agreed to deal with it according to the regulations before the Fire-Cock year of the Tibetan calendrical cycle. But they were in dispute on the problem of whether the Tashilhunpo should provide a quarter of Tibetan army provisions. The Panchen's side said that this had been added after the Fire-Cock Year, so it should be remitted, while the Dalai's side said it was added for fighting against the invasion of British imperialism, that is, for national defence, so the Tashilhunpo had the duty to shoulder it, and that it would be unfair to make the Dalai's side take the whole expense of the national defence of Tibet on its shoulders.

In order to calm down the dispute, Zhang Jingwu, by order of the Central People's Government, informed the Dalai and the Panchen that the PLA units stationed in Tibet were responsible for the national defense, and the ordinary army provisions were remitted for Tibet, but in the case of the invasion by a strong enemy that required it to participate in national defence, Tibet should provide the provisions according to established regulations. By this principle the Panchen's side was absolved of responsibility to fund one-quarter of army provisions.

With the solving of these two major problems, the restoration of the Panchen's status, functions and power was fundamentally in place. The other problems were of minor importance and could be left to be decided in the future.

On June 9, 1952, I was ordered to escort the Tenth Panchen back to the Tashilhunpo. The 18th Corps sent a company to be on guard duty for the Panchen. The Panchen and his entourage went via Gyantse and arrived at the Tashilhunpo on June 23, to the enthusiastic welcome of tens of thousands of lay and monastic Tibetan people. In Shigatse, people, singing and dancing, performed the waist-drum dance, five-star red flags fluttered atop all buildings in the city and portraits of Mao Zedong were hung in almost all the rooms in Tashilhunpo Monastery—this being the way that the lay and monastic residents of the city expressed their love of and gratitude to the People's Republic of China, the Chinese Communist Party and Chairman Mao.

Twenty-nine years had passed since the Ninth Panchen left the Tashilhunpo in 1923. It took the Central People's Government under the Chinese Communist Party only one year (from the signing of the peace accord to the Panchen's return to the Tashilhunpo) to solve the problem that had not been solved by the

Northern Government and the Nationalist government during twenty-odd years. Apparently, the Panchen's return to Tibet was closely related to the liberation of Tibet. When Tibet came back into the big family of the motherland, the normal relationship between Tibet and the motherland was clearly defined and the problem of the Panchen's return to Tibet was readily solved. I attended the celebrations held by the Tashilhunpo and, on behalf of the Northwest Military and Administrative Committee, offered sweet buttered-tea and alms to the four thousand Tashilhunpo monks. After staying for half a year in Shigatse I came back to Lhasa in late 1952. When I bid farewell to him, the Panchen asked the monks to hold for me a grand religious sending-off ceremony by lining up, reading prayers and burning incense to express their sincere thanks to me.

The peaceful liberation of Tibet and the Panchen's return to the Tashilhunpo were a great victory for the policies of the Chinese Communist Party towards national minorities and religious belief.

*Appendices*
# I. The Ming Dynasty's Administration of Tibet and the Reappraisal of the Phagdru Regime

The first four Panchens lived in the time of the Ming Dynasty, covering 259 years from the eighteenth year of the Hongwu reign period of Ming Emperor Taizu (1385) to the seventeenth year of the Chongzhen reign period of Ming Emperor Sizong (1644). (Fourth Panchen Lazang Choskyi lived to 1662, eighteen years after the suicide of the last Ming Emperor, Sizong.) Chinese and Tibetan historical books, however, do not give systematic accounts of the Ming administration of Tibet and Tibet's political situation in that period. In view of this, an account is given here to fill in the gaps.

In the middle of the 1360s Zhu Yuanzhang overthrew the Yuan Dynasty and established the Ming Dynasty. Zhu Yuanzhang, the first emperor of the Ming Dynasty, or Ming Emperor Taizu, ascended the throne in 1368, naming this the first year of his Hongwu reign period. At that time the Ming Dynasty took over the Yuan territory, of which Tibet was a part.

The Ming Emperor Taizu attached much importance to Tibet and paid much attention to the areas inhabited by Tibetan people in the northwest and southwest of China as well. Early in the Hongwu reign period the Emperor dispatched several hundred thousand troops under the command of General-in-Chief Deng Yu to the Tibetan-inhabited areas. The Yuan army stationed there fled helter-skelter before the Ming troops and the Yuan officials there pledged allegiance to the Ming imperial court. The Pacification Commissioner of Do-Kham (who governed Gansu, Qinghai and Xikang), and the Pacification Commissioner in the Three Regions of U, Tsang and Ngari Korsum also switched their allegiance to the Ming Dynasty. The *Imperial Records of the Ming Dynasty* has the following record:

> On the *yi-you* day of the sixth month of the third year of the Hongwu reign period [July 21, 1370] Sonam-pu, the original Pacification Commissioner of the Yuan, with gold and silver plates and seals of authority granted to him by the Yuan court, also came with Tibetan tribes to pledge his allegiance to the Ming court. Before that, an official of Shaanxi Province by the name of Xu Yunde had been dispatched to Dashimen, Tiecheng, Taozhou and Minzhou with an edict ordering the eighteen Tibetan tribes to give allegiance to the Ming court. Thus Sonam-pu came to surrender....
>
> [In the same year] Kunga Sonam was sent to order Tibet to surrender. Thirteen Yuan officials, including Sonam-pu, the Yuan's Pacification Commissioner of Tubo, pledged their allegiance by offering tribute to the Ming court....
>
> In the fourth year of the Hongwu reign period [1371] the Ming court set up a Hezhou Commandery and let Sonam-pu, who had had his headquarters there, retain command as Vice-Commander. This position was then made hereditary....
>
> [In the same year] the court set up the Do-Kham Commandery [Do means Amdo, the areas of Tibetan people in Gansu and Qinghai; *Kham* was later called Xikang]....
>
> In the sixth year of the Hongwu reign period [1373], according to the report of the Hezhou Commandery, Pacification Commissioner of Do-Kham Commandery Changchub Gyaltsen recommended twenty-two Tibetan chiefs to be officials of the commandery. His recommendation was approved by the Emperor, and seals of authority were granted to the officials.

In addition, the fourteenth Imperial Preceptor, Namgyal Palzangpo, submitted to the Ming Emperor. The central regime of the Yuan Dynasty had established the position of Great Yuan Imperial Preceptor, giving the holder social status almost as high as the Emperor's. Though the Imperial Preceptor had no actual power, this action had great appeal for Tibetans. There were altogether fourteen Imperial Preceptors successively—Phagspa was the first Imperial Preceptor and the succeeding preceptors were selected for the most part from the lamas of the Sakya sect. They lived in Beijing. In the fifth year of the Hongwu reign period (1372)

Namgyal Palzangpo sent men to offer tribute to the Ming imperial court. The Ming Emperor conferred on him the title of Brilliant Treasure Buddha State Tutor. Ming Emperor Taizu asked him to summon the Tibetan tribes to surrender. All sixty former Yuan officials that the Tutor recommended to the Emperor were given new official posts by the Emperor.

According to the *Imperial Records of the Ming Dynasty*, in the sixth year of the Hongwu reign period (1373) the Ming court set up two pacification commissions, a marshal's office, four pacification offices (used in aboriginal areas), thirteen *wan hu* and fourteen *qian hu* for Do-Kham and U-Tsang; Namkha Tenpa Gyaltsen, the original Yuan governor, was appointed Pacification Commissioner, and sixty former Yuan officials were given new posts. The Emperor gave an edict to explain the policy of pacification towards Tibet.

On the *ji-mao* day of the seventh month of the seventh year of the Hongwu reign period (1374) the Xi'an Regional Military Commission was set up in Hezhou (modern Linxia County of Gansu Province). The original Commander of the Hezhou Commandery, Wei Zheng, was appointed the Commander of the Xi'an Regional Military Commission in charge of Hezhou, Do-Kham and the three regions of U, Tsang and Ngari. The Do-Kham and U-Tsang commanderies were changed to Regional Military Commissions, which were headed respectively by their original Vice-Commanders, Sonam Odser and Konchok Odser, who were to be subordinate to Commander Wei Zheng. The Emperor said in an edict that he was glad to see that many local officials in U and Tsang came to request reappointment and to receive various offices, and he ordered that they be satisfied, hoping that these officials would be devoted to their duties and people live and work in peace (see *Imperial Records of the Ming Dynasty*).

From the historical records cited above it was evident that the areas inhabited by the Tibetan people in northwest and southwest China and U-Tsang (Tibet) were part of Ming territory.

By the end of the Yuan Dynasty the Sakya regime, the local regime of Tibet, had been replaced by the Phagmo Drupa (or Phagdru for short) regime of the Kagyu sect, which enjoyed the Yuan Emperor Shundi's recognition. Its ruling lama was called *desi*, or popularly Prince of the Dharma. When the Ming Dynasty was founded, Changchub Gyaltsen, the first Desi of the Phagdru regime, had died. He had been succeeded by the second Desi, Shakya Gyaltsen (referred to in historical books of the Ming Dynasty as "Jamyang Shakya Gyaltsen, the original Yuan Imperial Initiation Master of Phagmo Drupa in U-Tsang"). According to the *Imperial Records of the Ming Dynasty*,

> In the sixth year of the Hongwu reign period [1373], the former Yuan Imperial Initiation Master of Phagmo Drupa in U-Tsang, Jamyang Shakya Gyaltsen, sent a tribal chief by name of Sonam Zangpo to bring images of the Buddha, Buddhist sutras and *sarira* [bodily relics or ashes of the Buddha] to the imperial court. By order of the Emperor, Sonam Zangpo was entertained in a Buddhist monastery. The Emperor gave him gifts.

In the same year Ming Emperor Taizu granted Jamyang Shakya Gyaltsen the same title, "Imperial Initiation Master," as that given by the Yuan Emperor, and a jade seal of authority. This showed that the Ming court recognized the legal status of the Phagdru regime in Tibet.

Though both the Yuan and Ming dynasties attached great importance to Tibet, yet they were different in their administration of Tibet:

(1) The central regime of the Yuan Dynasty established the Political Council as the authority in charge of Tibet. But the council was abolished in the Ming Dynasty. During the Ming Dynasty the paying of tribute by Tibetan political and religious leaders was handled by the Ministry of Rites; and the appointment and dismissal of local officials of Tibet, by the Ministry of Personnel. More important matters were managed by the Emperor himself.

(2) The central regime of the Yuan Dynasty established the position of Great Yuan Imperial Preceptor, but the Ming Dynasty replaced it with "State Tutor," a position of a lower rank. This showed the Ming court did not put Tibetan Lamaism on the same high position as in the Yuan court, though the Ming also took it seriously.

(3) The Yuan Dynasty stationed a Mongol army in Tibet with four Mongol marshals, two in U-Tsang and two in Ngari Korsum. The Ming Dynasty did not station an army in Tibet, because the

Phagdru regime in Tibet peacefully submitted itself to the central government of the Ming Dynasty. Tibet experienced no invasion from the outside during the Ming Dynasty, either, so on this count there was also no need for the imperial court to send an army to Tibet.

On the other hand, as Tibet was a part of China's territory during the two dynasties, the Yuan and Ming dynasties were similar in their administration of Tibet in the following aspects:

(1) The central regime of the Ming Dynasty established in Tibet the U-Tsang Regional Military Commission, which was the equivalent of the Pacification Commission for the Three Regions of U, Tsang and Ngari Korsum in the Yuan Dynasty. The first Vice-Commander (i.e., local commander) of the U-Tsang Regional Military Commission, Konchok Odser, appointed by Ming Emperor Taizu, was probable one of the pacification commissioners for the Three Regions of U, Tsang, and Ngari Korsum appointed by the Yuan court. In 1385 (the eighteenth year of Hongwu), Paljor Zangpo was made the head of the U-Tsang Regional Military Commission. Since then the Ming court did not again make an appointment to this post. What probably occurred was that, because the Phagdru regime was loyal to the central government and explicitly recognized that Tibet was subordinate to the central government, the position of Vice-Commander of the U-Tsang Regional Military Commission was probably taken concurrently by the Desi of the Phagdru regime.

(2) By institution each new Desi of the Phagdru regime should ask the central government of the Ming Dynasty for recognition, and the latter gave its recognition of the new Desi's legal status by conferring on him an imperial certificate and a seal of authority.

(3) The Ming Dynasty instituted that the Phagdru regime should pay tribute to the imperial court every three years. The tribute was in fact the local taxes paid by the Phagdru regime to the central government.

(4) The Phagdru regime, along with the chieftains of Tibetan areas in Xikang and Qinghai, was duty-bound to repair and maintain the post-staging stations that had been built for communication between Tibet and the inland. The stations had been built in the Yuan Dynasty, but were damaged in the early Ming Dynasty.

In the reign of Ming Emperor Chengzu, the fifth Desi of the Phagdru regime, Drakpa Gyaltsen, who was granted the title of Propagation Prince of Persuasion, and local chieftains had the damaged stations repaired. Thus, the roads from Tibet to inland China were passable and the envoys could travel tens of thousands of *li* in safety and peace (see "The Biographies of the Propagation Princes of Persuasion" in the *History of the Ming Dynasty*).

(5) The Ming Dynasty's policy towards religion in Tibet was based on the belief that the best approach was to make use of the traditional influence of the ecclesiastics among the populace. To manifest the policy the Ming court conferred various honorific titles on the leaders of all Buddhist sects in Tibet. According to the *History of the Ming Dynasty*, the title of Prince of the Dharma went to many Tibetans, modified with such epithets as "Great Treasure" (granted by Ming Emperor Chengzu to the fifth ruling lama of the Black Hat line of the Karmapa sect), "Great Vehicle" (granted by Ming Emperor Chengzu to the ruling lama of the Sakya sect, Kunga Drashi), "Great Mercy" (granted by Ming Emperor Xuanzong to Sakya Yeshe, the disciple of Tsongkhapa), "Great Benevolence" (granted by Ming Emperor Daizong to Tibetan monk Sakya), "Great Augur" (granted by Ming Emperor Wuzong to Tibetan monk Lingtsang Palden), "Great Virtue" (granted by Ming Emperor Wuzong to Tibetan monk Choskyi Odser), "Great Enlightenment" (granted by Ming Emperor Xianzong to Tibetan monk Drakpa Gyaltsen), "Great Wisdom" (granted by Ming Emperor Wuzong to Tibetan monk Palden Drashi), and so on.

In addition, there were five princes. Those given the title of prince included "Propagation Prince of Persuasion" (granted by Ming Emperor Chengzu in the fourth year of Yongle to Drakpa Gyaltsen, the fourth Desi of the Phagdru regime), "Promotion Prince of Virtue" (granted by Ming Emperor Chengzu in the fifth year of Yongle to Chosphel Gyaltsen, who was the Commander of Do-Kham Commandery in charge of modern Qinghai and Xikang), "Guardian Prince of the Doctrine" (granted by Ming Emperor Chengzu in the fifth year of Yongle to Namgyal Palzangpo), "Assistance Prince of the Doctrine" (granted by Ming Emperor Chengzu in the eleventh year of Yongle to Namkha Legpa, a monk of the Sakya sect from Dachang, south of Sakya Monastery) and

"Propagation Prince of the Doctrine" (granted by Ming Emperor Chengzu in the eleventh year of Yongle to Rinchen Paljor Gyaltsen, a monk of the Drigung Kagyu sect from Medrogungkar of Tibet). Apart from the titles mentioned above, the titles of "Son of the Buddha in West Heaven," "Great State Tutor," "State Tutor," "Buddhist Master," etc., granted to ruling lamas of various lamaseries, were even more numerous. All these titles were hereditary. When a title was passed on from one generation to the next, the old certificate and seal of authority had to be replaced with new ones. Only leaders with these titles were qualified to pay tribute to the central government of the Ming Dynasty. As the number of tribute payers increased year by year, it was difficult for the post-staging stations to provide service. The Ming court thus began to apply restrictions on them. It was stipulated that Tibetan leaders with honorific titles paid tribute every three years and that only the leaders were allowed to go to the capital to present the tribute, while their entourages were to be left at the borders of the areas inhabited by Tibetans (Tachienlu of Sichuan, Xining of Qinghai and Hezhou of Gansu).

The first five Desis of the Phagdru regime of the Kagyu sect ruled Tibet during the period of time from Yuan Emperor Shundi to Ming Emperor Chengzu. This was a period of development for the feudal serf system in Tibet, with economic growth and social stability. At that time serf owners did not treat serfs so cruelly as they did afterwards, so serfs engaged in production comparatively actively.

The social mode was improved by Tsongkhapa's religious reform. Tsongkhapa stressed respect for discipline, and all his disciples were required to examine themselves daily for violations of discipline. After Tsongkhapa's death his disciples spared no effort to develop the Yellow Hat sect with the support of the Phagdru regime.

The Phagdru regime of the Kagyu sect ruled over Tibet for 264 years (from the fourteenth year of the Zhizheng reign period of Yuan Emperor Shundi to the forty-sixth year of the Wanli reign period of Ming Emperor Shenzong, or 1354-1618). The Karmapa branch of the Kagyu sect, together with Tsangpa Khan, then overthrew the Phagdru regime and founded the Karma regime.

The Karma regime ruled Tibet for twenty-four years (from the forty-sixth year of Wanli to the fifteenth year of the Chongzhen reign period of Ming Emperor Sizong, or 1618-1642). In other words, Tibet was ruled by the Kagyu sect, branches of which held power in both the Phagdru and Karma regimes, for at last 288 years —about three centuries.

The Kagyu sect was founded in Tibet in the late eleventh century (in the reign of Northern Song Emperor Zhezong), being based on teachings newly introduced from India. According to *Highlights of the History of Tibetan Buddhism* by Wang Furen, this sect derived its name from its major teaching method of oral instruction—*kagyu* meaning "oral instruction in Buddhist concepts." The Kagyu engaged in the main in Esoteric Buddhism, the doctrines of which must be studied by disciples through oral instruction from a tutor. So oral instruction became its major teaching method, from which the sect derived its name. "Ka" is also sometimes interpreted as meaning white colour. The reason was that Marpa and Milarepa, the founders of the sect, wore white monk robes in practising Buddhism, a custom from India. Since then all followers of the Kagyu sect wore white monk robes. That was why the Kagyu was otherwise called the White sect. In short, Kagyu was a sect of Esoteric Buddhism which had been introduced from India and had become a branch of Tibetan Esoteric Buddhism.

As the sect's major teaching method was oral instruction given by tutor to disciple, and as the oral instruction was different from tutor to tutor, the Kagyu sect had a number of sub-branches. Two branches formed soon after its founding. One was the Shangpa Kagyu, founded by Khyungpo Nagyapa. In 1086, he built Samding Monastery in Nakartse Dzong near Gyantse, where the Dorje Phagmo, a female Living Buddha, has been reincarnated till now. But the Shangpa Kagyu has had only a small number of followers and no great impact on Tibetan religious circles.

The other branch was the Dakpo Kagyu, founded by Marpa (1012-1097, or from the fifth year of the Dazhong-Xiangfu reign period of Northern Song Emperor Zhenzong to the fourth year of the Shaosheng reign period of Northern Song Emperor Zhezong). Marpa died at the age of eighty-five. He had many disciples, of whom the most influential was Milarepa (1040-1123, from the third year of the Baoyuan reign period of Northern Song Emperor Renzong to the fifth year of the Xuanhe reign period of Northern Song Emperor Huizong). Milarepa died at the age of eighty-three. He also had many disciples, of whom the most influential was Dakpo Lhaje (1097-1153, from the fourth year of the Shaosheng reign period of Northern Song Emperor Zhezong to the twenty-third year of the Shaoxing reign period of Southern Song Emperor Gaozong). Dakpo Lhaje, who died at fifty-six, founded the Dakpo Kagyu sect. The Dakpo Kagyu and Shangpa Kagyu were the two major branches of the Kagyu sect in its early years. The Dakpo Lhaje established Gampo Monastery in the Dakpo region, where he preached Buddhism and recruited many disciples for thirty years. His four leading disciples founded four branches of the sect:

(1) Dusum Khyen (from the fourth year of the Daguan reign period of Northern Song Emperor Huizong to the fourth year of the Shaoxi reign period of Southern Song Emperor Guangzong, or 1110-1193) founded the Karma Kagyu branch;

(2) Shang Tsalpa (from the fifth year of the Xuanhe reign period of Northern Song Emperor Huizong to the fifth year of the Shaoxi reign period of Southern Song Emperor Guangzong, or 1123-1194) constructed Tsalpa (also called Tselgungtang) Monastery, from which developed the Tsalpa Kagyu branch;

(3) Darma Wangchuk (in the twelfth century, precise dates unknown) established Barom Monastery and the Barom Kagyu branch;

(4) Phagmo Drupa Dorje Gyalpo (from the fourth year of the Daguan reign period of Northern Song Emperor Huizong to the sixth year of the Qiandao reign period of Southern Song Emperor Xiaozong, or 1110-1170) was born in Zhelongnaixue of the Jinsha valley in the Kham region. He became a monk in Lhakang Monastery of Gyalche at the age of nine, went to U at nineteen and began studies under the guidance of Dakpo Lhaje in 1152. In 1158, he founded Dansa Thel Monastery at Phagmodru in Shannan, and he himself became known as Phagmo Drupa (a man from Phagmodru), where the Phagdru Kagyu branch, the most influential branch of the Dakpo Kagyu, was established. Afterwards, the Phagdru Kagyu, Karma Kagyu, Tsalpa Kagyu and Barom Kagyu became

known as the four major branches of the Dakpo Kagyu order.

Eight disciples of Phagmo Drupa founded eight sub-branches: the Drigung Kagyu, Taklung Kagyu, Drukpa Kagyu, Yazang Kagyu, Tsurpu Kagyu, Shoshe Kagyu, Yelpa Kagyu and Matsang Kagyu. During the fourteenth and fifteenth centuries many religious sects gradually vanished; only some big sects—the Phagdru Kagyu, Karma Kagyu, Drigung Kagyu, Tsalpa Kagyu, Taklung Kagyu, Drukpa Kagyu and Yazang Kagyu, etc.—remained. The most influential of them was the Phagdru Kagyu.

The history of Tibet shows that a religious sect would not be able to hold its ground and develop itself in the society without the support of a local temporal power (slave owners or serf-owners). The most important of the reasons why Phagdru Kagyu could be founded and developed in Shannan was that it enjoyed great support of the Lang family, a big feudal manorial lord in Nedong of Shannan. So Phagmo Drupa had enough manpower and material and financial resources to build Dansa Thel Monastery. The monastery was said to have had eight hundred monks. This was a great achievement at that time (the twelfth century), though the number was much less than that of the Three Major Monasteries of Lhasa founded afterwards by the Gelug sect. The abbot of the Dansa Thel was called *chen-nga*, a title analogous to *tripa*, the abbotship of each of the Three Major Monasteries of Lhasa founded later by the Gelug sect. As a result of the close relationship between the Phagdru Kagyu and the local feudal manorial lords—the Lang family—all the abbots of Dansa Thel Monastery were selected from the monk members of the family.

Kublai Khan sent Akon and Milin to Tibet to make a census in 1268. On the basis of this census, thirteen *wan hu* (myriarchy) were installed in U-Tsang. Six *wan hu* were installed in U: Phagmo Drupa, Drigung, Tsalpa, Yazang, Gyama and Thangpoche; another six were installed in Tsang: Latulo, Latu-gyang, Gumo, Chumig, Shang and Shalu; and one in the Yamdrok Lake region. For each *wan hu* a chief was installed. The chiefs were nominated by the Sakya ruling lama and appointed by the Yuan Emperor. It deserves attention that of the thirteen *wan hu* chiefs, four—that of the Phagmo Drupa, Drigung, Tsalpa and Yazang—belonged to the Kagyu sect.

The *Biography of Fifth Dalai Lozang Gyatso* has a record of the census of ten of the thirteen *wan hu* as follows:

The subjects of Latu-gyang *wan hu*: 1,990 households.
The subjects of Latulo *wan hu*: 2,250 households.
The subjects of Chumig *wan hu*: 3,003 households.
The subjects of Shalu *wan hu*: 3,892 households.
The subjects of Yamdrok *wan hu*: 750 households.
The subjects of Drigung *wan hu*: 3,630 households.
The subjects of Tsalpa *wan hu*: 3,700 households.
The subjects of Phagmo Drupa *wan hu*: 2,438 households.
The subjects of Yazang *wan hu*: 3,000 households.
The subjects of Gyama *wan hu*: 5,900 households.

The censuses of the other three *wan hu*—Thangpoche, Shang and Gumo—were not recorded. The households in the record cited above each had to make one person available for unpaid labour under a system called *ula*. So the numbers do not include monks, the inhabitants under the jurisdiction of monasteries or feudal manorial lords, who were, as the Yuan court stipulated, exempt from taxes and service. Incidentally, the number mentioned above shows that Phagmo Drupa had relatively few households—only 2,438—eligible for *ula* service.

The local power of Phagmo Drupa *wan hu*, both secular and spiritual, was in the hands of the Lang family, who handled local affairs through the Chen-nga (abbot) of Dansa Thel Monastery. When the Yuan court established Phagmo Drupa *wan hu*, the abbot of Dansa Thel Monastery, Jewa Rinchen, recommended Dorjepal, caretaker of the cattle of the monastery, to be the chief of the *wan hu* and sent him to offer tribute to Kublai in Beijing. Thus, Dorjepal was appointed by the Yuan court as the first chief of Phagmo Drupa *wan hu*. Dorjepal, who observed strict Buddhist discipline and was always in monk's attire, was a fine example for the monastic and secular populace. He set up twelve manorial estates (known as the *shika* in Tibetan). His good administration of the *shika* promoted the *shika* system. Thereafter, when manorial estates began to enjoy development, Phagdru *wan hu* became stronger.

Rinchen Dorje succeeded Jewa Rinchen to be the abbot of the Dansa Thel. Dorjepal, the first chief of Phagdru *wan hu*, was succeeded, when he died, by his brother Shunu Gyaltsen. The second chief of Phagdru *wan hu* abandoned himself to carefree living and debauchery and died before long. He was not good for the interests of the Lang family. Being recommended by Rinchen Dorje and appointed by the Yuan court, Changchub Shunu became the third chief of Phagdru *wan hu*. He was succeeded by Shunu Yonten. The third and fourth chiefs of Phagdru *wan hu* also behaved themselves badly. Abbot Rinchen Dorje was succeeded by his nephew Drakpa Yeshe, who was in turn succeeded by his brother Drakpa Rinchen. Drakpa Rinchen was on good terms with Great Yuan Imperial Preceptor Drakpa Odser. The Imperial Preceptor recommended Drakpa Rinchen to be concurrently the fifth chief of Phagdru *wan hu*. The Yuan Emperor approved the recommendation.

Chen-nga Drakpa Rinchen, after his death, was succeeded by his nephew Drakpa Gyaltsen (1293-1360, from the thirtieth year of the Zhiyuan reign period of Yuan Emperor Shizu to the twentieth year of the Zhizheng reign period of Yuan Emperor Shundi), who recommended his own brother Drakpa Zangpo to be the sixth chief of Phagdru *wan hu*. But soon Drakpa Zangpo was replaced by Gyaltsen Gyalpo as the seventh chief of that *wan hu*. Later in 1349 (the ninth year of the Zhizheng reign period of Yuan Emperor Shundi), Changchub Gyaltsen was appointed the eighth chief of Phagdru *wan hu*.

Changchub Gyaltsen spared no effort to bolster the growth of manorial estates. At that time the manorial estates had produced a good impact on the economy, because the serfs, having been granted pieces of land, were actively engaged in farming production. This resulted in economic growth and better life in Phagdru district. Phagdru *wan hu* thus became stronger and stronger. During the six years of his reign Changchub annexed the other five *wan hu* in U and the seven *wan hu* in Tsang and the Yamdrok region. Finally in the fourteenth year of the Zhizheng reign period of Yuan Emperor Shundi (1354), he overthrew the Sakya regime, which had been supported by the Yuan court, and thus founded the Phagmo Drupa regime of the Kagyu sect.

According to *Records of Tibetan Kings and Ministers* by the Fifth Dalai Lama, since then U and Tsang were under the rule of the

Phagdru regime and all chiefs in U and Tsang paid tribute and taxes to it.

The chiefs of the other twelve *wan hu*, Imperial Preceptor Kunga Gyaltsen, *Atcharin* Sonam Lodro and governors of the Yarang and Chaba districts all sent delegates to the national capital to denounce Changchub, the head of Phagdru *wan hu*, for his armed invasions. Changchub also lodged several appeals to the Yuan Emperor. In order to remove the Emperor's misgivings, he sent Drongchen Sherab Drashi to take a whole skin of a white lion as a gift for the Yuan Emperor. At that time the Yuan Dynasty, which was close to disintegration, had no power to handle Tibetan affairs, so the Yuan Emperor had to recognize the Phagdru regime in Tibet.

When the Sakya regime was toppled by the Phagdru, the Pacification Commissioners were still in U, Tsang and Ngari Korsum. Changchub appealed to the commissioners as well. According to *The Phagdru's Lineal Description*, the commissioners said to him: "You should go yourself or send people to report to His Majesty." In response, the Yuan Emperor sent to him Dargyas as an imperial envoy with a gold album of certification, granting him the title of Ta Situ and a seal of authority (*Records of Tibetan Kings and Ministers*). Thus, the Phagdru regime of the Kagyu sect began to rule over Tibet.

Changchub Gyaltsen, the first Desi of the Phagdru regime, was born in the sixth year of the Dade reign period of Yuan Emperor Chengzong (1302) and died at sixty-two in the twenty-fourth year of the Zhizheng reign period of Yuan Emperor Shundi (1364). He reigned as Desi for ten years (1354-64, from the fourteenth to the twenty-fourth year of Zhizheng).

After establishing the Phagdru regime, Changchub Gyaltsen set the capital at Nedong of Shannan and built Tsethang Monastery at Tsethang of the same reign. The monastery was mainly engaged in preaching Exoteric Buddhism. Its first abbot was Shakya Gyaltsen, nephew of Changchub Gyaltsen.

Desi Changchub Gyaltsen, in a political reform he initiated, appointed a drongchen under the Desi to handle day-to-day political and religious affairs, a post comparable to that of the *ponchen* under the Sakya ruling lama. Besides, he established thirteen *dzong* (districts) in Tibet. The heads of the *dzong*, called *dzongpon*, were directly appointed by the Phagdru regime. The *dzong*, increasing in number later, became organizations of political power at the grass-root level. The post of *dzongpon* at first was not hereditary, but later, when local independent regimes (the Rinpungpa, for example) seized the power of certain *dzong*, it became hereditary.

Another political reform Changchub made was that he spared no effort to develop the system of manorial estates, which, in turn, promoted economic growth in Phagdru districts. As a result, the reigns of the first five Desis (totalling seventy-eight years, 1354-1432) were called the piping times of peace—the golden age of the Phagdru regime.

The Phagdru's second Desi was Shakya Gyaltsen, son of Changchub's brother Sonam Zangpo. He was born in the sixth year of the Zhiyuan reign period of Yuan Emperor Shundi (1340) and died at thirty-three in the sixth year of the Hongwu reign period of Ming Emperor Taizu (1373).

Shakya Gyaltsen (or Jamyang Shakya Gyaltsen, as he is referred to in the *History of the Ming Dynasty*), who had been a Buddhist monk from childhood, was at thirteen, the abbot of Tsethang Monastery, and at twenty-four (the twenty-fourth year of the Zhizheng reign period of Yuan Emperor Shundi, or 1364), the Phagdru's second Desi. He was granted the title of "Imperial Initiation Master" by the Yuan court, and by the Ming court as well, in the fifth year of the Hongwu reign period of the Ming Dynasty (1372). He died in the sixth year of the Ming Hongwu reign period (1373), having ruled for nine years.

Drakpa Changchub, the regime's third Desi, was a grandson of Changchub Gyaltsen and son of Rinchen Dorje, nephew of Changchub Gyaltsen. He was born in the sixteenth year of the Zhizheng reign period of Yuan Emperor Shundi (1356) and died at thirty in the nineteenth year of the Hongwu reign period of Ming Emperor Taizu (1386).

Drakpa Changchub, who in his childhood became a monk, was respectfully called "Chogshipa" in Tibetan. He was installed by ministers as the regime's third Desi in 1373, when the second Desi, Shakya Gyaltsen, died.

According to *Imperial Records of the Ming Dynasty*: "In the seventh year of Hongwu [1374], U-Tsang Phagmo Drupa Rinchen Drakpa Changchub Gyaltsen Palzangpo sent men to offer tribute." Drakpa Changchub Gyaltsen Palzangpo was none other than Drakpa Changchub. And again: "In the eighth year of Hongwu [1375], by an imperial decree...the Phagmo Drupa *wan hu* was installed." And in the twelfth year of the same reign period (1379): "Phagmo Drupa *wan hu* sent men to offer tribute." These historical records show that Ming Emperor Taizu appointed Drakpa Changchub head of Phagmo Drupa *wan hu*.

In the fourteenth year of the Hongwu reign (1381), Drakpa Changchub resigned his position as Desi and went back to Dansa Thel Monastery to be its Chen-nga (abbot). He had stayed in power for only eight years. During his reign as the Chen-nga, Tsongkhapa studied under his guidance. According to *Records of Tibetan Kings and Ministers*, Tsongkhapa had the greatest esteem for his tutor, Drakpa Changchub, and Master Chen-nga praised Tsongkhapa for his superior wisdom in learning sutras.

The regime's fourth Desi, Sonam Drakpa (brother of the third Desi, Drakpa Changchub), was born in the nineteenth year of the Zhizheng reign period of Yuan Emperor Shundi (1359), and died at forty-nine in the sixth year of the Yongle reign period of Ming Emperor Chengzu (1408). Sonam Drakpa, who in his childhood became a Buddhist monk, became the abbot of Tsethang Monastery from the age of nine for thirteen years (1368-1381). When his brother Drakpa Changchub resigned the position of Desi in 1381, he became the fourth Desi.

There were some mistakes in the records about Sonam Drakpa in the *History of the Ming Dynasty*. According to the *History of the Ming Dynasty*: "When Jamyang Shakya died, his title of Imperial Initiation Master was passed to his successor, Sonam Drakpa Yeshe Zangpo." Jamyang Shakya was Shakya Gyaltsen, the regime's second Desi. In actuality, he was succeeded by the third Desi, Drakpa Changchub, who, in turn, was succeeded by the fourth Desi, Sonam Drakpa—therefore, mention of the third Desi is missing from the record.

The *History of the Ming Dynasty* records:

In the twenty-first year of Hongwu, Sonam Drakpa informed the

Emperor of his succession by his younger brother Drakpa Gyaltsen Palzangpo on account of his illness. Drakpa Gyaltsen Palzangpo was granted the title of Imperial Initiation Master.

The *Imperial Records of the Ming Dynasty* has the same record:

On the *yi-hai* day of the first month of the twenty-first year of Hongwu . . . Phagmo Drupa Imperial Initiation Master Sonam Drakpa Gyaltsen sent a memorial to the Emperor, reporting his succession by his younger brother Drakpa Gyaltsen Palzangpo on account of his illness. The Emperor approved his report.

Thus, Sonam Drakpa appealed to Ming Emperor Taizu for approval for his resignation in the twenty-first year of Hongwu (1388). But in fact he had given his position of Desi to his brother Drakpa Gyaltsen in the eighteenth year of Hongwu (1385). He had actually stayed in the position for only four years (1381-1385). Following his resignation from the position of Desi, Sonam Drakpa became the Chen-nga of Dansa Thel Monastery for nineteen years (1385-1404). In 1404 he resigned his position as the Chen-nga. Four years later, the sixth year of the Yongle reign period (1408), he died.

Phagdru's fifth Desi was Drakpa Gyaltsen (or Drakpa Gyaltsen Palzangpo, as he is referred to in the *History of the Ming Dynasty*), whose father was Shakya Renpa, second Desi Shakya Gyaltsen's younger brother. He was born in the seventh year of the Hongwu reign period (1374) and died at fifty-eight in the seventh year of the Xuande reign period of Ming Emperor Xuanzong (1432). He reigned as Desi for forty-seven years, from the eighteenth year of Hongwu (1385) to the seventh year of Xuande (1432). Drakpa Gyaltsen became a monk in his childhood. At the age of seven he became the abbot of Tsethang Monastery and at eleven took the position of the fifth Desi of the Phagdru regime. His reign marked the piping times of peace of the Phagdru regime, and Tibetan historical works have many references to him.

Of Drakpa Gyaltsen's many deeds, two stand out as his greatest accomplishments. One was that he restored the post-staging stations that had fallen into disrepair at the end of the Yuan Dynasty. The *History of the Ming Dynasty* makes a high assessment of this, and describes how Ming Emperor Chengzu granted him the title of Propagation Prince of Persuasion. The *Imperial Records of the Ming Dynasty* records: "In the twenty-seventh year of Hongwu [1394] U-Tsang Imperial Initiation Master and Prince Drakpa Gyaltsen Palzangpo sent men to offer suits of armour and other tribute."

The *History of the Ming Dynasty* records:

Drakpa Gyaltsen sent men to offer tribute to Emperor Chengzu in the first year of the Yongle reign period and was granted by the Emperor in the fourth year of the same reign period the titles of Propagation Prince of Persuasion and Imperial Initiation Master along with a jade seal with a hydra-shaped top-knob, five hundred taels of silver, three brocade robes, fifty bolts of silk and two hundred *jin* of tea. The next year he was assigned by the Emperor the task of restoring post-staging stations in conjunction with the Guardian Prince of the Doctrine, the Promotion Prince of Virtue, the Imperial Initiation Master of Drigung, the governors of Beri, Do-Kham and Longda and the tribes in Sichuan and Tibet. In the eleventh year of the same reign period, Yang Sanbao, who had been sent as imperial envoy to U-Tsang, came back. The Prince sent his nephew Dargye to come with the envoy to offer tribute. The next year Yang Sanbao was again sent to U-Tsang to restore all the post-staging stations that had not been restored, along with the Propagation Prince of Persuasion, Guardian Prince of the Doctrine and the Promotion Prince of Virtue, as well as the tribes in Sichuan and Tibet. From then on, the roads stretched unobstructed for thousands of *li* and government envoys in transit travelled along these roads without fear of being attacked by bandits. Later the Prince's offering of tribute was frequent. To praise him for his loyalty the Emperor sent Yang Sanbao with images of the Buddha, Buddhist articles, monk robes, silk and cloth and money to the Prince. After that, Dai Xing was also sent to give him money.

His restoration of post-staging stations was indeed a very important contribution to the close relationship between the local regime of Tibet and the central government of the Ming Dynasty.

After that, in 1408, 1409, 1413, 1415, 1416, 1418, and 1423 (in the Yongle reign period), and in 1429 and 1431 (in the Xuande reign period), Propagation Prince of Persuasion Drakpa Gyaltsen sent men to offer tribute to the imperial court and the Ming emperors granted him money and other gifts.

Some of his subordinates went to Beijing to offer their service to the Emperor. For instance, in the fifth year of the Xuande reign period (1430), Gongkar Gyaltsen, an official of Yapulu Garrison under the U-Tsang Propagation Prince of Persuasion, sent Samdrasje to the capital, who said he was willing to work for the Emperor. Samdrasje was granted by the Emperor an official suit, fine clothes, money, silver, a saddled horse and a house. In the same year, Samdrup, who was sent by the Prince to the capital, said he was willing to stay and offer his service to the Emperor. He was also generously treated.

The other great achievement Drakpa Gyaltsen made was that he was a patron of the Gelug sect founded by Tsongkhapa, although the Desi himself belonged to the Kagyu sect. In 1409 (the seventh year of Yongle in Ming Emperor Chengzu's reign), Desi Drakpa Gyaltsen helped Tsongkhapa institute the Monlam Prayer Festival with all the financial and material resources Tibet could provide at that time. In addition, he was also the most important donor to the building of Ganden Monastery, the first monastery of the Gelug sect, in the same year. He gave many manorial estates to the monastery to support its monks.

Although the reign of Drakpa Gyaltsen was the golden age of the Phagdru regime, the seed that caused the regime's decline was also being sown—meaning the growth of the Rinpungpa. After being entitled the Propagation Prince of Persuasion, Drakpa Gyaltsen appointed Namkha Gyaltsen the *dzongpon* of Rinpung Dzong (since then Namkha Gyaltsen's family had been known as Rinpungpa) and concurrently the *ponchen* of Sakya Monastery. Since the time of Ta Situ Changchub Gyaltsen each *dzongpon* of Rinpung Dzong had been concurrently the *ponchen* of Sakya Monastery, which was a political measure taken to place the descendants of the Sakya ruling lama under surveillance.

Afterwards, Namkha Gyaltsen's son Namkha Gyalpo succeeded his father as the Rinpung *dzongpon*. In the fourteenth year of Yongle (1416) Ming Emperor Chengzu established a Regional Military Commission in Rinpung Dzong and appointed Namkha Gyalpo its Assistant Commander (a rank subordinate to the Commander and Vice-Commander), granting him the title of "Wise and Brave General."

In the first year of the Xuande reign period (1426) of Ming

Emperor Xuanzong, Namkha Gyalpo's son, Norbu Zangpo, became the Rinpung *dzongpon* and by order of Ming Emperor Xuanzong inherited the position of the Assistant Commander of Rinpung and the title of "Wise and Brave General".

Norbu Zangpo had five sons. His second son, Kundu Rangpo, was Rinpung *dzongpon*. His third son, Dondrup Dorje, was appointed *dzongpon* of Samdrutse (modern Shigatse). His fourth son, Tsokye Dorje, was appointed *dzongpon* of Yalung Khothor Dzong (later to become the acting Desi of the Phagdru regime). Thus the Rinpungpa became a strong local power.

Phagdru's sixth Desi was Drakpa Jungne. He was the son of Sangye Gyaltsen, brother of Drakpa Gyaltsen. He was born in the twelfth year of the Yongle reign period of Ming Emperor Chengzu (1414) and died at thirty-four in the thirteenth year of the Zhengtong reign period of Ming Emperor Yingzong (1448).

Drakpa Jungne became a monk in his childhood, and at the age of fourteen took the position of abbot of Tsethang Monastery for three years (1428-1431). In the seventh year of Xuande in Ming Emperor Xuanzong's reign (1432) he was appointed Phagdru's sixth Desi. In the eleventh year of Zhengtong in Emperor Yingzong's reign (1446) his father, Sangye Gyaltsen, usurped the position of Desi by forcing him to resign. He had reigned as Desi for fourteen years.

In the fourth year of Zhengtong of Ming Emperor Yingzong's reign (1439) Drakpa Jungne sent the Commander of U-Tsang Garrison, Trulgyi Drupa, to offer tribute to the imperial court. The Emperor bestowed money and the title of Imperial Initiation Master on Drakpa Jungne Gyaltsen Palzangpo (*Imperial Records of the Ming Dynasty*).

In the fifth year of Zhengtong (1440) the central government of the Ming Dynasty again sent Buddhist masters Kelzang and Kun Ling as envoys to bring approval for Phagmo Drupa Imperial Initiation Master Drakpa Jungne Gyaltsen to inherit his uncle's title of "Propagation Prince of Persuasion" and bestowed upon him a royal edict, brocade, Buddhist religious articles and monk robes (*Imperial Records of the Ming Dynasty*).

In the tenth year of Zhengtong (1445), "U-Tsang Imperial Initiation Master and Prince of Persuasion Drakpa Jungne Gyaltsen

Palzangpo sent Drashi Shingji and other Tibetan monks to offer horses and other tribute to the imperial court. The Emperor gave a banquet to the envoys and ordered them to take gifts and money to the Propagation Prince of Persuasion" (*Imperial Records of the Ming Dynasty*).

The first Desi of the Phagdru regime, Changchub Gyaltsen, had stipulated that only a monk, usually the Chen-nga of Dansa Thel Monastery, or the abbot of Tsethang Monastery, was to assume the office of Desi. But this institution was violated by Sangye Gyaltsen, sixth Desi Drakpa Jungne's father. Sangye Gyaltsen, who was a layman, was married and had two sons—Drakpa Jungne and Kunga Legpa. By the institution he was not qualified to be the Desi. Nevertheless, in order to usurp Phagdru power, he forced his son Drakpa Jungne, the sixth Desi, to pass the office of Desi to him. In the eleventh year of Zhengtong (1446) Sangye Gyaltsen became the seventh Desi of the Phagdru regime. He reigned as Desi for twenty-two years until his death in the fourth year of Chenghua in Ming Emperor Xianzong's reign (1468).

Tibetan historical books have records different from Chinese books concerning Sangye Gyaltsen's assumption of the post of Desi. The *Records of Tibetan Kings and Ministers*, written by the Fifth Dalai Lama, does not mention that Sangye Gyaltsen was a Desi, but says that his two sons (Drakpa Jungne and Kunga Legpa) had been Desi, one after the other. But the *Imperial Records of the Ming Dynasty* says:

> In the eleventh year of Zhengtong (1446) Temporary Successor to Prince of Persuasion Sangye Gyaltsen Palzangpo, father of the preceding Prince of Persuasion, Drakpa Jungne Gyaltsen Palzangpo, was granted by the Emperor a royal edict and money, which were taken to him by the officials from the Ministry of Rites and Gos Gongpa, the envoy sent to the capital by the Prince of Persuasion.

Here "temporary successor" probably means Sangye Gyaltsen was only an acting Desi.

The Phagdru's seventh Desi was Sangye Gyaltsen, Prince of Persuasion Drakpa Gyaltsen's brother. He was born in the twenty-ninth year of Hongwu in Ming Emperor Taizu's reign (1396) and died at seventy-two in the fourth year of Chenghua in Ming Emperor Xianzong's reign (1468). From the time of Sangye Gyaltsen, Phagdru's Desi was allowed to be a layman and the post became hereditary.

The eighth Desi, Kunga Legpa, who was Sangye Gyaltsen's second son and Drakpa Jungne's younger brother, was born in the eighth year of Xuande in Ming Emperor Xuanzong's reign (1433) and died at sixty-two in the eighth year of Hongzhi in Ming Emperor Xiaozong's reign (1495). As Phagdru's eighth Desi, he reigned for twenty-seven years (1468-1495, from the fourth year of Chenghua in Ming Emperor Xianzong's reign to the eighth year of Hongzhi in Ming Emperor Xiaozong's reign). Before becoming the Desi, he had been the abbot of Tsethang Monastery for four years (1444-1448). According to *Records of Tibetan Kings and Ministers*, his wife was from an aristocratic Rinpung family and bore him a son by the name of Rinchen Dorje Wangyal—so he evidently resumed secular life after his reign.

Kunga Legpa was authorized by the Ming court to inherit the title of Propagation Prince of Persuasion. Says *Imperial Records of the Ming Dynasty*:

In the fifth year of Chenghua [1469], by an imperial order, Kunga Legpa Jungne Lingzan Gyaltsen Palzangpo, son of the Imperial Initiation Master, Sangye Gyaltsen, succeeded to his father's title.

Kunga Legpa also had close relations with the central government of the Ming Dynasty. According to *Imperial Records of the Ming Dynasty*, in 1477, 1479, 1480, 1481, 1482 and 1485 (in the Chenghua reign period), and in 1488 and 1495 (in the Hongzhi reign period), Kunga Legpa sent envoys to offer tribute to the Ming court and the emperors gave gifts, including brocades and money, in return upon each presentation of tribute, in addition to banquets to his envoys.

In his remaining years Kunga Legpa was in discord with his wife. Says *Records of Tibetan Kings and Ministers*:

Later the King of Tsang believed in slanders made by the Geshepa brothers. Thus the slanders sowed discord between the king and queen. Yagong Gyalwa and Sandewa stood on the queen's side, while Lewu Ngog on the king's side. The discord caused many troubles. Fortunately Jungjepa Dorje Tseten, who did not stand on either side, mediated between the king and queen. His effort brought goodwill between the ministers. He performed meritorious service for the regime of Tibet.

The background of the struggle between the king's party and the queen's party was the scramble of the king's family, Lang, and the queen's family, Rinpung, for power and profit. Kunga Legpa had no son, so after his death Ngagi Wangpo, Chen-nga of Dansa Thel Monastery, succeeded him to be the ninth Desi. Whose son was Ngagi Wangpo? He was perhaps the son of the sixth Desi Drakpa Jungne or Gongrang Robi Dorje, according to *Records of Tibetan Kings and Ministers*. But the question remains to be solved by those who engage in the genealogical study of the Phagdru regime.

After he had been enthroned as the ninth Desi, Ngagi Wangpo, taking his ministers' advice, took the worldly life again by getting married. According to *Records of Tibetan Kings and Ministers*:

He married Tsongkhapa's daughter...who bore him a son named Nga-wang Drashi Drakpa.... Not long after his son's birth Ngagi Wangpo fell seriously ill. On his deathbed, Ngagi Wangpo was very anxious about his son. Chosje Drakpa, Chen-nga of Dansa Thel Monastery, said to the dying Desi that he would be loyal to the young crown prince and be devoted to his own duty to maintain the dynasty's high reputation.

According to tradition, Ngagi Wangpo should have requested the central government to let him inherit the title of Propagation Prince of Persuasion as soon as he assumed the post of the ninth Desi in 1495. But, owing to the damaged post-staging stations and obstructed roads, he did not send envoys to Beijing until two years later. He never received the title of Propagation Prince of Persuasion the Ming Emperor Xiaozong conferred on him in response to his application for the title in 1497 (the tenth year of the Emperor's reign); he died before the Emperor's envoy reached Tibet for the title-conferring ceremony. The *History of the Ming Dynasty* says:

In the tenth year of Hongzhi [1497] U-Tsang Prince of Persuasion died. His [eighth Desi Kunga Legpa's] son Ngagi Wangpo Drakpa applied to inherit the title of the Prince of Persuasion. The Emperor sent Tibetan monks Tsematsan Mantashri and Sonam Odser as envoy and vice-envoy, together with Tsemon Drashi Gyaltsen and eighteen other people, to grant Ngagi Wangpo Drakpa a title-conferring imperial edict and gifts, such as brocades, clothes and tea. But he died before the envoys arrived for the title-conferring ceremony after a journey of three years. His son Ngawang Drashi Drakpa Gyaltsen Palzangpo requested to receive the edict and the gifts from the Emperor. The envoys could not but satisfy him and brought back his father's seal and document granted by the Ministry of Rites. The governor of Sichuan accused the envoys of violating the established rules by making the granting without the permission of the Emperor. So they were arrested in Sichuan and sent to the capital to be beheaded. They begged the Emperor again and again for mercy. The Emperor thought it was not good to punish Tibetans severely and thus decided to exile the envoys to Pingliang of Shaanxi instead of execution and set the others free.

According to historical records, Phagdru's ninth Desi Ngagi Wangpo was born in the third year of Zhengtong in Ming Emperor Yingzong's reign (1438) and died at seventy-two in the fifth year of Zhengde of Ming Emperor Wuzong's reign (1510). He reigned for fifteen years (1495-1510, from the eighth year of Hongzhi in Ming Emperor Xiaozong's reign to the fifth year of Zhengde in Ming Emperor Wuzong's reign).

Phagdru's tenth Desi Ngawang Drashi Drakpa, son of Ngagi Wangpo, was born in the twelfth year of Hongzhi in Ming Emperor Xiaozong's reign (1499) and died at seventy-two in the fifth year of Longqing in Ming Emperor Muzong's reign (1571, at Yangpachen, according to *New Red Annals*).

When Ngagi Wangpo died, his son Ngawang Drashi Drakpa was only a little boy. So the fourth ruling lama of the Red Hat line of the Karma Kagyu sect, Chosdrak Yeshe, and Rinpungpa Norbu Zangpo's son Chosje Dorje acted for the Desi in handling Phagdru's politico-religious affairs for eight years (1510-1518).

Kunga Legpa's marriage brought the Rinpungpa family's power into the Phagdru regime. In fact, a large part of Phagdru power fell into the hands of the Rinpungpa family. Donyo Dorje, son of Rinpungpa Norbu Zangpo's second son, Kundu Rangpo (Chosje Dorje's nephew), seized by force Tsagar Chu, Lunpoz and other *shikas* of the Nedong *dzongpon*, Phagdru's personal attendant. In order to win the support of the fourth ruling lama of the Red Hat line of the Karma Kagyu sect, Chosdrak Yeshe (who was one of Phagdru's acting regents), Donyo Dorje donated many *shikas*, large tracts of pastoral land and a large amount of wealth to help the ruling lama build a monastery in Yangpachen. Thus the Rinpungpa colluded with the Red Hat line ruling lama of the Karma Kagyu sect, and they changed from the Phagdru regime's patronizing attitude towards the Gelug sect to indulging in relentless persecution of the Gelug.

In the thirteenth year of Zhengde in Ming Emperor Wuzong's reign (1518), Ngawang Drashi Drakpa became the tenth Desi of the Phagdru regime. The situation was turning for the better for the Gelug sect. The Phagdru regime gave its support to the Gelug once again.

The tenth Desi of the Phagdru regime, who had not received formal recognition from the central government of the Ming Dynasty, offered tribute to the imperial court in the name of his father, Ngagi Wangpo (the assumption of a title without the Emperor's permission as mentioned above was ineffective, of course). As the *Imperial Records of the Ming Dynasty* says, Ngawang Drashi Drakpa offered tribute to the imperial court in the fourth year (1509) and ninth year (1514) of Zhengde and the third year (1524), thirty-third year (1554) and fortieth year (1561) of Jiaqing in his father's name. It was not until the forty-second year of Jiaqing (1563) that the tenth Desi was granted the title of Propagation Prince of Persuasion. The *History of the Ming Dynasty* says:

> In response to the request of U-Tsang Prince of Persuasion, the Emperor, following an established precedent, sent twenty-two Tibetan monks, including Yonten Padma and others, as envoys under an official, Zhu Tingdui, with a title-conferring imperial edict to Tibet. But the monks did not obey Zhu Tingdui on the journey. Zhu reported it to the court. So the Ministry of Rites proposed that from then on such edicts would be taken back to Tibet by the envoy from the Prince who requested for it or by monks under his jurisdiction, instead of sending monks from the inland. The proposal was approved by the Emperor.

For all the trouble, Ngawang Drashi Drakpa gained the recognition of the central regime of the Ming Dynasty.

In the fifth year of Longqing in Ming Emperor Muzong's reign (1571) Ngawang Drashi Drakpa died. He reigned for fifty-three years (1518-1571). In his reign the Phagdru regime was coming close to disintegration and the Rinpungpa was also declining in power. At that time a serf owner of Tsang by the name of Shingshapa (Tsangpa Khan's forefather) rose.

In the forty-fourth year of Jiaqing in Ming Emperor Shizong's reign (1565) Ngawang Namgyal, son of Rinpungpa Chosje Dorje, lost his manorial estates in Nedong and had to go back to be the Rinpung *dzongpon* because he had offended the king of Tsang, Ngawang Drashi Drakpa. His son Ngawang Jigme Drakpa succeeded him as the Rinpung *dzongpon*. His personal attendant, Shingshapa Tseten Dorje, being hand in glove with local chiefs of western Tsang, then overthrew the Rinpungpa rule and claimed himself as the King of Upper Tsang (Tsang-tod Gyalpo). So only U still remained under tenth Desi Ngawang Drashi Drakpa's rule.

The Phagdru's eleventh and last Desi was Drowai Gongpo (or Drashi Zangpo, as he is referred to in the *History of the Ming Dynasty*), son of tenth Desi Ngawang Drashi Drakpa. According to *Records of Tibetan Kings and Ministers*, King of Tsang Ngawang Drashi Drakpa married Rinpungpa's daughter and she bore him two sons, who were King of Tsang Drowai Gongpo and Chen-nga Drajungwa. Drowai Gongpo went to Kunga and got married there. Drowai's son was Ngawang Drakpa.

According to the *New Red Annals*, Drowai Gongpo was born in the Earth-Dragon year of the tenth Tibetan calendrical cycle, or the second year of Longqing in Ming Emperor Muzong's reign (1568) and died at fifty in the forty-sixth year of Wanli of Ming Emperor Shenzong (1618).

Says *Records of Tibetan Kings and Ministers*: "After the death of Drowai Gongpo, a stupa decorated with jewels was built to contain his remains and for it was built Kongri Gapo [meaning 'white'] Palace."

But the date of his death was not mentioned. Drowai Gongpo's last tribute was paid, according to the *Imperial Records of the Ming Dynasty*, in the forty-sixth year of the Wanli reign period (1618), when the Phagdru regime was overthrown by Tsangpa Khan, so Drowai Gongpo was perhaps killed in that year.

As to when Drowai Gongpo was granted the honorific title by the Ming Dynasty, says the *History of the Ming Dynasty*:

> In the seventh year of Wanli [1579] the Tibetan envoy who brought the tribute to Beijing said that the eldest son of the Prince of Persuasion, Drashi Zangpo, asked to succeed to his father's office. Emperor Shenzong approved his request and granted him, by taking minister Shen Yiguan's advice, the title of Imperial Initiation Master and Propagation

Prince of Persuasion of Phagmo Drupa in U-Tsang.

From then on Drowai Gongpo kept close relations with the central regime of the Ming Dynasty, as the *Imperial Records of the Ming Dynasty* notes:

In the fifteenth year of Wanli [1587] the Propagation Prince of Persuasion in U-Tsang sent six hundred Tibetan monks headed by Rinchen to offer tribute and was granted gifts....

In the sixteenth year of Wanli [1588] the Propagation Prince of Persuasion of U-Tsang sent one thousand people, headed by Tse Dorje, to offer tribute....

In the twenty-fifth year of Wanli [1597] banquets were given to fifteen Tibetan monks sent by the U-Tsang Propagation Prince of Persuasion to offer tribute....

In the thirty-ninth year of Wanli [1611] brocade, silk, silver and money were given to the fifteen envoys headed by Gyentso Dorje who were sent to pay tribute by the Propagation Prince of Persuasion of U-Tsang....

In the forty-fifth year of Wanli [1617] the Propagation Prince of Persuasion in U-Tsang sent one thousand people, headed by Sonam Gyaltsen, a State Tutor, to offer coral, Tibetan woolen cloth and other tribute. Silk and money were given in return to the envoys....

In the forty-sixth year of Wanli [1618] the Propagation Prince of Persuasion of U-Tsang sent fifteen Tibetan monks, Samten Dorje, etc., to offer coral, rhinoceros horns, Tibetan woolen cloth, etc.

It merits our attention that the book has no record of the Prince offering tribute after the forty-sixth year of Wanli. According to the *Autobiography* of Fourth Panchen Lama Lozang Choskyi, Tsang-pa Khan captured the Nedong palace and overthrew the Phagdru regime, which had ruled over Tibet for 264 years, in that year.

Drowai Gongpo reigned as Desi for forty-seven years (1571-1618, from the fifth year of Longqing in Ming Emperor Muzong's reign to the forty-sixth year of Wanli in Ming Emperor Shenzong's reign).

After the death of the last Desi, Drowai Gongpo, his descendants still lived in the Nedong palace. According to *Records of Tibetan Kings and Ministers*, Drowai Gongpo's son was Ngawang Drakpa (called prince instead of king in that book), who had two sons —Kagyu Langpa Gyalwa and Namgyal Drakpa. Not long after, Langpa Gyalwa died. His son Mipham Sonam Wangchuk Drakpa

Namgyal lived in the Nedong palace. When the Fifth Dalai wrote the *Records of Tibetan Kings and Ministers*, Mipham Sonam Wangchuk Drakpa Namgyal was still alive.

As to the descendants of the Phagmo Drupa rulers, the *Imperial Records of the Qing Dynasty* has a record of them. In the fourteenth year of Shunzhi (1657) Qing Emperor Shizu said in an edict to Fifth Dalai Lama Lozang Gyatso:

> Since I came to the throne, the Propagation Prince of Persuasion has offered tribute three times, with one thousand envoys each time. I gave him two seals in recognition of his loyalty. Now he has sent Gyentso Napo to offer tribute with a jade seal and imperial certificate granted by the Ming Dynasty in order to exchange them for a new seal and certificate. I have been told that the Propagation Prince of Persuasion was originally King of Tubbat and then was overthrown by Tsangpa Khan. Tsangpa Khan was overthrown later by Gushri Khan of Oylut. The latter put the Prince of Persuasion under the Fifth Dalai Lama, who again put the Prince under the Depa. The Prince of Persuasion was then ordained into full monkhood by the Dalai.... According to the envoy, Gyentso Napo, the Prince has been put under the Depa for a long time. But he still offered tribute and made reports to the court in the name of the Propagation Prince of Persuasion. Now he has come to ask that the seals and certificate be exchanged without reporting the truth. You shall tell me the truth in a report to the court through Lama Samten Gelong.

The edict showed that the central regime of the Qing Dynasty did not recognize the former status of the Prince of Persuasion in Tibet and put the former prince under the Depa's jurisdiction. After that, Phagmo Drupa's lineage vanished from the political stage of Tibet.

# II. An Account of the Qing Dynasty's Administration of Tibet and the Qing Resident Officials in Tibet

The period from the latter part of Fourth Panchen Lozang Choskyi's life to the beginning of Ninth Panchen Choskyi Nyima's life covered the 269 years of the rule of the Qing Dynasty, from the seventh year of Chongde in Qing Emperor Taizong's reign (1642) to the third year of Xuantong Emperor's reign (1911). The Qing's administration of Tibet, and particularly the role of its resident officials (Ambans) in Tibet, deserves further discussion.

During the Qing Dynasty, Tibetan affairs were managed by the Board for National Minority Affairs, a government department in charge of affairs of national minorities not only in Tibet, but also in Outer and Inner Mongolia, Xinjiang, the northwest and other areas of China. It had been established by the Manchus before the Qing Dynasty was officially founded in Beijing. The board was headed by a minister and two vice-ministers, and it consisted of several *si* (bureau). Tibetan affairs were originally handled by the *Rouyuan Si*, but later they became too many for one *si* to cope with, so the *Rouyuanhou Si* was established to specially manage the affairs of the Gurkha, Oylut and Tangut.

As there was a great deal of correspondence from Tibet, a Tangut Office (equal to a *si* in status) was set up under the board to do the translation, and a number of Manchu young aristocrats were selected to study Tibetan in this office.

As to the installation of Qing Imperial Residents—the Ambans as they are known in Tibetan—it was a matter occurring afterwards. There were no Qing resident officials in Tibet for a period of eighty-four years, from the first year of Shunzhi (1644) to the sixth year of Yongzheng (1728). Tibetan affairs at that time were handled by officials of the Board for National Minority Affairs, who were sent from Beijing to Tibet periodically and came back to report after the completion of the task. For instance, in the first year of Yongzheng (1723) E Lai, senior secretary of the Board for National Minority Affairs, after being promoted to an Academician of the Grand Secretariat and concurrently Vice-Minister of Rites, was sent to Tibet to cope with local affairs. In the fifth year of Yongzheng (1727) Academician of the Grand Secretariat Sengge and Vice-Commander Mala were sent to the Dalai Lama after Vice-Commander E Qi had made an inspection tour of Tibet. In the sixth year of Yongzheng (1728) Yue Zhongqi, Governor-General of Sichuan and Shaanxi, mentioned in a memorial to the Emperor that Imperial Residents in Tibet Mala and Sengge had gone to the Potala to protect the Dalai Lama. Thus appeared for the first time the term "Imperial Residents in Tibet."

At that time a singular incident broke out in Tibet. Ngabopa, Lumpanas and Jaranas allied with each other in an armed clash and killed Khangchennas. The Qing court sent Jalangga, Minister of Personnel, to handle the aftermath of the incident. Jalangga said in a memorial:

> By Your Majesty's order we started with an army from Xining on the sixth of the fifth month and arrived in Tibet on the first of the eighth month. We immediately formed a court of justice with Vice-Commander Mala and Academician of the Grand Secretariat Sengge to interrogate Ngabopa, Lumpanas and Jaranas.

In this memorial the term "Imperial Resident in Tibet" was not mentioned.

In the seventh year of Yongzheng (1729) Qing Emperor Shizong issued an order: "To the Ministry of War: Vice-Commander Mala shall stay in Litang along with Naige to take care of the Dalai Lama."

Later in the same year another order was given to the Ministry of War: "Mala shall reside in Tibet and Tibetan affairs be handled by Mala and Sengge with Mailu and Bao Jinzhong as their assistants." Thus, Mala and Sengge were in fact resident officials in Tibet. It is not known in which year the official installation of Imperial Residents began in Tibet. But there is no doubt that the first two Residents in Tibet were Mala and Sengge.

In the ninth year of Yongzheng (1731) Qing Emperor Shizong instructed:

Vice-Commander Mala and Academician of the Grand Secretariat Sengge have been in Tibet for several years. I order that Qing Bao, the Mongolian Vice-Commander of the Blue Banner, and Miao Shou, Chief Minister of the Court of Judicial Review, be sent to replace them. But if both Mala and Sengge come back at the same time, it will be difficult for the newcomers to handle local affairs because of not knowing local conditions. So Mala will come back first and Sengge will stay for another year to help Qing Bao and Miao Shou.

In the first year of Qianlong (1736) ministers reported in a memorial to the Emperor:

There had been no resident officials in Tibet before the armed conflict between Khangchennas and Pholhanas. Owing to the incident, ministers with troops were sent to reside in Tibet temporarily. Now the Dalai Lama has gone back to Tibet and the army has also withdrawn. There is no need to have resident officials in Tibet anymore.

Nevertheless, in view of the importance of Tibetan affairs, Emperor Qianlong, in the second year of his reign (1737), ordered to

call back Vice-Commander Nasutai, who has been in Tibet for many years. Han Yilu shall stay in Tibet. He, together with Regional Commander Zhou Qifeng, shall be in charge of Tibetan affairs in Tibet. Other minor officials under them such as *zhangjing* and *bichiche* shall be rotated home according to the established system.

It is evident at that time the Imperial Resident's Office (yamen) had already been established, and there were such subalterns as *zhangjing* and *bichiche* for handling the daily affairs in the office.

In the forty-fifth year of Qianlong (1780) resident ministers began to be clearly defined as "Imperial Resident" and "Assistant Resident." In most cases the former was promoted from the latter's position. The first Assistant Resident was Bao Tai. From then on it became gradually clear that there was only one Resident and one Assistant Resident, with the term of office usually being three years. Thus, the institution was clearly defined in the tenth year of Qianlong (1745). The last Resident Lian Yu, made a proposition to the imperial court to cancel the post of Assistant Resident in Tibet.

His proposal was approved. At the same time, though, two counselors were installed. But less than a year afterwards the Revolution of 1911 broke out. With the revolution, gone was the institution of Imperial Residents in Tibet.

Under the Imperial Residents was installed the post of *zhangjing*, which was always filled by a Yuanwailang (second-class secretary) or a *zhushi* (assistant) of the Board for National Minority Affairs and whose tenure of office was also three years. In addition, there were *bichiche*— who dealt with the translation of the Manchu, Tibetan and Chinese languages—a Tibetan language interpreter and a Gurkha language interpreter.

As to the number of guards, Fukand'an stipulated in the fifty-seventh year of the Qianlong reign period (1792): thirty for the Imperial Resident's Office, eight for the *youji* (an army officer with the rank of lieutenant-colonel), six for the *dusi* (an army officer one rank below *youji*), four for the *shoubei* (second captain), four for the *zhangjing*, two for the *bichiche*, one for the *qianzong* (lieutenant), one for the *bazong* (sergeant) and eight for the grannery in U (*Historical Records of the Ming and Qing Dynasties*).

Imperial Residents acted on behalf of the central government and kept watch on the local regime of Tibet. In the fifty-seventh year of the Qianlong reign period (1792), Fukang'an, together with the Dalai Lama and the Panchen Lama, worked out the Twenty-nine Article Ordinance for More Effective Governing of Tibet. It had the following regulations concerning the functions and powers of the resident officials:

> The Imperial Resident in Tibet, being the supervisor of Tibetan administration, shall have the power and authority equal to that of the Dalai Lama and the Panchen Erdeni, and all those working under the Kalons, including the chief lamas, are subject to the Resident's supervision and authorization regardless of their position or rank.
>
> When vacancies arise in the office of *kalon, dapon, tsepon* or *changzod*, candidates shall be selected by the Imperial Resident and the Dalai Lama and shall be submitted to His Majesty for approval and appointment. The relatives of the Dalai and the Panchen shall be barred from holding public office.
>
> The *khenpos* of the major monasteries shall be appointed jointly by the Dalai Lama and the Resident and be given documents of authorization. The appointment of the *khenpos* in small monasteries shall

continue to be the responsibility of the Dalai Lama.

In order to exercise effective control, the Imperial Resident's Office and the Dalai Lama shall each be provided with a complete list of the names of monks of the monasteries in the charge of the Dalai Lama, and two other lists, to be prepared by the Kalons and Hutuktus, of the names of the inhabitants in the villages under the latters' charge.

In the Tashilhunpo the position left vacant by the *changzod* shall be filled by the *solpon* lama or the *zimpon* lama, the position left vacant by the *solpon* shall be filled by the *jedrung* lama, and the position left vacant by the *zimpon* lama shall be filled by the *dronyer*. The appointment of the *changzod*, *solpon* and *zimpon* shall be the joint responsibility of the Panchen Erdeni and the Imperial Resident.

The rent and taxes paid in U and Tsang shall be given to the Dalai Lama and the Panchen Erdeni. Checking the *Shangshang*'s expenses shall be the responsibility of the Imperial Resident.

No lay or monastic officials shall be allowed to use the *ula* (unpaid labour) service when they travel on private business. The *ula* service entitlement papers issued to those travelling on government duties shall bear the seals of the Imperial Resident and the Dalai Lama and shall bear the number.

The rich and Hutuktus have been given papers exempting them from corvée. All these papers shall be withdrawn.... Only those who deserve the corvée-exempting privilege for their meritorious service shall be eligible for these papers, which shall be issued to them jointly by the Dalai Lama and the Resident.

All the negotiations with foreign tribes, such as the Gurkha, Brukpa and Drenjong, will be the responsibility of the Resident. Correspondence from foreign countries contiguous to Tibet to be forwarded to the Dalai Lama or the Panchen Erdeni shall be subject to censorship by the Resident, who then will prepare the necessary reply to be delivered by courier. The Kalons shall not be allowed to maintain private correspondence with foreign countries.

Travellers and traders from Balebu, Kashmir and other places shall be allowed to do business in Tibet. A list of their names and numbers shall be forwarded to the Imperial Resident's Office to be put on file for reference.

Foreign traders must have travel permits issued to them by the Resident, and they shall produce their papers for inspection when passing through Gyantse and Dingri. The two checkpoints shall register the names and numbers of foreign traders who come to Tibet from outside and report this to the Resident to be put on file for reference.

In addition to the functions and powers mentioned above, the Imperial Resident had overall command of the Qing armed forces stationed in Tibet. The Qing government made several campaigns in Tibet over a period of more than a hundred years in the reign periods from Kangxi to Qianlong. However, because Tibet was too poor to support them, the troops were almost all withdrawn after each campaign. Only a few troops and officers were left behind on garrison duty. In Lhasa were 455 resident Qing troops stationed under a *youji*, a *shoubei*, two *qianzong*, two *bazong* and five *waiwei* (corporal). In Shigatse were 140 soldiers and officers, including a *dusi*, a *bazong* and a *waiwei*. In Gyantse were twenty soldiers and officers, a *shoubei* and a *waiwei*. In Dingri were forty soldiers and officers, including a *shoubei*, a *bazong* and a *waiwei*. In Chamdo and other places were 618 soldiers and officers, including a *youji*, a *qianzong*, a *bazong* and a *waiwei*, in addition to a *shoubei* and a *bazong* in Gyankha Xun (a *Xun* was a place which had resident troops), a *waiwei* in Lishu Xun, a *bazong* and a *waiwei* in Shibangou Xun, a *bazong* in Angdi Xun, a *qianzong* and a *waiwei* in Shuoban-do Xun, a *bazong* and a *waiwei* in Lhali Xun, and a *waiwei* in Gyamda Xun.

Fukang'an said in a memorial in the fifty-seventh year of Qian-long (1792):

Investigation shows that Gyantse and Dingri are two important places on the way for foreigners to come into Tibet, but there are no troops stationed there. So I propose to set up two *xuns* there, with forty troops under a *shoubei*, a *bazong* and a *waiwei* in Dingri, and twenty troops under a *shoubei* and a *waiwei* in Gyantse. Of the troops, forty will be sent from Chamdo, ten from Lhali and ten from Tsang, and the officers will be sent from Sichuan Province. They will be substituted with newcomers according to the traditional rotation system. On his inves-tigation tour, the Imperial Resident will supervise their military training.

The proposal was approved.

Besides, Fukang'an proposed in a memorial to the Emperor to set up a standing army of three thousand Tibetan soldiers in Tibet under the command of six *dapons*. According to the authorized organization of the Tibetan troops, a *dapon* was in charge of 500 men and had under him two officers with the rank of *rupon;* each *rupon* was in charge of 250 men; under the *rupon* were two officers with the rank of *gyapon*, each with 125 men in his charge; and under a *gyapon* were five officers with the rank of *dingpons*, who were in charge of 25 men each. Of the army's military equipment 50 percent, as he proposed, was guns, 30 percent bows and arrows, and 20 percent swords and spears.

Of the three thousand Tibetan troops, one thousand were stationed in Lhasa, one thousand in Shigatse, five hundred in Gyantse and five hundred in Dingri. They were under the control of the Dalai Lama and the Resident. The *dapons* were given estates by the Dalai Lama. The *rupons* were each paid 30 taels of silver annually, the *gyapons* 20 taels, and the *dingpons* 14.8 taels. The silver for this purpose was provided by the Tibetan government, and the payment was made by the Resident in the spring and autumn seasons. Each of the Tibetan soldiers was annually provided with 2.5 piculs of Tibetan barley and every day a *jin* (500 grams) of *tsamba* (parched barley flour) by the Tibetan government. The food rations and wages for the three thousand Tibetan troops and officers came mainly from the property of Shamarpa and Gyumey Namgyal, which had been confiscated by the Tibetan government.

All the military food rations and weapons (guns, powder, shot, bows and arrows, swords and spears, etc.) for resident troops in Tibet were transported from the inland. The transportation was a hard task, particularly in the war against the Gurkhas' second invasion of Tibet in the fifty-sixth year of Qianlong (1791). To solve the problem of transportation, six grain-transportation stations were established—one each in Tachienlu, Litang, Batang, Chamdo, Lhali and Lhasa. The *liangwu* (officials in charge of grain-transportation stations) in Tachienlu and Lhasa were selected from *tongzhis* (sub-prefects) and *tongpans* (assistant sub-prefects), and those in the other four places from *xiancheng* (assistant county heads) and *zhoutong* (first-class assistant department magistrate). Sometime later in Lhasa was installed a deputy *liangwu* in charge of coining money. The *liangwu* installed in Shigatse was responsible for the issuing of provisions to Tibetan soldiers and the fulfillment of tasks entrusted by the Imperial Resident. The term of office for each *liangwu* was three years. All *liangwu* were sent by Sichuan Province.

The six grain stations were under the jurisdiction of Sichuan Province and Tibet, respectively: the stations in Tachienlu, Litang and Batang were under the charge of the Office of the General of Sichuan Province; the stations in Chamdo, Lhali and Lhasa were under the Imperial Resident in Tibet.

The main task of the grain station was the transportation of grain, provisions and weapons to Tibet. The traditional *ula* corvée system was still the main method for the transportation—that is, grain, provisions and weapons were carried from station to station by manpower and pack animals rendered by the local people. Nevertheless, rather than being unpaid, the service for this transportation was hired at a fair wage. The Sichuan Governor-General Li Shijie said in a memorial in the fifty-third year of Qianlong (1788): "The pay for the service rendered for grain transportation, according to my judgment, will be 26.8 taels of silver for each picul of grain carried from Tachienlu to Tibet."

Sun Shiyi, Governor-General of Sichuan Province, who was sent to do rear service in Lhasa in the fifty-sixth year of Qianlong (1791), said in a report to the Emperor: "For each picul of army provisions, if it is carried from the inland, more than thirty taels of silver will be paid, but if bought in Tibet, only three taels are enough for one picul."

Evidently, the expenses on the grain for the army would be reduced by 90 percent if the grain was bought in Tibet. So Sun's proposal was accepted by the Qing Emperor Gaozong. Since then a part of the army provisions was bought in Tibet—ten thousand piculs at most, owing to Tibet's low-level production of grain. For instance, it was stipulated that the grain stations in Chamdo, Shuobando and Lhali each should buy two thousand piculs of grain locally every year. This shows that most of the army provisions were still carried from the inland.

Between every two major grain stations were set up several sub-stations, with a total of fifty from Tachienlu to Lhasa. The pay to every porter was according to how many sub-stations he had passed. The line of grain stations was extended from Lhasa westwards to Shegar in the war against the Gurkhas' second invasion in the fifty-seventh year of the Qianlong reign period (1792). According to the *Imperial Records of the Qing Dynasty:*

Originally, twenty-two army service stations were set up between Lhasa and Shegar. The transportation of army provisions, however, is quite different from that of soldiers. Considering the complexity and difficulty of the grain transportation, Fukang'an proposed to set up twenty-four grain stations from Lhasa to Shigatse and twenty-four from Shigatse to Shegar. Fukang'an's proposal was accepted.

The grain stations from Lhasa to Shegar were dismantled after the war. Those from Tachienlu to Lhasa were maintained until the end of the Qing Dynasty.

The post-staging stations, also called *tangpu*, in Tibet were also under the charge of the Imperial Resident. The Resident's reports to the imperial court and imperial edicts to the Resident were all transmitted by messengers on horseback from station to station.

The post-staging transportation was different in speed, ranging from four-hundred *li*, five hundred *li* or six hundred *li* for a day and night. According to the *Imperial Records of the Qing Dynasty*, at the speed of six hundred *li* a day it took ten days from Beijing to Chengdu and about twenty-odd days from Chengdu to Lhasa. For that time such a speed of postal delivery was quite impressive.

In order to meet the urgent needs of the postal deliveries, the post-staging stations were well-stocked with horses. According to the *Imperial Records of the Qing Dynasty*, each post-staging station was provided in ordinary circumstances with five horses; later, five more were added. During the war against the Gurkhas each station was provided with twenty horses, while sub-stations were provided with ten. All the horses were supplied by the local Tibetan inhabitants. The annual fee for each horse was eight taels of silver, according to the *Imperial Records of the Qing Dynasty*.

The messengers of post-staging stations were selected from officers and soldiers. Says the *Imperial Records of the Qing Dynasty*:

> The post-staging stations are run by a *youji*, a *shoubei*, ten *qianzong*, ten *bazong* and one thousand soldiers.... When positions become vacant, the Resident shall select candidates from officers and soldiers in Tibet.... It is 1,960 *li* from Jiayuqiao (west of Enda and east of Lhorong Dzong) to Lhasa...and all the area is Tibetan-inhabited. There are altogether twenty-five post-staging stations and three *xuns* on the road. Supplies for the men stationed in the stations are provided by *depas*.

According to *A General History of U-Tsang*, there were fifty-three post-staging stations from Tachienlu to Lhasa with one thousand officers and soldiers (on average, each with about eighteen men). The messengers and their horses were required to be strong enough to meet the urgent needs of postal delivery. The expenses of the post-staging stations in Chamdo for three years were 34,700 taels of silver, and those in Lhali 36,000 taels. The funds for the stations in Chamdo and Lhali were provided by the Imperial Resident's Office, while those in Tachienlu, Litang and Batang, by the Office of the General of Chengdu.

In addition, the Tsoba Sogu (the Thirty-Nine Tribes) and the Dam Mongols were also in the charge of the Resident in Tibet. The daily affairs concerning them were managed by the *zhangjing* of the Imperial Resident's Office.

A General History of U-Tsang says:

> An official of the Board for National Minority Affairs was responsible for the affairs of the Tsoba Sogu and the Eight Banners of Dam Mongols and for the Manchu files from the Imperial Resident's Office. His term of office was three years....
>
> The Eight Banners of Dam Mongols consisted of 538 households. Of the Dam Mongols eighty-three men were sent to be officers and soldiers in Lhasa and paid by the local Tibetan government, while the rest led a pastoral life in Dam....
>
> Dam Mongols were under the jurisdiction of eight chiefs with the rank of *gushanda*, eight chiefs with the rank of *zuoling* and eight with the rank of *xiaoqixiao*.

As to their origin, *A General History of U-Tsang* says:

> During the Fifth Dalai's reign, Tenzin, a Mongol Khan from Qinghai, led his troops to Tibet to subdue a rebellion. The Khan left behind 538 households, a part of his troops, in the Dam grassland to graze cattle.

The Mongols were originally under the administration of Gushri Khan, and then were put under the charge of Pholhanas. After Pholhanas' death, his son Gyumey Namgyal was in charge of the Dam Mongols. When Gyumey Namgyal was executed, they were put under the administration of the Imperial Resident in Tibet, as Celeng, Governor-General of Sichuan Province, Vice-Minister of Revenue and Population Zhao Hui and Resident Bandi and Namgyal proposed to the imperial court.

Each of the eight Mongol *zuoling* sent to Lhasa ten men (a total of eighty) for service as the Resident's guards. Their food provisions were provided by the local government of Tibet. The eight banners of Dam Mongols offered one hundred loads of salt as tribute to the local government of Tibet every year.

The Thirty-Nine Tribes (Tsoba Sogu) consisted of 4,889 households. Each of the households paid annually 0.08 taels of silver, totaling 391.12 taels, in taxes to the local government of Tibet. The Thirty-Nine Tribes were headed by a *qianhu*, thirteen *baihu* and fifty-three *baizhang*.

Says *A General History of U-Tsang:*

In the areas of Nangchen and Bayan Between Sichuna, Tibet and Qinghai lived seventy-nine Tibetan tribes, who had been slaves of the Qinghai Mongols. After the incident of Lozang Tenzin they accepted amnesty and were pacified. In the ninth year of Yongzheng [1731] Danai, a minister of Xining in charge of national minority affairs, made a proposition to the imperial court that officials from Sichuan and Shaanxi should be sent to make a survey of the areas and delimit the borders. It was decided that the areas be temporarily put under the jurisdiction of Xining and Tibet, each administrating the part of the areas neighbouring it.

After this, every one thousand households of them were put under a *qianhu*, every one hundred households were put under a *baihu*, and a *baizhang* was installed if the number of households was less than a hundred. The chieftains were given written certificates by the Ministry of War and their posts were made hereditary.

It was stipulated that every hundred households should offer eight taels of silver annually as a tribute, equivalent to the price of a horse. The households in the area adjacent to the Xining offered their tribute to the Xining administration, and those adjacent to Tibet paid it to the Grain Affairs Department of the local government of Tibet.

The Thirty-Nine Tribes under the Tibetan administration consisted of 4,889 households with a population of 17,606 people. They paid an annual tribute of 391.12 taels of silver to the Grain Affairs Department of the local government of Tibet.

If any position of the chiefs of the Thirty-Nine Tribes became vacant, the Imperial Resident in Tibet was to inform the superintendent of Qinghai and the latter was to report to the Ministry of War, arrangements then being made for a certificate to be given to the successor. In the twenty-eighth year of Qianlong (1763), Emperor Gaozong, accepting Resident Funai's proposal, ordered that the Imperial Resident could appoint the successors and then inform the Ministry to issue certificates, so that a vacant position could be filled as expediently as possible. From then on, with Emperor Gaozong's approval, the Thirty-Nine Tribes were under the administration of the Imperial Resident in Tibet.

According to the *Imperial Records of the Qing Dynasty*, from the time of Qing Emperor Shizong to the end of the Qing Dynasty, there were appointed altogether 135 Residents and Assistant Residents, of whom eleven did not assume office for various reasons. Of the 124 who took up the post, one filled the post three times and ten twice. Since some books, such as *On Resident Officials in Tibet* and *A Study of Qing's Resident Officials in Tibet*, have given a review of them, only a brief account of them is given here.

Except for a few sagacious and a few weak and incompetent resident officials, most of them acted with prudence. They clearly knew that Tibet was a part of the territory of the Qing Empire and the local government of Tibet should submit itself to the central regime of the Qing court. When they dealt with important matters of Tibet, they would ask the imperial court for instructions in advance and submit reports afterwards. They were loyal to the Qing court and devoted to their duties.

It is a fact that they adopted a policy of humiliating the country by forfeiting its sovereignty to imperialism instead of supporting the Tibetan people's anti-imperialistic patriotic struggle—a criticism some people have made. But it was not they but the Qing imperial court that was to blame. Only a few of them had corrupt morals and went too far in currying favour with foreigners, and these were punished severely afterwards.

Imperial Resident Qi Shan accomplished a task that was the most important of a resident official since Fukang'an. In the twenty-fourth year of Daoguang (1844) he made, in the light of specific conditions, twenty-eight additional regulations to the Twenty-Nine-Article Ordinance drawn up by Fukang'an. The supplementary regulations were important measures which the Qing took in dealing with Tibetan affairs in the middle and late Qing Dynasty. The following are the twenty-eight points Qi Shan proposed in his memorials to the Qing imperial court:

(1) As Emperor Gaozong said in an edict dated the fifty-seventh year of his reign, quite a few officials that had been sent to Tibet had ignored the interests of the country and yielded precedence to the Dalai Lama. Because of this the Dalai Lama and Hutuktus were able to do whatever they wished in the administration of Tibetan affairs, ignoring the existence of these officials. For example, E Hui and He Lin, as imperial envoys, should have been equal in power and authority with the Dalai Lama and the Panchen Erdeni in handling Tibetan affairs. In the nineteenth year of Jiaqing, Minister Hutuli, when sent to Tibet, also should have been equal with the Dalai and the Panchen. Besides, the ministers sent to Tibet were given the power to supervise the conduct of Tibetan officials and to punish them if they dared to engage in malpractices. Instead, the ministers sent to Tibet did nothing to contend with the Dalai for power, but merely flattered the Dalai. As a result, the Dalai and the Hutuktus monopolized power in everything they dealt with and acted arbitrarily and wildly. The Imperial Resident should henceforth be equal in status to the Dalai Lama and the Panchen Erdeni in supervising the administration of Tibetan affairs. As a guarantee against usurpation of authority, the Regent and Hutuktus should, without exception, seek the instructions of the Resident in the execution of their duties.

(2) Tibet is adjacent to the tribes of Gurkha, Drukpa, Drenjong, Lo Menthang and Lhadak, and it is only natural that many foreigners come to Tibet to give alms to the monasteries or make contacts with Tibetan officials. However, all the communications with them should be reported to the Imperial Resident. Private correspondence with foreign countries shall not be allowed.

(3) If there is any trouble in Tibet made by tribes of Tibet or foreign countries, a survey of it should be made before taking any high-handed measures. If the trouble is triggered by some official's misconduct, the official must be severely punished. No troops will be sent to suppress the trouble before the cause of it is made clear through investigation. Those who violate the stipulation will be punished.

(4) The Dalai's chief and deputy sutra-tutors were frequently not recommended to the imperial court for title-granting during the Qianlong reign period. The favour will be done to those who

have been the Dalai's sutra-tutors for many years by His Majesty himself, when the Dalai begins to engage in political affairs. Imperial Residents will not be allowed to recommend the tutors, as was frequently done before.

(5) The Dalai Lama shall take over political power at the age of eighteen, as the eighth Dalai did, with His Majesty's approval through the Imperial Resident. His Regent should then be dismissed. All the seals of authority of the regent will be sent to the national capital or kept in *Shangshang* (the local government of Tibet). The Regent will not be allowed to monopolize power.

(6) By tradition, the Dalai's parents should receive estates and houses from *Shangshang*. The Dalai's father, Tsewang Dondrup, originally a poor man, came with the Dalai to Lhasa and was given by His Majesty the title of Duke in the twenty-first year of the Daoguang reign period. But the Nomihan (reference to the then Regent, Tsemonling Ngawang Jampal Tsultrim) did not give him the estates he should have received, so he has had to appeal again and again. As of last winter after three years, only a few poor estates had been given to him. A survey showed the Nomihan had given the estates of more than forty *gang* in areas that were to be allocated to the Dalai's father by *Shangshang* to his nephew-in-law Sakya Hutuktu. The incident naturally caused great anger and indignation among the people. From now on, as soon as a reincarnation of the Dalai is decided upon through formal procedure, his parents will receive the estates and houses they should be given from *Shangshang*.

(7) The power of the Regent is already very great. If he is concurrently the Dalai's tutor or the Ganden Tripa, the most privileged lama, he will be powerful enough to do anything he wishes. So the Regent henceforth will not be allowed to be concurrently the Dalai's tutor or the abbot of the Ganden.

(8) From now on, the Ganden Tripa will be selected in the light of old tradition, that is, from the lamas who have made a thorough and careful study of sutras. Nomihan Hutuktu should not be allowed to take the post, so that the appointment will be made according to one's moral character instead of authority of office.

(9) The Dzasa Lama under the Regent shall only manage the affairs of his own monastery. He is not to be allowed to interfere

in the public affairs of *Shangshang*. He or other lamas under the Regent can be selected to fill the vacant posts of their own monastery, but not those of *Shangshang*.

(10) The Regent has his own manors and many inhabitants in his charge, who provide him with various labour service, so he will not be allowed to use the public *ula* service of *Shangshang*. When he gives alms to monasteries, he shall use his own money, but not the money of *Shangshang*.

(11) The Regent shall have his seal of authority preserved in his own monastery and the key for the box of the seal shall be kept by the chief *khenpo*. The use of the seal will be managed by both the Regent and the chief *khenpo*. The Regent's *drungyig* (secretary) who works in *Shangshang* should live in the residence provided by *Shangshang*, but not in the Regent's monastery, in order to prevent malpractices.

(12) The Regent will not be allowed to grant the *Shangshang* estates with their inhabitants to his monastery nor to his relatives and friends. Nor will his monastery, relatives and friends be allowed to apply for the granting. Those who violate the stipulation will be punished and the granted estates will be returned to *Shangshang*.

(13) The farmland the Dalai has given to aristocratic families and common people shall not be privately offered to or sold to the Regent's monastery. Those who violate the stipulation will return the farmland to *Shangshang*.

(14) The number of *tsedrung* lamas (monk officials) working in *Shangshang*, which was fixed at 160 in the eleventh year of Jiaqing, will not be increased.

Now the Dalai is in his minority. He does not need too many lamas to serve him. The present number of 140 is enough for the time being. When the Dalai is old enough to assume temporal power, twenty more *tsedrung* lamas will be added to that number.

The *tsedrung* lamas have not been granted official posts and they have no official rank. They should not be put in high official posts of the fourth or fifth rank, as Fukang'an proposed in the Qianlong reign period. Those who have been *tsedrung* lamas for three years may be appointed monk officials of the seventh rank.

(15) It was not until Nomihan became the Regent that candi-

dates for the posts of *tsedrung* in *Shangshang* were selected from among the monks of other monasteries. This was done against the will of the monks, who preferred to practise Buddhism in monasteries. The Kalons tried in vain to talk Nomihan out of doing it. Henceforth the candidates for *tsedrung* shall be selected, if necessary, from no other monastery than Namgyal Dratsang, the monastery of *Shangshang*. Monk officials of *Shangshang* will be selected from the monastery under the direct jurisdiction of *Shangshang* —this is in accordance with traditional regulations and good for preventing evil practices.

(16) The ranks of Tibetan lay and monk officials are now in a state of confusion, so a system should be set up in accordance with traditional regulations. The chief *khenpo* is to be of the third rank, equivalent to the Kalons.

The officials of the fourth rank are as follows: a monk *solpon*, a monk *zimpon*, a monk *chopon*, five senior *khenpos* as the Dalai's close attendants, four junior *khenpos* as the Dalai's *drungyig*, three lay *tsepons*, two *Shangshang shangdrotepa*, two Jokhang *shangdrotepa*, a lay *shangdrotepa*, a junior *solpon*, a lay *popon* and a monk *popon* in charge of Tibetan soldiers' provisions, a senior *dronyer* in *Shangshang*, a senior physician and eight junior *khenpos* as the Dalai's close attendants.

The officials of the fifth rank are as follows: ten *Shangshang tsedrung dronyers*, four interpreters, a junior physician, three *Shangshang nyertsangpas*, a Jokhang *nyertsangpa*, three lay *nyertsangpas*, two *shipons*, a lay and a monk *shodepa* and two lay *mipons*.

The officials of the sixth rank are as follows: two lay *drungyig chenpo* of the Kashag, three *dronyers*, two lay *dapons* in charge of horses, two *tsedrungs* in charge of sutras, two *tsedrungs* in charge of brocades and a *khenpo* of the Dedan Khil.

The officials of the seventh rank are as follows: three junior lay *drungyigs*, three *depas* in charge of firewood, grass and *tsamba*, two lay *depas* in charge of tents, three *depas* in charge of sheep and cattle, four trader-*depas*, two *depas* in charge of making images of the Buddha, a *depa* in charge of dress-making, a *depa* in charge of joss-stick making, a *depa* in charge of offering sacrifices and two *khangnyers* (housekeepers), one in Jokhang and the other in Norbulingka.

(17) The promotion of monk officials has not been clearly prescribed. Even Fukang'an's report did not give a clear account of it. From now on the position left vacant by the chief *khenpo* shall be filled by a senior *solpon*, *zimpon* or *chopon*, or by a senior *khenpo*. The vacancy left by a senior *solpon* shall be filled by a junior *solpon*. The vacancy left by a *zimpon* shall be filled by a senior *khenpo* or a junior *khenpo*. The vacancy left by a *chopon* shall be filled by a senior *khenpo* who has a good knowledge of the sutras or by a junior *khenpo*. The position left vacant by a senior *khenpo* shall be filled by a junior *khenpo*. As to the position left vacant by the *Shangshang shangdrotepa*, *Jokhang shangdrotepa*, *popon* in charge of Tibetan soldiers' provisions or the senior *dronyer* of *Shangshang*, it shall be filled by a junior *khenpo* or by a civil official or officer of the fifth rank. The vacancy left by the officials of the fifth rank will be filled by those of the sixth rank. The vacancy left by the officials of the sixth rank shall be filled by those of the seventh rank. The vacancy left by the officials of the seventh rank shall be filled by *tsedrung* lamas who have no fixed office and no official rank. To promote more than one rank at a time is prohibited.

(18) According to the existing regulation, the position left vacant by a *tsepon* or *shangdrotepa* is filled by a *nyertsangpa*, a *shipon*, a senior *drungyig* or a *jedrung* lama. But, as a survey shows, *tsepon* and *shangdrotepa* are officials of the fourth rank, while the senior *drungyig* are of the sixth rank—too low to be promoted to the fourth rank. Besides, there are no *jedrung* lamas in U. There are *tsedrung* in U, but they have never been officially put in an office, so it is improper to promote them to the fourth rank. Henceforth the vacancy left by a *tsepon* or *shangdrotepa* will be filled by a *nyertsangpa*, a *shipon*, a *shodepa* or a *mipon*—officials of the fifth rank.

According to the existing regulation, the position left vacant by a *shodepa*, *mipon* or *dapon* is filled by an officer of the fifth rank. But a *dapon* is an officer of the sixth rank. So from now on the position left vacant by *shodepa* will be filled by officers of the fifth or the sixth rank. The vacancy left by *dapon* will be filled by officers of the sixth or the seventh rank.

According to the existing regulation, the position left vacant by commanding officers of the fifth rank on the border are filled by officers of the seventh rank or junior *drungyig* of the seventh rank. From now on the vacancy left by commanding officers of the fifth rank on the border will be filled by officers and officials of the sixth rank. The vacancy left by officers of the sixth rank will be filled by officers and officials of the seventh rank.

Also according to the existing regulation, the vacancy left by a junior *drungyig* or *dronyer* in the Kashag is filled by a *dongkar*. But in fact it is not proper for a *dongkar* to fill the post of a *dronyer*, an official of the sixth rank, because it is in contradiction to the stipulation that a *dongkar* can only be promoted to a post of the seventh rank. From now on the vacancy left by a *kashag dronyer* will be filled by officials of the seventh rank. *Dongkar* will be able to be promoted only to the post of the seventh rank. To promote more than one rank at a time will not be allowed.

(19) The position left vacant by a *drungyig* whose task is the translation of documents in *Shangshang* will be filled by a junior *khenpo* or by an officer or official of the fifth rank who has good moral character and has a good knowledge of foreign languages.

The senior physician should have a thorough understanding of medicine. He can be granted only the title of junior *khenpo*.

The position of interpreters will be filled by those who know well more than one language and act honestly regardless of their original official ranks. *Lotsawas* (interpreters) will be promoted by rank.

The appointment of all lay and monk Tibetan officials of the sixth rank and above shall be authorized by the Resident.

(20) The positions of the officials in charge of the Dalai's food are usually filled by *tsedrungs*. They can be promoted to minor *solpon* at most. The *depa* in charge of gatekeeping should be strongly built. Their status is rather low, so their appointment is not restricted.

(21) A clear line should be made between the lay and monk officers. Their appointments should not be confused with each other. The vacancy left by a lay officer should not be filled by a monk.

(22) As to the appointment of *khenpos* of the monasteries, five to seven *khenpos* will be selected for a major monastery and three to five for a minor one. The appointment should be in accordance

with the traditional regulations. The *khenpos* should be men of great learning who have been monks for more than twenty years, enjoyed the respect of others and have the academic title of *geshe*. Those who are young and do not have great learning nor an adequate record of service should not be appointed as *khenpos*.

(23) The appointment of the *Gegu* Lama (the Dean of Discipline, or popularly called the Iron-Club Lama) of the Drepung, Sera and Ganden should be made in accordance with traditional regulations. The candidates for the *Gegu* Lama should be those who have been monks for more than a dozen years, know the Buddhist disciplines very well, are held in great respect and have had good performance while in the post of *nyertsangpa*. Those who violate the regulation and have gotten the post by bribery will be stripped of the title of lama and be driven out of the monastery. The Regent will be accused of the violation of rules if he does not abide by the regulations and instead appoints men lacking ability as *gegus* after receiving bribes.

(24) The appointment of the Ganden Tripa should be made strictly in accordance with traditional regulations.

(25) The building of monasteries, no matter by whom, should not be detrimental to the farmland and houses of the common people. Those who have suffered from such unauthorized construction may bring an accusation against the monastery, and the occupied land and houses will be returned.

Monks are prohibited to interfere in public affairs, speak for other people in a report to the government or carry out revenge for other people, as they have often done. In case of violation, the offenders shall be severely punished and the *khenpo* of the monastery will be repudiated and dismissed from his post.

(26) In handling lawsuits, the decisions should be compatible with the seriousness of the offence. Illegal confiscation of an offender's property is not allowed. The ruling on such cases made by Nomihan in recent years was unfair and there were many cases concerning the confiscation of the property of people on false charges. In order to stop all illegal practice in the handling of lawsuits, new regulations should be set up. The size of fines will be restricted to twenty taels of silver, as a measure to warn the Tibetan offenders not to make further mistakes. In dealing with

serious cases the fine for common people will not exceed thirty Tibetan *taels*, and for officials, three hundred Tibetan *taels*. The confiscation of an offender's property will be done only to those who have been involved in serious graft. As to others, no matter whether the persons involved are civilians or holders of public office, no confiscation is allowed. It is forbidden to confiscate an offender's property on the excuse of getting back his property given by *Shangshang*.

(27) *Ula* corvée has plunged Tibetan people into misery. Fukang'an prohibited Tibetan officials from using *ula* corvée, but he did not mention the Regent. Tibetan soldiers and officers scattered over an area of about three thousand *li* cannot all be issued notices by the Imperial Resident concerning the use of *ula*. The Regent has estates and subjects in possession. He will not be allowed to use *ula* corvée except for urgent needs. Stationed troops can use *ula* according to regulations made by Amban Yu Lin in the twenty-third year of Jiaqing (1544). Tibetan officials can use *ula* corvée according to regulations made by Amban Song Yun in the second year of Jiaqing (1523). Tibetan officials' families, relatives and attendants will not be allowed to use *ula*.

(28) The number of Tibetan soldiers should be guaranteed. The old and the weak are to be replaced. The soldiers who have been sent on official business will be called back. All the soldiers must undergo rigorous training. Those who violate the regulations will be punished.

Foreigners who are engaged in trade in Tibet should pay taxes in accordance with traditional regulations. Kalons will not be allowed to levy more than ordinary taxes on them in order to show our concern for them and to avoid disputes.

Qi Shan's twenty-eight articles, after being carefully examined by the Board for National Minority Affairs, were approved by the Emperor. They were produced on the basis of the Twenty-Nine-Article Ordinance in accordance with the new conditions. They were a supplement to the former "Imperial Ordinance." When Fukang'an was in Tibet, the power was in the hands of the Eighth Dalai and there was no Regent. Therefore, the Twenty-Nine-Article Ordinance did not mention the Regent. Things in Tibet had changed much after the Eighth Dalai's death. The Ninth Dalai and the Tenth Dalai died at only eleven and twenty-two years of age, respectively, and the political and religious power was being held by the Regent. With the "Imperial Ordinance," the Regent could do anything he wished. When Qi Shan was appointed the Resident in Tibet, the Eleventh Dalai was only five years old and Regent Tsemonling Ngawang Jampal Tsultrim had seized the secular and religious power of Tibet. Qi Shan thought it necessary to put the power of the Regent under control. That was why he proposed the twenty-eight articles. The articles were essential for consolidating the relationship of the local government of Tibet and the central regime of the Qing Dynasty and safeguarding China's sovereignty. In the appraisal of Qi Shan's twenty-eight articles, it is proper to give them a positive assessment in the main.

# III. Bibliography

## Monographs

1. *The Biography of the Fourth Panchen Lama, Lozang Choskyi* (in Tibetan), printed from the woodblocks of the Tashilhunpo.
2. *The Biography of the Fifth Panchen Lama, Lozang Yeshe* (in Tibetan), printed from the woodblocks of the Tashilhunpo.
3. *The Biography of the Sixth Panchen Lama, Palden Yeshe* (in Tibetan), printed from the woodblocks of the Tashilhunpo.
4. *The Biography of the Seventh Panchen Lama, Tenpai Nyima* (in Tibetan), printed from the woodblocks of the Tashilhunpo.
5. *The Biography of the Eighth Panchen Lama, Tenpai Wangchuk* (in Tibetan), printed from the woodblocks of the Tashilhunpo.
6. Liu Jiaju, *The Complete Works of the Panchen Lamas*, the Panchen's Council of Khenpo, 1943.
7. Chen Wenjian, *A Fifteen-Year Chronicle of Major Events of the Great Master Panchen Lama's Eastern Journey*, Dafalun Book Co., Shanghai, 1925.
8. The Entertaining Group of the Panchen, *Records of the Panchen Lama's Eastern Journey*, World Book Co., Shanghai, 1925.
9. Wu Fengpei, "A Brief Account of the Panchen Lama's Journey to India," *A Collection of Historical Documents on Tibet During the Qing Period*, Vol. 1, Commercial Press, 1936.
10. Zhang Bozheng, *The Biographies of the Panchen Erdenis*, Canghai Series, No. 3(a), Canghai Library Press, 1934.
11. *The Biography of the First Dalai Lama, Gedun Truppa* (in Tibetan), printed from the woodblocks of the Drepung, Lhasa.
12. *The Biography of the Third Dalai Lama, Sonam Gyatso* (in Tibetan), printed from the woodblocks of the Drepung, Lhasa.
13. *The Biography of the Fifth Dalai Lama, Lozang Gyatso* (in Tibetan), printed from the woodblocks of the Drepung, Lhasa.

14. *The Biography of the Seventh Dalai Lama, Kelzang Gyatso* (in Tibetan), printed from the woodblocks of the Drepung, Lhasa.

15. *The Biography of the Thirteenth Dalai Lama, Thubten Gyatso* (in Tibetan), printed from the woodblocks of the Potala's Buddhist Scripture Printing Office.

16. Zhang Bozheng, *The Biographies of the Dalai Lamas*, Canghai Series, No. 3(a), Canghai Library Press, 1934.

17. *History of the Ming Dynasty*: "Biographies of the Pacification Princes."

18. Tibet Academy of Social Sciences, *Documents on the Tibetan Nationality Collected from the "Imperial Records of the Ming Dynasty"* (two volumes), Tibet People's Press, 1982.

19. Tibet Academy of Social Sciences, *Documents on the Tibetan Nationality Collected from the "Imperial Records of the Qing Dynasty"* (ten volumes), Tibet People's Press, 1982.

20. History Department of the Tibet Institute for Nationalities, *A Collection of Historical Documents on the Tibetan Nationality from the "Imperial Records of the Qing Dynasty"* (five volumes), 1982.

21. Fazun, *The Political and Religious History of the Tibetan Nationality*, 1940.

22. Liu Liqian, *Sequel to the Illuminating History of Tibet*, West China University Press, Chengdu, 1941.

23. *Records of Tibet* and *A General History of U-Tsang* (bound volume), Tibet People's Press, 1982.

24. *An Illustrated History of Tibet* and *A Brief Illustrated History of Tsang* (bound volume), Tibet People's Press, 1982.

25. Wu Fengpei, *Dispatches and Memorials to the Throne Concerning Tibet in the Qing Period*, Commercial Press, 1938.

26. Zhang Qiqing and Wu Fengpei, *Historical Documents on Tibet in the Qing Dynasty (1)*, Tibet People's Press, 1983.

27. Wu Fengpei, *Sequel to the Historical Documents on Tibet in the Qing Dynasty*, Sichuan Nationality Press, 1984.

28. Wu Fengpei, *Memorials to the Throne from Zhao Erfeng in Sichuan*, Sichuan Nationality Press, 1984.

29. Wu Fengpei, *Telegraphic Messages on Tibetan Affairs in the First Year of the Republic of China*, Tibet People's Press, 1982.

30. Wu Fengpei, *Four Versions of Details on the Riots in Tibet*, Library of the Central Institute for Nationalities, 1979.

31. Wu Fengpei, *Telegraphic Messages on Tibetan Affairs in the Second Year of the Republic of China* (manuscript).

32. Wu Fengpei, *Appendixes to the Telegraphic Messages on Tibetan Affairs in the Second Year of the Republic of China* (manuscript).

33. Wu Fengpei, *Memorials to the Throne from Qing Resident Lian Yu*, Tibet People's Press, 1980.

34. Wu Fengpei, *An Account of Eminent Tibetan Monks* and *The Origin and Development of Tibet's Religions* (bound volume), Tibet People's Press, 1982.

35. Wang Furen and Suo Wenqing, *Highlights of Tibetan History*, Sichuan Nationality Press, 1981.

36. Hong Dichen, *An Outline History and Geography of Tibet*, Zhengzhong Book Co., 1936.

37. Xiao Jinsong, *A Study of Qing's Resident Officials in Tibet*, Taiwan.

38. Ting Shicun, *On Resident Officials in Tibet*, Commission for Mongolian and Tibetan Affairs of the Nationalist Government, 1943.

39. Huang Musong, *My Mission to Tibet*, Commercial Press, 1944.

40. Wu Zhongxin, *Highlights of Tibet*, Zhonghua Press Co., Nanjing.

41. Gao Changzhu, *Essays on the Frontier Questions*, Zhengzhong Book Co., 1948.

42. Ma Hetian, *A Survey of the Borderland in Gansu, Qinghai and Tibet*, Vol. 2, Commercial Press, Shanghai, 1947.

43. MacDonald, David, *Twenty Years in Tibet*, translated into Chinese by Sun Meisheng and Huang Cishu, Commercial Press, Shanghai, 1936.

44. Liu Manqing, *My Mission to Xikang and Tibet*, Commercial Press, Shanghai, 1933.

45. Zhu Shaoyi, "Lhasa Reports," *Exploration of Northwest China*, No. 1, Vol. 2, July 1934.

46. Zhu Xiu, *A Sixty-Year Chronicle of Major Events in Tibet*, 1925.

47. Xie Guoliang, *A Brief Account of Tibetan Affairs*.

48. The Fifth Dalai Lama, *Records of Tibetan Kings and Ministers*, translated into Chinese by Guo Heqing, Nationality Press, Beijing, 1983.

49. Younghusband, Francis, *India and Tibet*, translated into Chinese by Sun Zhaochu, Commercial Press, Shanghai, 1934.

50. She Suo, *History of the British Invasion of Tibet in the Qing Period*,

World Knowledge Press, Beijing, 1959.

51. Bell, Charles, *Tibet: Past and Present*, translated into Chinese by Gong Tingzhang, Commercial Press, Peiping, 1930.

52. Richardson, Hugh, *Tibet and Its History*, translated into Chinese by Li Youyi.

53. Tucci, Giuseppe, *Tibetan Painted Scrolls*, translated into Chinese by Li Youyi and Deng Ruiling, Institute of Nationality Studies of the Chinese Academy of Social Sciences, 1980, (pp.3-80).

54. Wang Sen, *Ten Articles About the History of Tibetan Buddhism*, Institute of Nationality Studies of the Chinese Academy of Social Sciences, 1965.

55. Wang Sen, *The Biography of Tsongkhapa*, Institute of Nationality Studies of the Chinese Academy of Social Sciences, 1965.

56. Fifth Dalai Lama Lozang Gyatso, *The Sakya's Lineal Description and the Phagdru's Lineal Description*, translated into Chinese by Wang Yao, Institute of Nationality Studies of the Chinese Academy of Social Sciences, 1965.

57. Cai Zhicun and Gao Wende, *Mongolian Lineage*, China Social Sciences Publishing House, Beijing, 1979.

58. Dungkar Lozang Trinley, *On Tibetan Theocracy*, translated from Tibetan into Chinese by Guo Guanzhong and Wang Yuping, Institute of Nationality Studies of the Chinese Academy of Social Sciences, 1983.

59. Sumpa Khenpo Yeshe Paljor, "A History of the Kokonor Region," *Journal of the Northwestern Institute for Nationalities*, translated into Chinese by Huang Hao, No. 3, 1983, and No. 1-2, 1984.

60. Pan-chen Sonam Drakpa, *New Red Annals*, translated into Chinese by Huang Hao, Tibet People's Press, Lhasa, 1985.

# Essays

1. Du Jiang, "A Brief Account of the Homage Paid to Emperor Qianlong by the Sixth Panchen Lama," *Tibet Studies*, No. 1, 1984.

2. Li Keyu, "The Qing Policy Towards Tibet Reflected in the Two Imperial Poems Inscribed on Wooden Boards in the Temple of Sumeru Happiness and Longevity," *Tibet Studies*, No. 1, 1984.

3. Liu Ruzhong, "On the Painted Scrolls About the Western Cam-

paign of General Fuyuan," *Tibet Studies*, No. 1, 1984.

4. Wu Fengpei, "On the Discord Between the Dalai Lama and the Panchen Erdeni."

5. Wang Meixia, "The Ninth Panchen's Return to Tibet," Taiwan.

6. Ma Ruheng and Ma Dazheng, "A Brief Account of Gushri Khan," *Nationality Studies*, No. 2, 1983.

7. Cai Zhicun, "A Research into the Dates of Gushri Khan," *Nationality Studies*, No. 2, 1984.

8. Huang Hao and Wu Biyun, "A Research into Sixth Dalai Lama Tsangyang Gyatso," *Tibet Studies*, inaugural number, 1981.

9. Wu Fengpei, "On the Batang Riot in the Thirty-First Year of the Guangxu Reign Period," *Yugong Fortnightly*, No. 12, Vol. 6.

10. Wu Fengpei, "On the Dalai Lama's Self-Exile in the Qing Period."

11. Wang Furen, "On the Five Entries About the Ngabopa Incident in Tibet in the Early Qing Dynasty," *A Collection of Tibetological Articles*, Institute of Tibetology of the Central Institute for Nationalities, 1985.

12. Zhao Yuntian, "A Brief Account of the Administration of Tibet by the Qing Board for National Minority Affairs," *Tibet Studies*, No. 3, 1984.

13. Zhao Weibang, "How Manning, the First Among Englishmen Who Came into Lhasa, Was Expelled Out of Lhasa," *Tibet Studies*, No. 2, 1984.

14. Ren Shugui, "On the Gansu Mission to Tibet in 1919," *Tibet Studies*, No. 4, 1984.

15. Kong Qingzong, "A Review of the Kuomintang Government's Administration of Tibet," *Selected Cultural and Historical Materials*, Vol. 93.

16. Kong Qingzong, "How Tibet Interfered in the Conflicts Between Greater Jinchuan and Beri in Xikang," *Selected Cultural and Historical Materials*, Vol. 93.

17. Kong Qingzong, "Records of Huang Musong's Errand to Tibet," *Selected Cultural and Historical Materials*, Vol. 93.

18. Chen Xizhang, "A Brief Account of My Political Career in Tibet," *Selected Cultural and Historical Materials*, Vol. 79.

19. Chang Xiwu, "Kuomintang Spies in Tibet," *Selected Cultural and Historical Materials About Tibet*, Vol. 3.

20. Li Su and Jigme Wangchuk, "The Tibetan Political Situation After the Thirteenth Dalai Lama's Death," *Selected Cultural and Historical Materials About Tibet*, Vol. 3.

21. Lhawu Dare Thubten Tenthar, "I Took Part in the Lungshar Incident," *Selected Cultural and Historical Materials About Tibet*, Vol. 3.

22. Lungshar Ugyen Dorje, "How Regent Radreng was Murdered in Prison," *Selected Cultural and Historical Materials About Tibet*, Vol. 3.

23. Lhazong Drokhor, "Something About Jamchen Thubten Kunphel," *Selected Cultural and Historical Materials About Tibet*, Vol. 3.

24. Jampa Dorje Ngodrup, "The Inside Story About the Tibetan Local Government Sending a Mission to Convey Greetings and Appreciation to the Allied Nations and to Attend the National Congress in Nanjing." *Selected Cultural and Historical Materials About Tibet*, Vol. 2

25. Zangpo Tenzin Dondrup and others, "The Real State of Affairs Concerning the Tibetan Mission Participating in the 'Asian Relations Conference,'" *Selected Cultural and Historical Materials About Tibet*, Vol. 2.

26. Lhalu Tsewang Dorje, "My Memories of My Father, Lungshar Dorje Trije," *Selected Cultural and Historical Materials About Tibet*, No. 3.

27. Shartse Yeshe Thubten, "I Was a Warden When Regent Radreng Was a Prisoner," *Selected Cultural and Historical Materials About Tibet*, No. 2.

28. Thubten Chosje, "My Memories of Champa Paksu, the Physician to the Thirteenth Dalai Lama," *Selected Cultural and Historical Materials About Tibet*, Vol. 2.

29. Fan Zhisheng, "Memoirs of the Garze Incident," *Kangdao Monthly*, No. 8, Vol. 2.

30. Shou Mei, "I Survived the Garze Incident," *Kangdao Monthly*, No. 8, Vol. 2.

31. Li Jingxuan, "Who Was to Blame for the Garze Incident," *Kangdao Monthly*, No. 8, Vol. 2.

32. Liu Wenhui, "How the Garze Incident Was Solved," *Kangdao Monthly*, No. 8, Vol. 2.

33. Yang Zexian, "The Garze Incident," *Kangdao Monthly*, No. 8, Vol. 2.
34. Chi Yurui, "How the Peace-Making Mission Went into Tibet."
35. Zhou Xiyin, "Getag Rimpoche Gave His Life for the Peaceful Liberation of Tibet," *Tibet Studies*, No. 3, 1984.
36. Zhou Runnian, "Getag Rimpoche, a Well-Known Tibetan Patriot," *A Collection of Papers on Tibetan Studies*, Institute of Tibetology of the Central Institute for Nationalities, Vol. 2.
37. Li Weihan, "The Road to the Liberation of the Tibetan Nationality," *People's Daily*, May 23, 1981.
38. Zhang Guohua, "Records of the Actual Events of the Marching of the 18th Corps into Tibet," *Selected Cultural and Historical Materials About Tibet*, Vol. 2.
39. Thubten Tenthar, "Before and After the Signing of the Agreement on Measures for the Peaceful Liberation of Tibet," *Selected Cultural and Historical Materials About Tibet*, Vol. 1.
40. Le Yuhong, "Selected Pages from My Diary About the Peaceful Liberation of Tibet," *Memoirs of the Revolution in Tibet*, Vol. 2.
41. Xi Jinwu, "The Advance Troops Marching into Tibet," *Memoirs of the Revolution in Tibet*, Vol. 1.
42. Chen Zizhi, "The Battle for the Liberation of Chamdo," *Selected Cultural and Historical Materials About Tibet*, Vol. 1.
43. Chen Bing, "Marching to Zayu, Chamdo," *Memoirs of the Revolution in Tibet*, Vol. 2.
44. Zhai Jinzhen and others, "In Memory of the Commander Li Disan of the Heroic Advance Company Marching into Ngari," *Selected Cultural and Historical Materials About Tibet*, Vol. 3.
45. Wei Ke, "A Brief Description of the 18th Corps Marching to Tibet," *Selected Cultural and Historical Materials*, Vol. 3.
46. Dergе Kelzang Wangdu, "How I Led My Troops to Uprising," *Selected Cultural and Historical Materials About Tibet*, Vol. 3.
47. Lhalu Tsewang Dorje, "After the PLA Came into Lhasa," *Selected Cultural and Historical Materials About Tibet*, Vol. 1.
48. Zhou Shilong, "Escorting the Panchen Erdeni Back to Shigatse," *Selected Cultural and Historical Materials About Tibet*, Vol. 1.
49. Wang Xianmei, "The PLA Advance Troops Marching from Chamdo to Lhasa," *Memoirs of the Revolution in Tibet*, Vol. 2.
50. Yang Yizheng, "Vow to Erect the Red Flag on the Himalayas,"

*Memoirs of the Revolution in Tibet*, Vol. 2.

51. Chen Jingbo, "A Political Contest," *Selected Cultural and Historical Materials About Tibet*, Vol. 1.

52. Li Chuan'en, "The Building of the Sichuan-Tibet Highway," *Selected Cultural and Historical Materials About Tibet*, Vol. 1.

53. Yang Zonghui, "The Surveying of the Southern Route of the Sichuan-Tibet Highway," *Memoirs of the Revolution in Tibet*, Vol. 2.

54. Yao Zhaolin, *Tibet Is an Inalienable Part of China* (a collection of historical materials), Tibet People's Press, Lhasa, 1986.

39624 $ 9.20

**班禅额尔德尼传**

牙含章　著

\*

外文出版社出版

（中国北京百万庄路 24 号）

邮政编码 100037

北京外文印刷厂印刷

中国国际图书贸易总公司发行

（中国北京车公庄西路 35 号）

北京邮政信箱第 399 号　邮政编码 100044

1994 年(大 32 开)第一版

（英）

ISBN 7－119－01687－3 /K・117（外）

02700

ISBN 7－119－01688－1 /K・118（外）

02300

11－E－2883